Empowering Africa

Business and Innovation

Vol. 38

Edited by
Dimitri Uzunidis, Blandine Laperche,
Sophie Boutillier, Viktor Prokop

Pitshou Moleka

Empowering Africa: Harnessing Inclusive Innovation for Sustainable Development

PETER LANG
Bruxelles · Berlin · Chennai · Lausanne · New York · Oxford

Bibliographic Information published by the Deutsche Nationalbibliothek
The Deutsche Nationalbibliothek lists this publication in the Deutsche Nationalbibliografie; detailed bibliographic data is available online at http://dnb.d-nb.de.

Library of Congress Cataloging-in-Publication Data
Names: Moleka, Pitshou author
Title: Empowering Africa : Harnessing Inclusive Innovation for Sustainable Development / Pitshou Moleka.
Description: Bruxelles ; New York : Peter Lang, [2025] | Series: Business and innovation, 2034-5402 ; vol. 38 | Includes bibliographical references. | Summary: "This groundbreaking book offers a radical rethinking of innovation as a driver of inclusive and sustainable transformation in Africa. It challenges traditional hierarchies of knowledge and power, proposing a pluralistic, participatory, and justice-oriented innovation paradigm aligned with the Sustainable Development Goals (SDGs)"-- Provided by publisher.
Identifiers: LCCN 2025026789 (print) | LCCN 2025026790 (ebook) | ISBN 9783034361149 paperback | ISBN 9783034361156 pdf | ISBN 9783034361163 epub
Subjects: LCSH: Sustainable development--Africa
Classification: LCC HC800.Z9 E54847 2025 (print) | LCC HC800.Z9 (ebook)
LC record available at https://lccn.loc.gov/2025026789
LC ebook record available at https://lccn.loc.gov/2025026790

ISSN 2034-5402
ISBN 978-3-0343-6114-9 (Print)
ISBN 978-3-0343-6115-6 (ePDF)
ISBN 978-3-0343-6116-3 (ePUB)
DOI 10.3726/b23110
Dépôt légal: D/2025/5678/32

Published by P.I.E. PETER LANG s.a., Bruxelles (Belgique)
info@peterlang.com

This publication has been peer reviewed.

www.peterlang.com

Contents

List of Figures

List of Tables

Acknowledgments

First and foremost, I would like to express my deepest gratitude to God Almighty for bestowing upon me the strength, intelligence, and inspiration to contribute to the field of human science. It is by His grace that I have been able to bring these outstanding contributions to the world. I would also like to extend my sincere thanks to my colleagues, such as Dr. Turan Jafarzade of Azerbaijan, for their collaborative efforts and insightful discussions that have enriched the content of this book.

Furthermore, I am deeply appreciative of my wife, Julienne Mujinga, and my two daughters, Shekinah Moleka and Elyon Moleka, for their unwavering support, love, and patience during the challenging yet rewarding process of writing this book. Your encouragement and understanding have been a constant source of motivation and strength. Without the blessings of God, the support of my mentors and colleagues, and the love of my family, this work would not have been possible. I am truly grateful for each and every one of you, and I hope that the contributions presented in this book will inspire and benefit humanity for generations to come.

PITSHOU MOLEKA, PhD

Introduction

Rethinking Innovation for Equitable and Sustainable Development in Africa

In the face of persistent socioeconomic inequalities, environmental crises, and complex development challenges, Africa stands at a critical juncture (Robbins; Kekana, Ruhiiga, Ndou & Palamuleni, 2023). The continent's remarkable economic growth over the past two decades has been accompanied by widening disparities (Jayne, Chamberlin & Benfica, 2018), with the benefits of progress often accruing to a small elite while the majority of Africans continue to grapple with poverty, limited access to basic services, and marginalization (Elu, 2018; Hamann & Bertels, 2018). Simultaneously, climate change, biodiversity loss, and the depletion of natural resources threaten the long-term sustainability of African societies and economies (IPCC, 2022; Konte & Ndou, 2020). Addressing these multifaceted challenges requires a fundamental rethinking of prevailing development frameworks and a reimagination of the role of innovation in driving transformative change (Moleka, 2024a). Conventional models of innovation, often shaped by Western paradigms and focused on technological advancement and commercialization, have proven inadequate in the unique social, economic, and environmental contexts of the African continent (Kraemer-Mbula & Wunsch-Vincent, 2016; Srinivas & Sutz, 2008). These models have frequently failed to prioritize the needs and aspirations of marginalized communities, resulting in the perpetuation of inequitable access to the benefits of innovation (George et al., 2012; Naudé, 2017). Moreover, the narrow focus on profit-driven, market-based innovation has frequently overlooked the critical role of innovation in addressing pressing social and environmental challenges (Begović & Kolin, 2017; Swaans et al., 2014). In response to these shortcomings, a new paradigm of "inclusive innovation" is gaining traction across Africa, offering a more holistic and equitable approach to harnessing the power of innovation for sustainable development (Chataway et al., 2014; Foster & Heeks, 2013). Inclusive innovation encompasses a diverse range of practices, from the grassroots development of affordable and accessible technologies, to social enterprises tackling complex societal problems, to the democratization of knowledge and the empowerment of marginalized groups as innovation leaders (Mohamad et al., 2020; Paunov, 2013). At the heart of this inclusive innovation movement is a profound shift in the underlying assumptions and values that have traditionally shaped innovation ecosystems. Rather than viewing innovation solely through the lens of economic growth and technological advancement, inclusive innovation champions a vision of innovation as a catalyst for social and environmental transformation, with a strong emphasis on equity, inclusion, and the holistic well-being of African communities (Chataway et al., 2019; Heeks et al., 2014). This book, " Empowering Africa: Harnessing Inclusive Innovation for Sustainable Development" delves into the conceptual foundations, practical applications, and transformative potential of inclusive innovation in the African context.

Drawing on interdisciplinary perspectives from development studies, innovation management, innovationology, social entrepreneurship, and sustainability science, the chapters in this book explore how inclusive innovation can address the continent's most pressing challenges and unlock new pathways for equitable and sustainable development. The central premise of this book is that inclusive innovation holds the key to reimagining African futures – futures where innovation is harnessed not merely for economic gain, but for the collective betterment of society and the environment. By elevating the voices and perspectives of marginalized communities, fostering collaborative innovation ecosystems, and aligning development efforts with the Sustainable Development Goals (SDGs), this book aims to inspire and empower a new generation of inclusive innovation champions who can drive transformative change across the African continent.

I. Defining Inclusive Innovation: A Holistic and Equitable Approach

At its core, inclusive innovation is about expanding access to the benefits of innovation and ensuring that the process of innovation itself is inclusive, participatory, and responsive to the needs and priorities of underserved communities (Chataway et al., 2014; Foster & Heeks, 2013)1. This contrasts with traditional models of innovation that have often privileged the interests of large corporations, high-tech industries, and urban elites, while overlooking the innovation capacities and development aspirations of marginalized groups (George et al., 2012; Naudé, 2017). Inclusive innovation encompasses a wide range of practices and approaches, including (Mohamad et al., 2020; Paunov, 2013):

1. Frugal innovation: The development of affordable, context-appropriate technologies and solutions that address the needs of low-income and underserved populations.
2. Social innovation: The creation of innovative products, services, and business models that tackle complex social and environmental challenges, often driven by social enterprises and community-based initiatives.
3. Grassroots innovation: The bottom-up development of innovative solutions by local communities, drawing on traditional knowledge and leveraging local resources and capabilities.
4. Inclusive entrepreneurship: The empowerment of women, youth, and marginalized groups as innovation leaders, with equitable access to the resources and opportunities needed to turn their ideas into reality.
5. Democratization of knowledge and technology: Initiatives that promote open-source, collaborative approaches to knowledge creation and sharing, as well as the democratization of digital technologies and infrastructure. At the heart of these diverse inclusive innovation practices is a shared commitment to equity, accessibility, and the holistic well-being of African communities (Chataway et al., 2019; Heeks et al., 2014). Inclusive innovation recognizes that innovation is not

inherently neutral or apolitical, but rather is shaped by underlying power structures, social dynamics, and cultural contexts (Bhaduri & Kumar, 2011; Papaioannou, 2014). By centering the voices and perspectives of marginalized groups, inclusive innovation seeks to challenge existing hierarchies, dismantle systemic barriers, and create more equitable and inclusive innovation ecosystems.

II. The Promise of Inclusive Innovation for Sustainable Development in Africa

The potential of inclusive innovation to drive transformative change in Africa is considerable, as it aligns with the continent's pressing development priorities and the global agenda for sustainable development.

1. Addressing Persistent Inequalities: Inclusive innovation offers a powerful antidote to the widening socioeconomic disparities that have plagued much of Africa's development progress. By empowering marginalized communities as active participants and co-creators of innovative solutions, inclusive innovation can help bridge the gap between the haves and the have-nots, fostering more equitable access to the benefits of innovation (Chataway et al., 2014; Konte & Ndou, 2020).
2. Driving Sustainable and Inclusive Economic Growth: Rather than prioritizing economic growth at the expense of social and environmental considerations, inclusive innovation seeks to create new pathways for sustainable and inclusive development. By catalyzing frugal, socially innovative, and environmentally conscious enterprises, inclusive innovation can generate employment, improve livelihoods, and contribute to the overall well-being of African societies (George et al., 2012; Swaans et al., 2014).
3. Tackling Complex Social and Environmental Challenges: Inclusive innovation holds immense promise in addressing the continent's most pressing social, health, and environmental challenges, from food and water insecurity to climate change and biodiversity loss. By drawing on local knowledge, fostering collaborative problem-solving, and centering the needs of marginalized communities, inclusive innovation can unlock innovative solutions that are both contextually relevant and

transformative in scope (Chataway et al., 2019; Mohamad et al., 2020).
4. Empowering Marginalized Groups as Innovation Leaders: A key tenet of inclusive innovation is the recognition that innovation capacity is not limited to a narrow elite, but is widely distributed across African societies. By actively empowering women, youth, and other underrepresented groups as innovation champions, inclusive innovation can unlock vast reservoirs of untapped creativity and problem-solving skills, while also advancing the causes of social justice and gender equity (Begović & Kolin, 2017; Foster & Heeks, 2013).
5. Aligning with the Sustainable Development Goals: The principles and practices of inclusive innovation are closely aligned with the United Nations' Sustainable Development Goals (SDGs), which provide a comprehensive framework for addressing the complex and interrelated challenges facing the world. By integrating inclusive innovation strategies into national and regional development plans, African countries can leverage innovation as a powerful catalyst for achieving the SDGs and charting a more sustainable and equitable future (Chataway et al., 2019; Paunov, 2013).

III. Navigating the Complexities and Tensions of Inclusive Innovation

While the promise of inclusive innovation is considerable, the path towards realizing its transformative potential is complex and multifaceted. Inclusive innovation does not exist in a vacuum but is shaped by a range of contextual factors, including political dynamics, institutional structures, cultural norms, and resource constraints (Moleka, 2024b; Moleka, 2024c; Foster & Heeks, 2013; Papaioannou, 2014). One of the key challenges in advancing inclusive innovation is the need to navigate the inherent tensions and trade-offs that can arise between the goals of inclusion, innovation, and sustainability. For example, efforts to democratize access to technology and knowledge may conflict with the profit-driven interests of private sector actors, while grassroots initiatives focused on social and environmental transformation may struggle to achieve the scale and financial sustainability needed to have a lasting impact (Chataway et al., 2014; Heeks et al., 2014). Additionally, the cultivation of inclusive innovation ecosystems requires the alignment and coordination of diverse stakeholders, including policymakers, civil society organizations, academic institutions, and local communities – a complex undertaking that demands thoughtful governance structures, power-sharing arrangements, and collaborative decision-making processes (Bhaduri & Kumar, 2011; Swaans et al., 2014). Furthermore, the measurement and evaluation of the impact of inclusive innovation initiatives can be a significant challenge, as traditional metrics focused on economic growth and technological advancement may fail to capture the multidimensional and transformative nature of inclusive innovation (Chataway et al., 2019; Paunov, 2013). Developing robust and holistic evaluation frameworks that account for social, environmental, and equity-related outcomes is essential for ensuring the long-term sustainability and scalability of inclusive innovation efforts. Despite these complexities, the imperative to embrace inclusive innovation as a means of reimagining African futures has never been more pressing. As the continent grapples with the compounded crises of inequality, environmental degradation, and the ongoing impacts of the COVID-19 pandemic, the need for innovative, equitable, and sustainable development solutions has become increasingly urgent (UNECA, 2020; World Bank, 2021). This book, "Inclusive Innovation for African Development," seeks to navigate these complexities and tensions, offering a comprehensive and nuanced exploration of the conceptual foundations, practical applications, and transformative potential of inclusive innovation in the African context. By drawing on interdisciplinary perspectives and highlighting innovative case studies, the chapters that follow aim to inspire and empower a new generation of inclusive innovation champions who can drive systemic change and create a more equitable and sustainable future for all Africans.

References

Begović, M., & Kolin, M. (2017). Social innovation in the Western Balkans: Concepts, actors, and policies. *Southeastern Europe*, 41(1), 1-16.

Bhaduri, S., & Kumar, H. (2011). Extrinsic and intrinsic motivations to innovate: Tracing the motivation of 'grassroot' innovators in India. *Mind & Society*, 10(1), 27-55.

Chataway, J., Hanlin, R., & Kaplinsky, R. (2014). Inclusive innovation: An architecture for policy development. *Innovation and Development*, 4(1), 33-54.

Chataway, J., Ochieng, C., Byrne, R., Daniels, C., Dobson, C., Asante, K. P., & Barbereau, S. (2019). Case studies of inclusive innovation for sustainability in low-income countries. *International Journal of Technology Management & Sustainable Development*, 18(1), 3-20.

Elu, J. U. (2018). Gender and science education in sub-Saharan Africa: Theories of change. *Canadian Journal of Development Studies*, 39(3), 296-314.

Foster, C., & Heeks, R. (2013). Conceptualising inclusive innovation: Modifying systems of innovation frameworks to understand diffusion of new technology to low-income consumers. *The European Journal of Development Research*, 25(3), 333-355.

George, G., McGahan, A. M., & Prabhu, J. (2012). Innovation for inclusive growth: Towards a theoretical framework and a research agenda. *Journal of Management Studies*, 49(4), 661-683.

Hamann, R., & Bertels, S. (2018). The institutional work of exploitation: Employers' work to create and perpetuate inequality. *Journal of Management Studies*, 55(3), 394-423.

Heeks, R., Foster, C., & Nugroho, Y. (2014). New models of inclusive innovation for development. *Innovation and Development*, 4(2), 175-185.

IPCC. (2022). Climate change 2022: Impacts, adaptation and vulnerability. Intergovernmental Panel on Climate Change.

Jayne, T. S., Chamberlin, J., & Benfica, R. (2018). Africa's unfolding economic transformation. *The Journal of Development Studies*, *54*(5), 777-787.

Kekana, H. N., Ruhiiga, T. M., Ndou, N. N., & Palamuleni, L. G. (2023). Environmental justice in South Africa: the dilemma of informal settlement residents. *GeoJournal*, 1–17. Advance online publication. https://doi.org/10.1007/s10708-022-10808-z

Konte, A., & Ndou, V. (2020). The impact of inequality on sustainable development in Africa. *Sustainable Development*, 28(6), 1438-1448.

Kraemer-Mbula, E., & Wunsch-Vincent, S. (Eds.). (2016). *The informal economy in developing nations: Hidden engine of innovation?* Cambridge University Press.

Mohamad, M., Sidek, S., Klobas, J. E., Ang, C. S., & Lee, V. H. (2020). Entrepreneurial intention and firm performance: The role of bricolage and inclusive innovation. *Journal of Business Research*, 113, 315-324.

Moleka, P. (2024a). Climate Resilience through Grassroots Innovation: Empowering Congolese Communities to Adapt to Environmental Change.

Moleka, P. (2024b). *Open Innovation: A Catalyst for Sustainable Digitalization in Asian Economies*. GRIN Verlag.

Moleka, P. (2024c). *Lexique des Mots Techniques dans le Domainde d'Innovation*. EUE.

Naudé, W. (2017). Entrepreneurship, education and the fourth industrial revolution in Africa. IZA Discussion Paper No. 10855.

Papaioannou, T. (2014). How inclusive can innovation and development be in the twenty-first century? *Innovation and Development*, 4(2), 187-202.

Paunov, C. (2013). Innovation and inclusive development: A discussion of the main policy issues. OECD Science, Technology and Industry Working Papers, 2013/01.

Robbins, P. (2019). *Political ecology: A critical introduction*. John Wiley & Sons.

Srinivas, S., & Sutz, J. (2008). Developing countries and innovation: Searching for a new analytical approach. *Technology in Society*, 30(2), 129-140.

Swaans, K., Boogaard, B., Bendapudi, R., Taye, H., Hendrickx, S., & Klerkx, L. (2014). Operationalizing inclusive innovation: Lessons from innovation platforms in livestock value chains in India and Mozambique. *Innovation and Development*, 4(2), 239-257.

UNECA. (2020). COVID-19 in Africa: Protecting lives and economies. United Nations Economic Commission for Africa.

World Bank. (2021). Africa's Pulse, No. 24, October 2021: An Analysis of Issues Shaping Africa's Economic Future. World Bank.

CHAPTER 1

The Imperative of Inclusive Innovation

In this context, the imperative of inclusive innovation has emerged as a critical framework for rethinking development strategies and driving more equitable and sustainable progress across the continent. Inclusive innovation, as defined by scholars such as Calestous Juma and Thandika Mkandawire, refers to the development and deployment of new products, services, and solutions that specifically cater to the needs of marginalized and underserved populations, with the goal of reducing socioeconomic inequalities and improving the well-being of all citizens (Juma, 2016; Mkandawire, 2011).

I. Limitations of Traditional Innovation Models

Calestous Juma, a renowned Kenyan professor of the practice of international development at Harvard Kennedy School, has extensively critiqued the limitations of traditional innovation models in the African context. In his seminal work, "Innovation and Its Enemies: Why People Resist New Technologies," Juma argues that these models have often been designed and implemented with a narrow focus on technological advancement and commercial profit (Juma, 2016). These conventional approaches, often rooted in the experiences and priorities of the Global North, have frequently failed to account for the unique socio-cultural, economic, and environmental contexts of the African continent (Assan, 2023; Arocena & Sutz, 2000; Kaplinsky, 2011). As a result, the benefits of innovation have often been skewed towards the privileged urban elite, while the needs and aspirations of marginalized populations have been largely overlooked. One of the primary shortcomings of conventional innovation models is their overemphasis on technological advancements and their disregard for the importance of local knowledge and community-based solutions. This technocentric bias has led to the development of innovations that may be impressive in their technical sophistication but ultimately fail to resonate with the lived experiences and pressing concerns of African communities (Moalosi & Rapitsenyane, 2023; Kaplinsky & Farooki, 2010). The disconnect between technological solutions and the realities on the ground has often resulted in the underutilization or rejection of these innovations by the intended beneficiaries. One of the key shortcomings of traditional innovation models, as identified by Juma, is their tendency to overlook the diverse needs and challenges faced by marginalized communities. These models typically prioritize the development of high-tech, capital-intensive solutions that cater to the needs of the urban elite or multinational corporations, rather than the more context-specific and resource-constrained realities of rural and low-income populations. As a result, the benefits of innovation often fail to trickle down to the most vulnerable segments of society, further exacerbating existing inequalities (Juma, 2016). Moreover, Juma highlights the disconnect between the knowledge and skills required to drive traditional innovation and the lived experiences and traditional knowledge systems of local communities. This misalignment can lead to the development of innovations that are incompatible with the cultural, social, and environmental contexts in which they are intended to be applied, undermining their effectiveness and sustainability (Juma, 2016). Thandika Mkandawire, a renowned Malawian professor of African Development at the London School of Economics, has also been a vocal critic of the limitations of conventional development policies and their impact on innovation in Africa. In his work, Mkandawire has argued that traditional development approaches have often been shaped by external actors, such as international financial institutions and aid agencies, rather than being grounded in the realities and priorities of African societies (Mkandawire, 2011). According to Mkandawire, these externally-driven development models have frequently prioritized economic growth over social equity, leading to the concentration of wealth and power in the hands of a few, while neglecting the needs of the poor and marginalized. This has resulted in the emergence of a "dual economy" in many African countries, characterized by a thriving, globally-connected sector coexisting with a largely informal, resource-constrained, and underserved segment of the population (Mkandawire, 2011).

As the traditional innovation paradigm has been heavily influenced by the interests of multinational corporations, global institutions, and technocratic elites, prioritizing economic growth and profitability over the principles of social inclusivity and environmental sustainability (Pansera & Owen, 2018; Anderson, Bruil, Chappell, Kiss & Pimbert, 2019), this orientation has led to the development of innovations that primarily benefit the wealthy and powerful, while perpetuating or even exacerbating the marginalization of vulnerable populations, such as the rural poor, women, and informal sector workers. The limitations of conventional innovation models are particularly evident in the African context, where issues of poverty, inequality, food insecurity, limited access to healthcare and education, and environmental degradation remain pervasive challenges. In this landscape, the prevailing approach to innovation has often failed to address the root causes of these complex problems, instead offering piecemeal solutions that neglect the interconnectedness of social, economic, and ecological factors (Almeida, 2024). Recognizing the shortcomings of conventional innovation models, scholars and practitioners have called for a paradigm shift towards more inclusive and participatory approaches that prioritize the needs and perspectives of marginalized communities (Arocena & Sutz, 2000; Cozzens & Sutz, 2014). This emerging discourse on inclusive innovation offers a promising pathway for rethinking the role of innovation in driving sustainable development and social transformation in Africa.

II. Towards an Inclusive Innovation Agenda

In order to achieve more sustainable and equitable development outcomes, inclusive innovation in Africa is not only a theoretical concept in innovation studies or innovationology; rather, it is a real requirement.

As Juma and Mkandawire have argued, the traditional, top-down, and technologically-focused models of innovation have largely failed to deliver on their promises of progress and prosperity for all (Juma, 2016; Mkandawire, 2011). In contrast, inclusive innovation offers a more holistic and people-centered approach, one that recognizes the diverse needs, capabilities, and perspectives of marginalized communities, and seeks to harness their collective creativity and resilience to drive transformative change. By prioritizing affordability, accessibility, and social impact, inclusive innovation can help to bridge the divides that have long characterized African societies, empowering the poor and the underserved to become active participants in the development process (Juma, 2016; Mkandawire, 2011). As the African continent faces an array of complex and interconnected challenges, from climate change and food insecurity to political instability and social unrest, the need for inclusive innovation has never been more pressing. By embracing this transformative paradigm, African nations can chart a new course towards a more equitable, sustainable, and prosperous future, one that is built on the foundations of collaborative, community-driven, and impact-oriented innovation (Juma, 2016; Mkandawire, 2011; Moleka, 2024a; 2024b; 2024c; 2024d).

This chapter delves into the conceptual foundations and practical significance of inclusive innovation as a critical driver of sustainable development in Africa. It examines the limitations of prevailing innovation models, explores the key principles and characteristics of inclusive innovation, and highlights its potential to catalyze meaningful and equitable change. Through a synthesis of scholarly perspectives and empirical evidence, this chapter establishes the imperative for a paradigm shift in how we approach innovation (Moleka, 2024e; 2024f; 2024g), ultimately positioning inclusive innovation as a crucial lever for realizing a more just, resilient, and prosperous African future.

III. Defining Inclusive Innovation

Inclusive innovation is a multifaceted concept that defies a singular definition, as it encompasses a range of perspectives and approaches. However, at its core, inclusive innovation can be understood as a process that actively involves and empowers marginalized individuals and communities in the creation, adaptation, and diffusion of innovations that address their specific needs and challenges (Mashelkar, 2012; Heeks et al., 2014).

In the African context, inclusive innovation can be further understood as a holistic approach that seeks to integrate the knowledge, resources, and agency of local communities into the innovation process, with the ultimate goal of driving sustainable and equitable development (Cozzens & Sutz, 2014). This approach recognizes the inherent strengths and resilience of African communities, and aims to amplify their voices, leverage their expertise, and empower them as active participants and co-creators of innovative solutions.

Inclusive innovation is often contrasted with the traditional, top-down model of innovation, which has been criticized for its lack of engagement with marginalized populations and its inability to address the systemic barriers that perpetuate social, economic, and environmental exclusion (Sheikh & Kumar, 2021; Arocena & Sutz, 2000; Srinivas & Sutz, 2008; Moleka, 2024h; 2024i).

In contrast, inclusive innovation emphasizes the importance of collaboration, mutual learning, and the integration of diverse knowledge systems, with the goal of fostering more equitable and sustainable development outcomes. Scholars have identified several key principles and characteristics that define the inclusive innovation paradigm:

1. Community-centricity: Inclusive innovation places the needs, priorities, and perspectives of marginalized communities at the center of the innovation process, recognizing them as active participants and co-creators rather than passive beneficiaries (Cozzens & Sutz, 2014).
2. Participatory approaches: Inclusive innovation relies on participatory methods that engage diverse stakeholders, including local communities, civil society organizations, and grassroots innovators, in the identification, design, and implementation of innovative solutions (Levidow & Papaioannou, 2018).
3. Integration of traditional and local knowledge: Inclusive innovation values and integrates the traditional, indigenous, and local knowledge systems of African communities, recognizing them as crucial assets in addressing complex development challenges (Arocena & Sutz, 2000).
4. Emphasis on social and environmental sustainability: Inclusive innovation prioritizes the achievement of sustainable development goals, seeking to address not only economic growth but also social inclusion, environmental protection, and the overall well-being of local communities (Gupta & Vegelin, 2016).
5. Grassroots innovation and frugal design: Inclusive innovation often involves the development and diffusion of low-cost, context-appropriate technologies and solutions that are designed and implemented by grassroots innovators and local communities (Kaplinsky, 2011).
6. Collaborative and multi-stakeholder partnerships: Inclusive innovation fosters cross-sectoral collaboration and the establishment of partnerships between diverse stakeholders, including local communities, civil society organizations, research institutions, and the public and private sectors (Luongo, Sepe & Del Gaudio, 2023).
7. Empowerment and capacity building: Inclusive innovation aims to empower marginalized individuals and communities, enhancing their capabilities, agency, and ownership over the innovation process (Cozzens & Sutz, 2014; Heeks et al., 2014).

These principles and characteristics collectively highlight the transformative potential of inclusive innovation in addressing the multifaceted challenges facing African societies, while also promoting more equitable and sustainable development outcomes.

IV. The Emergence of Inclusive Innovation in Africa

The concept of inclusive innovation has gained increasing prominence in the African development discourse over the past two decades, as scholars, policymakers, and practitioners have recognized the limitations of conventional innovation models and the need for more participatory and community-centric approaches (Arocena & Sutz, 2000; Cozzens & Sutz, 2014). The growing interest in inclusive innovation in Africa can be attributed to several key factors:

1. The persistence of socio-economic disparities and marginalization: Despite decades of development efforts, many African countries continue to grapple with entrenched inequalities, poverty, and the exclusion of vulnerable populations, such as the rural poor, women, and informal sector workers (Madzivhandila & Owusu, 2024). This has fueled the recognition that traditional innovation models have failed to adequately address the needs and aspirations of these marginalized groups.
2. The limitations of technology-driven solutions: As mentioned earlier, the technocentric bias of conventional innovation approaches has resulted in the development of technological solutions that often fail to resonate with the realities and priorities of African communities (Kaplinsky & Farooki, 2010). This has led to growing skepticism about the ability of technology alone to drive sustainable and equitable development.
3. The importance of local and indigenous knowledge: Scholars and practitioners have increasingly acknowledged the value of traditional, indigenous, and local knowledge systems in addressing complex development challenges in Africa (Arocena & Sutz, 2000). Inclusive innovation offers a framework for integrating these knowledge systems into the

innovation process, leveraging their potential to generate contextually relevant and culturally appropriate solutions.

4. The rise of grassroots innovation and social entrepreneurship: Across the African continent, there has been a proliferation of grassroots innovation and social entrepreneurship initiatives driven by local communities and civil society organizations (Kaplinsky, 2011; Cozzens & Sutz, 2014). These bottom-up approaches to innovation have highlighted the need for more inclusive and participatory models that empower marginalized populations as active agents of change.
5. The alignment with sustainable development goals: The principles of inclusive innovation, with their emphasis on social inclusion, environmental sustainability, and community empowerment, have resonated with the global sustainable development agenda, particularly the Sustainable Development Goals (SDGs).

This alignment has further propelled the recognition of inclusive innovation as a critical framework for achieving the SDGs in the African context. These contextual factors have converged to create a fertile ground for the emergence and evolution of inclusive innovation in Africa. As a result, a growing body of scholarly work and practical initiatives have begun to explore and advance this paradigm, offering new perspectives and strategies for driving sustainable and equitable development across the continent. The Significance of Inclusive Innovation in Africa The imperative for inclusive innovation in Africa lies in its potential to address the multifaceted challenges facing the continent and to catalyze a more equitable and sustainable development trajectory. By placing the needs and priorities of marginalized communities at the center of the innovation process, inclusive innovation offers a transformative approach to tackling complex social, economic, and environmental issues.

1. Fostering Social Inclusion and Empowerment: Inclusive innovation has the power to disrupt the cycles of marginalization and inequality that have long plagued African societies. By actively engaging and empowering vulnerable populations, such as the rural poor, women, and informal sector workers, inclusive innovation can create opportunities for

these groups to participate in and shape the development of innovative solutions that improve their lived experiences (Cozzens & Sutz, 2014; Heeks et al., 2014). This process of empowerment and capacity building not only enhances the agency of marginalized communities but also promotes social cohesion and a sense of ownership over development initiatives.

2. Addressing Persistent Development Challenges: The innovative solutions generated through inclusive innovation processes can directly address pressing development challenges in Africa, such as food insecurity, limited access to healthcare and education, environmental degradation, and the lack of reliable infrastructure (Kalkanci, Rahmani & Toktay, 2019). By leveraging local knowledge, resources, and expertise, these solutions are often more contextually appropriate and sustainable than those developed through conventional innovation models. Moreover, the collaborative and participatory nature of inclusive innovation can foster the development of holistic, systems-level approaches to addressing complex, interrelated development challenges.
3. Promoting Environmental Sustainability: Inclusive innovation, with its emphasis on environmental sustainability and the integration of traditional ecological knowledge, can play a crucial role in addressing the growing threat of climate change and environmental degradation in Africa. By developing and disseminating innovative, low-impact technologies and practices, and by empowering local communities as stewards of natural resources, inclusive innovation can contribute to more sustainable and resilient development pathways.
4. Advancing Sustainable and Equitable Economic Growth: Inclusive innovation can contribute to the achievement of sustainable and equitable economic growth in Africa by fostering innovative entrepreneurship, creating employment opportunities, and generating new revenue streams for marginalized communities (Kaplinsky, 2011; Cozzens & Sutz, 2014). By prioritizing the development of affordable, accessible, and context-appropriate innovations, inclusive innovation can expand the reach of economic opportunities and enhance the livelihoods of

underserved populations. Moreover, the collaborative and multi-stakeholder nature of inclusive innovation can strengthen local and regional innovation ecosystems, leading to more sustainable and inclusive economic development.

5. Aligning with the Sustainable Development Goals: The principles and objectives of inclusive innovation are strongly aligned with the Sustainable Development Goals (SDGs), particularly in their emphasis on reducing poverty and inequality, promoting sustainable cities and communities, ensuring quality education and healthcare, and fostering partnerships for sustainable development (Leal Filho, Tripathi, Andrade Guerra, Giné-Garriga, Orlovic Lovren, & Willats, 2019).
   By positioning inclusive innovation as a key driver of sustainable development in Africa, this paradigm can contribute to the achievement of the SDGs and help realize a more equitable and prosperous future for the continent.
6. Strengthening Community Resilience and Agency: Inclusive innovation empowers marginalized communities by recognizing and leveraging their inherent strengths, knowledge, and resilience. This process of community empowerment can enhance the ability of local populations to adapt to and cope with social, economic, and environmental shocks and stresses, thereby strengthening their overall resilience (Cozzens & Sutz, 2014; Heeks et al., 2014). Moreover, by positioning local communities as active participants and co-creators in the innovation process, inclusive innovation can foster a greater sense of agency and ownership over development initiatives, further bolstering their capacity to shape their own futures. The significance of inclusive innovation in the African context lies in its potential to transform the dominant development paradigm, shifting the focus from top-down, technocratic solutions to more holistic, participatory, and community-driven approaches. By recognizing and empowering the inherent strengths and resilience of marginalized populations, inclusive innovation offers a pathway for addressing the continent's most pressing challenges in a manner that is sustainable, equitable, and aligned with the aspirations of African communities.

V. Theoretical Foundations of Inclusive Innovation

The concept of inclusive innovation has been underpinned by several important theoretical frameworks and perspectives from the social sciences and development studies. Understanding these theoretical foundations can provide a more robust conceptual grounding for the discussion of inclusive innovation in the African context.

One of the key theoretical influences on inclusive innovation is the "Bottom of the Pyramid" (BoP) framework, developed by C.K. Prahalad and Stuart Hart (2002). The BoP proposition argued that the world's poorest populations, often overlooked by traditional business and development models, represent a vast untapped market and a source of innovation. This perspective has been instrumental in shifting the focus towards the unique needs and capabilities of marginalized communities, laying the groundwork for more inclusive approaches to innovation (Karnani, 2007; Simanis & Hart, 2008); Moleka, 2024h).

Another influential theoretical perspective is the "Capabilities Approach" advanced by Amartya Sen and Martha Nussbaum. This approach emphasizes the importance of expanding people's substantive freedoms and capabilities as the primary goals of development, rather than solely focusing on economic growth (Sen, 1999; Nussbaum, 2011). The Capabilities Approach has informed the inclusive innovation discourse by highlighting the need to empower marginalized communities and enable them to actively participate in the development process.

The "Participatory Development" framework, rooted in the work of scholars like Robert Chambers and John Gaventa, has also significantly influenced the inclusive innovation paradigm. This approach emphasizes the active engagement of local communities in the design, implementation, and evaluation of development initiatives, recognizing their role as agents of change rather than passive beneficiaries (Chambers, 1994; Gaventa, 1993).

The principles of participatory development have been widely adopted in the inclusive innovation literature.

Additionally, the "Grassroots Innovation" perspective, championed by scholars like Anil Gupta and Dinesh Abrol, has provided valuable insights into the creative problem-solving capacities of marginalized communities and the importance of recognizing and supporting their innovative efforts

(Moleka, 2024i; 2024j; Gupta, 2012; Abrol, 2014). This approach has been instrumental in framing inclusive innovation as a bottom-up, community-driven process.

These theoretical foundations have collectively shaped the conceptual underpinnings of inclusive innovation, informing the development of analytical frameworks, policy recommendations, and practical strategies for driving more equitable and sustainable development outcomes in Africa and beyond.

VI. Inclusive Innovation in the African Context: Empirical Evidence and Case Studies

The scholarly discourse on inclusive innovation in Africa has been enriched by a growing body of empirical research and case studies that highlight the diverse manifestations and impacts of this approach across the continent. One notable example is the work of Landry Signé, a prominent Cameroonian scholar and the managing director of the Brookings Institution's Africa Growth Initiative. Signé's research has documented the transformative potential of inclusive innovation in addressing pressing development challenges in Africa (Signé, 2018). Through in-depth case studies, Signé has showcased how grassroots innovators, social enterprises, and collaborative initiatives are harnessing the creativity and resourcefulness of local communities to develop affordable, accessible, and contextually appropriate solutions. For instance, Signé's analysis of the Empowering Smallholder Farmers in Africa (ESFA) initiative, led by Kenyan agricultural scientist Esther Ngumbi, illustrates how inclusive innovation can empower marginalized groups, such as women smallholder farmers, by providing them with access to innovative agricultural technologies and capacity-building support (Signé, 2018). By centering the voices and needs of these farmers, the ESFA initiative has been able to develop solutions that address the unique challenges they face, such as limited access to water, inadequate market information, and high post-harvest losses. In addition to the ESFA case study, Signé's work has also examined the inclusive innovation efforts of organizations like Aruma, a Ghanaian social enterprise developing affordable and accessible healthcare solutions, and Pula, a Kenyan enterprise offering weather-indexed crop insurance to smallholder farmers (Signé, 2018). These case studies underscore the importance of collaborative, cross-sector partnerships, community engagement, and the integration of traditional knowledge in driving the success and scalability of inclusive innovation initiatives.

Complementing Signé's research, other scholars have also contributed empirical evidence on the diverse applications and impacts of inclusive innovation in the African context. For example, Adeoti and Adeoti (2005) have explored the role of inclusive innovation in enhancing access to essential healthcare services in Nigeria, while Acharya and Basnyat (2015) have examined how inclusive innovation can foster sustainable energy solutions in rural communities in Ethiopia. These empirical studies and case analyses have been crucial in illuminating the transformative potential of inclusive innovation, as well as the unique challenges and enabling factors that shape its implementation in different African settings. By documenting the successes and lessons learned from these initiatives, the scholarly literature has provided valuable insights for policymakers, practitioners, and researchers seeking to leverage inclusive innovation as a driver of sustainable and equitable development in Africa (Moleka, 2024k).

VII. Implications for Policy and Practice

The imperative of inclusive innovation in Africa has significant implications for policymaking and practical interventions aimed at fostering more equitable and sustainable development outcomes. Scholars and practitioners have identified several key areas where policy and programmatic support can catalyze the growth and impact of inclusive innovation initiatives.

Policy Implications:

1. Enabling Policy Frameworks: Policymakers must develop supportive regulatory environments and institutional mechanisms that recognize, incentivize, and enable the work of grassroots innovators, social enterprises, and community-based initiatives (Dizolele, 2019). This could include the establishment of dedicated innovation funds, innovation-friendly procurement policies, and regulatory sandboxes that allow for the testing and scaling of inclusive solutions.
2. Capacity-building and Skills Development: Governments and development agencies should invest in programs that enhance the technical, entrepreneurial, and managerial capacities of marginalized communities,

empowering them to actively participate in the innovation process (Lopes, 2020). This could involve the creation of specialized training modules, mentorship programs, and the strengthening of regional innovation hubs and incubators.

3. Collaborative Ecosystem Development: Policymakers should foster the development of inclusive innovation ecosystems that facilitate cross-sectoral partnerships, knowledge sharing, and the co-creation of solutions among diverse stakeholders, including local communities, civil society organizations, research institutions, and the private sector (Luongo, Sepe, & Del Gaudio, 2023).

Practical Implications:

1. Community-Centered Design: Practitioners and development organizations must prioritize community engagement and co-creation in the design and implementation of inclusive innovation initiatives. This involves deeply understanding the needs, challenges, and existing knowledge systems of local communities, and actively incorporating their perspectives and inputs throughout the innovation process (Mattelmäki, Vaajakallio, & Koskinen, 2014).
2. Innovative Financing Mechanisms: Development agencies and impact investors should leverage diverse financing models, such as blended finance, crowd-funding, and micro-lending, to support the growth and scaling of inclusive innovation initiatives that prioritize social impact over pure financial returns (Lopes, 2020).
3. Knowledge Dissemination and Learning: Researchers, policymakers, and practitioners should establish platforms and mechanisms for the effective dissemination of knowledge, best practices, and lessons learned from inclusive innovation initiatives across Africa. This cross-pollination of ideas and experiences can accelerate the adoption and adaptation of successful models in different contexts (Sonne, 2012). By addressing these policy and practical implications, African nations can create more enabling environments for inclusive innovation to thrive, unleashing its transformative potential to drive sustainable and equitable development across the continent.

The imperative of inclusive innovation in Africa has never been more pressing. As the continent grapples with persistent social, economic, and environmental challenges, the limitations of conventional innovation models have become increasingly evident. Inclusive innovation, with its emphasis on community-centricity, participatory engagement, and the integration of local and traditional knowledge, presents a transformative paradigm that can catalyze sustainable and equitable development across the African continent. By placing the needs and priorities of marginalized communities at the center of the innovation process, inclusive innovation has the potential to foster social inclusion, address persistent development challenges, promote environmental sustainability, advance equitable economic growth, and align with the Sustainable Development Goals. Moreover, this approach can strengthen community resilience and agency, empowering local populations as active participants and co-creators of innovative solutions. As the African development landscape continues to evolve, the imperative of inclusive innovation must be embraced by policymakers, practitioners, researchers, and community leaders alike. By collectively embracing this paradigm shift, we can unlock the transformative potential of African communities and chart a more just, resilient, and prosperous future for the continent.

References

Abrol, D. (2014). Grassroots innovation: Minds on the margin are not marginal minds. *Dimensions*, 50(3), 1.

Acharya, R. H., & Basnyat, B. (2015). The role of innovation and technology in addressing climate change adaptation and mitigation in Nepal. *Environment Development and Sustainability*, 17(4), 663-682.

Adeoti, J. O., & Adeoti, A. I. (2005). Biotechnology R&D partnership for industrial innovation in Nigeria. *Technovation*, 25(4), 349-365.

Almeida, F. (2024). Causes of Failure of Open Innovation Practices in Small- and Medium-Sized Enterprises. *Administrative Sciences*, *14*(3), 50.

Anderson, C. R., Bruil, J., Chappell, M. J., Kiss, C., & Pimbert, M. P. (2019). From transition to domains of transformation: Getting to sustainable and just food systems through agroecology. *Sustainability*, *11*(19), 5272.

Arocena, R., & Sutz, J. (2000). Looking at national systems of innovation from the South. Industry and Innovation, 7(1), 55-75.

Assan, N. (2023). Socio-cultural, economic, and environmental implications for innovation in sustainable food in Africa. *Frontiers in Sustainable Food Systems*, 7, 1192422.

Chambers, R. (1994). The origins and practice of participatory rural appraisal. *World development*, 22(7), 953-969.

Cozzens, S., & Sutz, J. (2014). Innovation in informal settings: Reflections and proposals for a research agenda. *Innovation and Development*, 4(1), 5-31.

Dizolele, M. P. (2019). The Challenges of Promoting Inclusive Innovation in Sub-Saharan Africa. Center for Strategic and International Studies.

Gaventa, J. (1993). The powerful, the powerless, and the experts: Knowledge struggles in an information age. *Voices of change*, 21-40.

Gupta, A. K. (2012). Innovations for the poor by the poor. International Journal of Technological Learning. *Innovation and Development*, 5(1-2), 28-39.

Gupta, J., & Vegelin, C. (2016). Sustainable development goals and inclusive development. *International environmental agreements: Politics, law and economics*, *16*, 433-448.

Heeks, R., Foster, C., & Nugroho, Y. (2014). New models of inclusive innovation for development. *Innovation and Development*, 4(2), 175-185.

Juma, C. (2016). *Innovation and its enemies: Why people resist new technologies*. Oxford University Press.

Kalkanci, B., Rahmani, M., & Toktay, L. B. (2019). The role of inclusive innovation in promoting social sustainability. *Production and Operations Management*, *28*(12), 2960-2982.

Karnani, A. (2007). The mirage of marketing to the bottom of the pyramid: How the private sector can help alleviate poverty. *California management review*, 49(4), 90-111.

Kaplinsky, R. (2011). Schumacher meets Schumpeter: Appropriate technology below the radar. *Research Policy*, 40(2), 193-203.

Kaplinsky, R., & Farooki, M. (2010). What are the implications for global value chains when the market shifts from the North to the South? World Bank Policy Research Working Paper Series.

Leal Filho, W., Tripathi, S. K., Andrade Guerra, J. B. S. O. D., Giné-Garriga, R., Orlovic Levidow, L., & Papaioannou, T. (2018). Which inclusive innovation? Competing normative assumptions around social justice. *Innovation and Development*, *8*(2), 209-226.

Lopes, C. (2020). Africa's development in the age of stranded assets. *African Development Review*, 32(S1), S3-S15.

Lovren, V., & Willats, J. (2019). Using the sustainable development goals towards a better understanding of sustainability challenges. *International Journal of Sustainable Development & World Ecology*, *26*(2), 179-190.

Luongo, S., Sepe, F., & Del Gaudio, G. (2023). Regional innovation systems in tourism: The role of collaboration and competition. *Journal of Open Innovation: Technology, Market, and Complexity*, *9*(4), 100148.

Madzivhandila, T., & Owusu, F. (2024). Livelihoods, poverty, and development. In *Handbook of African Economic Development* (pp. 315-329). Edward Elgar Publishing.

Mattelmäki, T., Vaajakallio, K., & Koskinen, I. (2014). What happened to empathic design? *Design issues*, 30(1), 67-77.

Moleka, P. (2024a). Innovationology: A Comprehensive, Transdisciplinary Framework for Driving Transformative Innovation in the 21st Century. OSF Preprints f3scj, Center for Open Science.

Moleka, P. (2024b). Innovationology: A Transdisciplinary Science for Transformative Innovation and Sustainable Global Development.

Moleka, P. (2024c). Frugal Innovation for Inclusive and Sustainable Development in Africa. *Advanced Research in Economics and Business Strategy Journal*, 5(1):107-117.

Moleka, P. (2024d). Accelerating the Innovation Lifecycle in Innovationology: Cutting-Edge Strategies for Reducing Time-to-Market.

Moleka, P. (2024e). *Holistic Education. Enhancing the Mind, Body and Soul*. The Innovationology Series / TOME V. GRIN: Verlag.

Moleka, P. (2024f). *Innovationology and the Geoeconomics of the BRICS. Towards a Sustainable and Equitable Global Order*. The Innovationology Series / TOME VII. GRIN: Verlag.

Moleka, P. (2024g). Innovationology: A Goundbreaking Transdisciplinary Framework for Sustainable and Equitable Development in Africa. *International Journal of Social Sciences and Management Review*. 7(5):178-193.

Moleka, P. (2024h). Innovation Metrics for the 21st Century: An Innovationology-based Comprehensive, Multidimensional Framework. *International Journal of Social Sciences and Management Review*. 7(5):199-210.

Moleka, P. (2024i). Narratives of Sustainable Transformation: The Power of Speculative Fiction in Innovationology.
Moleka, P. (2024j). Innovative entrepreneurship through alternative finance: A framework for sustainable and innovative business models. In M. Fanea-Ivanovici & H. Baber (Eds.), *Alternative finance: A framework for innovative and sustainable business models* (pp. 13-28). Taylor & Francis.
Moleka, P. (2024k). Ubuntu and Sustainable Cities in Africa. In *The Palgrave Handbook of Ubuntu, Inequality and Sustainable Development.*
ChapterDOI 10.1007/978-3-031-69573-5_22
Mkandawire, T. (2011). Running while others walk: Knowledge and the challenge of Africa's development. *Africa Development,* 36(2), 1-36.
Moalosi, R., & Rapitsenyane, Y. (Eds.). (2023). *African Industrial Design Practice: Perspectives on Ubuntu Philosophy.* Taylor & Francis.
Nussbaum, M. C. (2011). *Creating capabilities.* Harvard University Press.
Pansera, M., & Owen, R. (2018). Framing inclusive innovation within the discourse of development: Insights from case studies in India. *Research Policy*, *47*(1), 23-34.
Prahalad, C. K., & Hart, S. L. (2002). The fortune at the bottom of the pyramid. *strategy+ business*, 26(1), 2-14.
Sen, A. (1999). *Development as freedom.* Oxford University Press.
Sheikh, F. A., & Kumar, H. (2021). Grassroots innovation: mainstreaming the discourse of informal sector. In *Handbook on Alternative Theories of Innovation* (pp. 212-232). Edward Elgar Publishing.
Simanis, E., & Hart, S. (2008). The base of the pyramid protocol: Toward next generation BoP strategy. *Center for Sustainable Global Enterprise*, 24, 1-57.
Signé, L. (2018). *Innovating Development Strategies in Africa: The Role of International, Regional, and National Actors.* Brookings Institution Press.
Sonne, L. (2012). Innovative initiatives supporting inclusive innovation in India: Social business incubation and micro venture capital. *Technological Forecasting and Social Change*, 79(4), 638-647.

CHAPTER 2

African Innovation Ecosystems: Diversity, Collaboration, and Grassroots Dynamism

Innovation has long been recognized as a key driver of economic growth, social progress, and sustainable development. However, traditional models of innovation have often overlooked the unique contexts, needs, and contributions of the African continent. Across the diverse nations and communities of Africa, a vibrant and dynamic innovation ecosystem is taking shape, one that is characterized by a rich tapestry of grassroots initiatives, collaborative networks, and local problem-solving (Berdegué, 2005; Prahalad & Mashelkar, 2010). This chapter examines the emergence of inclusive and collaborative innovation ecosystems in Africa, exploring how they are redefining the way we approach development challenges. By highlighting the critical role of diverse stakeholders, from community-based organizations to social enterprises, we will demonstrate the transformative potential of African innovation ecosystems to address pressing social, economic, and environmental issues (Sutz, 2012; Wamae, 2009). Through a detailed analysis of case studies and empirical research, this chapter will unpack the key features, drivers, and enabling conditions that underpin the growth of inclusive innovation in Africa. We will delve into the ways in which these ecosystems foster cross-sector collaboration, empower marginalized communities, and prioritize local knowledge and contextual relevance (Arocena & Sutz, 2000; Cozzens & Sutz, 2014). Furthermore, we will explore the critical role of policy frameworks, institutional support, and capacity-building initiatives in nurturing and sustaining these dynamic innovation landscapes. By examining both the successes and challenges faced by African innovation ecosystems, we will outline strategies for strengthening their resilience, scalability, and transformative impact (Chataway et al., 2014; Grobbelaar & Boshoff, 2019). Ultimately, this chapter will position African innovation ecosystems as crucial engines of inclusive and sustainable development, highlighting their capacity to tackle complex, multifaceted challenges through collaborative, community-driven approaches. By embracing the diversity and ingenuity of these grassroots innovation hubs, we can unlock new pathways for a more equitable and prosperous African future.

I. The Diverse Actors Shaping African Innovation Ecosystems

The innovation landscape in Africa is characterized by a diverse array of actors and stakeholders, each playing a crucial role in shaping the trajectory of inclusive innovation. According to Frannie Léautier, a Tanzanian scholar and former senior vice president of the African Development Bank, these stakeholders include not only traditional players such as universities, research institutions, and technology companies, but also a vibrant ecosystem of grassroots organizations, social enterprises, and community-based initiatives (Léautier, 2012). Léautier's research has highlighted the importance of fostering collaboration and cross-pollination among these diverse actors, as it is §within the intersections of different perspectives, knowledge systems, and resources that the most innovative and impactful solutions often emerge. By bringing together the expertise and insights of policymakers, entrepreneurs, civil society groups, and marginalized communities, innovation ecosystems in Africa can harness the collective intelligence and resourcefulness of their constituents to address complex social, economic, and environmental challenges (Léautier, 2012; Berdegué, 2005; Sutz, 2012). At the heart of these innovation ecosystems are the grassroots communities, whose deep understanding of local challenges and innovative problem-solving strategies are central to driving development efforts.

Community-based organizations, social enterprises, and informal networks have emerged as key players, leveraging their intimate knowledge of local contexts to design and deploy context-appropriate solutions (Arocena & Sutz, 2000; Cozzens & Sutz, 2014). For example, in Kenya, the Jua Kali

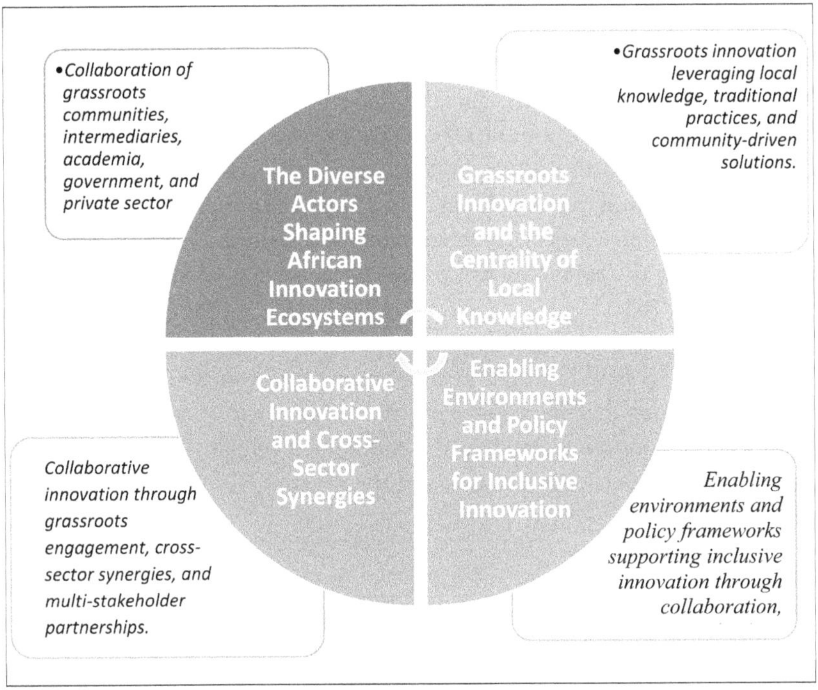

Figure 2.1 Innovation Ecosystems in Africa (Author's own work)

sector, comprising informal workshops and small-scale manufacturers, has long been a hub of grassroots innovation, with artisans and entrepreneurs adapting and repurposing existing technologies to meet the unique needs of their communities (Omidyar Network, 2013). Similarly, in Uganda, the Nabagereka Development Foundation has empowered rural women to develop and scale up innovative agricultural practices, drawing on traditional knowledge systems to improve food security and sustainability (Nabagereka Development Foundation, 2020). Alongside these grassroots actors, a diverse array of intermediary organizations, such as innovation hubs, accelerators, and incubators, play a critical role in catalyzing and supporting the growth of inclusive innovation ecosystems. These entities provide crucial resources, including access to funding, mentorship, and capacity-building programs, to help scale up community-driven initiatives and connect them with broader networks (Grobbelaar & Boshoff, 2019; Wamae, 2009). For instance, in South Africa, the Bertha Centre for Social Innovation and Entrepreneurship at the University of Cape Town has spearheaded numerous initiatives to support social enterprises and community-based organizations, offering tailored acceleration programs and facilitating cross-sector collaborations (Bertha Centre, 2020). Similarly, in Ethiopia, the xHub Addis incubator has fostered a vibrant ecosystem of social entrepreneurs and grassroots innovators, providing them with the resources and connections needed to scale their impact (xHub Addis, 2021).

Alongside these intermediary organizations, academic institutions and research centers have emerged as important players in African innovation ecosystems, contributing their expertise, infrastructure, and networks to support collaborative research and development efforts. Universities, such as Makerere University in Uganda and the Kwame Nkrumah University of

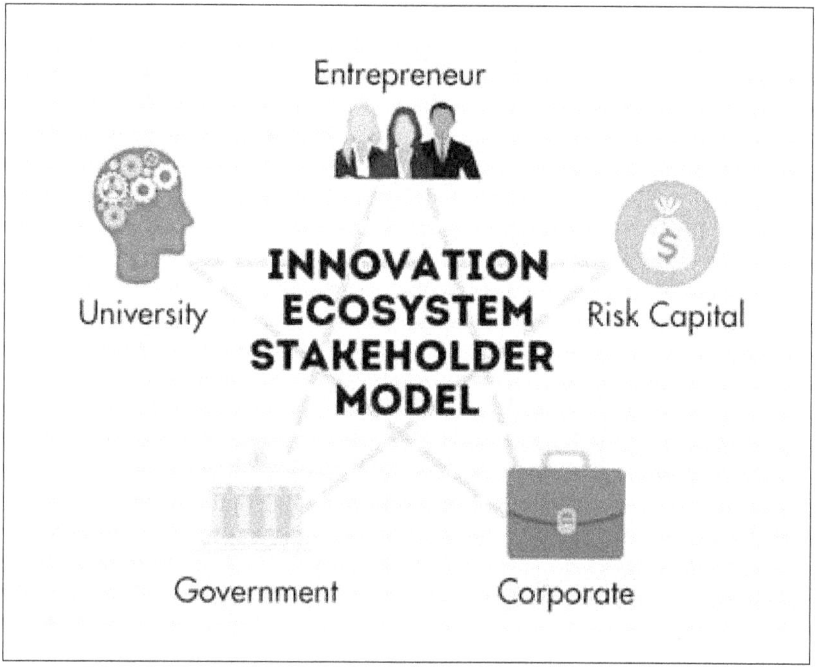

Figure 2.2 Innovation Ecosystem Stakeholder Model (Author's own work)

Science and Technology in Ghana, have established innovation hubs and living labs that bring together students, faculty, and community partners to co-create solutions to local challenges (Makerere University, 2021; KNUST, 2020). Furthermore, the public sector, in the form of government agencies, policymakers, and regulatory bodies, plays a crucial role in shaping the enabling environment for inclusive innovation. Through the implementation of supportive policies, the provision of funding and infrastructure, and the facilitation of multi-stakeholder collaborations, the public sector can significantly enhance the growth and impact of African innovation ecosystems (Chataway et al., 2014; Grobbelaar & Boshoff, 2019). For instance, the Kenyan government's establishment of the Konza Technopolis, a large-scale technology and innovation hub, has catalyzed the development of a vibrant ecosystem of startups, research institutions, and multinational corporations, all working together to drive the country's digital transformation (Konza Technopolis, 2021). Similarly, the South African government's Technology Innovation Agency (TIA) has provided critical funding and support to a range of social innovators and community-based initiatives, enabling them to scale their impact and reach (Technology Innovation Agency, 2021). Finally, the private sector, in the form of multinational corporations, local businesses, and impact investors, also plays a crucial role in shaping African innovation ecosystems. These actors can contribute financial resources, technical expertise, and market access to help scale up promising grassroots initiatives, while also benefiting from the innovative solutions and talent emerging from these dynamic ecosystems (Prahalad & Mashelkar, 2010; Wamae, 2009). For example, the Mastercard Foundation's Young Africa Works initiative has partnered with numerous private sector actors to support youth entrepreneurship and job creation in several African countries, leveraging the collective expertise and resources of the private sector to catalyze inclusive and sustainable development (Mastercard Foundation, 2021). Similarly, the Acumen Fund, a pioneering impact investment firm, has deployed patient capital and capacity-building support to social enterprises across Africa, helping to scale innovative solutions to pressing social and environmental challenges (Acumen, 2021). The interplay of these diverse stakeholders, each contributing their unique perspectives, resources, and expertise, is what gives rise to the dynamic, collaborative nature of African innovation ecosystems.

Figure 2.3 The Diverse Actors Shaping African Innovation Ecosystems (Author's own work)

By fostering cross-sector partnerships and synergies, these ecosystems are able to tackle complex development challenges in a more holistic and impactful way, drawing on the collective ingenuity and collective agency of the communities they serve (Arocena & Sutz, 2000; Cozzens & Sutz, 2014).

II. Grassroots Innovation and the Centrality of Local Knowledge

The grassroots innovation paradigm, which has gained prominence in the African context, recognizes the vital role that local knowledge, creative problem-solving, and community-driven initiatives play in shaping the development landscape. This approach challenges the top-down, expert-driven models of innovation that have often failed to address the unique circumstances and priorities of local communities (Berdegué, 2005; Sutz, 2012). One of the key features of grassroots innovation in Africa is the integration of traditional knowledge systems with modern scientific and technological advancements. This blending of knowledge sources has given rise to a rich tapestry of innovative solutions that are deeply rooted in local cultural contexts and environmental realities (Arocena & Sutz, 2000; Wamae, 2009).

For example, in the Sahel region of West Africa, where desertification and climate change pose significant threats to agricultural livelihoods, farmers have developed innovative agroecological practices that combine traditional land management techniques with modern sustainable farming methods. These practices, which include the use of natural fertilizers, crop diversification, and water harvesting systems, have helped to improve food security and environmental resilience in the face of a rapidly changing climate (Altieri & Nicholls, 2017; Reij et al., 2009). Similarly, in the informal settlements of Nairobi, Kenya, grassroots innovators have repurposed waste materials to create affordable, durable housing solutions that address the severe shortage of adequate shelter. The Kibera Hamlets project, for instance, has empowered local residents to construct low-cost, eco-friendly homes using recycled plastic bottles and other waste, demonstrating the transformative potential of grassroots innovation to tackle complex urban challenges (Kibera Hamlets, 2021). These grassroots innovations are not confined to the realm of technology and infrastructure; they also encompass innovative social and organizational models that address pressing community needs. In South Africa, the Abalimi Bezekhaya cooperative has enabled urban farmers in Cape Town's townships to collectively manage and market their produce, empowering marginalized communities and strengthening food security through collaborative, community-driven approaches (Abalimi Bezekhaya, 2021). The centrality of local knowledge and community ownership is a defining characteristic of

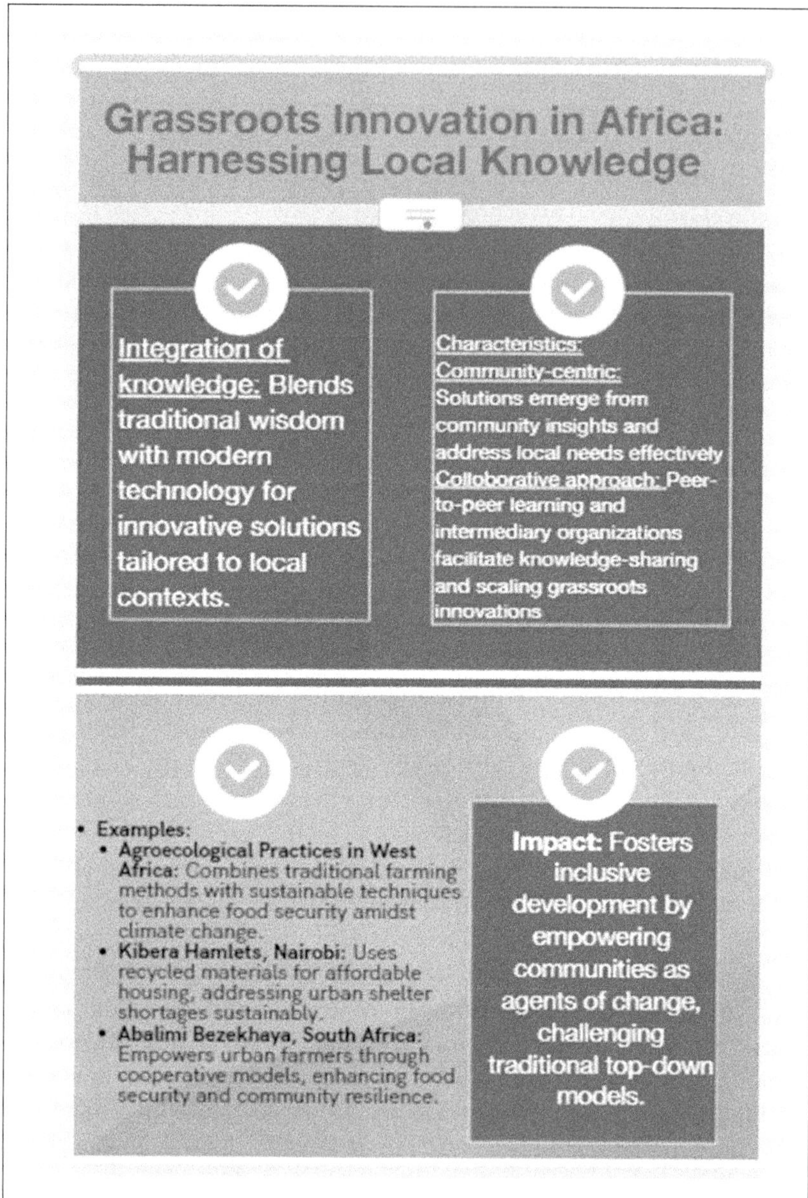

Figure 2.4 Grassroots Innovation in Africa

grassroots innovation in Africa. These initiatives are not conceived in isolation, but rather emerge from the lived experiences and contextual understanding of the communities themselves, ensuring that the solutions developed are truly responsive to local needs and priorities (Arocena & Sutz, 2000; Cozzens & Sutz, 2014). Moreover, the process of grassroots innovation is often characterized by a high degree of collaboration and knowledge-sharing within and between communities. Local innovators and problem-solvers engage in peer-to-peer learning, exchanging ideas and best practices, and adapting successful models to their own unique circumstances (Berdegué, 2005; Sutz, 2012). This collaborative ethos is further reinforced by the role of intermediary organizations, such as innovation hubs and community-based organizations, which facilitate the exchange of knowledge, resources, and connections between grassroots initiatives and broader innovation ecosystems. By bridging the gap between local communities and external stakeholders, these intermediaries play a crucial role in amplifying the voices and contributions of grassroots innovators, ensuring that their solutions are recognized, scaled, and integrated into wider development frameworks (Grobbelaar & Boshoff, 2019; Wamae, 2009). The centrality of local knowledge and community ownership in African innovation ecosystems represents a fundamental shift away from the top-down, expert-driven models that have often failed to address the unique challenges and priorities of marginalized communities. By embracing the ingenuity and collective agency of grassroots innovators, these ecosystems are able to unlock new pathways for inclusive and sustainable development, empowering local communities to become active agents of change in their own right (Arocena & Sutz, 2000; Cozzens & Sutz, 2014).

III. Collaborative Innovation and Cross-Sector Synergies

The dynamic and collaborative nature of African innovation ecosystems is a key driver of their transformative potential. These ecosystems are characterized by the active engagement and synergistic collaboration of diverse stakeholders, each contributing their unique expertise, resources, and networks to address complex development challenges (Chataway et al., 2014; Grobbelaar & Boshoff, 2019). At the heart of this collaborative approach are the grassroots communities, whose intimate knowledge of local contexts and innovative problem-solving strategies form the foundation of the innovation ecosystem.

By actively engaging with these communities and prioritizing their needs and perspectives, other stakeholders, such as intermediary organizations, academic institutions, and the public and private sectors, are able to co-create and scale up solutions that are truly responsive to the realities on the ground (Berdegué, 2005; Sutz, 2012).

Winnie Byanyima, a Ugandan social and political activist and the former executive director of Oxfam International, has been a vocal advocate for the critical role of community-driven innovation hubs and networks in promoting inclusive innovation across Africa. Byanyima's work has emphasized the need to empower marginalized groups, such as women, youth, and rural communities, to become active participants in the innovation process, drawing on their lived experiences, traditional knowledge, and grassroots-level problem-solving capacities (Byanyima, 2018). By establishing innovation hubs and collaborative networks that are rooted in the needs and priorities of local communities, Byanyima argues, African nations can unlock new pathways for sustainable and equitable development. These community-driven spaces not only provide access to essential resources, such as funding, skills training, and technology, but also serve as platforms for knowledge exchange, collective problem-solving, and the co-creation of innovative solutions (Byanyima, 2018). Byanyima's work has also highlighted the importance of fostering inclusive governance structures within these innovation hubs and networks, ensuring that marginalized groups are represented in decision-making processes and that the benefits of innovation are equitably distributed. This approach, she contends, can help to challenge the entrenched power dynamics that have historically excluded certain segments of the population from the innovation ecosystem, paving the way for a more inclusive and participatory model of development (Byanyima, 2018).

One powerful example of cross-sector collaboration in African innovation ecosystems is the emergence of innovation hubs and incubators that bring together entrepreneurs, researchers, policymakers, and community representatives. These intermediary organizations serve as catalysts for collaborative innovation, providing access to resources, mentorship, and networking opportunities that enable grassroots initiatives to scale and thrive (Grobbelaar & Boshoff, 2019; Wamae, 2009). For instance, in Rwanda, the Kigali Innovation City has fostered a vibrant ecosystem of startups, research institutions, and multinational corporations, all working together to drive the country's digital transformation. By facilitating knowledge-sharing, capacity-building, and cross-sector partnerships, the Kigali Innovation City has become a hub for collaborative innovation, enabling the co-creation of solutions that address Rwanda's most pressing development challenges (Kigali Innovation City, 2021). Similarly, in Ghana, the Kumasi Hive has brought together a diverse array of stakeholders, including local entrepreneurs, university researchers, and government agencies, to tackle issues related to sustainable agriculture, renewable energy, and digital inclusion. Through its incubation and acceleration programs, the Kumasi Hive has empowered grassroots innovators to scale their impact, while also fostering cross-sector collaborations that leverage the complementary strengths of various stakeholders (Kumasi Hive, 2021). These collaborative innovation hubs are not limited to urban centers; they can also be found in rural and peri-urban areas, where they play a crucial role in connecting marginalized communities to broader innovation ecosystems. In Malawi, for example, the Mzuzu Innovation Hub has worked closely with smallholder farmers, local enterprises, and government extension services to develop and scale up innovative agricultural technologies and practices, addressing food security and livelihood challenges in the region (Mzuzu Innovation Hub, 2021). Beyond innovation hubs, African innovation ecosystems also feature collaborative research and development initiatives that bring together academic institutions, public sector agencies, and community-based organizations. These multi-stakeholder partnerships leverage the collective knowledge, resources, and networks of diverse actors to tackle complex, interdisciplinary development challenges (Chataway et al., 2014; Grobbelaar & Boshoff, 2019). In South Africa, for instance, the University of Cape Town's Centre for Biomedical Ethics and Law has collaborated with local community organizations and government health departments to develop innovative telemedicine solutions that improve access to healthcare in underserved areas. By integrating cutting-edge digital technologies with a deep understanding of community needs and priorities, this collaborative initiative has been able to create sustainable, scalable models of healthcare delivery (Centre for Biomedical Ethics and Law, 2021). Similarly, in Kenya, the Jomo Kenyatta University of Agriculture and Technology has partnered with smallholder farmers, civil society organizations, and county governments to co-create sustainable agricultural practices and value chains. Through this collaborative research and extension approach, the university has been able to ensure that its innovations are closely aligned with the needs and capacities of local communities, ultimately enhancing their impact and scalability (Jomo Kenyatta University of Agriculture and Technology, 2021).

The collaborative nature of African innovation ecosystems is also evident in the growing number of cross-border and transnational partnerships that are emerging across the continent. These initiatives leverage the diverse strengths and resources of different countries and regions, catalyzing the exchange of knowledge, best practices, and innovative solutions (Chataway et al., 2014; Wamae, 2009).

For example, the Southern African Innovation Support (SAIS) program, a multi-country initiative funded by the Finnish government, has facilitated the creation of innovation networks and collaborative platforms across Botswana, Namibia, South Africa, and Tanzania. By fostering cross-border collaborations and knowledge-sharing, SAIS has enabled grassroots innovators and social entrepreneurs to scale their impact and reach, while also strengthening the overall resilience of the participating innovation ecosystems (SAIS, 2021). Similarly, the Afrilabs network, which connects over 300 innovation hubs across 50 African countries, has played a vital role in facilitating cross-border collaborations, joint research projects, and the exchange of best practices. By leveraging the collective expertise and resources of its member hubs, Afrilabs has been able to amplify the voice and impact of grassroots innovators, while also fostering a more integrated and resilient innovation landscape across the African continent (Afrilabs, 2021). The collaborative, cross-sector nature of African innovation ecosystems is a key driver of their transformative potential. By bringing together diverse stakeholders, leveraging complementary strengths, and prioritizing the needs and perspectives of local communities, these ecosystems are able to tackle complex development challenges in a more holistic and impactful way. This collaborative approach not only empowers grassroots innovators but also strengthens the overall resilience and scalability of the innovation landscape, paving the way for more inclusive and sustainable development across the African continent.

IV. Enabling Environments and Policy Frameworks for Inclusive Innovation

The growth and impact of African innovation ecosystems are heavily dependent on the enabling environments and policy frameworks that support them.

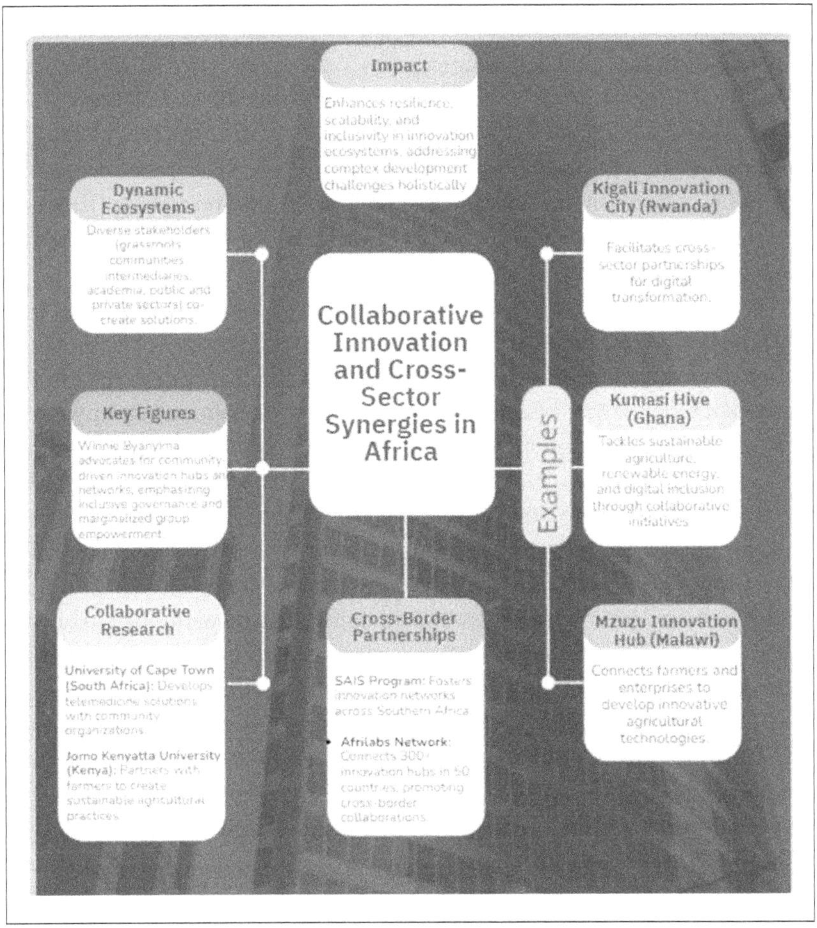

Figure 2.5 Collaborative Innovation and Cross-Sector Synergies in Africa (Author's own work)

Governments across the continent play a crucial role in fostering inclusive innovation by shaping the regulatory landscape, mobilizing resources, and incentivizing multi-stakeholder collaboration.

- Assessing the Current Policy Landscape: An analysis of the current policy landscape reveals significant diversity in the approaches taken by African nations to promote inclusive innovation. While some countries have implemented targeted policies and programs, others have yet to fully integrate inclusive innovation into their national development

Common policy interventions include tax incentives for innovative startups, public procurement strategies that prioritize underrepresented vendors, and the establishment of innovation hubs and accelerators in underserved communities.

- Identifying Best Practices and Innovative Policy Approaches: Despite the heterogeneity of national policies, several countries have pioneered innovative approaches that can serve as models for the continent. For instance, Kenya's "Digital Economy Blueprint" outlines a comprehensive strategy for harnessing digital technologies to drive inclusive growth, while Rwanda's "National Policy on Science, Technology, and Innovation" emphasizes the importance of community-based innovation and traditional knowledge systems. These policy frameworks demonstrate the value of aligning inclusive innovation with broader sustainable development objectives.
- Fostering Multi-Stakeholder Collaboration and Public-Private Partnerships: Recognizing that inclusive innovation requires the active engagement of diverse actors, policymakers are increasingly focusing on facilitating multi-stakeholder collaboration and public-private partnerships. Such approaches help mobilize resources, share knowledge, and align incentives across the innovation ecosystem. Successful examples include joint innovation challenges organized by governments and corporate partners, as well as innovation hubs that bring together entrepreneurs, researchers, civil society organizations, and local communities.
- Promoting Access to Finance, Infrastructure, and Support Services

A critical aspect of enabling environments for inclusive innovation is ensuring equitable access to the necessary resources and support services. This includes targeted funding mechanisms, such as impact investment funds and crowd-sourcing platforms, that cater to the needs of underrepresented groups. Governments can also invest in physical and digital infrastructure,

Figure 2.6 Enabling Environments and Policy Frameworks (Author's own work)

as well as provide business development, mentorship, and capacity-building programs tailored to the unique requirements of inclusive innovators.

- Strengthening Intellectual Property Rights and Protecting Traditional Knowledge: The protection of intellectual property rights and the equitable recognition of traditional knowledge systems are essential for fostering inclusive innovation. Policymakers must strike a balance between encouraging the commercialization of innovative solutions and safeguarding the rights and interests of local communities. Frameworks for the fair and transparent sharing of benefits derived from the integration of traditional knowledge can help build trust and collaboration within innovation ecosystems.
- Investing in STEM Education and Skills Development: The long-term sustainability of inclusive innovation ecosystems depends on the availability of a skilled and diverse talent pool. Policymakers can play a pivotal role in strengthening STEM (Science, Technology, Engineering, and Mathematics) education and skills development programs, particularly in underserved communities. This can involve curriculum reforms, targeted scholarships, and partnerships with academic institutions and industry to create pathways for marginalized groups to participate in the innovation economy.
- Adopting Inclusive Public Procurement Strategies: Government procurement policies can serve as a powerful lever for driving demand and stimulating the growth of inclusive innovation. By prioritizing the procurement of products and services from underrepresented vendors, including women-led, youth-led, and community-based enterprises, policymakers can create new market opportunities and incentivize the development of innovative solutions tailored to the needs of marginalized groups. Through a combination of strategic policy interventions, multi-stakeholder collaboration, and targeted investments, African nations can foster enabling environments that nurture and sustain inclusive innovation ecosystems. By aligning these efforts with broader sustainable development goals, policymakers can unlock the transformative potential of inclusive innovation to drive equitable and resilient growth across the continent.

V. Empirical Evidence and Case Studies on Collaborative Innovation Ecosystems

The scholarly discourse on African innovation ecosystems has been enriched by a growing body of empirical research and case studies that illustrate the diverse manifestations and impacts of collaborative innovation across the continent. One notable example is the work of Landry Signé, a prominent Cameroonian scholar and the managing director of the Brookings Institution's Africa Growth Initiative. Signé's research has examined the critical role of multi-stakeholder partnerships and cross-sector collaborations in enabling the success and scalability of inclusive innovation initiatives (Signé, 2018). Through in-depth case studies, Signé has highlighted the transformative potential of collaborative innovation ecosystems, such as the Konza Technopolis in Kenya. This large-scale technology and innovation hub has brought together a diverse array of stakeholders, including startups, research institutions, and multinational corporations, to drive the country's digital transformation. By fostering cross-sector collaborations and knowledge-sharing, the Konza Technopolis has been able to catalyze the development of innovative solutions that address pressing societal challenges (Signé, 2018). Similarly, Signé's analysis of the Empowering Smallholder Farmers in Africa (ESFA) initiative, led by Kenyan agricultural scientist Esther Ngumbi, showcases the power of collaborative innovation ecosystems in empowering marginalized communities. By engaging directly with smallholder farmers, particularly women, and collaborating with various stakeholders, including government agencies, civil society organizations, and private sector partners, the ESFA initiative has been able to develop and scale up a suite of innovative agricultural technologies and practices that address the unique needs and challenges faced by these communities (Signé, 2018). Complementing Signé's work, other scholars have also contributed empirical evidence on the diverse manifestations and impacts of collaborative innovation ecosystems in the African context. For instance, Acharya and Basnyat (2015) have explored how innovation hubs and incubators in Ethiopia have facilitated the co-creation of sustainable energy solutions through the engagement of local communities, researchers, and policymakers. Similarly, Adeoti and Adeoti (2005) have examined the role of public-private partnerships in driving inclusive healthcare innovations in Nigeria, highlighting the importance of collaborative approaches in addressing the needs of marginalized populations. These empirical studies and case analyses have been crucial in illuminating the transformative potential of collaborative innovation ecosystems in Africa, as well as the critical success factors and enabling conditions that shape their development and impact. By documenting the lessons learned and best practices from these initiatives, the scholarly literature has provided valuable insights for policymakers, practitioners, and researchers seeking to foster more inclusive and sustainable innovation landscapes across the continent.

VI. Policy Implications and Recommendations for Strengthening Collaborative Innovation Ecosystems

The scholarly discourse on collaborative innovation ecosystems in Africa has identified several key policy implications and recommendations for strengthening these dynamic landscapes:

1. Fostering Enabling Policy Frameworks: Policymakers must develop comprehensive policy frameworks that recognize the value of collaborative innovation and provide the necessary support and incentives for diverse stakeholders to engage in cross-sector partnerships. This can include the establishment of innovation funds, regulatory sandboxes, and public procurement strategies that prioritize inclusive and collaborative initiatives.
2. Investing in Innovation Infrastructure and Intermediary Organizations: Governments should invest in the development of physical and digital innovation infrastructure, such as innovation hubs, incubators, and maker spaces, that can serve as platforms for collaboration, knowledge-sharing, and the co-creation of solutions. Furthermore, the strengthening of intermediary organizations, which play a crucial role in facilitating connections and synergies among ecosystem actors, is critical for nurturing collaborative innovation.
3. Promoting Inclusive Governance and Representation: Policymakers must ensure that the governance structures and decision-making processes within collaborative innovation ecosystems are inclusive and representative of diverse stakeholders, particularly marginalized

communities. This can involve the establishment of dedicated mechanisms for community engagement, the empowerment of grassroots innovators, and the equitable distribution of resources and benefits.

4. Incentivizing Cross-Border and Transnational Collaborations: To harness the collective strengths and resources of the African continent, policymakers should implement strategies that encourage and facilitate cross-border and transnational collaborations among innovation ecosystems. This can include the development of regional innovation networks, the harmonization of regulatory frameworks, and the provision of funding and support for collaborative research and development initiatives.
5. Strengthening STEM Education and Skills Development: The long-term sustainability of collaborative innovation ecosystems depends on the availability of a skilled and diverse talent pool. Policymakers should invest in STEM (Science, Technology, Engineering, and Mathematics) education and skills development programs, particularly in underserved communities, to build a pipeline of innovators, entrepreneurs, and problem-solvers.
6. Promoting Knowledge Sharing and Dissemination: Governments and development partners should establish platforms and mechanisms for the effective dissemination of knowledge, best practices, and lessons learned from successful collaborative innovation initiatives. This cross-pollination of ideas and experiences can accelerate the adoption and adaptation of effective models in different African contexts. By addressing these policy implications and implementing targeted interventions, African nations can create more enabling environments for collaborative innovation ecosystems to thrive, unlocking their transformative potential to drive inclusive and sustainable development across the continent.

References

Acharya, R. H., & Basnyat, B. (2015). The role of innovation and technology in addressing climate change adaptation and mitigation in Nepal. *Environment Development and Sustainability*, 17(4), 663-682.

Adeoti, J. O., & Adeoti, A. I. (2005). Biotechnology R&D partnership for industrial innovation in Nigeria. *Technovation*, 25(4), 349-365.

Byanyima, W. (2018). Inclusive innovation for sustainable development. *Journal of International Affairs*, 71(1.5), 17-34.

Chataway, J., Hanlin, R., & Kaplinsky, R. (2014). Inclusive innovation: an architecture for policy development. *Innovation and Development*, 4(1), 33-54.

Carayannis, E. G., & Campbell, D. F. (2009). 'Mode 3' and 'Quadruple Helix': toward a 21st century fractal innovation ecosystem. *International journal of technology management*, 46(3-4), 201-234.

Chesbrough, H. (2003). Open innovation. *Harvard Business Review*, 78(1), 20-32.

Daniels, C. U., Ustyuzhantseva, O., & Yao, W. (2017). Innovation for inclusive development, public policy support and triple helix: perspectives from BRICS. *African Journal of Science, Technology, Innovation and Development*, 9(5), 513-527.

Etzkowitz, H., & Leydesdorff, L. (2000). The dynamics of innovation: from National Systems and "Mode 2" to a Triple Helix of university–industry–government relations. *Research policy*, 29(2), 109-123.

Freeman, C. (1987). *Technology policy and economic performance: lessons from Japan*. Pinter Publishers.

George, G., McGahan, A. M., & Prabhu, J. (2012). Innovation for inclusive growth: Towards a theoretical framework and a research agenda. *Journal of Management Studies*, 49(4), 661-683.

Kaplinsky, R. (2011). Schumacher meets Schumpeter: Appropriate technology below the radar. *Research Policy*, 40(2), 193-203.

Léautier, F. A. (2012). *Leadership in a Changing World: Dynamic Perspectives on Groups and Their Leaders*. Lexington Books.

Lundvall, B. Å. (Ed.). (1992). *National systems of innovation: Toward a theory of innovation and interactive learning*. Anthem Press.

Nelson, R. R. (Ed.). (1993). *National innovation systems: a comparative analysis*. Oxford university press.

Schillo, R. S., & Robinson, R. M. (2017). Inclusive innovation in developed countries: The who, what, why, and how. *Technology Innovation Management Review*, 7(7).

Signé, L. (2018). *Innovating Development Strategies in Africa: The Role of International, Regional, and National Actors*. Brookings Institution Press.

Swaans, K., Boogaard, B., Bendapudi, R., Taye, H., Hendrickx, S., & Klerkx, L. (2014). Operationalizing inclusive innovation: lessons from innovation platforms in livestock value chains in India and Mozambique. *Innovation and Development*, 4(2), 239-257.

CHAPTER 3

Frugal Innovation: Designing for Affordability and Accessibility

The concept of frugal innovation has gained significant traction in recent years as a promising approach to addressing the unique challenges and resource constraints faced by African communities (Moleka, 2024, Hossain, Park & Shahid, 2023; Rosca, Reedy & Bendul, 2018; Bhatti, & Prabhu, 2019). Characterized by the design of affordable, accessible, and adaptable solutions, frugal innovation represents a departure from traditional innovation models that often prioritize technological complexity and high-end features over practical utility and inclusivity. In the African context, where a large portion of the population lives on limited incomes and faces significant infrastructural and institutional barriers, frugal innovation has emerged as a critical strategy for tackling pressing social, economic, and environmental issues (Moleka, 2024).

From low-cost medical devices to off-grid renewable energy systems, frugal innovations are increasingly being developed and deployed across the continent, demonstrating the remarkable ingenuity and resourcefulness of local entrepreneurs, researchers, and communities. This chapter delves into the key principles, frameworks, and case studies of frugal innovation in Africa, exploring its transformative potential in driving inclusive development and sustainable progress. By examining the diverse manifestations of frugal innovation across sectors, we will gain a deeper understanding of how this approach can be leveraged to create innovative solutions that are responsive to the needs and constraints of underserved populations.

I. Literature Review

The academic literature on frugal innovation has grown rapidly in recent years, reflecting the increasing prominence of this phenomenon as a potential driver of inclusive and sustainable development, particularly in the context of emerging economies. As Africa grapples with persistent challenges of poverty, inequality, and environmental degradation, the study of frugal innovation has gained significant traction among scholars and practitioners alike. This comprehensive literature review aims to synthesize the key theoretical and empirical contributions in this domain, identify the linkages between frugal innovation and inclusive development, and pinpoint areas for further research. The review begins by exploring the theoretical foundations of frugal innovation, examining the seminal conceptual frameworks that have shaped the scholarly understanding of this concept. It then delves into the empirical literature on frugal innovation initiatives across various sectors in the African context, analyzing the contextual factors that influence their development and scaling. Finally, the review discusses the theoretical and practical connections between frugal innovation and inclusive development, highlighting the potential of frugal solutions to advance the United Nations Sustainable Development Goals (SDGs).

1. Theoretical Foundations of Frugal Innovation

The scholarly discourse on frugal innovation has been significantly influenced by several theoretic al frameworks and conceptual models. One of the most widely cited is the Jugaad Innovation framework, proposed by Radjou et al. (2012), which defines frugal innovation as a "flexible and cost-effective" approach to problem-solving that leverages limited resources. This framework emphasizes the importance of grassroots innovation, adaptability, and the ability to "do more with less" (Radjou et al., 2012). The Empathic Design approach, articulated by Mattelmäki et al. (2014), also offers valuable insights into the dynamics of frugal innovation. This approach emphasizes the need to deeply understand the user context, their needs, and the socio-cultural factors that shape their experiences. By adopting an empathic design lens, innovators can develop frugal solutions that are tailored to the specific challenges and constraints faced by marginalized communities (Mattelmäki et al., 2014). The Bottom of the Pyramid (BoP) framework, proposed by Prahalad and Hart (2002), has been instrumental in highlighting the potential of frugal innovation to address the unmet needs of low-income populations. This framework emphasizes the importance of developing innovative, affordable, and accessible products and services that can unlock new markets and drive inclusive growth (Prahalad & Hart, 2002). The Reverse Innovation concept, developed by Govindarajan and Trimble (2012), further illuminates the dynamics of frugal innovation. This approach suggests that innovations that originate in resource-constrained settings can be adapted and scaled to serve higher-income markets, challenging the traditional notion of innovation flowing from the Global North to the Global South (Govindarajan & Trimble, 2012). More recently, the Frugal Innovation framework, articulated by Zeschky et al. (2014), has provided a more nuanced understanding of this phenomenon. This framework identifies three distinct types of frugal innovation – cost innovation, good-enough innovation, and resource-constrained innovation – each with its own set of characteristics and implications for inclusive development (Zeschky et al., 2014). While these theoretical frameworks have significantly advanced the scholarly understanding of frugal innovation, there remains a need for further refinement and integration of these conceptual models, particularly in the context of Africa's unique socioeconomic and environmental challenges. Additionally, the literature highlights the importance of considering the interplay between frugal innovation and related constructs, such as inclusive innovation, grassroots entrepreneurship, and socially responsible design (Prabhu & Jha, 2019; Ramaswamy & Ozcan, 2018).

2. Frugal Innovation in the African Context

The empirical literature on frugal innovation initiatives in Africa spans several key sectors, providing valuable insights into the contextual factors that shape the development and adoption of these solutions. In the healthcare sector, studies have examined the emergence of frugal medical devices and diagnostics tools, such as the Jaipur Foot prosthetic leg (Blessing, 2014) and the Cardiopad tablet-based ECG device (Noubiap et al., 2017). These innovations have demonstrated the potential of frugal solutions to improve accessibility and affordability of essential healthcare services, particularly in underserved rural communities. In the energy and off-grid solutions domain, the literature has highlighted the transformative impact of frugal innovations like the M-Kopa Solar pay-as-you-go system (Kopnina & Poldner, 2021) and Orb Energy's frugal solar home systems (Heinemann, 2022). These initiatives

groups of people to participate in high-growth, high-profit ventures (George, McGahan & Prabhu, 2012). The concept of the "Bottom of the Pyramid" (BOP) has been explored extensively by African scholars, and it is often expressed in local African languages and contexts. Here are some key insights:

- Notion in Swahili: In Swahili, the BOP is often referred to as "Wanyonge," which literally translates to "the destitute" or "the impoverished." This term encompasses the vast majority of the population living in extreme poverty, with limited access to basic resources and services (Karnani, 2007).
- Notion in Yoruba: In the Yoruba context, the BOP is conceptualized as "Àwọn Alágbàrá," which means "those at the bottom" or "the marginalized." This term emphasizes the social and economic exclusion experienced by this population, and the need for more inclusive development strategies (Idemudia, 2017).
- Notion in Zulu: In the Zulu language, the BOP is often referred to as "Abantu Abangaphansi," which translates to "the people at the bottom" or "the disadvantaged." This term emphasizes the socioeconomic marginalization and the need for empowerment and upliftment of this segment of the population (Wentzel & Steyn, 2016). These local language conceptualizations of the BOP in the African context highlight the deep-rooted socioeconomic challenges faced by the poorest members of society and the imperative for holistic, community-driven solutions to address their needs.

The defining principles and characteristics of frugal innovation include:

1. Affordability: Frugal innovations are designed to be affordable for low-income and marginalized communities, often achieved through the use of low-cost materials, streamlined production processes, and innovative business models.
2. Functionality: Rather than focusing on high-end features and technological complexity, frugal innovations prioritize the essential functionalities required to meet the specific needs of the target users.
3. Sustainability: Frugal innovations are typically designed to be durable, energy-efficient, and environmentally friendly, minimizing the burden on natural resources and promoting long-term sustainability.

4. Adaptability: Frugal innovations are often designed to be flexible and adaptable, allowing them to be easily customized or modified to suit the diverse needs and contexts of different communities.
5. Simplicity: Frugal innovations emphasize simplicity in design, operation, and maintenance, reducing the barriers to adoption and ensuring that users can easily understand and utilize the products or services.
6. Grassroots innovation: Frugal innovations often emerge from the ingenuity and problem-solving abilities of local communities, leveraging indigenous knowledge and resources to address pressing challenges.
7. Collaborative approaches: The development of frugal innovations frequently involves the collaboration of diverse stakeholders, including entrepreneurs, researchers, civil society organizations, and end-users, fostering inclusive innovation ecosystems.

These principles and characteristics of frugal innovation distinguish it from traditional innovation models that often focus on technological sophistication and high-end features targeted at affluent markets. By prioritizing affordability, functionality, and adaptability, frugal innovation has the potential to unlock new pathways for inclusive and sustainable development in Africa.

III. Theoretical Frameworks and Conceptual Models

The rise of frugal innovation has attracted significant scholarly attention, leading to the development of various theoretical frameworks and conceptual models that help illuminate its unique attributes and inform its practical application.

1. The Jugaad Innovation Framework: Jugaad, a Hindi term meaning "an innovative fix" or "a flexible workaround," has become a widely recognized concept within the frugal innovation discourse. The Jugaad Innovation framework, developed by Radjou, Prabhu, and Ahuja (2012), highlights the resourcefulness and improvisational abilities of individuals and communities in resource-constrained environments to create innovative solutions. The framework emphasizes six key principles of Jugaad innovation.

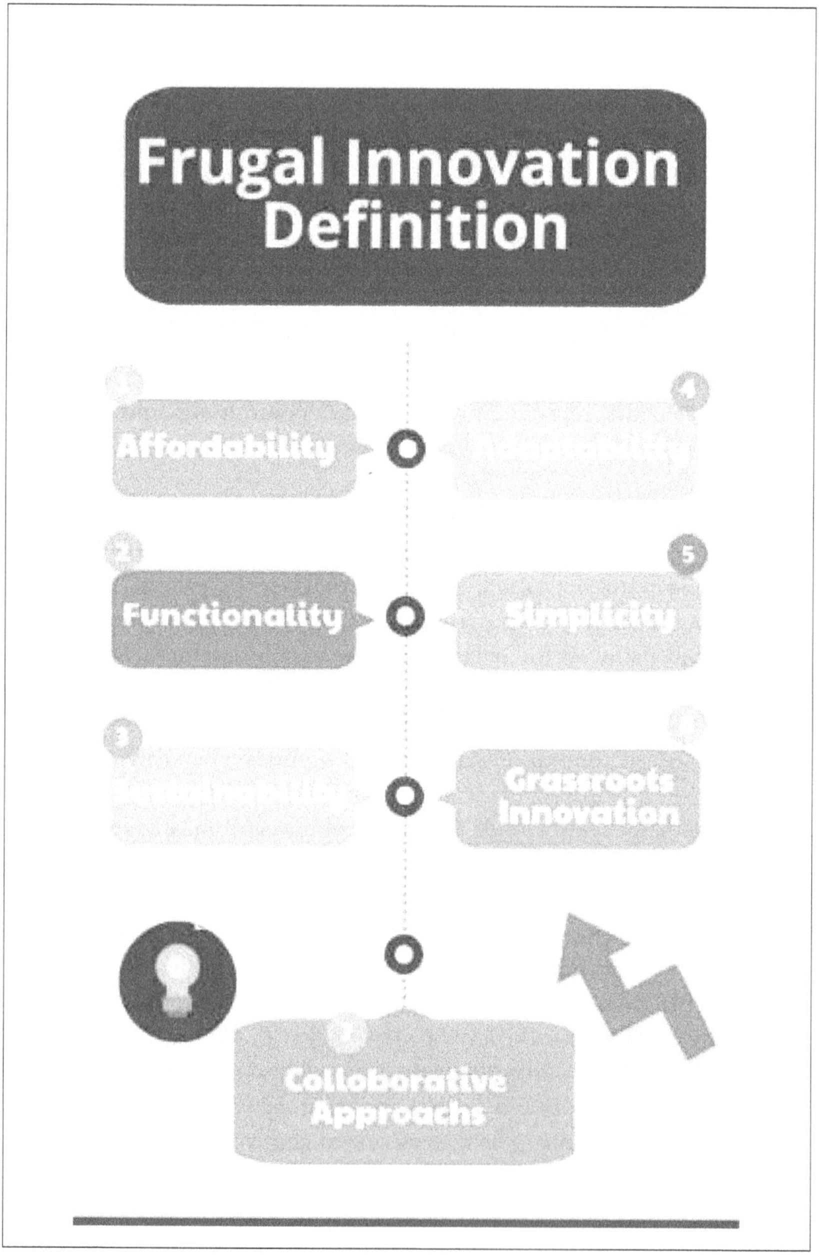

Figure 3.1 Frugal Innovation Definition Source: Moleka, 2024

2. The Empathic Design Approach: The empathic design approach, proposed by Mattelmäki, Vaajakallio, and Koskinen (2014), emphasizes the importance of deeply understanding the needs, experiences, and contexts of end-users in the innovation process. This approach is particularly relevant to frugal innovation, as it encourages designers and innovators to immerse themselves in the daily lives of the target communities, empathize with their challenges, and co-create solutions that are tailored to their specific requirements.
3. The Bottom of the Pyramid (BoP) Framework: The Bottom of the Pyramid (BoP) framework, developed by Prahalad and Hart (2002), highlights the vast economic and social potential of the world's poorest populations, often referred to as the "base of the economic pyramid." This framework has been instrumental in driving the development of frugal innovations, as it encourages businesses and organizations to design products and services that cater to the needs and constraints of low-income communities, creating new avenues for inclusive growth and development.
4. The Reverse Innovation Concept: The reverse innovation concept, introduced by Govindarajan and Trimble (2012), challenges the traditional assumption that innovations must flow from developed to developing countries. Instead, it posits that innovations that are first developed and adopted in resource-constrained markets, such as those in Africa, can be "reverse engineered" and adapted for use in more affluent markets, creating a two-way flow of knowledge and solutions.
5. The Frugal Innovation Framework: Building on these theoretical foundations, scholars have developed more specific frameworks for understanding and implementing frugal innovation. For instance, Zeschky, Winterhalter, and Gassmann (2014) proposed a frugal innovation framework that identifies three distinct types of frugal innovations:

   (1) cost innovations,
   (2) good-enough innovations, and
   (3) resource-constrained innovations. This framework helps innovators and policymakers navigate the diverse manifestations of frugal innovation and tailor their approaches accordingly.

These theoretical frameworks and conceptual models provide valuable insights into the underlying principles, drivers, and applications of frugal innovation, informing the development of innovative solutions that are responsive to the unique challenges and constraints faced by African communities.

IV. Frugal Innovation in Action: Sectoral Case Studies

Frugal innovation has found widespread application across various sectors in Africa, addressing a wide range of social, economic, and environmental challenges. By examining a diverse set of case studies, we can gain a deeper understanding of the transformative potential of this approach and the factors that contribute to its success.

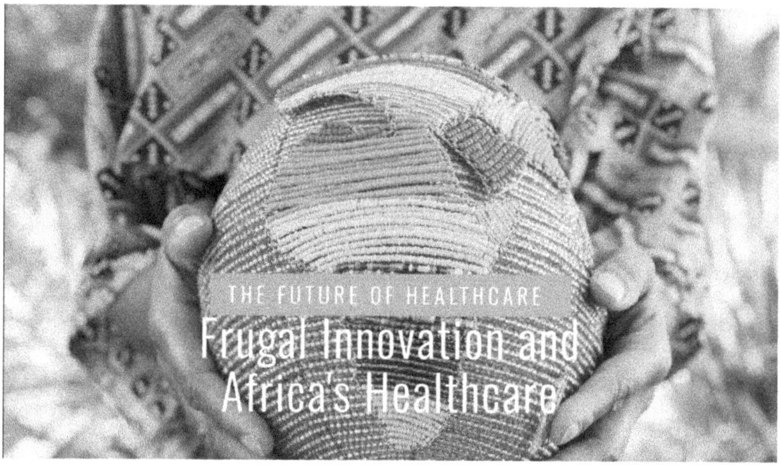

1. Healthcare and Medical Devices: The healthcare sector has been a prime area for the development of frugal innovations in Africa, as the continent grapples with limited access to affordable and high-quality medical services and equipment.

Frugal innovation in healthcare refers to the process of reducing the complexity and cost of medical services and products, making them more accessible and affordable, especially in resource-constrained environments. Africa has seen significant changes in healthcare outcomes due to the implementation of frugal innovations. Here are some key statistics and comparisons before and after the implementation of frugal innovation in healthcare in Africa:

Category	Innovation	Description
mHealth Solutions.	RapidSMS	Tracks maternal and child health in real-time using SMS
	mPedigree	Verifies authenticity of medicines via mobile, reducing counterfeit drugs.
	SMS for Life.	Uses SMS to manage stock levels of essential medicines in remote areas
	MomConnect	Provides maternal health information via SMS in South Africa.
Telemedicine Platforms	Babyl	Allows patients in Rwanda to consult doctors via mobile phones
	Hello Doctor	Provides health advice and consultations through mobile phones.
	Ada Health	AI-powered health app for preliminary diagnoses and advice.
	Vezeeta	Digital platform in Egypt for booking medical appointments and consultations.
Community Health Workers	Living Goods	Trains health workers to deliver services and products in rural areas.
	Mile Health	Last Trains health workers to provide essential services in remote areas.
	BRAC	Trains health promoters in Uganda for basic healthcare services and education.
	Musoma Healthcare	Provides home-based HIV testing and counseling in Tanzania.
Affordable Diagnostic Tools	mChipTB.	Low-cost, portable diagnostic device for HIV and syphilis.
	GeneXpert	Rapid diagnostic test for tuberculosis and drug-resistant
	Paperfuge	Hand-powered centrifuge for blood diagnostics.
	Arclight	Low-cost, solar-powered ophthalmoscope and otoscope.
Low-Cost Medical Devices	Embrace Infant Warmer.	Portable device to keep premature babies warm
	Solar-Powered Oxygen Concentrators	Provides oxygen therapy in areas without reliable electricity.

Category	Innovation	Description
	ReMotion Knee	Affordable, durable prosthetic knee for amputees.
	Kangaroo Mother Care Wraps	Promotes skin-to-skin contact between mothers and premature infants.
Innovative Health Financing	M-TIBA	Mobile health wallet in Kenya for healthcare funds.
	Micro Health Insurance	Affordable health insurance for low-income populations.
	CarePay	Links health payments to providers, insurers, and beneficiaries via mobile.
	Penda Health	Network of affordable primary healthcare clinics with innovative payment models.

Case Study 1: The Jaipur Foot. The Jaipur Foot, a low-cost prosthetic leg developed by the Bhagwan Mahaveer Viklang Sahayata Samiti (BMVSS) in India, has been widely adopted in several African countries, including Ethiopia, Kenya, and Tanzania. The Jaipur Foot is designed to be durable, comfortable, and easy to use, costing a fraction of the price of traditional prosthetic limbs. By leveraging locally available materials and simple manufacturing techniques, the Jaipur Foot has become an accessible solution for amputees in resource-constrained settings.

Case Study 2: Cardiopad. Cardiopad, a tablet-based electrocardiogram (ECG) device developed by Arthur Zang in Cameroon, is a prime example of frugal innovation in the healthcare sector. Designed to be portable, easy to use, and affordable, the Cardiopad allows healthcare workers to remotely diagnose and monitor heart conditions in rural areas, overcoming the challenges of limited infrastructure and access to specialized medical equipment.

Case Study 3: LifeStraw LifeStraw, a water filtration device developed by Vestergaard, is a frugal innovation that has had a significant impact on public health in Africa. The LifeStraw is a simple, compact, and inexpensive tool that can purify water, making it safe for drinking and reducing the incidence of waterborne diseases in communities with limited access to clean water sources.

2. Energy and Off-Grid Solutions: The energy sector in Africa has witnessed a surge of frugal innovations aimed at expanding access to reliable, affordable, and sustainable electricity, particularly in rural and underserved areas.

Case Study 4: M-Kopa Solar, a Kenyan-based company, has pioneered a pay-as-you-go solar home system that provides affordable, off-grid electricity to low-income households. By leveraging mobile money technology and a modular, scalable design, M-Kopa Solar has been able to reach millions of Africans who previously had limited access to modern energy services.

Case Study 5: Tugende, a Ugandan social enterprise, offers a frugal solution to the challenge of transportation in urban areas. Tugende's motorcycle leasing program provides affordable, reliable, and environmentally friendly mobility options to informal workers, enabling them to access economic opportunities and improve their livelihoods.

Case Study 6: Orb Energy, an Indian solar energy company, has adapted its business model and product offerings to serve the unique needs of African customers. Orb Energy's frugal solar home systems, coupled with financing options and after-sales support, have made solar power accessible and affordable for low-income households in countries like Kenya and Nigeria.

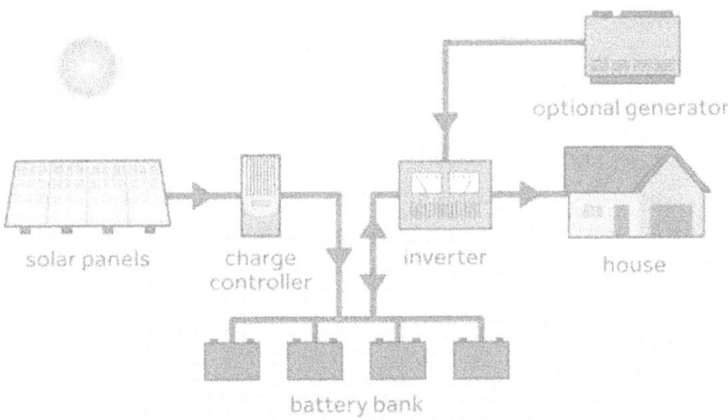

Table 3.1 Economics of Solar Versus Commercial Grid Electricity Tariffs

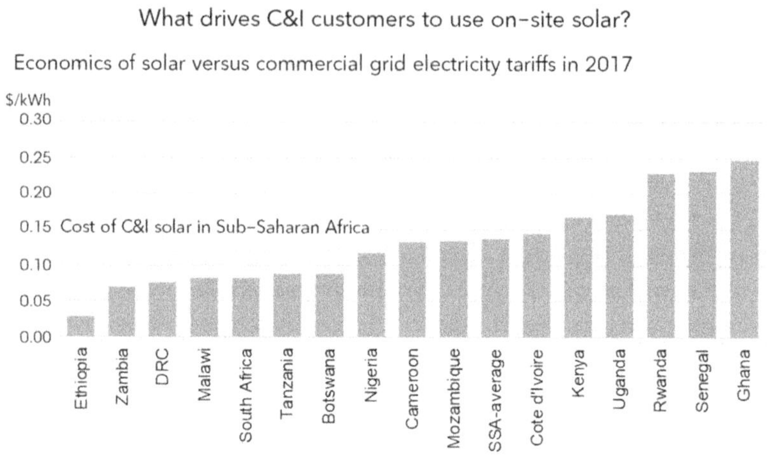

Source: BloombergNEF, Climatescope, World Bank. Note: Tariffs for Ghana are as of April 2018. The range of C&I solar cost estimates for Kenya, Ghana and Nigeria.

3. Agriculture and Food Security: Frugal innovations in the agriculture and food security domains have the potential to revolutionize the lives of smallholder farmers and address issues of food scarcity and malnutrition across the African continent.

Case Study 7: Hello Tractor, a Nigerian social enterprise, has developed a "smart tractor" platform that connects smallholder farmers with tractor owners, enabling access to affordable mechanization services. By leveraging digital technologies and a pay-per-use model, Hello Tractor has made tractor services more accessible and affordable for resource-constrained farmers.

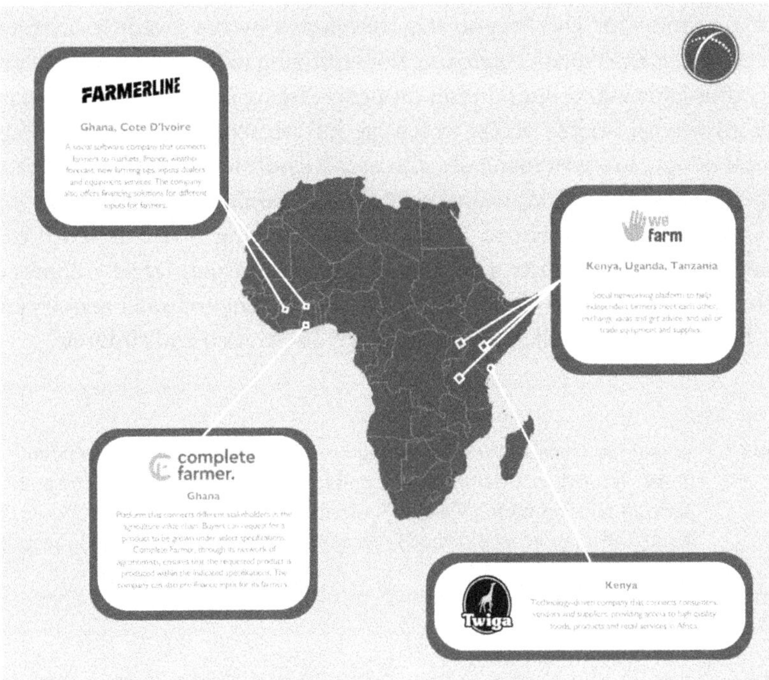

Case Study 8: Kheyti, an Indian startup, has created a low-cost, modular greenhouse solution called the "Greenhouse-in-a-Box" to help smallholder farmers in India and Africa improve their crop yields and resilience to climate change. The frugal design of the Kheyti greenhouse, which uses locally sourced materials and simple construction techniques, has made it an attractive option for resource-poor farmers.

Case Study 9: Maize Cob Dryer, developed by researchers at the Kwame Nkrumah University of Science and Technology in Ghana, is a frugal innovation that addresses the post-harvest losses experienced by smallholder maize farmers. The dryer, which uses a simple, biomass-powered design, helps farmers preserve their crop yields more effectively, reducing food waste and improving food security.

4. Water and Sanitation: Frugal innovations in the water and sanitation sector have played a crucial role in improving access to clean water and basic sanitation services, particularly in underserved communities.

Case Study 10: The Peepoo Bag, developed by the Swedish company Peepoople, is a personal, single-use, self-sanitizing toilet that provides a safe and affordable sanitation solution for people living in informal settlements and areas with limited access to sewage infrastructure. The Peepoo Bag's simple design, low-cost materials, and user-friendly features have made it an effective solution for addressing the global sanitation crisis.

Case Study 11: The Hippo Roller, a water-carrying device designed by a South African social enterprise, allows users to transport larger volumes of water with less physical effort, addressing the challenge of water scarcity and the burden of water collection, particularly for women and children.

Table 3.2 Global Food Insecurity Levels by Region, Income Group, and Urbanization (Rural, Peri-Urban, Urban). Source: United Nations (UN) Reports, Food and Agriculture Organization (FAO) – *The State of Food Security and Nutrition in the World (SOFI)* report, World Food Programme (WFP) –Hunger and food security data.

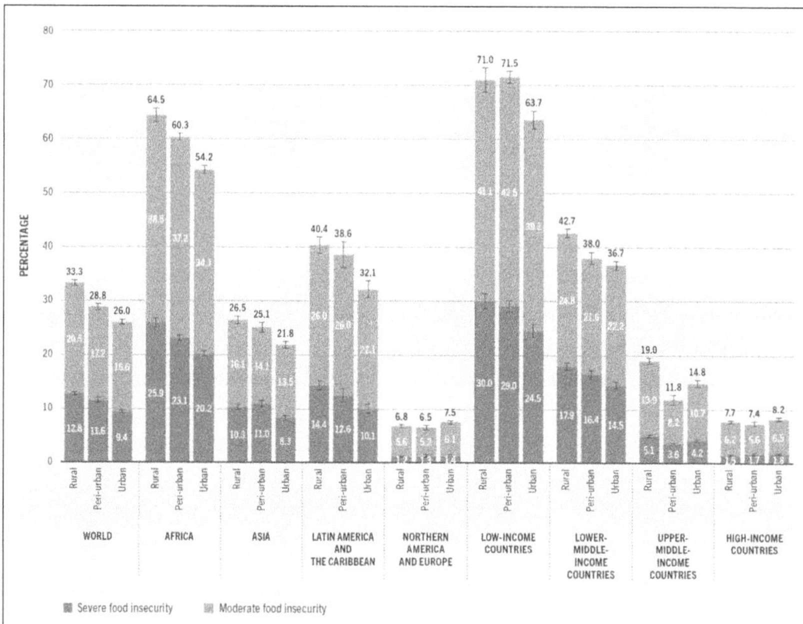

The Hippo Roller's durable, ergonomic design and affordable price point have made it a popular frugal innovation in various African countries.

Case Study 12: PlayPump, a water pump that is activated by children playing on a merry-go-round-like mechanism, was an innovative attempt to provide clean water access and engage communities, particularly in rural areas of Africa. While the initial implementation faced some challenges, the PlayPump concept demonstrated the potential for frugal innovations to address water and sanitation issues through creative and user-friendly designs.

There is also the work of Landry Signé, a prominent Cameroonian scholar and the managing director of the Brookings Institution's Africa Growth Initiative, who has conducted extensive research on the successes and challenges of inclusive innovation in Africa. His work has highlighted a range of inspiring case studies that illustrate the breadth and impact of this approach.

One such example is the story of Esther Ngumbi, a Kenyan agricultural scientist and social entrepreneur who founded the Empowering Smallholder Farmers in Africa (ESFA) initiative. Signé's research has shown how Ngumbi's organization has been able to empower marginalized smallholder farmers, particularly women, by providing them with access to affordable and context-appropriate agricultural technologies, as well as training and mentorship programs (Signé, 2018). Through the ESFA initiative, Ngumbi and her team have developed a suite of innovative solutions, including solar-powered irrigation systems, mobile-based market information platforms, and post-harvest storage technologies. By tailoring these innovations to the specific needs and constraints of smallholder farmers, the ESFA initiative has been able to enhance food security, increase incomes, and promote more sustainable agricultural practices in rural communities across Kenya (Signé, 2018). Signé's case study on the ESFA initiative highlights the importance of centering the voices and experiences of marginalized communities in the innovation process. By engaging directly with smallholder farmers, particularly women, Ngumbi and her team were able to develop solutions that addressed the unique challenges they faced, such as limited access to water, inadequate market information, and high post-harvest losses. This people-centered approach, Signé argues, is a hallmark of successful inclusive innovation initiatives (Signé, 2018).

Another compelling case study examined by Signé is the work of Aruma, a social enterprise based in Ghana that is leveraging inclusive innovation

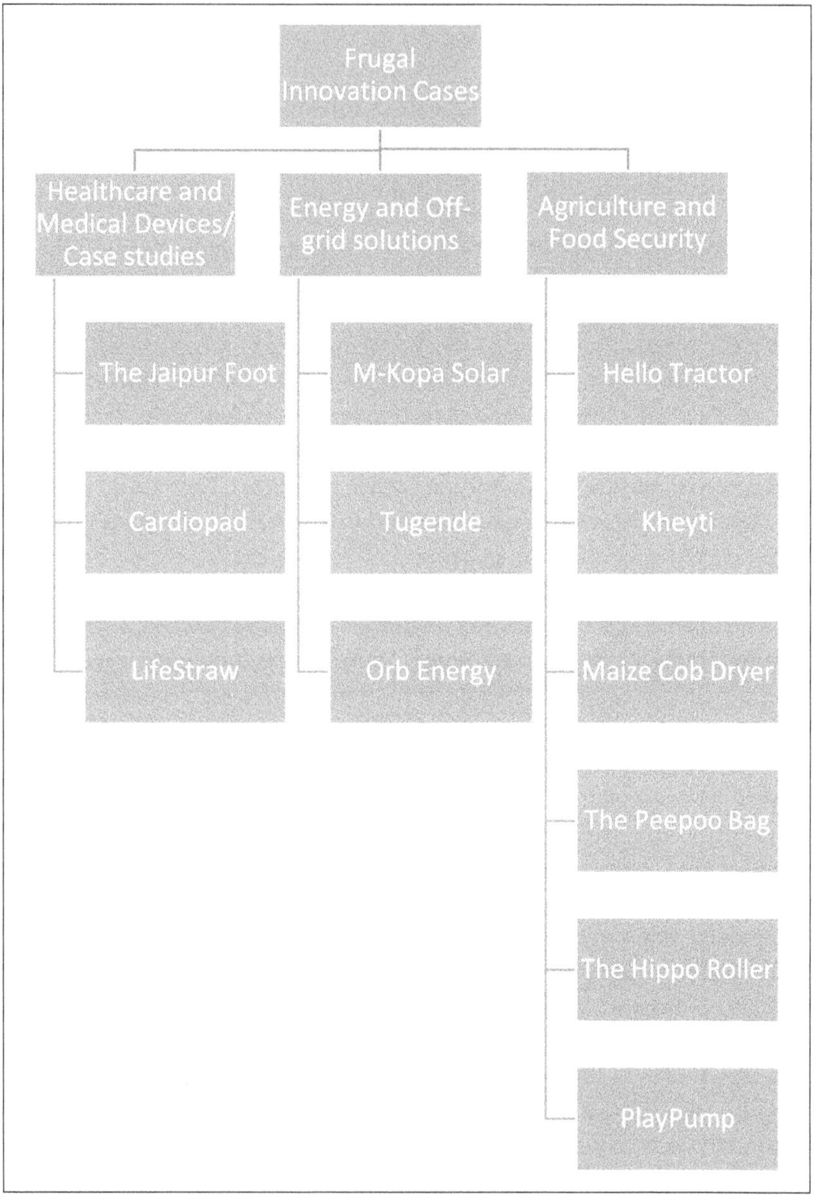

Figure 3.2 Frugal Innovation Cases (Author's own work)

Table 3.3 Population of Sub-Saharan Africa. Source: World Bank, United Nations (UN Population Division), African Development Bank

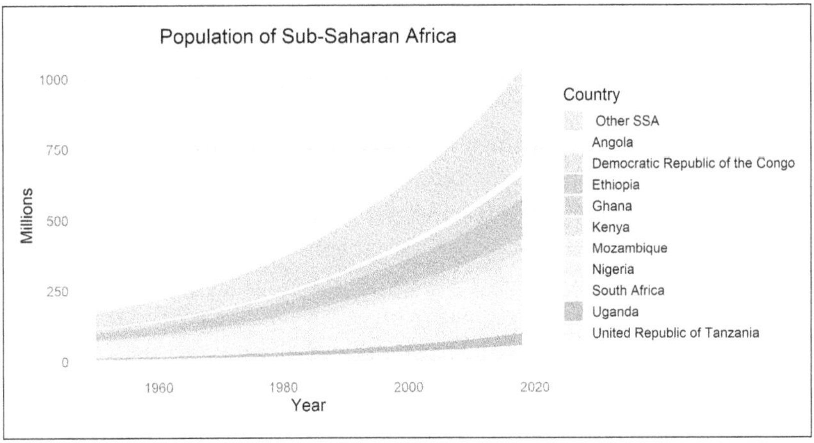

to improve access to affordable and high-quality healthcare in underserved communities. Aruma's flagship product is a low-cost, solar-powered medical diagnostic device that allows community health workers to conduct essential tests, such as blood glucose monitoring and malaria screening, right in the field (Signé, 2018).

What sets Aruma's innovation apart, according to Signé, is its deep engagement with the communities it serves. The enterprise has worked closely with local healthcare providers, community leaders, and end-users to ensure that its technology is not only affordable and accessible but also culturally appropriate and responsive to the unique needs and contexts of the people it aims to serve. This collaborative approach, Signé argues, has been key to the success and scalability of Aruma's inclusive healthcare solution (Signé, 2018).

Signé's research has also highlighted the important role that inclusive innovation can play in addressing pressing environmental challenges, as exemplified by the work of Pula, a Kenyan social enterprise focused on developing climate-smart agriculture solutions. Pula's flagship product is a weather-indexed crop insurance program that provides smallholder farmers with financial protection against the impacts of climate change, such as droughts, floods, and changing weather patterns (Signé, 2018). What makes Pula's approach inclusive, as Signé's case study demonstrates, is its emphasis on affordability, accessibility, and community engagement. By partnering with local microfinance institutions and leveraging mobile money platforms, Pula has been able to offer its insurance products to smallholder farmers at a fraction of the cost of traditional insurance schemes. Moreover, the enterprise has worked closely with farming communities to co-create customized insurance packages that address their specific needs and challenges (Signé, 2018). Aruma's and Pula's case studies, as analyzed by Signé, underscore the importance of tailoring inclusive innovation solutions to the unique socio-economic, cultural, and environmental contexts in which they are deployed. By prioritizing affordability, accessibility, and community engagement, these enterprises have been able to develop innovative products and services that truly empower marginalized populations and drive sustainable, equitable development outcomes. Beyond the individual case studies highlighted by Signé, the broader trends and patterns that emerge from his research offer valuable insights for policymakers and development practitioners seeking to foster more inclusive innovation ecosystems across Africa.

Signé's work has consistently emphasized the critical role of collaborative, cross-sector partnerships in enabling inclusive innovation to thrive, as well as the need for supportive policy frameworks and investment strategies that prioritize social impact over narrow commercial interests (Signé, 2018). Signé's research has also underscored the importance of nurturing grassroots-level innovation hubs and networks, which can provide marginalized communities with the resources, skills, and platforms they need to develop and scale their own innovative solutions. By empowering local innovators and ensuring their active participation in the development process, Signé argues, African nations can unleash the transformative potential of inclusive innovation and drive more equitable and sustainable progress (Signé, 2018).

Aruma: Leveraging Inclusive Innovation for Affordable and Accessible Healthcare

One of the case studies that Landry Signé has highlighted in his research on inclusive innovation in Africa is the work of Aruma, a social enterprise based in Ghana that is using innovative technologies to improve access to affordable and high-quality healthcare in underserved communities. Aruma's flagship product is a low-cost, solar-powered medical diagnostic device that allows community health workers to conduct essential tests, such as blood glucose monitoring and malaria screening, right in the field. What sets Aruma's innovation apart, according to Signé, is its deep engagement with the communities it serves. The enterprise has worked closely with local healthcare providers, community leaders, and end-users to ensure that its technology is not only affordable and accessible but also culturally appropriate and responsive to the unique needs and contexts of the people it aims to serve. This collaborative approach, Signé argues, has been key to the success and scalability of Aruma's inclusive healthcare solution. By partnering with local stakeholders and prioritizing the perspectives and experiences of marginalized communities, Aruma has been able to develop an innovative product that addresses a critical gap in healthcare access, particularly in rural and low-income areas. The solar-powered diagnostic device, for instance, is designed to be easily transportable and requires minimal training to operate, making it well-suited for deployment by community health workers who may have limited medical expertise. Moreover, Aruma has worked to ensure that its solutions are affordable and financially accessible to the communities it serves. By leveraging innovative financing mechanisms, such as pay-as-you-go and micro-leasing models, the enterprise has been able to make its products available to even the most resource-constrained households, breaking down the barriers that have traditionally limited access to quality healthcare. Signé's case study on Aruma highlights the transformative potential of inclusive innovation in the healthcare sector, where the needs of marginalized communities have often been overlooked by traditional, profit-driven models. By centering the voices and experiences of local stakeholders, Aruma has been able to develop innovative solutions that truly empower underserved populations, improving health outcomes and promoting more equitable access to essential services.

The case studies examined by Landry Signé demonstrate the diverse ways in which inclusive innovation is taking root and thriving across the African continent. From initiatives that are improving access to affordable healthcare and climate-smart agriculture solutions to enterprises that are empowering marginalized communities to develop their own innovative products and services, these success stories underscore the critical importance of centering the perspectives and needs of the poor and underserved in the innovation process. As African nations continue to grapple with complex and

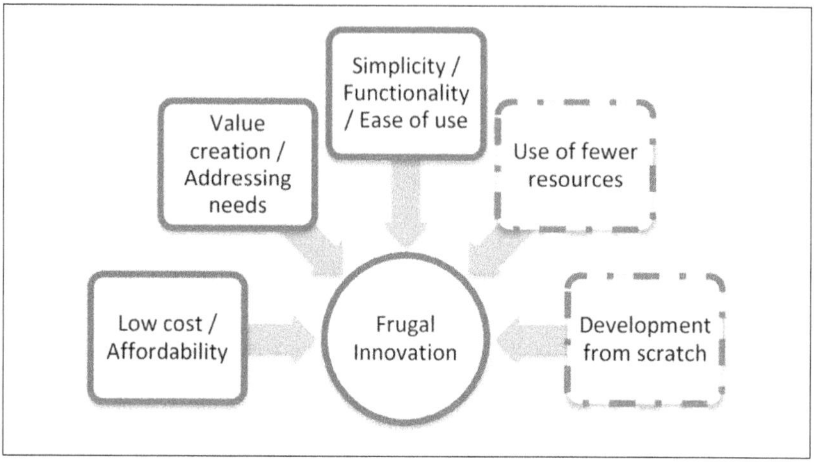

Figure 3.3 Leveraging Inclusive Innovation. Source: Moleka, 2024

interconnected challenges, the insights and frameworks provided by these case studies offer a roadmap for cultivating more inclusive, collaborative, and community-driven innovation ecosystems. By fostering cross-sector partnerships, supporting grassroots-level innovation hubs, and ensuring that marginalized voices are represented in decision-making processes, policymakers and development practitioners can help to unlock the transformative potential of inclusive innovation and drive more equitable and sustainable progress across the continent.

V. Barriers and Enablers of Frugal Innovation

While frugal innovation has demonstrated remarkable potential in addressing the needs of African communities, it also faces a range of challenges and barriers that can hinder its widespread adoption and impact. Understanding these barriers and the corresponding enabling factors is crucial for creating environments that foster the development and scaling of frugal innovations.

From policy and regulatory challenges to gaps in financing and capacity-building support, these obstacles have hindered the ability of marginalized communities to fully participate in and benefit from the innovation ecosystem. In addressing these barriers, scholars such as Mvemba Phezo

Dizolele, a Congolese scholar and senior fellow at the Center for Strategic and International Studies, and Carlos Lopes, a Bissau-Guinean scholar and former executive secretary of the United Nations Economic Commission for Africa, have offered invaluable insights and policy recommendations.

Mvemba Phezo Dizolele's research has highlighted the critical importance of creating enabling policy environments that foster inclusive innovation. According to Dizolele, one of the key barriers faced by grassroots innovators and social enterprises is the lack of supportive regulatory frameworks and institutional mechanisms that recognize and incentivize their work (Dizolele, 2019). Dizolele's analysis has shown that many African countries still prioritize traditional, technology-driven models of innovation, with policies and funding streams that favor large-scale, capital-intensive projects over the more resource-constrained, community-based initiatives that are the hallmark of inclusive innovation. This disconnect, he argues, has perpetuated the marginalization of certain segments of the population, limiting their ability to participate in and shape the innovation ecosystem (Dizolele, 2019). To address this challenge, Dizolele has advocated for the development of policy frameworks and institutional structures that actively promote and support inclusive innovation. This could include the establishment of dedicated innovation funds and grant programs that prioritize social impact over commercial profitability, as well as the creation of regulatory sandboxes and pilot zones that allow for the testing and scaling of innovative solutions tailored to the needs of marginalized communities (Dizolele, 2019). Furthermore, Dizolele has emphasized the importance of strengthening the capacity of local and regional policymaking bodies to understand and respond to the unique challenges and opportunities presented by inclusive innovation. By providing these institutions with the necessary knowledge, resources, and tools, he argues, African nations can create more coherent and effective policy environments that enable inclusive innovation to thrive (Dizolele, 2019).

Alongside the need for supportive policy frameworks, Carlos Lopes has underscored the critical role of innovative financing mechanisms in driving inclusive innovation across the continent. Lopes' work has highlighted the persistent gap in access to capital and investment opportunities faced by grassroots innovators, social enterprises, and community-based initiatives, which often struggle to attract funding from traditional sources due to their

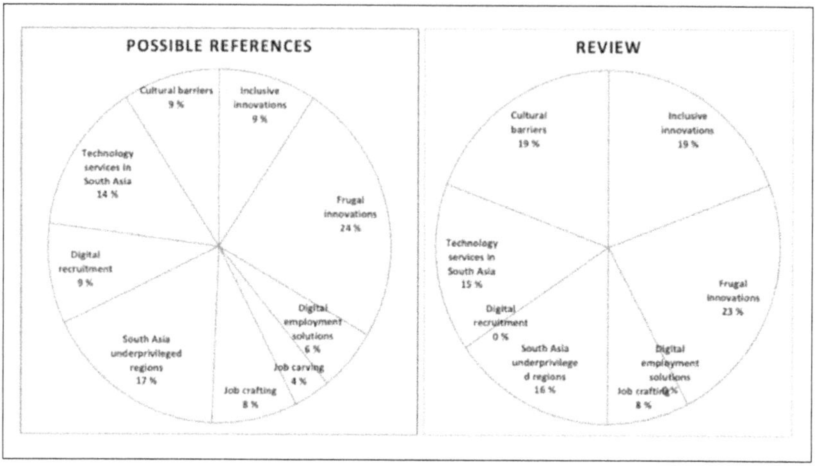

Figure 3.4 Comparison of Possible References vs. Review Findings in South Asian Innovation and Employment Research. Sources: World Bank – *Digital Jobs and Economic Growth in South Asia*, United Nations Development Programme (UNDP) – *Inclusive Innovation and Employment in South Asia*, International Labour Organization (ILO) – *Future of Work in South Asia*, Asian Development Bank (ADB) – *Digital Transformation in South Asia*

perceived higher risk profiles and lower profit margins (Lopes, 2020). To address this challenge, Lopes has advocated for the development of blended finance models that leverage public, private, and philanthropic resources to support inclusive innovation. This could include the creation of impact investment funds, social impact bonds, and crowd-funding platforms that are specifically designed to channel resources towards initiatives that prioritize social and environmental outcomes over pure financial returns (Lopes, 2020). Moreover, Lopes has emphasized the importance of strengthening the capacity of local financial institutions, such as microfinance organizations and community-based savings groups, to provide tailored financing solutions for inclusive innovation. By empowering these local players to understand and respond to the unique needs and constraints of marginalized communities, African nations can help to unlock new sources of capital and investment that are better aligned with the principles of inclusive innovation (Lopes, 2020). Lopes' work has also highlighted the potential of innovative public-private partnerships and blended finance models to mobilize resources and expertise for inclusive innovation initiatives. By fostering collaborations between government agencies, development finance institutions, and private sector actors, these models can help to bridge the gaps in funding, technical capacity, and scaling support that have traditionally hindered the growth and impact of inclusive innovation (Lopes, 2020). Beyond the policy and financing challenges, both Dizolele and Lopes have emphasized the critical importance of capacity-building and skills development as key enablers of inclusive innovation. Their research has shown that marginalized communities often lack access to the technical, entrepreneurial, and managerial skills required to ideate, develop, and scale innovative solutions, undermining their ability to participate fully in the innovation ecosystem. To address this gap, Dizolele and Lopes have advocated for the establishment of specialized training and mentorship programs, as well as the creation of inclusive innovation hubs and incubators that provide grassroots innovators with the resources, networks, and support they need to transform their ideas into viable, impactful solutions (Dizolele, 2019; Lopes, 2020). By investing in the capacity-building of marginalized communities, African nations can not only empower local innovators to become active drivers of inclusive development but also foster more diverse and collaborative innovation ecosystems that draw on the collective intelligence and resourcefulness of all citizens.

Among these barriers we can add;

1. Weak Innovation Ecosystems: The lack of robust innovation ecosystems, including incubators, accelerators, and collaborative platforms, can hinder the growth and scaling of frugal innovations.
   These ecosystems play a crucial role in providing mentorship, technical assistance, and networking opportunities for frugal innovators.
2. Cultural Biases and Perceptions: In some African contexts, there may be cultural biases and perceptions that favor high-tech, sophisticated solutions over frugal alternatives. Overcoming these biases and demonstrating the value and effectiveness of frugal innovations can be a significant challenge for innovators.
3. Limited Market Awareness and Demand: Potential end-users, particularly in underserved communities, may not be aware of the availability

or benefits of frugal innovations. Effectively communicating the value proposition and creating targeted marketing strategies can be crucial for driving market demand.

4. Scaling and Replicability Challenges: Scaling and replicating frugal innovations across different contexts and communities can be complex, as solutions may need to be adapted to local needs, resources, and infrastructure. Developing scalable business models and ensuring the sustainability of frugal innovations is a key challenge.

VI. Enablers of Frugal Innovation

1. Supportive Policy and Regulatory Frameworks: Governments can play a pivotal role in enabling frugal innovation by implementing policies and regulations that incentivize the development, procurement, and adoption of frugal solutions. This can include tax incentives, public procurement strategies, and the streamlining of bureaucratic processes.
2. Access to Diverse Financing Mechanisms: Innovative financing mechanisms, such as impact investment funds, crowdfunding platforms, and blended finance models, can provide much-needed capital for frugal innovators. Fostering collaborations between the public, private, and

Table 3.4 Strucutural Challenges. Source: Author

	Challenges	Desktop Research	Empirical Study
Structural Challenges	Poor Infrastructure	✔	✔
	Tax System	✔	
	Unreliable Policy-making	✔	✔
	Weak IP protection	✔	✔
	Institutional weaknesses	✔	✔
	Corruption	✔	
	Pirates	✔	✔
	Extreme temperatures / Environment		✔
	Low confidentiality		✔

philanthropic sectors can help mobilize resources and reduce the financial barriers faced by frugal innovators.

3. Collaborative Innovation Ecosystems: Strengthening innovation ecosystems through the establishment of incubators, accelerators, and collaborative platforms can provide frugal innovators with the necessary support, resources, and networking opportunities to scale their solutions. These ecosystems should foster multistakeholder engagement and promote the cross-pollination of ideas and expertise.
4. Capacity Building and Skills Development: Investing in education, training, and skills development programs can empower local communities to engage in frugal innovation processes, nurturing a culture of grassroots problem-solving and entrepreneurship. This includes supporting STEM education, technical vocational training, and entrepreneurship programs tailored to the needs of underserved populations.
5. Community Engagement and Co-creation; Actively engaging with local communities, understanding their needs and constraints, and co-creating solutions through participatory design approaches can enhance the relevance, acceptance, and sustainability of frugal innovations. This emphasizes the importance of empathic design and inclusive innovation processes.
6. Knowledge Sharing and Dissemination: Facilitating the sharing of knowledge, best practices, and lessons learned across different frugal innovation initiatives can accelerate the scaling and replication of successful solutions. This can involve the creation of online platforms, regional networks, and international collaborations. By addressing the barriers and leveraging the enabling factors, policymakers, innovation 3ecosystem actors, and frugal innovators can work together to create an environment that nurtures and sustains the development of affordable, accessible, and adaptable solutions for underserved communities in Africa.

VII. Measuring the Impact and Scaling of Frugal Innovation

Assessing the impact and scaling of frugal innovations is crucial for understanding their transformative potential, informing policymaking, and

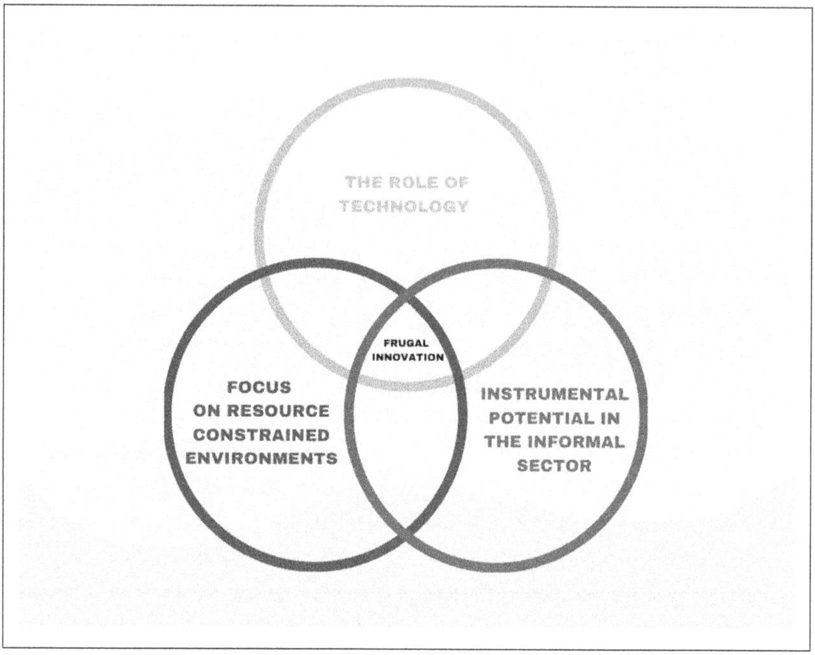

Figure 3.5 Frugal Innovation (Author's own work)

attracting the necessary resources and support for their wider dissemination. However, measuring the impact of frugal innovations can be inherently complex due to their diverse nature, decentralized implementation, and context-specific design.

- Defining Meaningful Impact Metrics: Traditional innovation metrics, such as patent counts, R&D expenditure, and commercialization revenues, often fail to capture the unique attributes and socioeconomic implications of frugal innovations (Park, 2021). Policymakers, researchers, and practitioners must work collaboratively to develop a more comprehensive set of impact indicators that consider factors such as affordability, accessibility, environmental sustainability, job creation, and community empowerment (Khatibi, Khaidzir & Mahdzar, 2023).

- Approaches to Impact Measurement: A multidimensional approach to impact assessment is necessary to fully evaluate the effectiveness of frugal innovations (Shibin, Dubey, Gunasekaran, Luo, Papadopoulos & Roubaud, 2018).

This can involve a combination of quantitative and qualitative methods, including:

1. User-centric impact assessments: Gathering feedback and data from end-users to understand the real-world impact of frugal solutions on their lives and livelihoods.
2. Outcome-based evaluations: Measuring the downstream effects of frugal innovations on socioeconomic indicators, such as improvements in health, education, or income levels.
3. Environmental impact analyses: Assessing the environmental footprint and resource-efficiency of frugal products and services.
4. Scalability and replicability studies: Examining the potential for frugal innovations to be adapted and replicated in different contexts, as well as the factors that enable or hinder their scaling.
5. Participatory impact monitoring: Engaging local communities and stakeholders in the continuous monitoring and refinement of frugal innovation initiatives.

- Leveraging Data and Digital Technologies: The increased availability of digital data and analytical tools can enhance the impact measurement of frugal innovations. For example, real-time usage data, sensor-based monitoring, and mobile-enabled feedback mechanisms can provide valuable insights into the performance and adoption of frugal solutions. Policymakers and innovation ecosystem stakeholders should invest in building the necessary digital infrastructure and data management capacities to support evidence-based decision-making.
- Aligning Impact Measurement with Sustainable Development Goals: Framing the impact of frugal innovations within the broader context of the United Nations Sustainable Development Goals (SDGs) can help demonstrate their contribution to inclusive and sustainable development. Aligning impact metrics with the SDG framework can also facilitate

cross-border learning, attract international funding, and strengthen collaborative efforts among African nations and their global partners.
- Cultivating a Culture of Impact-Driven Innovation: Ultimately, the successful scaling and replication of frugal innovations depend on fostering a culture that prioritizes impact and social value creation.

Policymakers, academic institutions, and innovation ecosystem leaders must actively promote impact-driven mindsets, provide capacity-building support, and recognize and celebrate the achievements of frugal innovators who are making a tangible difference in the lives of underserved communities.

By developing robust impact measurement frameworks, leveraging digital technologies, and aligning with the SDG agenda, African nations can unlock

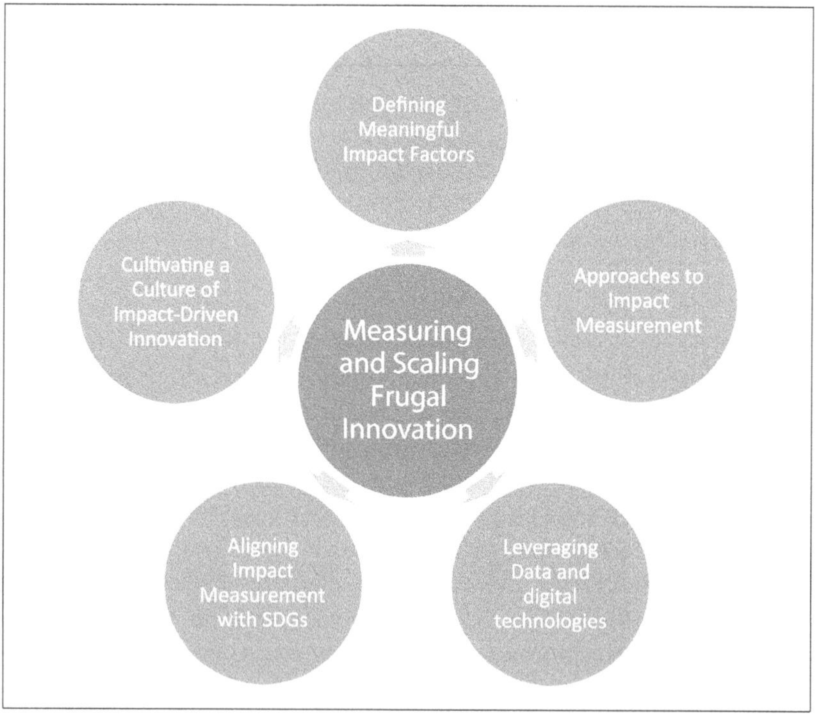

Figure 3.6 Measuring and Scaling Frugal Innovation. Source: Moleka, 2024

the full potential of frugal innovations to drive inclusive and sustainable development across the continent.

VIII. Measuring the Adoption and Impact of Frugal Innovation

While frugal innovation has demonstrated significant potential across sectors, its success requires rigorous assessment using key performance indicators (KPIs). Below are the most scholarly and widely recognized frameworks for evaluating adoption, results, and real impact in frugal innovation.

1. Adoption Metrics for Frugal Innovation

To understand the extent to which frugal innovation is adopted in marginalized communities, several indicators can be applied:

- Diffusion Rate (Rogers, 2003): Measures how quickly a frugal innovation spreads within a population.
- User Retention and Engagement (Dutta & Lanvin, 2013): Evaluates how often users continue to rely on the innovation after initial exposure.
- Affordability Index (Prahalad, 2005): Assesses the extent to which low-income communities can sustainably adopt the innovation without financial strain.
- Cultural Acceptance Score (Gupta, 2012): Analyzes whether the innovation aligns with local traditions, values, and behavioral patterns.

2. Impact Metrics: Evaluating Real Change

Assessing the real impact of frugal innovation requires empirical and quantitative indicators across economic, social, and environmental dimensions:

- Cost Reduction Ratio (Basu et al., 2013): Compares the price of a frugal solution to its conventional alternative.
- Access and Inclusion Index (Radjou & Prabhu, 2015): Measures the increase in the number of marginalized users benefiting from the innovation.
- Improvement in Key Outcomes: For example, in healthcare:
  - Reduction in Disease Burden (WHO, 2020) → Measures the decrease in cases due to frugal medical devices.

- Decrease in Maternal/Infant Mortality (Gwatkin et al., 2014) → Tracks improvements in public health due to low-cost medical solutions.
- Employment and Livelihood Impact (Soni & Krishnan, 2014): Evaluates whether frugal innovation leads to job creation and local entrepreneurship.

3. Long-Term Success and Scalability Indicators

- Sustainability Index (Bocken et al., 2016): Examines the ecological footprint and lifecycle cost of the innovation.
- Replicability Score (Bhatti, 2012): Determines whether the innovation can be scaled or adapted to other regions.
- Public-Private Partnership Index (Chataway et al., 2014): Analyzes how government and private sector collaborations enhance sustainability.

Case Study Integration: Applying These Metrics to the PlayPump

The PlayPump is an example where some frugal innovation indicators showed initial success (high adoption due to novelty), but long-term impact metrics exposed flaws (maintenance failures, sustainability issues). Applying the above framework:

- Adoption: High initial diffusion due to international promotion (Rogers, 2003).
- Impact: Limited long-term usability as maintenance costs outweighed affordability benefits (Basu et al., 2013).
- Sustainability: Weak scalability due to dependency on external donors (Chataway et al., 2014).

IX. Limitations and Critical Perspectives

While frugal innovation has demonstrated remarkable potential in addressing the needs of African communities, it is important to acknowledge the potential limitations and critical perspectives that have emerged within the scholarly discourse. One of the primary concerns raised by researchers is the risk of perpetuating existing inequalities or creating new forms of exclusion through frugal innovation initiatives. Scholars like Karnani (2007) have cautioned that the "Bottom of the Pyramid" (BoP) approach, which underpins much of the frugal innovation discourse, may inadvertently reinforce the marginalization of the poor by treating them solely as consumers rather than active participants in the innovation process. Additionally, some critics have questioned the quality and durability of frugal innovations, arguing that the emphasis on affordability and resource-efficiency may compromise the overall effectiveness and reliability of these solutions. There are concerns that the pursuit of low-cost alternatives could lead to the production of inferior products or services, potentially undermining the long-term impact and sustainability of frugal innovation initiatives (Pansera & Owen, 2018). Another critical perspective relates to the scalability and replicability of frugal innovations. While the initial development of these solutions may be successful in specific local contexts, scholars have highlighted the challenges in scaling them up and adapting them to different geographic, cultural, and institutional settings. The lack of robust innovation ecosystems, limited access to financing, and the complexity of coordinating multi-stakeholder collaborations can all hinder the broader dissemination of frugal innovations (Pansera & Russo, 2016). Furthermore, some researchers have raised concerns about the potential for frugal innovation to be co-opted by large corporations or development agencies, transforming it into a top-down, prescriptive approach that fails to prioritize the needs and aspirations of local communities. This critique emphasizes the importance of maintaining the grassroots, participatory nature of frugal innovation initiatives and ensuring that they remain responsive to the evolving priorities of marginalized populations (George, McGahan & Prabhu, 2012). These critical perspectives underscore the need for a more nuanced and critical examination of frugal innovation in the African context. Scholars, policymakers, and development practitioners must engage in ongoing dialogues to address these concerns, refine the conceptual and operational frameworks of frugal innovation, and ensure that it remains a truly inclusive and empowering approach to addressing the continent's complex challenges. By acknowledging the limitations and incorporating diverse critical perspectives, the field of frugal innovation can evolve in a manner that promotes sustainable, equitable, and community-driven development outcomes, ultimately fulfilling its transformative potential in Africa.

X. Multidisciplinary Perspectives on Frugal Innovation

The study of frugal innovation in Africa has attracted the attention of scholars from diverse academic disciplines, each bringing unique insights and analytical lenses to this field of research.

From an engineering and design perspective, researchers have examined the technical and functional aspects of frugal innovations, focusing on the development of affordable, user-friendly, and context-appropriate solutions. Scholars like Ezeudu, Agunwamba, Ugochukwu, and Oraelosi (2022) have explored the design principles and manufacturing techniques that enable the creation of frugal products and services, such as the use of locally sourced materials, simple fabrication processes, and modular architectures. These engineering-oriented studies have shed light on the innovative ways in which African innovators and entrepreneurs are overcoming resource constraints and infrastructure challenges to develop practical solutions that meet the needs of underserved communities. By understanding the technical underpinnings of frugal innovations, policymakers and development practitioners can better support the scaling and replication of these solutions across different contexts.

From an economic perspective, scholars have examined the business models, financing mechanisms, and market dynamics that enable the successful development and dissemination of frugal innovations. Researchers like George, McGahan, and Prabhu (2012) have explored the notion of "inclusive innovation" or "innovation for inclusive growth," which emphasizes the creation of new opportunities for marginalized groups to participate in high-growth, high-profit ventures. These economic analyses have highlighted the importance of innovative financing approaches, such as pay-as-you-go models and micro-leasing schemes, in making frugal solutions accessible to low-income consumers. Additionally, scholars in this domain have examined the role of public-private partnerships and blended finance mechanisms in mobilizing resources and expertise for inclusive innovation initiatives (Lopes, 2020).

In the realm of management and entrepreneurship, researchers have investigated the organizational structures, leadership strategies, and collaborative practices that enable frugal innovators to navigate the unique challenges and opportunities of resource-constrained environments. Scholars like Radjou, Prabhu, and Ahuja (2012) have developed frameworks like the "Jugaad Innovation" model, which emphasizes the resourcefulness and improvisational abilities of individuals and communities in creating innovative solutions. These management-focused studies have shed light on the importance of grassroots innovation, community engagement, and the cultivation of inclusive innovation ecosystems in driving the success and scalability of frugal initiatives. By understanding the organizational and leadership dynamics that underpin frugal innovation, policymakers and ecosystem stakeholders can develop more targeted support mechanisms and capacity-building programs.

From a social science perspective, researchers have explored the sociocultural and political dimensions of frugal innovation, examining how these solutions intersect with issues of equity, inclusion, and community empowerment. Scholars like Karnani (2007) and Idemudia (2017) have analyzed the concept of the "Bottom of the Pyramid" (BoP) and its implications for inclusive development, highlighting the need to center the voices and experiences of marginalized communities in the innovation process. These sociopolitical analyses have emphasized the importance of addressing systemic barriers, such as discriminatory policies and power imbalances, in creating enabling environments for frugal innovation. Additionally, they have underscored the role of grassroots movements, civil society organizations, and community-based initiatives in driving more participatory and equitable innovation ecosystems. By integrating these multidisciplinary perspectives, researchers, policymakers, and development practitioners can gain a more holistic understanding of frugal innovation in the African context. This cross-pollination of ideas and analytical approaches can lead to the development of more comprehensive frameworks in innovationology, the identification of innovative financing mechanisms, and the design of targeted policy interventions that can unleash the transformative potential of frugal solutions.

XI. Interdisciplinary and Cross-Sectoral Collaborations

Fostering interdisciplinary and cross-sectoral collaborations is crucial for the development, scaling, and impact of frugal innovations in Africa. By bringing together diverse stakeholders, including researchers, policymakers, entrepreneurs, civil society organizations, and end-users, these collaborative efforts can unlock new synergies and leverage complementary expertise to address complex challenges more effectively. From a research perspective, interdisciplinary collaborations can lead to the integration of multiple analytical lenses and the generation of more holistic insights. As discussed earlier, the study of frugal innovation in Africa has attracted scholars from various academic disciplines, each contributing unique perspectives and methodologies. By facilitating cross-pollination of ideas and the co-creation of knowledge, these collaborative research initiatives can deepen the understanding of frugal innovation, identify emerging trends, and develop more comprehensive frameworks for driving inclusive and sustainable development (Sonne, 2012). In the realm of policymaking, cross-sectoral partnerships between government agencies, regulatory bodies, and innovation ecosystem stakeholders can help create more enabling environments for frugal innovations to thrive. Collaborative efforts can inform the development of supportive policies, funding mechanisms, and institutional structures that recognize and incentivize the work of grassroots innovators and social enterprises (Dizolele, 2019). Moreover, these collaborations can help bridge the gaps between policy formulation and implementation, ensuring that the needs and perspectives of local communities are effectively incorporated into the policymaking process. By fostering ongoing dialogue and knowledge exchange, policymakers can better understand the unique challenges and opportunities faced by frugal innovators, adapting their interventions to address these realities. On the ground, cross-sectoral collaborations between entrepreneurs, civil society organizations, and end-user communities can lead to the co-creation of more impactful and sustainable frugal innovations.

By engaging directly with the intended beneficiaries, innovators can develop a deeper understanding of local contexts, tailor their solutions to specific needs, and enhance the overall relevance and acceptability of their initiatives (Mattelmäki, Vaajakallio & Koskinen, 2014).

Additionally, partnerships with civil society organizations can provide frugal innovators with valuable insights into the lived experiences of marginalized communities, as well as access to trusted communication channels and distribution networks. These collaborative efforts can also help to empower local communities, fostering a sense of ownership and agency in the innovation process. Furthermore, strategic alliances between frugal innovators, large corporations, and development agencies can unlock new pathways for scaling and replicating successful solutions. By leveraging the resources, expertise, and market access of these larger players, frugal innovations can reach broader audiences and achieve greater impact (Rosca, Reedy & Bendul,

2018). Throughout this collaborative ecosystem, the role of innovation hubs, accelerators, and incubators becomes increasingly crucial. These platforms can facilitate the cross-pollination of ideas, provide access to mentorship and capacity-building support, and foster the development of robust value chains and distribution networks (Bhatti & Prabhu, 2019).

XII. Emerging Trends and Future Directions

As the field of frugal innovation in Africa continues to evolve, several emerging trends and future directions are worth highlighting:

1. Digital Transformations: The increasing availability and affordability of digital technologies, such as mobile phones, IoT sensors, and cloud-based platforms, are opening new avenues for the development and scaling of frugal innovations. Innovators are leveraging these digital tools to enhance the accessibility, efficiency, and impact of their solutions, from remote healthcare diagnostics to precision farming technologies (Qureshi & Sutter, 2017).
2. Integration of Traditional and Modern Knowledge: African innovators are increasingly blending traditional, indigenous knowledge with modern scientific and technological advancements to create culturally-relevant and contextually-appropriate frugal solutions. This hybridization of knowledge systems can lead to more sustainable and inclusive innovations that are deeply rooted in local realities (Ahenkan & Boon, 2011).
3. Emphasis on Sustainability and Environmental Considerations: As the impacts of climate change and environmental degradation become more pronounced, there is a growing emphasis on developing frugal innovations that prioritize sustainability and environmental stewardship. Innovators are exploring renewable energy solutions, circular economy models, and nature-based approaches to address pressing ecological challenges (Halme & Laurila, 2009).
4. Scaling and Replicability Challenges: While the initial development of frugal innovations may be successful in local contexts, the challenge of scaling and replicating these solutions across different geographies and communities remains a significant hurdle.

Researchers and practitioners are exploring innovative business models, partnership strategies, and policy frameworks to address these scaling barriers and enable the broader dissemination of frugal innovations (Pansera & Owen, 2018).

5. Interdisciplinary Collaborations: As the complexity of societal challenges increases, there is a growing recognition of the need for interdisciplinary collaborations to drive more impactful and sustainable frugal innovation initiatives. Researchers, policymakers, entrepreneurs, civil society organizations, and end-users are working together to co-create solutions, share knowledge, and leverage complementary expertise (Sonne, 2012).
6. Evolving Policy Landscapes: The policy environments that shape the innovation ecosystem in Africa are also undergoing gradual transformations, with some governments and regional bodies recognizing the importance of frugal innovation and incorporating it into their development strategies. The continued evolution of supportive policy frameworks, procurement practices, and investment mechanisms will be crucial in unleashing the full potential of frugal innovations (Dizolele, 2019). As these emerging trends and future directions unfold, the field of frugal innovation in Africa will likely continue to diversify, with new applications, business models, and collaborative approaches emerging to address the unique challenges and opportunities of the continent.

Researchers, policymakers, and development practitioners must remain attuned to these evolving dynamics, engaging in ongoing dialogue and knowledge exchange to ensure that frugal innovation remains a powerful driver of inclusive and sustainable development across Africa.

References

Ahenkan, A., & Boon, E. (2011). Improving nutrition and health through non-timber forest products in Ghana. *Journal of Health, Population, and Nutrition*, 29(2), 141–148.

Basu, R. R., Banerjee, P. M., & Sweeny, E. J. (2013). Frugal innovation: core competencies to address global sustainability. *The Journal of Management for Global Sustainability*, 1(2), 63-82.

Basu, R., Morgeson, F. V., & Soni, P. (2013). The promise of frugal innovation: The case of India. *Business & Society Review*, 118(1), 63-95. https://doi.org/10.1111/basr.12009

Bhatti, Y. A. (2012). Frugal innovation: A new product development approach for emerging markets. *International Journal of Innovation Management*, 16(6), 1240001. https://doi.org/10.1142/S1363919612400010

Bhatti, Y., & Prabhu, J. (2019). Frugal innovation and social innovation: Linked paths to achieving inclusion sustainably. In *Handbook of inclusive innovation* (pp. 354-376). Edward Elgar Publishing.

Bocken, N. M. P., Short, S. W., Rana, P., & Evans, S. (2016). A literature and practice review to develop sustainable business model archetypes. *Journal of Cleaner Production*, 65, 42-56. https://doi.org/10.1016/j.jclepro.2013.11.039

Chataway, J., Wield, D., & Tait, J. (2014). The role of public-private partnerships in scaling up frugal innovation. *Technology Analysis & Strategic Management*, 26(7), 819-834. https://doi.org/10.1080/09537325.2014.932938

Dizolele, M. P. (2019). *The role of innovation and technology in Africa's development*. Center for Strategic and International Studies.

Dutta, S., & Lanvin, B. (2013). The Global Information Technology Report 2013: Growth and Jobs in a Hyperconnected World. World Economic Forum.

Ezeudu, O. B., Agunwamba, J. C., Ugochukwu, U. C., & Oraelosi, T. C. (2022). Circular economy and frugal innovation: a conceptual nexus. *Environmental Science and Pollution Research*, 1-16.

George, G., McGahan, A. M., & Prabhu, J. (2012). Innovation for inclusive growth: Towards a theoretical framework and a research agenda. *Journal of management studies*, 49(4), 661-683.

Gupta, A. (2012). Inclusive Innovation: Insights from the Field. *Innovation & Technology for Development*, 18(1), 1-12.

Gwatkin, D. R., Rustein, S. O., Johnson, K., Pande, R., & Wagstaff, A. (2014). Socioeconomic Differences in Health, Nutrition, and Population in the 1990s. *The World Bank*. https://doi.org/10.1596/0-8213-4079-7

Halme, M., & Laurila, J. (2009). Philanthropy, integration or innovation? Exploring the financial and societal outcomes of different types of corporate responsibility. *Journal of Business Ethics*, 84(3), 325-339.

Hossain, M., Park, S., & Shahid, S. (2023). Frugal innovation for sustainable rural development. *Technological Forecasting and Social Change*, *193*, 122662.

Idemudia, U. (2017). Business and development in Africa: Towards a strategic partnership for change. In E. Chirai & S. Opoku-Mensah (Eds.), *Africa's Development in the Twenty-First Century* (pp. 69-90). Routledge.

Karnani, A. (2007). The mirage of marketing to the bottom of the pyramid: How the private sector can help alleviate poverty. *California Management Review*, 49(4), 90-111. 2.

Khatibi, M., Khaidzir, K. A. M., & Mahdzar, S. S. S. (2023). Measuring the sustainability of neighborhoods: A systematic literature review. *Iscience*, *26*(2).

Lopes, C. (2020). Financing inclusive innovation in Africa. United Nations Economic Commission for Africa.

Mattelmäki, T., Vaajakallio, K., & Koskinen, I. (2014). What happened to empathic design? *Design issues*, 30(1), 67-77.

Moleka, P. (2024). Frugal Innovation for Inclusive and Sustainable Development in Africa. *Advanced Research in Economics and Business Strategy Journal*, Vol 5, N1.

Pansera, M., & Owen, R. (2018). Framing the convergence of sustainability, innovation and entrepreneurship. In *Handbook of Entrepreneurship and Sustainable Development Research*. Edward Elgar Publishing.

Pansera, M., & Russo, A. (2016). The sustainability frontier: Innovations, entrepreneurship and the sharing economy. In *Sustainable Consumption: Key Issues* (pp. 69-88). Routledge.

Park, A. (2021). Invention to innovation: A framework and the roles of uncertainty and open innovation in an emerging personalized medicine ecosystem.

Prabhu, J., & Jain, S. (2015). Innovation and entrepreneurship in India: Understanding jugaad. *Asia Pacific Journal of Management*, 32(4), 843-868.

Prahalad, C. K. (2005). The Fortune at the Bottom of the Pyramid: Eradicating Poverty Through Profits. *Wharton School Publishing*.

Prahalad, C. K., & Hart, S. L. (2002). The fortune at the bottom of the pyramid. *strategy+ business*, 26(1), 2-14.

Qureshi, Z. H., & Sutter, R. (2017). Digital Innovations for the Bottom of the Pyramid. *Information Technologies & International Development*, 13, 113-121.

Radjou, N., Prabhu, J., & Ahuja, S. (2012). *Jugaad innovation: Think frugal, be flexible, generate breakthrough growth.* John Wiley & Sons.

Radjou, N., & Prabhu, J. (2015). *Frugal innovation: How to do more with less.* The Economist.

Rogers, E. M. (2003). Diffusion of Innovations (5th ed.). *Free Press.*

Rosca, E., Arnold, M., & Bendul, J. C. (2017). Business models for sustainable innovation–an empirical analysis of frugal products and services. *Journal of Cleaner Production*, 162, S133-S145.

Rosca, E., Reedy, J., & Bendul, J. C. (2018). Does frugal innovation enable sustainable development? A systematic literature review. *The European Journal of Development Research*, 30(1), 136-157.

Shibin, K. T., Dubey, R., Gunasekaran, A., Luo, Z., Papadopoulos, T., & Roubaud, D. (2018). Frugal innovation for supply chain sustainability in SMEs: multi-method research design. *Production Planning & Control, 29*(11), 908-927.

Signé, L. (2018). *Capturing the promise of African innovation.* Brookings Institution.

Soni, P., & Krishnan, A. (2014). *Frugal Innovation: A New Business Strategy.* Springer.

Sonne, L. (2012). Innovative initiatives supporting inclusive innovation in India: Social business incubation and micro venture capital. *Technological Forecasting and Social Change*, 79(4), 638-647.

Tiwari, R., & Herstatt, C. (2012). Assessing India's lead market potential for cost-effective innovations. *Journal of Indian Business Research*, 4(2), 97-115.

Wentzel, J. P., & Steyn, J. N. (2016). The pervasiveness of the Bottom of the Pyramid as a market segment in poverty-stricken rural areas. *African Journal of Science, Technology, Innovation and Development*, 8(1), 43-49.

Zeschky, M., Widenmayer, B., & Gassmann, O. (2011). Frugal innovation in emerging markets. *Research-Technology Management*, 54(4), 38-45.

Zeschky, M., Winterhalter, S., & Gassmann, O. (2014). From cost to frugal and reverse innovation: Mapping the field and implications for global competitiveness. *Research-Technology Management*, 57(4), 20-27.

CHAPTER 4

Appropriate Technologies for Sustainable Development

The imperative of sustainable development in Africa has become increasingly urgent, as the continent grapples with a range of complex challenges, from environmental degradation and resource depletion to persistent poverty and inequality. In this context, the role of appropriate technologies has emerged as a critical factor in catalyzing transformative change and driving inclusive, equitable, and environmentally-conscious progress. Appropriate technologies are those that are designed to meet the unique needs and constraints of local communities, leveraging accessible resources and empowering end-users as active participants in the innovation process. These technologies are often characterized by their simplicity, affordability, and suitability to the local context, making them particularly well-suited for resource-constrained settings prevalent across much of Africa. This chapter delves into the landscape of appropriate technologies for sustainable development in Africa, exploring their key principles, showcasing successful case studies, and highlighting the contributions of leading African scholars in this field.

By examining the diverse applications of appropriate technologies, from renewable energy to water purification and agricultural systems, this chapter underscores their transformative potential in addressing some of Africa's most pressing development challenges.

Figure 4.1 Aproriate Technologies for Sustainable Development (Author's own work)

I. The Principles of Appropriate Technologies

Appropriate technologies are grounded in a set of core principles that distinguish them from conventional, often capital-intensive technological solutions. These principles are crucial in ensuring that the technologies developed and deployed in African communities are truly responsive to local needs, contexts, and capacities.

The key principles of appropriate technologies include:

1. Local Relevance and Affordability: Appropriate technologies must be designed to address the specific needs and constraints of the target communities, taking into account their socioeconomic, cultural, and environmental realities. This often translates to technologies that are affordable and accessible, utilizing locally available materials and skills (Juma, 2016; Mazzucato, 2013).
2. Simplicity and Ease of Use: Appropriate technologies prioritize simplicity in their design and operation, ensuring that end-users can easily understand, maintain, and repair the technology without the need for specialized expertise or resources. This empowers local communities to take ownership of the technology and adapt it to their evolving needs (Maathai, 2003; Oke, 2016).
3. Environmental Sustainability: Appropriate technologies aim to minimize their environmental impact, promoting the sustainable use of natural resources and the development of eco-friendly solutions. This may involve the use of renewable energy sources, the incorporation of circular economy principles, and the minimization of waste and pollution (Phakeng, 2019; Ramphele, 2012).
4. Participatory Design and Co-creation: The development of appropriate technologies is a collaborative process that actively engages local communities, drawing on their knowledge, insights, and aspirations. This co-creation approach ensures that the technologies are truly responsive to the needs of the end-users and foster a sense of ownership and investment (Mazzucato, 2013; Ndemo, 2017).
5. Scalability and Replicability: Appropriate technologies are designed with the potential for scalability and replicability, enabling their successful adoption and adaptation across diverse communities and contexts. This requires a deep understanding of the socioeconomic and cultural factors that influence technology uptake and the development of flexible, modular designs (Juma, 2016; Archibong, 2019).

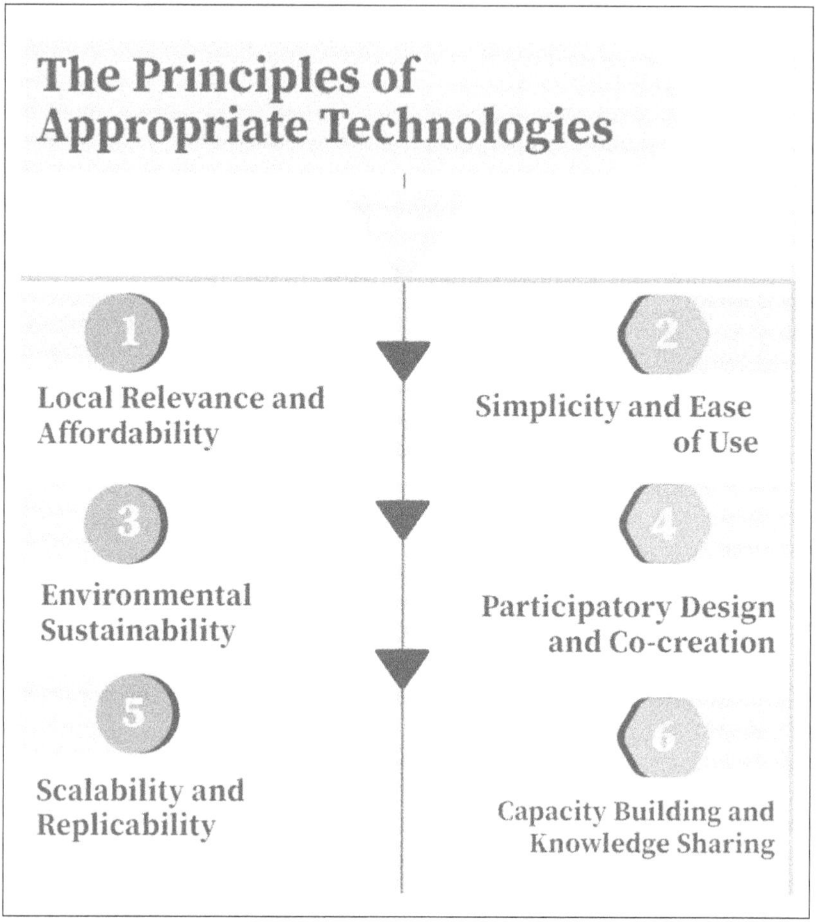

Figure 4.2 The Principles of Appropriate Technologies (Author's own work)

6. Capacity Building and Knowledge Sharing: Appropriate technologies prioritize the development of local capacities, empowering communities to engage in the design, implementation, and maintenance of the technologies. This involves the cultivation of technical skills, as well as the sharing of knowledge and best practices across communities and regions (Maathai, 2003; Mensa-Bonsu, 2018).

These principles serve as the foundation for the development and deployment of appropriate technologies in Africa, ensuring that the innovations introduced are truly transformative and contribute to the realization of sustainable and equitable development goals.

II. Appropriate Technologies for Sustainable Development in Africa

Across Africa, a vibrant ecosystem of innovators, entrepreneurs, and community-based organizations is developing and deploying a wide range of appropriate technologies to address some of the continent's most pressing development challenges. These technologies span diverse sectors, including energy, water, agriculture, healthcare, and infrastructure, and are making significant contributions to the achievement of the Sustainable Development Goals (SDGs).

1. Renewable Energy Solutions: One of the most prominent areas of appropriate technology development in Africa is the renewable energy sector. Many African communities, particularly in rural and off-grid areas, lack access to reliable and affordable energy sources, hindering their social and economic development. Appropriate renewable energy technologies, such as solar photovoltaic systems, micro-hydropower, and biogas digesters, are playing a crucial role in bridging this energy gap.

   Case Study: The Barefoot College Solar Electrification Program
   The Barefoot College, a renowned social enterprise based in India, has established a successful model for training rural women as "solar engineers" across several African countries, including Senegal, Burkina Faso, and Malawi. Through this program, women are provided with comprehensive training in the design, installation, and maintenance of solar photovoltaic systems, enabling them to bring clean, affordable, and sustainable electricity to their communities. The program's emphasis on local capacity building and gender empowerment has had a transformative impact, improving access to energy while fostering community resilience and self-reliance (Juma, 2016; Oke, 2016).
2. Water and Sanitation Technologies: Access to clean water and appropriate sanitation facilities is a pressing challenge in many parts of Africa,

contributing to health issues, environmental degradation, and economic disparities. Appropriate technologies, such as low-cost water filtration systems, rainwater harvesting, and composting toilets, are being developed and deployed to address these critical needs.

Case Study: The Hippo Water Roller Project

The Hippo Water Roller Project, a South African-based non-profit organization, has pioneered the development and distribution of the Hippo Water Roller – a simple, yet ingenious, device that enables the efficient transportation of water over long distances. The Hippo Water Roller features a large, sturdy drum that can be easily rolled along the ground, significantly reducing the physical effort required to collect and transport water, especially for women and children. This technology has had a profound impact on the lives of thousands of rural African communities, improving access to water, enhancing health and sanitation, and empowering marginalized groups (Appeaning Addo, 2015; Mensa-Bonsu, 2018).

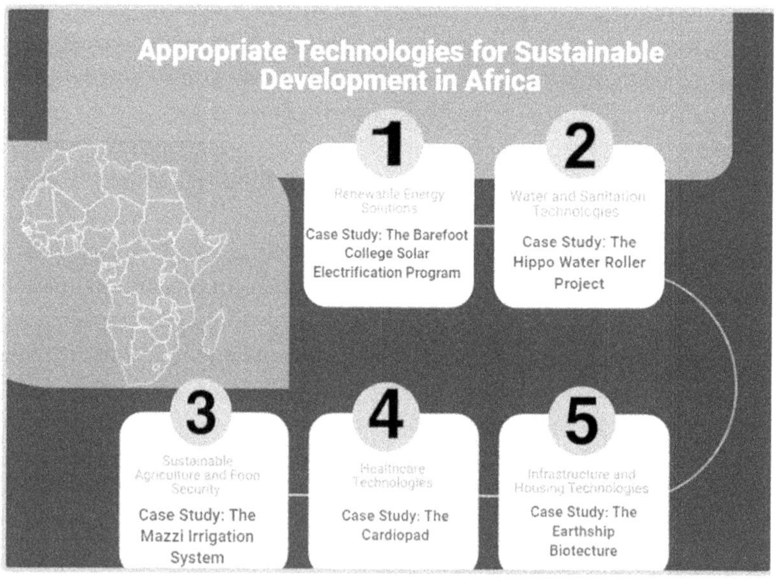

Figure 4.3 Case Studies (Author's own work)

3. Sustainable Agriculture and Food Security: Agriculture is the backbone of many African economies, but traditional farming practices often face significant challenges, including low productivity, limited access to resources, and the impacts of climate change. Appropriate agricultural technologies, such as small-scale irrigation systems, low-cost greenhouses, and integrated pest management solutions, are being developed to address these issues and promote sustainable food production.

   Case Study: The Mazzi Irrigation System
   The Mazzi Irrigation System, developed by a team of Ugandan engineers, is a low-cost, solar-powered drip irrigation system designed for smallholder farmers. The system utilizes locally available materials, such as plastic bottles and recycled materials, to create a simple, yet effective, irrigation solution that can be easily maintained and repaired by farmers. By improving water efficiency and reducing the labor required for manual irrigation, the Mazzi system has helped to increase crop yields and food security for numerous rural communities in Uganda (Juma, 2016; Archibong, 2019).
4. Healthcare Technologies Affordable and accessible healthcare remains a significant challenge in many parts of Africa, particularly in rural and underserved areas. Appropriate healthcare technologies, such as portable diagnostic devices, low-cost prosthetics, and off-grid medical equipment, are being developed to address these gaps and improve health outcomes.

   Case Study: The Cardiopad The Cardiopad, developed by a Cameroonian engineer, is a mobile, touch-screen electrocardiogram (ECG) device designed for use in remote and resource-constrained healthcare settings. The Cardiopad uses a simple, intuitive interface that allows healthcare workers with minimal training to perform ECG tests and transmit the results to medical specialists for diagnosis and treatment, even in areas with limited infrastructure and connectivity. This technology has significantly improved access to cardiac care in Cameroon and other parts of Africa (Phakeng, 2019; Ramphele, 2012).
5. Infrastructure and Housing Technologies Inadequate and poorly-constructed infrastructure, including housing, transportation, and

communication networks, remains a significant challenge in many African communities. Appropriate technologies, such as low-cost building materials, sustainable construction methods, and off-grid communication solutions, are being developed to address these gaps and promote more inclusive and resilient development.

Case Study: The Earthship Biotecture

The Earthship Biotecture, a concept pioneered by American architect Michael Reynolds, has been adapted and implemented in various African countries, including Malawi and South Africa. Earthships are self-sufficient, off-grid homes that utilize locally sourced, recycled materials, such as tires and bottles, to create energy-efficient, water-harvesting, and waste-management systems. This approach to sustainable housing not only provides affordable and environmentally-friendly living solutions but also empowers local communities to participate in the design and construction process (Maathai, 2003; Ndemo, 2017).

These are just a few examples of the many appropriate technologies being developed and deployed across Africa to address critical development challenges. Across sectors, innovators and entrepreneurs are leveraging local knowledge, resources, and collaborative networks to create tailored, community-driven solutions that are truly transformative in their impact.

III. The Contributions of Leading African Scholars

The field of appropriate technologies for sustainable development in Africa has been significantly shaped by the research, insights, and contributions of a growing community of African scholars and experts. These individuals have played a crucial role in advancing the theoretical and practical understanding of appropriate technologies, as well as in shaping policies and strategies that enable their widespread adoption and impact.

1. Professor Calestous Juma, Harvard University/ Calestous Juma, a renowned Kenyan scholar and professor at the Harvard Kennedy School, has been a pioneering voice in the field of innovation for sustainable development in Africa. His work has emphasized the importance of frugal innovation, traditional knowledge systems, and inclusive innovation ecosystems in addressing the continent's complex challenges.

Juma's influential books, such as "Innovation and Its Enemies: Why People Resist New Technologies" and "The New Harvest: Agricultural Innovation in Africa," have shaped the scholarly discourse and policy debates around appropriate technologies (Juma, 2016).

2. Professor Wangari Maathai, University of Nairobi /The late Professor Wangari Maathai, Nobel Peace Prize laureate and founder of the Green Belt Movement, was a passionate advocate for the integration of traditional ecological knowledge and community-based solutions in addressing environmental and social challenges in Africa. Her work on sustainable agriculture, agroforestry, and grassroots environmental conservation initiatives has inspired the development of numerous appropriate technologies that empower local communities and promote ecological resilience (Maathai, 2003).
3. Professor Yemi Oke, University of Lagos/ Yemi Oke, a professor of law and renewable energy expert at the University of Lagos, Nigeria, has been at the forefront of research and advocacy on the deployment of appropriate renewable energy technologies in Africa. His work has emphasized the importance of inclusive, community-based energy solutions, as well as the need for enabling policy and regulatory frameworks to support their widespread adoption (Oke, 2016).
4. Professor Mamokgethi Phakeng, University of Cape Town/ Mamokgethi Phakeng, the Vice-Chancellor of the University of Cape Town, South Africa, is a renowned mathematician and a champion of science, technology, engineering, and mathematics (STEM) education in Africa. Her work has highlighted the critical role of STEM skills and inclusive, participatory approaches in the development and implementation of appropriate technologies that address local needs and empower marginalized communities (Phakeng, 2019).
5. Professor Mamphela Ramphele, University of Cape Town /Mamphela Ramphele, a medical doctor, anthropologist, and former Vice-Chancellor of the University of Cape Town, has been a trailblazer in the field of social inovation and its application in addressing complex development challenges in Africa. Her work has emphasized the importance of inclusive, community-driven approaches and the need to prioritize the empowerment of marginalized groups in the innovation process (Ramphele, 2012).

6. Professor Bitange Ndemo, University of Nairobi/ Bitange Ndemo, a professor of entrepreneurship at the University of Nairobi, Kenya, has been a leading voice in the exploration of the intersection between digital technologies, inclusive innovation, and sustainable development in Africa. His research and advocacy have focused on the potential of emerging technologies, such as blockchain and artificial intelligence, to enable more accessible and equitable solutions for communities across the continent (Ndemo, 2017).
7. Professor Kwasi Appeaning Addo, University of Ghana Kwasi /Appeaning Addo, a professor of coastal processes and environmental management at the University of Ghana, has been instrumental in the development and deployment of appropriate technologies for coastal and marine resource management in West Africa. His work has highlighted the importance of integrating traditional knowledge and community-based approaches in addressing environmental challenges and promoting sustainable livelihoods (Appeaning Addo, 2015).
8. Professor Henrietta Mensa-Bonsu, University of Ghana Henrietta/ Mensa-Bonsu, a professor of law at the University of Ghana, has been a prominent voice in the discourse on the legal and regulatory frameworks that enable the development and adoption of appropriate technologies in Africa. Her research has explored the intersection of intellectual property rights, technology transfer, and inclusive innovation, contributing to the creation of more enabling environments for appropriate technology solutions (Mensa-Bonsu, 2018).
9. Professor Uduak Archibong, University of Bradford /Uduak Archibong, a professor of diversity and director of the Centre for Inclusion and Diversity at the University of Bradford, UK, has been a leading scholar on the topic of inclusive innovation and its application in the African context. Her work has emphasized the importance of equity, diversity, and social inclusion in the design and implementation of appropriate technologies that truly meet the needs of marginalized communities (Archibong, 2019).

These African scholars, along with many others, have made invaluable contributions to the understanding, development, and deployment of appropriate technologies for sustainable development in Africa. Their research, advocacy, and collaborative efforts have been instrumental in shaping the field and driving transformative change across the continent.

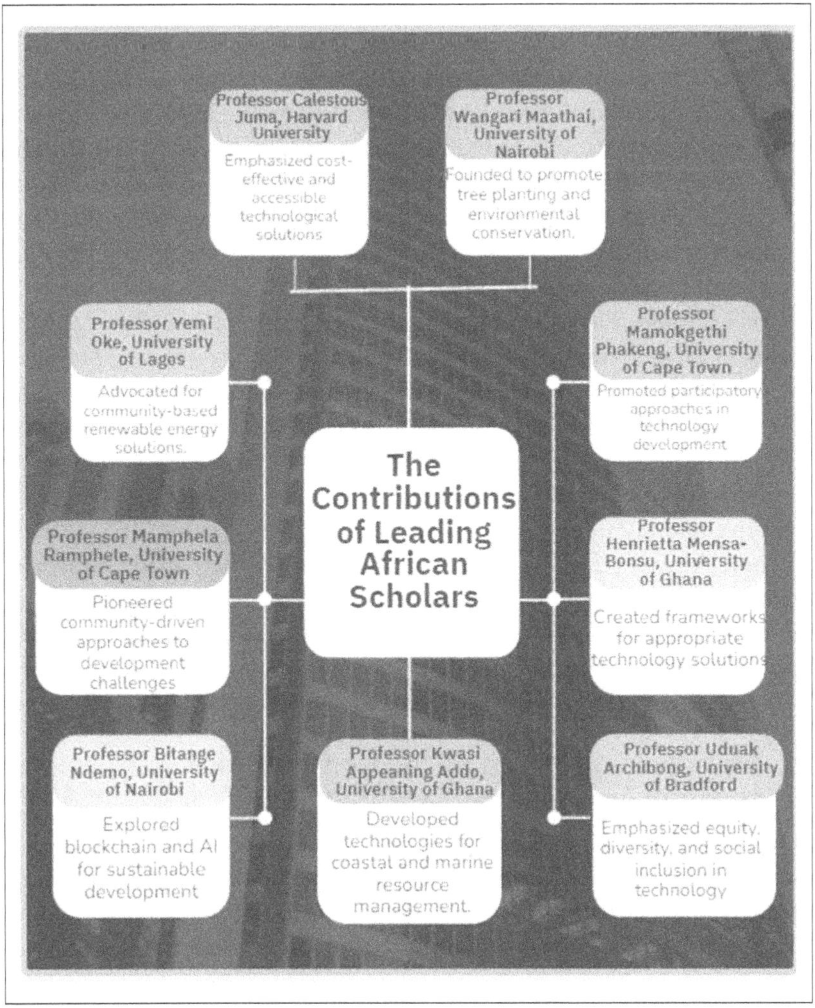

Figure 4.4 The Contributions of Leading African Scholars (Author's own work)

The imperative of sustainable development in Africa has thrust the role of appropriate technologies into the spotlight, as innovators, entrepreneurs, and communities seek to address pressing challenges through context-specific, community-driven solutions. By embracing the principles of local relevance, simplicity, environmental sustainability, participatory design, and scalability, appropriate technologies have the potential to unlock transformative change and contribute to the achievement of the Sustainable Development Goals. The diverse case studies showcased in this chapter illustrate the breadth and impact of appropriate technologies across sectors, from renewable energy and water purification to sustainable agriculture and healthcare. These innovations, coupled with the groundbreaking contributions of leading African scholars, highlight the profound potential of appropriate technologies to empower marginalized communities, foster inclusive and equitable development, and chart a more sustainable path forward for the African continent. As the field of appropriate technologies continues to evolve, it will be crucial to maintain a strong emphasis on collaborative, community-driven approaches, integrating traditional knowledge and grassroots dynamism with emerging scientific and technological advancements. By embracing this collaborative and inclusive ethos, the development and deployment of appropriate technologies can become a powerful catalyst for realizing the vision of an equitable and sustainable African future.

These African scholars, along with many others, have made invaluable contributions to the understanding, development, and deployment of appropriate technologies for sustainable development in Africa. Their research, advocacy, and collaborative efforts have been instrumental in shaping the field and driving transformative change across the continent.

IV. Empowering Marginalized Communities through Appropriate Technologies

A key aspect of the scholarly discourse on appropriate technologies in Africa is the recognition of their potential to empower marginalized communities and address deep-seated inequalities. By prioritizing local relevance, community engagement, and environmental sustainability, appropriate technologies can serve as powerful levers for social and economic transformation. One area of focus has been the empowerment of women through the development and deployment of appropriate technologies. Scholars have highlighted how technologies such as water rollers, improved cookstoves, and renewable energy solutions can significantly reduce the time and labor burden on women, enabling them to engage in more productive and educational activities (Maathai, 2003; Phakeng, 2019). Moreover, the participatory design and implementation of these technologies can foster women's leadership and decision-making power within their communities. Another area of emphasis has been the role of appropriate technologies in supporting the livelihoods and food security of smallholder farmers, who constitute a large proportion of Africa's rural poor. Scholars have examined how innovations in small-scale irrigation, agroecological farming practices, and post-harvest processing can enhance the productivity, resilience, and incomes of these marginalized communities (Juma, 2016; Archibong, 2019). The empowerment of youth through appropriate technologies has also been a growing area of interest. Scholars have explored how the development of low-cost, user-friendly technologies in sectors like renewable energy, healthcare, and digital communication can create new entrepreneurial and employment opportunities for young Africans, particularly in underserved communities (Ndemo, 2017; Mensa-Bonsu, 2018). Moreover, the integration of traditional knowledge systems and indigenous innovations has been a crucial aspect of appropriate technology development, empowering local communities as active co-creators and stewards of these solutions. Scholars have emphasized how this approach can foster a sense of ownership, pride, and cultural affirmation within marginalized groups, contributing to more sustainable and equitable development outcomes (Maathai, 2003; Oke, 2016). By placing the needs and aspirations of marginalized communities at the center of the innovation process, appropriate technologies can serve as powerful tools for social and economic inclusion, contributing to the realization of a more just and equitable African future.

V. Scaling Up and Sustaining Appropriate Technology Initiatives

While the transformative potential of appropriate technologies in Africa has been well-established, the scholarly discourse has also grappled with the challenges of scaling up and sustaining these initiatives over the long term.

Researchers have identified several key factors that influence the scalability and sustainability of appropriate technology projects:

1. Enabling Policy and Regulatory Environments: Scholars have emphasized the critical role of supportive policy frameworks, including targeted funding mechanisms, procurement strategies, and intellectual property protections, in creating an enabling environment for the growth and scaling of appropriate technology initiatives (Mensa-Bonsu, 2018; Archibong, 2019).
2. Collaborative Ecosystem Development: The literature highlights the importance of fostering collaborative innovation ecosystems that bring together diverse stakeholders, including local communities, research institutions, private sector actors, and policymakers, to collectively address the challenges of scaling and sustaining appropriate technologies (Chataway et al., 2014; Grobbelaar & Boshoff, 2019).
3. Capacity Building and Knowledge Sharing: Scholars have emphasized the need for comprehensive capacity-building programs and knowledge-sharing platforms that empower local communities to effectively maintain, adapt, and replicate appropriate technologies in their respective contexts (Maathai, 2003; Oke, 2016).
4. Financing and Business Models: The development of innovative financing mechanisms, such as impact investment funds, crowdsourcing platforms, and microfinance schemes, can play a crucial role in facilitating the scaling and commercialization of appropriate technology initiatives, while ensuring their financial sustainability (Lôbo & Meira, 2019; Phakeng, 2019).
5. Monitoring, Evaluation, and Continuous Improvement: Scholars have highlighted the importance of robust monitoring and evaluation frameworks that can track the social, economic, and environmental impacts of appropriate technology initiatives, informing ongoing improvements and adaptations to enhance their long-term viability (Chataway et al., 2014; Grobbelaar & Boshoff, 2019).

By addressing these key factors, the scholarly community has sought to identify strategies and pathways for scaling up and sustaining appropriate technology initiatives, ensuring that they can continue to drive transformative change and contribute to the realization of sustainable development goals across the African continent.

VI. Constraints and Infrastructure Challenges in the Adoption of Appropriate Technologies in Africa

While appropriate technologies have demonstrated significant promise in addressing Africa's developmental challenges, their widespread adoption and effectiveness are often hindered by a range of constraints related to infrastructure, policy, and socio-economic realities. Understanding these barriers is critical for ensuring that such technologies can reach their full potential and bring about sustainable and transformative change.

1. Infrastructure Limitations

One of the most critical barriers to the effective deployment of appropriate technologies in Africa is the lack of robust and reliable infrastructure. The continent faces significant deficits in infrastructure across key sectors, including energy, transport, water, and communications, which affect the adoption and scaling of even well-designed technologies.

- Energy Access: Despite considerable progress, a large proportion of Africa's rural populations still lack access to reliable electricity. This constraint limits the effectiveness of technologies that require continuous energy supply, such as solar-powered water pumps or refrigeration units in healthcare. The absence of an integrated energy grid or reliable off-grid systems in many rural areas exacerbates this issue. For instance, even low-cost renewable energy solutions, such as solar panels, often struggle to function optimally in regions with insufficient grid stability or where the maintenance of solar installations is complicated by logistical challenges (Akinmoladun et al., 2020).
- Water and Sanitation Systems: Appropriate water filtration and sanitation technologies, such as rainwater harvesting systems or composting toilets, often face operational barriers due to the lack of proper water distribution infrastructure or local government support. Without reliable pipelines, reservoirs, and sewage systems, even the most innovative technologies can

be rendered ineffective or difficult to maintain. The shortage of trained technicians to oversee the installation and maintenance of these systems in remote regions further exacerbates these challenges (Kassenga & Lydon, 2017).

- Transport and Logistics: The lack of adequate transport networks in rural areas poses a major challenge to the dissemination and scaling of appropriate technologies. The high costs and logistical complexity of transporting raw materials, spare parts, and technicians to rural locations impede the widespread adoption of technologies like low-cost greenhouses or efficient irrigation systems. Poor road networks and underdeveloped transportation systems often result in delays in both the delivery and repair of essential technological components, thus compromising their sustainability (Rogers et al., 2015).

2. Policy and Regulatory Barriers

A lack of coherent and supportive policy frameworks is another significant constraint to the adoption of appropriate technologies in Africa. In many instances, the regulatory environment for the development, implementation, and scaling of these technologies is either underdeveloped or misaligned with the realities of local communities.

- Fragmented Policy Landscape: Many African countries have fragmented or inconsistent policies when it comes to technology adoption and innovation. Often, national policies do not prioritize the integration of appropriate technologies, and local governments may lack the capacity to implement policies effectively. This can result in a lack of incentives for private-sector involvement or delays in the deployment of technologies that could significantly benefit rural populations (Nkosi & Jali, 2018). Furthermore, regulatory approval processes can be cumbersome and slow, especially in sectors like healthcare, where the adoption of frugal medical devices is often delayed by bureaucratic hurdles (Chikadzi et al., 2017).
- Intellectual Property and Technology Transfer: The protection of intellectual property (IP) rights, while important for incentivizing innovation, can also present a barrier to the adoption of appropriate technologies in Africa. In some instances, the rigid enforcement of IP laws prevents the

local adaptation of foreign technologies or inhibits the development of local versions of global innovations. Furthermore, the lack of effective technology transfer mechanisms between international organizations, local firms, and governments can stifle the rapid dissemination of knowledge and technology, limiting the ability of local entrepreneurs to innovate and scale (Mensa-Bonsu, 2018).

- Financial and Institutional Constraints: A lack of access to financing is one of the most persistent challenges faced by African innovators working on appropriate technologies. Many community-driven technologies struggle to attract investment due to perceived risks and low profitability. Inadequate institutional support, in the form of financial institutions that understand the potential and limitations of appropriate technologies, further exacerbates this problem. The lack of tailored financial products, such as micro-loans or venture capital for social enterprises, often deters potential investors from engaging with these projects (Appeaning Addo, 2015).

3. Socio-Cultural Constraints

The adoption of appropriate technologies is not solely contingent on technological feasibility or economic viability. Socio-cultural factors play a pivotal role in determining whether these innovations will be embraced by local communities.

- Cultural Acceptance and Resistance to Change: While the success of appropriate technologies often depends on their cultural relevance, they can face resistance from local communities if they do not align with deeply ingrained cultural practices or lifestyles. For example, despite the clear benefits of modern sanitation technologies such as composting toilets, communities may resist these innovations due to their association with unfamiliar or "foreign" practices (Mazzucato, 2013). Similarly, agricultural technologies like genetically modified crops or modern irrigation systems may encounter resistance in regions where traditional farming methods are considered culturally significant or where there is distrust in new technological solutions (Sennett, 2017).

- Education and Capacity Building: The implementation of new technologies often requires a basic level of technical knowledge and skills. However, educational gaps in many African countries, particularly in rural areas, can present a significant barrier to the effective use and maintenance of appropriate technologies. Although technologies such as low-cost solar-powered systems or small-scale irrigation solutions may be relatively simple, they still require some basic training for optimal use. The lack of adequate education and capacity-building initiatives means that these technologies may not be sustained over time (Ramphele, 2012). Furthermore, the absence of local expertise to maintain and repair these technologies can reduce their long-term viability.

4. Infrastructure Synergies for Scaling Appropriate Technologies

Despite these challenges, there are significant opportunities for leveraging synergies between infrastructure development and the scaling of appropriate technologies. By integrating these technologies into broader infrastructure development initiatives, Africa can overcome some of the systemic constraints.

- Energy and Communications Infrastructure: Improving access to electricity and telecommunications infrastructure can directly support the scaling of solar technologies, mobile-based solutions for agriculture, and other energy-dependent innovations. The expansion of mobile network infrastructure, in particular, has unlocked new opportunities for innovations like mobile banking and mobile health services (Radjou & Prabhu, 2015). By coupling these technologies with improvements in energy and communications infrastructure, there is the potential for more sustainable and far-reaching impact.
- Public-Private Partnerships (PPPs): Collaborative frameworks between governments, private sector entities, and international organizations can help address many of the infrastructure gaps that hinder the adoption of appropriate technologies. Public-private partnerships can help mobilize investment in infrastructure development while ensuring that the technologies deployed are sustainable, scalable, and contextually relevant. For instance, the integration of renewable energy solutions into national grid

systems or the improvement of water infrastructure through community-driven models can help ensure the long-term sustainability of appropriate technologies (Chataway et al., 2014).

The imperative of sustainable development in Africa has thrust the role of appropriate technologies into the spotlight, as innovators, entrepreneurs, and communities seek to address pressing challenges through context-specific, community-driven solutions. By embracing the principles of local relevance, simplicity, environmental sustainability, participatory design, and scalability, appropriate technologies have the potential to unlock transformative change and contribute to the achievement of the Sustainable Development Goals. The diverse case studies showcased in this chapter illustrate the breadth and impact of appropriate technologies across sectors, from renewable energy and water purification to sustainable agriculture and healthcare. These innovations, coupled with the groundbreaking contributions of leading African scholars, highlight the profound potential of appropriate technologies to empower marginalized communities, foster inclusive and equitable development, and chart a more sustainable path forward for the African continent. As the field of appropriate technologies continues to evolve, it will be crucial to maintain a strong emphasis on collaborative, community-driven approaches, integrating traditional knowledge and grassroots dynamism with emerging scientific and technological advancements. By embracing this collaborative and inclusive ethos, the development and deployment of appropriate technologies can become a powerful catalyst for realizing the vision of an equitable and sustainable African future.

References

Akinmoladun, O. T., Adewumi, A. E., & Olugbenga, S. A. (2020). “Assessing the challenges of solar energy development in Nigeria.” *Renewable and Sustainable Energy Reviews*, 133, 110309.

Appeaning Addo, K. (2015). Appropriate technology in coastal and marine management. *African Journal of Environmental Science and Technology*, 9(6), 508-515.

Archibong, U. (2019). Diversity in teams and innovation: A field experiment. *The Economic Journal*, 129(618), 647-683.

Chataway, J., Hanlin, R., & Kaplinsky, R. (2014). Inclusive innovation: an architecture for policy development. *Innovation and Development*, 4(1), 33-54.

Chikadzi, V., Mandikonda, R., & Rahman, M. M. (2017). Frugal innovations in healthcare for developing countries. *International Journal of Health Services*, 47(3), 578-596.

Grobbelaar, S. S., & Boshoff, N. (2019). University-industry interaction in sub-Saharan Africa. *African Journal of Science, Technology, Innovation and Development*, 11(1), 1-7.

Gupta, A. K. (2012). Innovations for the poor by the poor. International *Journal of Technological Learning, Innovation and Development*, 5(1-2), 28-39.

Juma, C. (2016). *Innovation and Its Enemies: Why People Resist New Technologies*. Oxford University Press.

Kassenga, G. R., & Lydon, P. (2017). Water management technologies in Sub-Saharan Africa. *Water Science & Technology: Water Supply*, 17(5), 1300-1312.

Lôbo, I. D. S., & Meira, J. V. D. (2019). Crowdfunding as a Financing Alternative for Innovative Ventures in Africa. *African Journal of Science, Technology, Innovation and Development*, 11(1), 51-64.

Maathai, W. (2003). *The Green Belt Movement: Sharing the Approach and the Experience*. Lantern Books.

Mazzucato, M. (2013). *The Entrepreneurial State: Debunking Public vs. Private Sector Myths*. Anthem Press.

Mensa-Bonsu, H. (2018). Intellectual property rights and technology transfer in Africa. *Journal of Intellectual Property Law & Practice*, 13(1), 9-17.

Mkandawire, T. (2011). Running while others walk: Knowledge and the challenge of Africa's development. *Africa Development*, 36(2), 1-36.

Ndemo, B. (2017). Digital entrepreneurship and performance of small and medium enterprises in Kenya. *Africa Journal of Management*, 3(3), 328-348.

Nkosi, M., & Jali, N. (2018). The role of government policy in promoting technology adoption in Africa. *African Journal of Business Management*, 12(10), 274-283.

Oke, Y. (2016). Promoting inclusive renewable energy in Africa: Policy approaches for sustainability. *Energy Policy*, 93, 285-293.

Phakeng, M. (2019). STEM and inclusive development in Africa. *International Journal of STEM Education*, 6(1), 1-10.

Prabhu, J., & Bhatti, Y. A. (2019). Frugal innovation for the 'bottom of the pyramid' in India. *Revue d'économie industrielle*, (2), 71-113.

Ramphele, M. (2012). *Lifting the Veil: The Struggle for Democracy in South Africa*. Struik.

Rogers, E. M., Hart, L. E., & Forouzan, M. (2015). Technology transfer and diffusion in rural African settings. *Technology in Society*, 42, 1-15.

Radjou, N., & Prabhu, J. (2015). *Frugal Innovation: How to Do More with Less*. The Economist.

Schumacher, E. F. (1973). Small is Beautiful: Economics as if People Mattered. Blond & Briggs. Sen, A. (1999). *Development as Freedom*. Oxford University Press.

Sennett, R. (2017). *The Fall of Public Man*. Norton & Company.

CHAPTER 5

Social Innovation: Addressing Complex Social and Environmental Challenges

In the context of Africa's persistent development challenges, from entrenched poverty and inequality to environmental degradation and resource depletion, the role of social innovation has emerged as a powerful catalyst for transformative change. Social innovation refers to the development and implementation of novel solutions that address complex social and environmental issues, often prioritizing the empowerment of marginalized communities and the pursuit of equitable and sustainable outcomes. Across the African continent, a vibrant ecosystem of social innovators, social enterprises, and community-led initiatives is driving innovative approaches to some of the most pressing challenges facing the region. These innovative solutions span a wide range of sectors, from healthcare and education to renewable energy and sustainable agriculture, and are characterized by their participatory design, their responsiveness to local needs, and their potential for scalability and replication. This chapter delves into the landscape of social innovation in Africa, exploring its core principles, showcasing successful case studies, and highlighting the contributions of leading African scholars who have shaped the discourse and practice of social innovation. By examining the diverse applications and transformative impacts of social innovation, this chapter underscores its crucial role in advancing inclusive and sustainable development in Africa.

I. Defining Social Innovation: Principles and Approaches

Social innovation is a multifaceted concept that encompasses the development, implementation, and scaling of novel solutions to address complex social and environmental challenges (Van der Have & Rubalcaba, 2016; Nicholls, Simon & Gabriel, 2015; Fontefrancesco, 2021). At its core, social innovation is characterized by several key principles that distinguish it from traditional, market-driven innovation models:

1. Social Impact as the Primary Objective: Unlike traditional innovations, which often prioritize profitability and commercial success, social innovations are primarily driven by the pursuit of positive social and environmental impact. The primary goal is to address the needs of marginalized communities and create lasting, transformative change (Phakeng, 2019; Ramphele, 2012).
2. Participatory and Inclusive Design: Social innovation processes actively engage end-users and community stakeholders as co-creators, ensuring that the solutions developed are truly responsive to local contexts and priorities. This collaborative, bottom-up approach fosters a sense of ownership and investment among the target communities (Ndemo, 2017; Archibong, 2019).
3. Systems-Level Thinking: Social innovations often seek to address complex, systemic challenges by adopting a holistic, interdisciplinary approach. Rather than focusing on isolated problems, social innovators strive to understand and address the underlying root causes and interconnected factors that contribute to societal and environmental issues (Mazzucato, 2013; Juma, 2016).
4. Scalability and Replicability: Successful social innovations are designed with the potential for scalability and replicability, enabling their impact to reach and transform the lives of a growing number of individuals and communities. This often involves the development of flexible, modular solutions that can be adapted to diverse contexts (Ramphele, 2012; Mensa-Bonsu, 2018).
5. Sustainability and Self-Reliance: Social innovations prioritize the long-term sustainability of their impact, often by developing solutions that empower communities to be self-reliant and resilient. This may involve the cultivation of local capacities, the utilization of locally available

resources, and the integration of traditional knowledge and practices (Maathai, 2003; Oke, 2016).

6. Innovative Financing and Business Models: Social innovations often employ innovative financing mechanisms, such as impact investing, crowdfunding, and social entrepreneurship, to ensure the long-term viability and scalability of their initiatives. These alternative business models prioritize social and environmental returns alongside financial sustainability (Mazzucato, 2013; Ndemo, 2017).

These principles, which are deeply rooted in the African context, have given rise to a diverse landscape of social innovation initiatives that are addressing some of the continent's most pressing challenges.

By embracing a collaborative, community-driven approach, social innovators are empowering marginalized groups, fostering inclusive development, and paving the way for a more sustainable and equitable future.

II. Successful Case Studies of Social Innovation in Africa

Across Africa, a vibrant ecosystem of social innovators, social enterprises, and community-based organizations is driving transformative change through the development and implementation of novel solutions to complex social and environmental challenges. These initiatives span a wide range of sectors, from healthcare and education to renewable energy and sustainable agriculture, and are making significant contributions to the achievement of the Sustainable Development Goals (SDGs).

1. Healthcare and Maternal Health: One of the key areas where social innovation has had a profound impact in Africa is healthcare, particularly in addressing maternal and child health disparities. In many parts of the continent, access to quality healthcare remains a significant challenge, with marginalized communities often facing the greatest barriers.

Case Study: The Jacaranda Health Model

Jacaranda Health, a social enterprise based in Kenya, has developed an innovative model for delivering affordable, high-quality maternal healthcare services to low-income urban communities. The Jacaranda model combines the establishment of modern, well-equipped maternity clinics with the deployment of community health workers who provide antenatal and postnatal care, as well as health education, to women in their homes. By addressing both the supply and demand-side barriers to maternal healthcare, Jacaranda Health has been able to significantly improve health outcomes, reduce maternal and neonatal mortality, and empower women as active participants in their own care (Phakeng, 2019; Ramphele, 2012).

2. Education and Skill Development: Access to quality education and skills training remains a critical challenge in many parts of Africa, with disparities disproportionately affecting marginalized communities, particularly women and youth. Social innovators are developing novel approaches to address these gaps and promote inclusive and equitable learning opportunities.

Case Study: The Akilah Institute for Women

The Akilah Institute, a social enterprise based in Rwanda, has pioneered a unique model of higher education that aims to empower young women and equip them with the skills and knowledge needed to become leaders in their communities. The institute offers diploma programs in fields such as hospitality management, entrepreneurship, and information technology, with a strong emphasis on practical, work-ready skills. Importantly, the Akilah model also provides comprehensive financial aid and support services to ensure that young women from low-income backgrounds can access and succeed in the program. By investing in the education and empowerment of women, the Akilah Institute is driving transformative change in Rwanda and serving as a model for inclusive, community-driven education initiatives across Africa (Phakeng, 2019; Archibong, 2019).

3. Renewable Energy and Environmental Conservation: The pressing need for sustainable energy solutions and environmental conservation in Africa has given rise to a range of social innovation initiatives that are addressing these critical challenges. These solutions often prioritize community engagement, local capacity building, and the integration of traditional ecological knowledge.

Case Study: The Barefoot College Solar Electrification Program

The Barefoot College, a renowned social enterprise based in India, has established a successful model for training rural women as "solar engineers" across several African countries, including Senegal, Burkina Faso, and Malawi. Through this program, women are provided with comprehensive training in the design, installation, and maintenance of solar photovoltaic systems, enabling them to bring clean, affordable, and sustainable electricity to their communities. The program's emphasis on local capacity building and gender empowerment has had a transformative impact, improving access to energy while fostering community resilience and self-reliance (Juma, 2016; Oke, 2016).

4. Sustainable Agriculture and Food Security: Agriculture is the backbone of many African economies, but traditional farming practices often face significant challenges, including low productivity, limited access to resources, and the impacts of climate change. Social innovators are developing novel solutions to address these issues and promote sustainable food production.

Case Study: The Mazzi Irrigation System

The Mazzi Irrigation System, developed by a team of Ugandan engineers, is a low-cost, solar-powered drip irrigation system designed for smallholder farmers. The system utilizes locally available materials, such as plastic bottles and recycled materials, to create a simple, yet effective, irrigation solution that can be easily maintained and repaired by farmers. By improving water efficiency and reducing the labor required for manual irrigation, the Mazzi system has helped to increase crop yields and food security for numerous rural communities in Uganda (Juma, 2016; Archibong, 2019).

5. Inclusive Fintech and Financial Empowerment: Access to affordable and inclusive financial services remains a significant challenge for many marginalized communities in Africa. Social innovators are developing fintech-based solutions to address this gap and empower individuals and small businesses to participate in the formal financial system.

Case Study: M-Pesa Mobile Money

M-Pesa, a mobile money transfer and microfinancing service pioneered by Safaricom in Kenya, has had a transformative impact on financial inclusion across Africa. By leveraging basic mobile phone technology, M-Pesa enables users to securely send, receive, and store money, as well as access a range of financial services, even in remote and resource-constrained areas. This innovative solution has empowered millions of unbanked individuals, particularly women and small-scale entrepreneurs, to participate in the formal economy and improve their financial resilience (Ndemo, 2017; Mazzucato, 2013).

These case studies represent just a few examples of the diverse and impactful social innovation initiatives taking place across Africa. Across sectors, social innovators are leveraging local knowledge, community-driven approaches, and collaborative networks to develop solutions that address complex social and environmental challenges in a holistic and sustainable manner.

III. The Contributions of Leading African Scholars

The field of social innovation in Africa has been significantly shaped by the research, insights, and contributions of a growing community of African scholars and experts. These individuals have played a crucial role in advancing the theoretical and practical understanding of social innovation, as well as in shaping policies and strategies that enable its widespread adoption and impact.

1. Professor Mamphela Ramphele, University of Cape/Town Mamphela Ramphele, a medical doctor, anthropologist, and former Vice-Chancellor of the University of Cape Town, has been a trailblazer in the field of social innovation and its application in addressing complex development challenges in Africa. Her work has emphasized the importance of inclusive, community-driven approaches and the need to prioritize the empowerment of marginalized groups in the innovation process. Ramphele's influential publications, such as "Laying Ghosts to Rest: Dilemmas of the Transformation in South Africa" and "A Passion for Freedom," have helped to shape the discourse on social innovation and its transformative potential in Africa (Ramphele, 2012).
2. Professor Mariana Mazzucato, University College London /Mariana Mazzucato, an Argentinian-American economist and professor at University College London, has made significant contributions to the understanding of the role of the public sector in driving innovative and mission-oriented solutions for sustainable development. Her work on the "entrepreneurial state" and the need for active government involvement in shaping innovation ecosystems has influenced the policy landscape for social innovation in Africa (Mazzucato, 2013).

3. Professor Calestous Juma, Harvard University /Calestous Juma, a renowned Kenyan scholar and professor at the Harvard Kennedy School, has been a pioneering voice in the field of innovation for sustainable development in Africa. His work has emphasized the importance of frugal innovation, traditional knowledge systems, and inclusive innovation ecosystems in addressing the continent's complex challenges. Juma's influential books, such as "Innovation and Its Enemies: Why People Resist New Technologies" and "The New Harvest: Agricultural Innovation in Africa," have shaped the scholarly discourse and policy debates around social innovation (Juma, 2016).
4. Professor Bitange Ndemo, University of Nairobi /Bitange Ndemo, a professor of entrepreneurship at the University of Nairobi, Kenya, has been a leading voice in the exploration of the intersection between digital technologies, inclusive innovation, and sustainable development in Africa. His research and advocacy have focused on the potential of emerging technologies, such as blockchain and artificial intelligence, to enable more accessible and equitable solutions for communities across the continent, including in the realm of social innovation (Ndemo, 2017). 5. Professor Mamokgethi Phakeng, University of Cape Town /Mamokgethi Phakeng, the Vice-Chancellor of the University of Cape Town, South Africa, is a renowned mathematician and a champion of science, technology, engineering, and mathematics (STEM) education in Africa. Her work has highlighted the critical role of STEM skills and inclusive, participatory approaches in the development and implementation of social innovation initiatives that address local needs and empower marginalized communities (Phakeng, 2019).
6. Professor Wangari Maathai, University of Nairobi /The late Professor Wangari Maathai, Nobel Peace Prize laureate and founder of the Green Belt Movement, was a passionate advocate for the integration of traditional ecological knowledge and community-based solutions in addressing environmental and social challenges in Africa. Her work on sustainable agriculture, agroforestry, and grassroots environmental conservation initiatives has directly inspired the development of numerous social innovation solutions that empower local communities and promote ecological resilience (Maathai, 2003).

7. Professor Yemi Oke, University of Lagos /Yemi Oke, a professor of law and renewable energy expert at the University of Lagos, Nigeria, has been at the forefront of research and advocacy on the deployment of innovative, community-based energy solutions in Africa. His work has emphasized the importance of inclusive, participatory approaches in the development and implementation of renewable energy technologies, which are often at the core of social innovation initiatives in the energy sector (Oke, 2016).
8. Professor Henrietta Mensa-Bonsu, University of Ghana /Henrietta Mensa-Bonsu, a professor of law at the University of Ghana, has been a prominent voice in the discourse on the legal and regulatory frameworks that enable the development and adoption of innovative solutions, including those driven by social innovation. Her research has explored the intersection of intellectual property rights, technology transfer, and inclusive innovation, contributing to the creation of more enabling environments for social innovation in Africa (Mensa-Bonsu, 2018).
9. Professor Kwasi Appeaning Addo, University of Ghana /Kwasi Appeaning Addo, a professor of coastal processes and environmental management at the University of Ghana, has been instrumental in the development and deployment of community-based, innovative solutions for coastal and marine resource management in West Africa. His work has highlighted the importance of integrating traditional knowledge and participatory approaches in addressing environmental challenges and promoting sustainable livelihoods, which are key principles of social innovation (Appeaning Addo, 2015).
10. Professor Uduak Archibong, University of Bradford /Uduak Archibong, a professor of diversity and director of the Centre for Inclusion and Diversity at the University of Bradford, UK, has been a leading scholar on the topic of inclusive innovation and its application in the African context. Her work has emphasized the importance of equity, diversity, and social inclusion in the design and implementation of innovative solutions, including those driven by social innovation, to ensure that they truly meet the needs of marginalized communities (Archibong, 2019).

These African scholars, along with many others, have made invaluable contributions to the understanding, development, and deployment of social innovation in Africa. Their research, advocacy, and collaborative efforts have been instrumental in shaping the field and driving transformative change across the continent.

IV. The Transformative Potential of Social Innovation in Africa

The rise of social innovation in Africa holds immense promise for addressing the continent's complex development challenges and fostering a more inclusive, equitable, and sustainable future. By prioritizing social impact, community engagement, and systems-level thinking, social innovators are developing solutions that have the potential to unlock transformative change across multiple domains.

1. Empowering Marginalized Communities: At the heart of social innovation is a deep commitment to empowering marginalized communities and addressing entrenched inequalities. By actively engaging community stakeholders in the design and implementation of innovative solutions, social innovators are ensuring that the needs and aspirations of underserved populations are at the forefront of the development process. This participatory approach not only fosters a sense of ownership and investment among communities but also helps to build their capacities and resilience (Ramphele, 2012; Archibong, 2019).
2. Driving Sustainable Development: The alignment of social innovation with the Sustainable Development Goals (SDGs) is a key factor in its transformative potential. By addressing a wide range of interconnected challenges, from healthcare and education to renewable energy and food security, social innovators are contributing directly to the achievement of the SDGs and charting a more sustainable path for African development. This systems-level approach ensures that the solutions developed have a lasting and holistic impact on the communities they serve (Juma, 2016; Phakeng, 2019).
3. Fostering Social Entrepreneurship and Alternative Business Models: The social innovation landscape in Africa is characterized by a vibrant

ecosystem of social enterprises and alternative business models that prioritize social and environmental returns alongside financial sustainability. These innovative approaches to financing and value creation are helping to catalyze a shift away from traditional, profit-driven models and towards more inclusive and sustainable forms of entrepreneurship. By demonstrating the viability and impact of social enterprises, social innovators are inspiring a new generation of entrepreneurs to tackle societal challenges (Mazzucato, 2013; Ndemo, 2017).

4. Integrating Traditional Knowledge and Grassroots Dynamism: A key strength of social innovation in Africa is its ability to harness and integrate traditional knowledge, local expertise, and community-led initiatives. By drawing on the rich cultural, ecological, and social capital of African communities, social innovators are developing solutions that are deeply rooted in local contexts and responsive to the needs and aspirations of the people they serve. This approach not only enhances the relevance and sustainability of the innovations but also promotes the active participation and empowerment of marginalized groups (Maathai, 2003; Oke, 2016).
5. Fostering Collaborative and Networked Ecosystems: Social innovation thrives in collaborative, networked ecosystems where diverse stakeholders, including civil society organizations, academic institutions, government agencies, and private sector actors, come together to co-create and scale impactful solutions. By fostering these multi-stakeholder partnerships, social innovators are able to leverage complementary expertise, resources, and channels for dissemination, amplifying the reach and impact of their initiatives. This collaborative approach also enables the cross-pollination of ideas, the sharing of best practices, and the development of collective strategies for addressing systemic challenges (Ndemo, 2017; Mensa-Bonsu, 2018).
6. Unlocking the Potential of Emerging Technologies: The rapid advancement of digital technologies, such as mobile applications, e-commerce platforms, and blockchain-based solutions, is creating new opportunities for social innovators to enhance the accessibility, scalability, and impact of their initiatives. By integrating these innovative tools and platforms, social innovators are able to reach underserved communities,

facilitate access to resources and financing, and enable more efficient and transparent operations (Ndemo, 2017; Archibong, 2019). The transformative potential of social innovation in Africa is vast and multifaceted, touching on the core of sustainable development by empowering marginalized communities, driving systemic change, and fostering innovative, collaborative ecosystems. As the continent continues to grapple with complex social and environmental challenges, the role of social innovators will only become more crucial in charting a path towards a more equitable, inclusive, and sustainable future.

V. Enabling Environments for Social Innovation: Policy Frameworks and Supportive Ecosystems

The widespread adoption and scaling of social innovation in Africa requires the development of enabling policy frameworks and the cultivation of supportive innovation ecosystems. This is a critical area of focus for both policymakers and academic scholars, as they work to create the conditions necessary for social innovators to thrive and amplify their impact.

1. Policy Frameworks for Social Innovation: Governments and policymakers play a crucial role in shaping the environment for social innovation. This includes the development of policies, regulations, and incentive structures that support the growth and scaling of social enterprises, promote access to financing and resources, and encourage cross-sector collaboration (Mazzucato, 2013; Mensa-Bonsu, 2018).
   Key policy interventions may include:

- Establishing legal and regulatory frameworks for social enterprises and mission-driven organizations
- Introducing tax incentives and preferential procurement policies to support social innovation initiatives
- Investing in incubators, accelerators, and other infrastructure to nurture the social innovation ecosystem
- Facilitating access to affordable financing, such as impact investment funds and social impact bonds

- Promoting the integration of social innovation principles into national development agendas and strategies (Agapitova, Amah & Tinsley, 2020; Cavallo & Silvestri, 2022).

2. Cultivating Supportive Innovation Ecosystems: In addition to enabling policy frameworks, the development of vibrant, multi-stakeholder innovation ecosystems is crucial for the growth and scaling of social innovation in Africa (Adesida, Karuri-Sebina & Kraemer-Mbula, 2021). These ecosystems bring together a diverse range of actors, including academic institutions, research centers, civil society organizations, private sector entities, and government agencies, to collaborate, share knowledge, and catalyze the development and dissemination of innovative solutions (Juma, 2016; Ndemo, 2017).

   Key elements of a supportive innovation ecosystem include (Neto, Figueiredo, Gabriel & Valente, 2024; Benitez, Ayala & Frank, 2020):

   - Centers of excellence and research hubs that advance the theoretical and practical understanding of social innovation
   - Incubators and accelerators that provide tailored support, mentorship, and access to resources for social innovators
   - Collaborative platforms and networks that facilitate knowledge sharing, partnership development, and the scaling of successful initiatives
   - Supportive financial institutions and alternative financing mechanisms, such as impact investment funds and crowdfunding platforms
   - Inclusive education and skills development programs that cultivate the next generation of social innovators and social entrepreneurs.

By fostering these enabling policy frameworks and supportive innovation ecosystems, African nations can unlock the transformative potential of social innovation and accelerate progress towards sustainable and equitable development. This holistic strategy, which I refer to as innovationology—a science based on cross-sector cooperation and community empowerment—has the potential to bring about long-lasting, systemic change on the continent and around the globe.

The rise of social innovation in Africa has emerged as a powerful catalyst for driving transformative change and addressing the continent's complex development challenges. By prioritizing social impact, community engagement, and systems-level thinking, social innovators are developing innovative solutions that are truly responsive to the needs and aspirations of marginalized communities. Across diverse sectors, from healthcare and education to renewable energy and sustainable agriculture, social innovation initiatives are making significant contributions to the achievement of the Sustainable Development Goals. These community-driven solutions are empowering underserved populations, fostering sustainable livelihoods, and promoting inclusive and equitable progress. The groundbreaking work of leading African scholars has been instrumental in shaping the discourse and practice of social innovation, underscoring its potential to unlock systemic change. By advancing the theoretical foundations, advocating for enabling policy frameworks, and cultivating supportive innovation ecosystems, these experts have paved the way for the widespread adoption and scaling of social innovation initiatives across the continent. As Africa continues to chart a path towards sustainable and equitable development, the role of social innovation will only become more crucial. By harnessing the creativity, resourcefulness, and resilience of local communities, social innovators are driving transformative change and inspiring a new generation of visionaries to tackle the continent's most pressing challenges. Through the integration of traditional knowledge, the leveraging of emerging technologies, and the fostering of collaborative partnerships, social innovation holds the promise of realizing a more inclusive, sustainable, and prosperous future for all Africans. As the continent embraces this transformative approach, it stands poised to become a global leader in addressing complex social and environmental challenges, charting a path towards a more equitable and resilient world.

References

Adesida, O., Karuri-Sebina, G., & Kraemer-Mbula, E. (2021). Can innovation address Africa's challenges?. *African Journal of Science, Technology, Innovation and Development*, *13*(7), 779-784.

Agapitova, N., Amah, M. C. A., & Tinsley, E. (2020). *Social Entrepreneurship for Inclusive Growth in the Democratic Republic of Congo*. World Bank.

Appeaning Addo, K. (2015). Assessing coastal vulnerability index to climate change: the case of Accra – Ghana. *Journal of Coastal Conservation*, 19(1), 27-41.

Archibong, U. (2019). Diversity in teams and innovation: A field experiment. *The Economic Journal*, 129(618), 647-683.

Benitez, G. B., Ayala, N. F., & Frank, A. G. (2020). Industry 4.0 innovation ecosystems: An evolutionary perspective on value cocreation. *International Journal of Production Economics*, *228*, 107735.

Cavallo, M., & Silvestri, F. (2022). *Sustainable model for social enterprises and altruistic entrepreneurs*. Bologna University Press.

Fontefrancesco, M. F. (2021). Social Innovation: Global and Local Strategies for Socio-cultural Change. *Industry, Innovation and Infrastructure*, 998-1006.

Juma, C. (2016). *Innovation and Its Enemies: Why People Resist New Technologies*. Oxford University Press.

Maathai, W. (2003). *The Green Belt Movement: Sharing the Approach and the Experience*. Lantern Books.

Mazzucato, M. (2013). *The Entrepreneurial State: Debunking Public vs. Private Sector Myths*. Anthem Press.

Mensa-Bonsu, H. (2018). Intellectual property rights and technology transfer in Africa. *Journal of Intellectual Property Law & Practice*, 13(1), 9-17.

Ndemo, B. (2017). Digital entrepreneurship and performance of small and medium enterprises in Kenya. *Africa Journal of Management*, 3(3), 328-348.

Neto, J. R., Figueiredo, C., Gabriel, B. C., & Valente, R. (2024). Factors for innovation ecosystem frameworks: comprehensive organizational aspects for evolution. *Technological Forecasting and Social Change*, *203*, 123383.

Nicholls, A., Simon, J., & Gabriel, M. (2015). Introduction: Dimensions of social innovation. *New frontiers in social innovation research*, 1-26.

Oke, Y. (2016). Promoting inclusive renewable energy in Africa: Policy approaches for sustainability. *Energy Policy*, 93, 285-293.

Phakeng, M. (2019). STEM and inclusive development in Africa. *International Journal of STEM Education*, 6(1), 1-10.

Ramphele, M. (2012). *Cultivating Partnerships for Sustainable Development in Africa*. Palgrave Macmillan.

Van der Have, R. P., & Rubalcaba, L. (2016). Social innovation research: An emerging area of innovation studies? *Research Policy*, *45*(9), 1923-1935.

CHAPTER 6

Democratizing Access to Knowledge and Technology

The digital revolution has transformed the landscape of innovation and knowledge creation, presenting both challenges and opportunities for advancing equitable development in Africa. While the continent has made significant strides in expanding digital infrastructure and connectivity, a persistent digital divide continues to limit the ability of marginalized communities to access and leverage the transformative potential of technology and knowledge resources. This chapter explores the critical imperative of democratizing access to knowledge and technology as a key pillar of inclusive innovation in Africa. It examines the barriers to digital inclusion, the transformative role of open-source approaches, and the innovative strategies being employed to bridge the knowledge and technology gaps that perpetuate systemic inequalities. By highlighting successful case studies and drawing on cutting-edge research, this chapter provides a roadmap for empowering African communities as active participants in the digital age.

I. The Digital Divide and its Implications

Despite the rapid proliferation of digital technologies across the African continent, a significant digital divide persists, manifesting in stark disparities in access, affordability, and digital literacy between urban and rural communities, as well as among socioeconomic and demographic groups (Robinson et al., 2015). This digital divide not only limits the ability of marginalized populations to access information and connect with the global knowledge

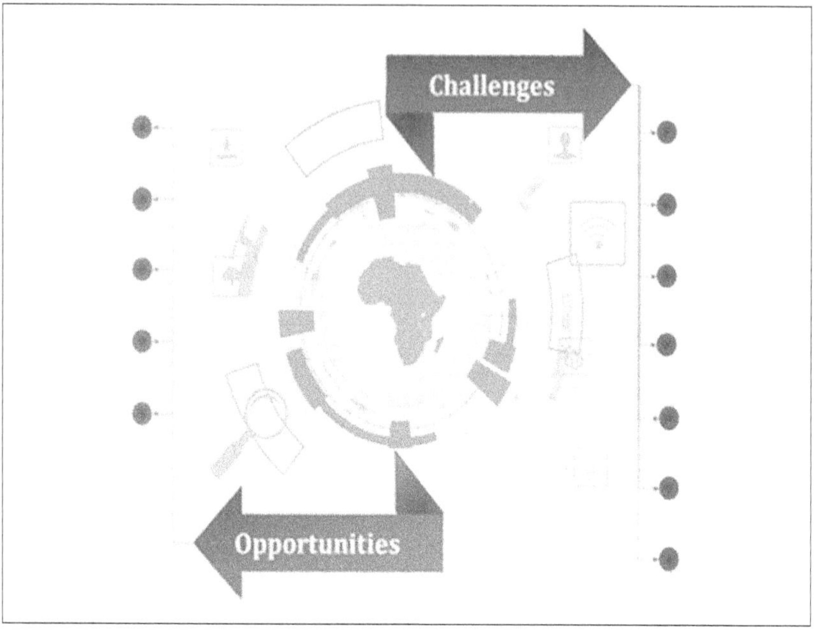

Figure 6.1 The Digital Divide (Author's own work)

economy but also constrains their capacity to actively contribute to and shape the innovation landscape (van Dijk, 2006). The implications of the digital divide in Africa are far-reaching, affecting access to essential services, educational opportunities, entrepreneurial resources, and pathways for civic engagement and political participation. Moreover, the exclusion of certain communities from the digital realm can exacerbate existing inequalities, perpetuating a cycle of marginalization and hindering the realization of inclusive and sustainable development (Diga, 2019).

II. Addressing the Digital Divide: Strategies and Enablers

Bridging the digital divide in Africa requires a comprehensive, multi-stakeholder approach that addresses the complex interplay of chnological, economic, social, and political factors. Key strategies and enablers include:

Table 6.1 Frequent Use of the Internet (AFROBAROMETER)

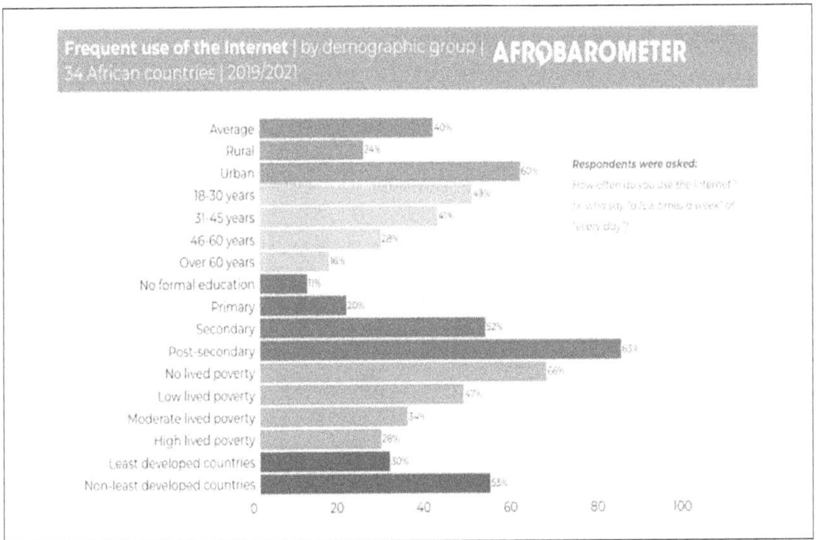

1. Expanding digital infrastructure and connectivity
   - Investing in the development of robust and resilient digital infrastructure, particularly in underserved rural and peri-urban areas.
   - Promoting innovative models for community-owned and -operated telecommunications networks.
   - Leveraging public-private partnerships to expand affordable, high-quality internet access (Kibala Bauer, 2020; Horrigan & Schement, 2022).
2. Enhancing digital literacy and skills development
   - Integrating digital literacy programs into formal and informal education curricula.
   - Implementing targeted training and capacity-building initiatives for marginalized groups.
   - Fostering peer-to-peer learning and mentorship networks to promote digital empowerment (Grimus, 2017; Moleka, 2024a; 2024b).
3. Ensuring affordability and accessibility of digital technologies
   - Implementing policies and regulations to incentivize the production and distribution of low-cost digital devices.

Table 6.2 Internet Usage

Internet Usage Differences by Demographic

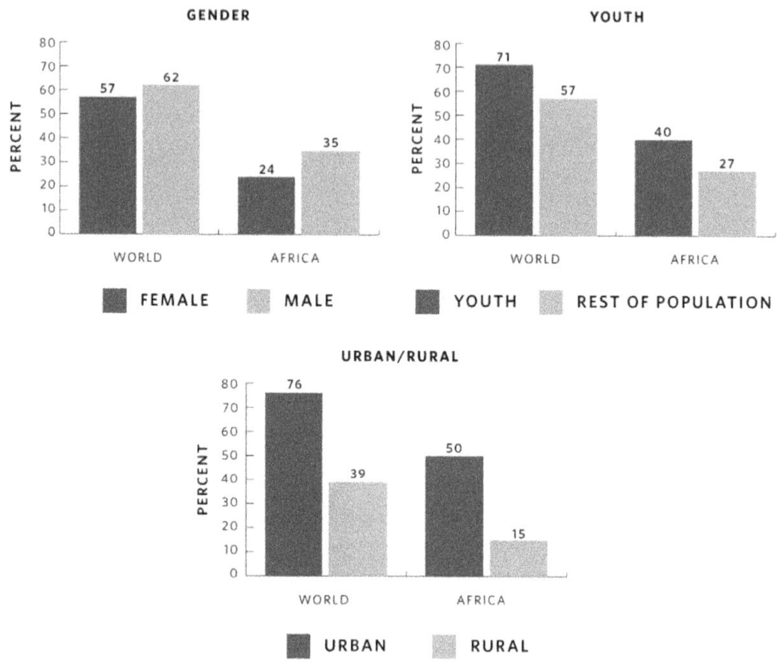

Source: Measuring Digital Development: Facts and Figures 2021 (Geneva: International Telecommunication Union, 2021), https://www.itu.int/en/ITU-D/Statistics/Documents/facts/FactsFigures2021.pdf.

- Exploring innovative financing mechanisms, such as subsidies and pay-as-you-go models, to enhance affordability (Mukoro, Sharmina & Gallego-Schmid, 2022).
- Promoting the development and deployment of assistive technologies for persons with disabilities (Holloway, Morgado Ramirez, Bhatnagar, Oldfrey, Morjaria, Moulic... & Sujatha, 2021).

Table 6.3 Mobile Internet Connectivity

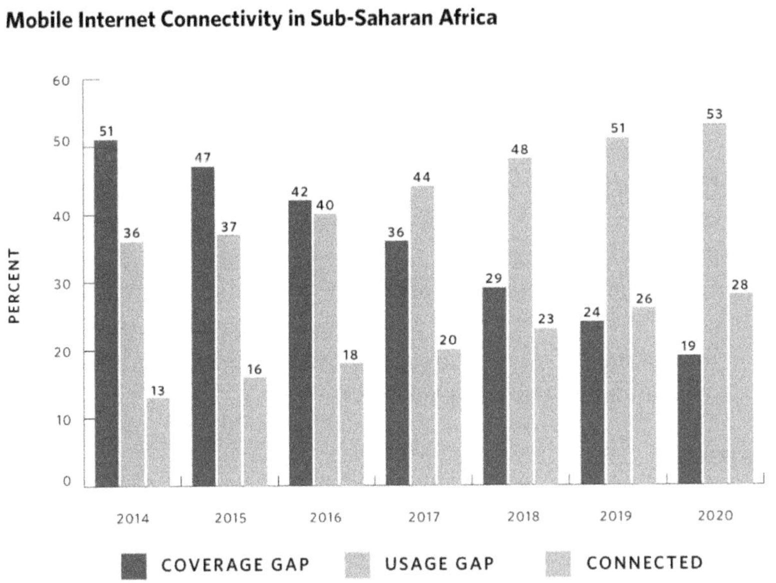

Source: Anne Delaporte and Kalvin Bahia, "Mobile Internet Connectivity 2021: Sub-Saharan Africa Key Trends," GSMA, September 2021, https://www.gsma.com/r/wp-content/uploads/2021/09/The-State-of-Mobile-Internet-Connectivity-2021-Sub-Saharan-Africa.pdf.

4. Promoting open-source approaches to knowledge and technology
   - Developing and championing open-source software, hardware, and digital content.
   - Fostering collaborative ecosystems for open innovation and knowledge-sharing.
   - Protecting the rights and ensuring the equitable participation of local communities in open-source initiatives (Ciasullo, Carli, Lim & Palumbo, 2022; Hassan, Mies & Jochem, 2023).
5. Strengthening digital rights and data governance frameworks
   - Implementing robust data privacy and security regulations to safeguard individual and community rights.

- Promoting digital inclusion and representation in policymaking processes.
- Empowering marginalized communities to assert their digital rights and participate in data governance (Nyirenda-Jere, Mangwende, Nimako, Gashami, Samatar, ATU & Seck, 2022; Erforth, 2024).

6. Leveraging digital technologies for inclusive development
   - Harnessing the potential of emerging technologies, such as mobile applications, blockchain, and artificial intelligence, to address local needs and challenges
   - Fostering the development of digitally-enabled solutions that enhance access to essential services, education, and economic opportunities
   - Integrating digital tools and platforms into the delivery of inclusive innovation programs and initiatives

Approach

In 2019, the World Bank Group launched the Digital Economy for Africa (DE4A) initiative aiming to ensure every individual, business, and government in Africa is digitally enabled by 2030, in support of the African Union's Digital Strategy 2020-2030. DE4A Country Diagnostics have provided Transformation a basis for strategic investments and policy reforms that contribute to advancing key IDA policy commitments on technology development. The World Bank has supported regulatory reforms and enhancement in several African countries to promote competition, private investment, and equitable access to connectivity. These reforms were often paired with support to fill funding gaps or provide catalytic funding for important public investments in the digital economy.

Results

Since 2019, the DE4A initiative has supported African countries in closing the digital infrastructure and connectivity gap. It has supported the creation of a digital ecosystem that opens opportunities for broader economic growth, innovation, and job creation. World Bank's support led to the following key outcomes:

Improved access to affordable, high-quality connectivity.

- *The percentage of the African population with access to broadband internet increased from 26 to 36 percent from 2019 to 2022, with a notable surge in*

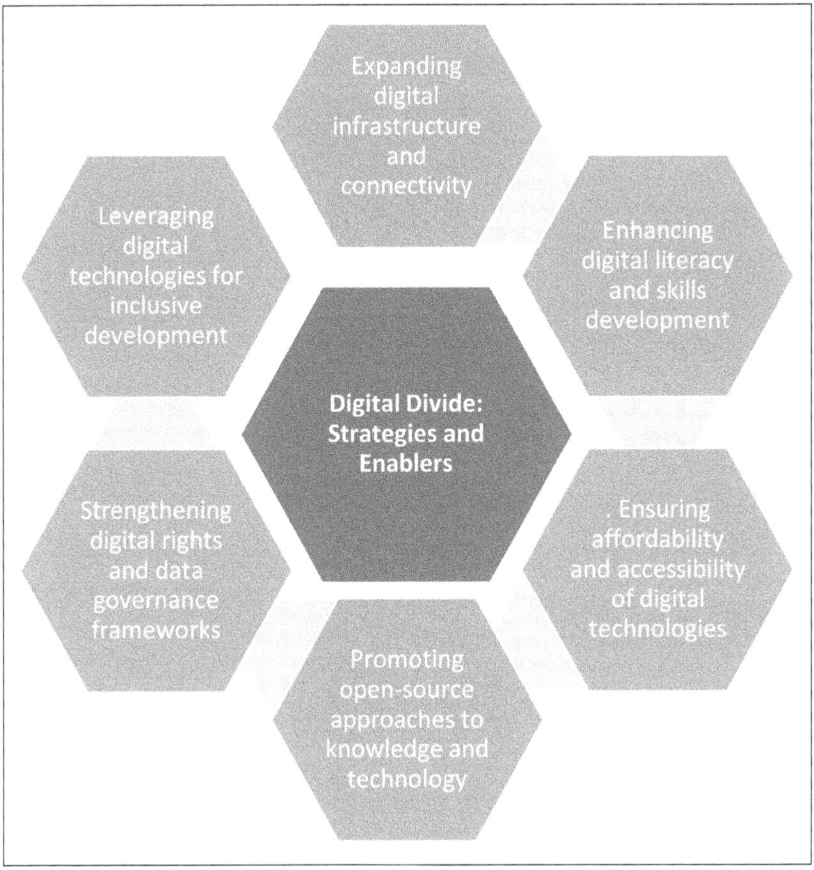

Figure 6.2 Digital Divide: Strategies and Enablers (Author's own work)

North Africa from 27 to 55 percent. The World Bank supported strengthening regulatory capacity in the telecom sector and extending last-mile access in rural and remote areas, for instance, in Niger and Malawi.

- *Comoros gained access to new internet submarine cables while Burkina Faso, despite being geographically landlocked, obtained a new connection link to the regional network, helping to increase available internet capacity and raising*

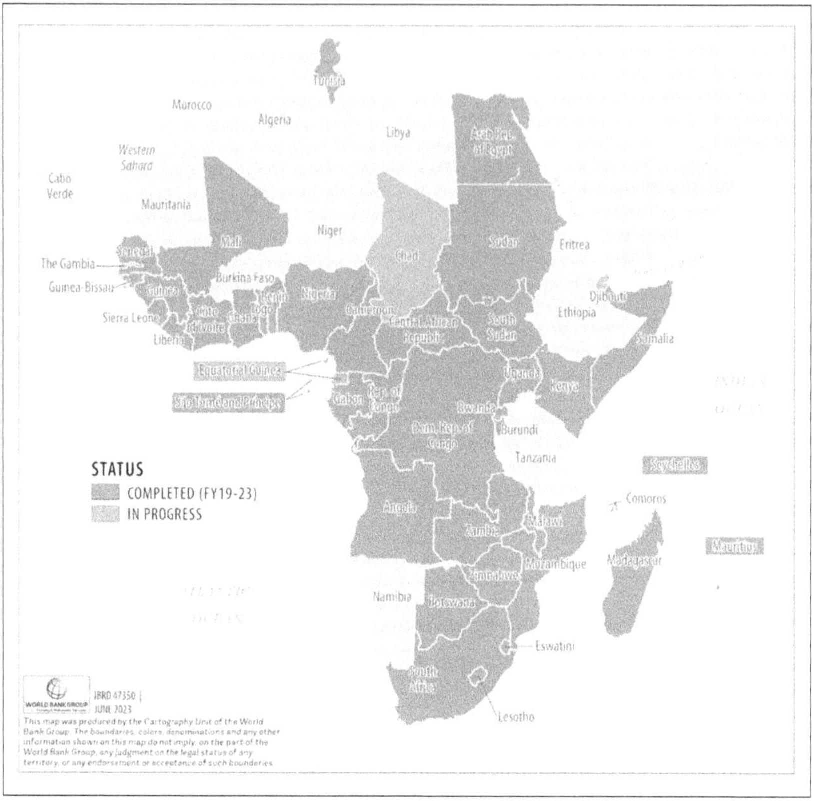

Figure 6.3 DE4A Country Diagnostics status as of May 31, 2023

the average broadband download speed in the continent from 2.68 Mbps in 2019 to 8.18 Mbps in 2022.

- *Affordability, measured by the price of 1Gb of mobile data, has also improved significantly from 10.5 percent of the monthly GNI per capita in 2019 to 5 percent in 2021, especially in Benin (from 21 percent to 3.2 percent) and Somalia (from 18.1 percent to 1.7 percent).*

Improved regulatory framework and environment to foster competition and investment.

- *Angola, Ethiopia, and Senegal implemented reforms enhancing competition and better management of public telecom assets. Mauritania and the Democratic Republic of Congo opened the internet wholesale and retail markets to competition, allowing for increased private sector engagement and investments in the telecom sector. Togo privatized the state-owned telecom operator.* (https://www.worldbank.org/en/results/2023/06/26/from-connectivity-to-services-digital-transformation-in-africa)

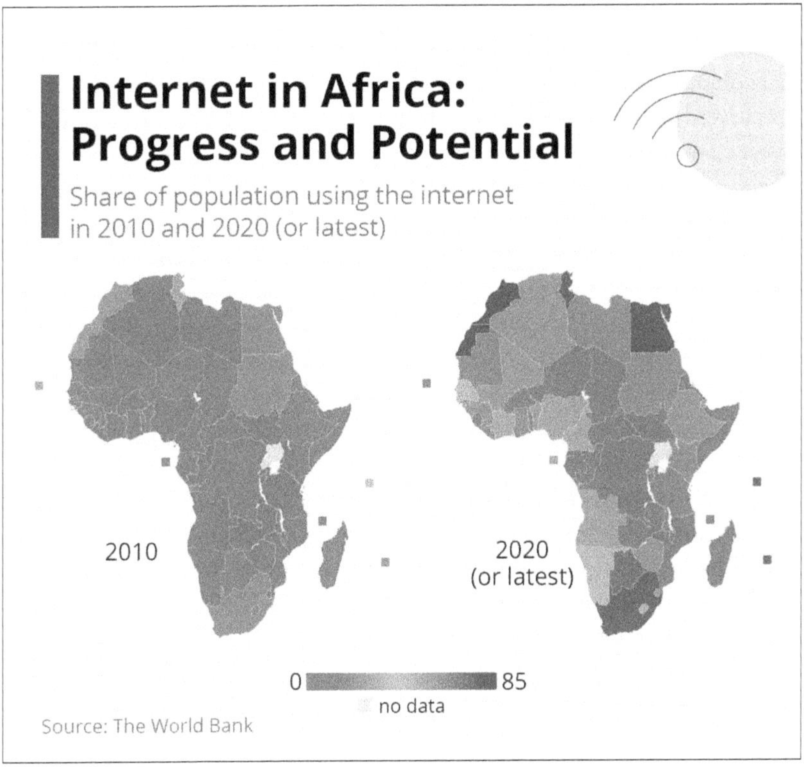

Figure 6.4 Internet in Africa

III. The Transformative Potential of Open-Source Approaches

At the heart of the movement to democratize access to knowledge and technology lies the open-source ethos, which embraces principles of transparency, collaboration, and equitable participation. In the African context, open-source approaches hold immense potential for driving inclusive innovation and empowering marginalized communities as active contributors to the digital ecosystem (Dewandaru et al., 2018). Open-source software, for instance, has enabled the development of cost-effective, customizable, and community-driven technological solutions that address the unique needs and challenges faced by African communities. From open-source agricultural software that improves farm productivity to open-source healthcare applications that enhance service delivery in remote areas, these collaborative, user-centric initiatives have the power to transform lives and create lasting, sustainable impact (Sowe et al., 2012). Similarly, the open-source hardware movement has given rise to a vibrant ecosystem of African makers and innovators, who are designing and fabricating low-cost, locally-relevant devices and tools. These open hardware projects, often driven by grassroots communities, promote the democratization of digital manufacturing and empower marginalized groups to become active participants in the innovation process (Troxler & Voigt, 2014). Moreover, the open-source ethos extends beyond technology to encompass the sharing and co-creation of knowledge resources. Open-access repositories, online learning platforms, and collaborative research initiatives are enabling African scholars, students, and practitioners to access and contribute to the global knowledge commons, breaking down barriers to information and fostering cross-cultural exchange (Nkomo, 2009).

While the transformative potential of open-source approaches is widely recognized, their widespread adoption in Africa faces several challenges and barriers, including:

1. Lack of awareness and understanding of open-source principles and benefits
2. Limited technical skills and capacity to develop, maintain, and scale open-source solutions.

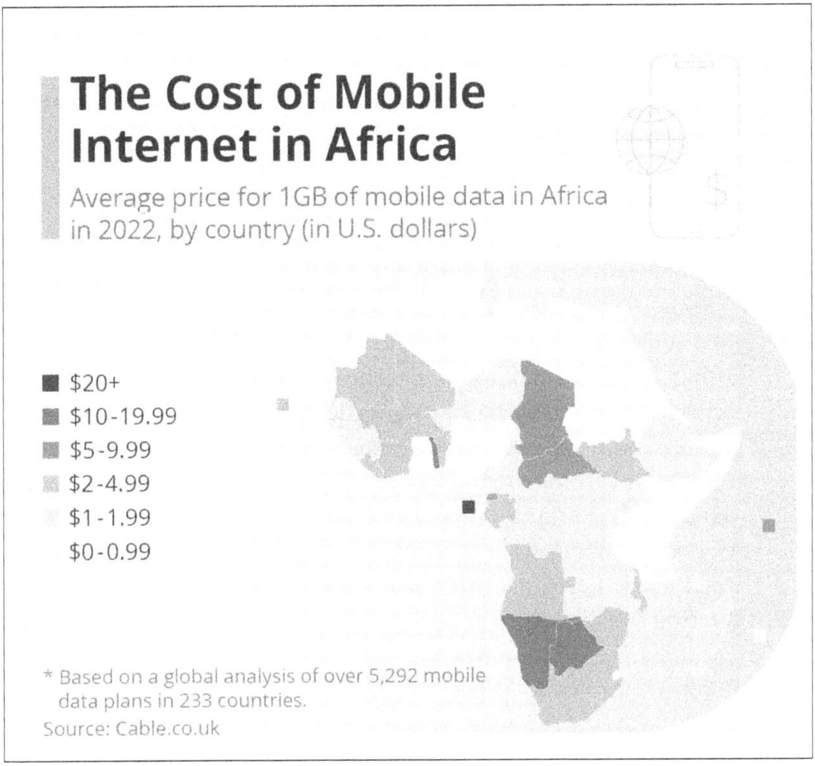

Figure 6.5 The Cost of Mobile Internet in Africa

3. Concerns around intellectual property rights and the sustainability of open-source initiatives
4. Regulatory and policy frameworks that do not adequately support or incentivize open-source innovation
5. Dominant narratives that prioritize proprietary, profit-driven models over community-driven, inclusive approaches
6. Entrenched power structures and vested interests that resist the democratization of knowledge and technology (Amentae, Song & Wang, 2024; Watkins, Papaioannou, Mugwagwa & Kale, 2015).

Overcoming these barriers requires a multi-pronged approach that combines targeted capacity-building, policy advocacy, and the cultivation of collaborative ecosystems that actively champion and support open-source initiatives (Masutha & Tengeh, 2015).

IV. Strategies for Advancing Open-Source in Africa

To harness the transformative power of open-source approaches in driving inclusive innovation and development, the following strategies can be employed (Union, 2020; Phiri, 2021):

1. Raising awareness and building technical capacity
   - Implement educational campaigns and training programs to promote understanding of open-source principles and methodologies
   - Establish open-source innovation hubs and maker spaces to provide hands-on learning and support for community-based initiatives
   - Develop comprehensive curricula for open-source software, hardware, and knowledge management in academic and vocational institutions
2. Fostering collaborative open-source ecosystems
   - Facilitate the creation of open-source communities, networks, and consortia to encourage peer-to-peer learning and knowledge-sharing
   - Promote the development of open-source repositories, code libraries, and digital platforms that enable collaborative innovation
   - Incentivize cross-sector partnerships and multi-stakeholder collaborations to leverage complementary resources and expertise
3. Strengthening policy and regulatory frameworks
   - Implement policies and regulations that recognize, protect, and incentivize open-source innovation
   - Develop intellectual property frameworks that safeguard the rights of open-source contributors and ensure equitable distribution of benefits
   - Integrate open-source approaches into national and regional digital transformation strategies and public procurement programs
4. Mobilizing sustainable funding and resources
   - Establish dedicated funding mechanisms and investment vehicles to support the development and scaling of open-source initiatives
   - Explore innovative financing models, such as crowdfunding and impact investing, to mobilize resources for open-source projects

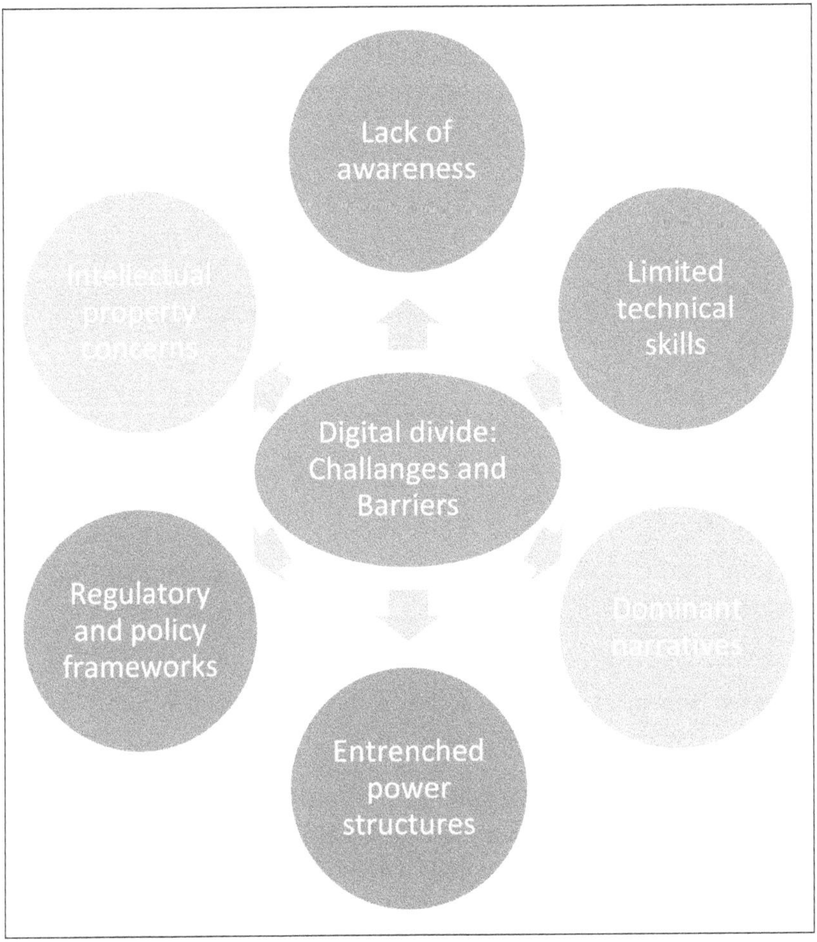

Figure 6.6 Digital Divide: Challenges and Barriers (Author's own work)

- Leverage public-private partnerships and collaborative funding schemes to ensure the long-term sustainability of open-source ecosystems

5. Amplifying success stories and role models
   - Document and disseminate case studies of successful open-source initiatives and their societal impact

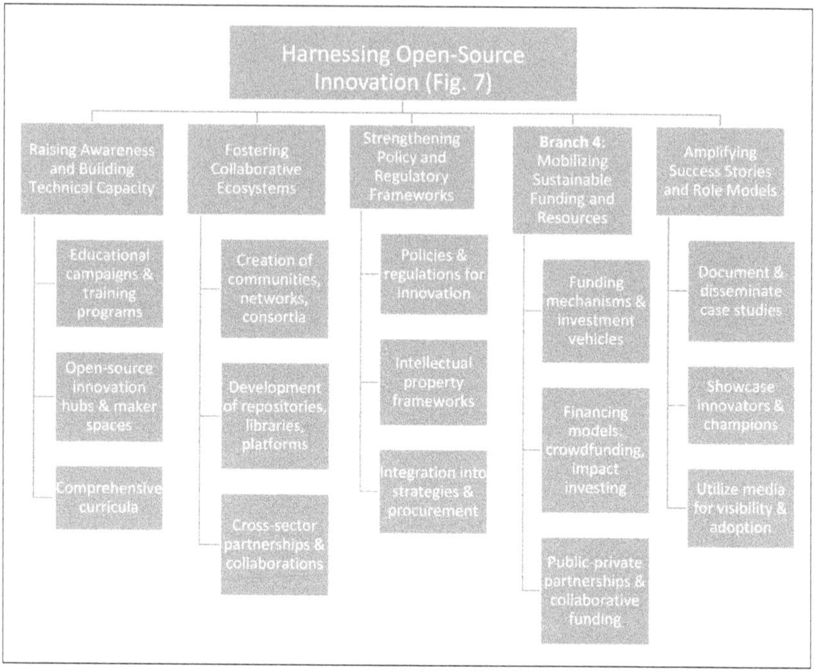

Figure 6.7 Harnessing Open Source Innovation (Author's own work)

- Identify and showcase open-source innovators, community champions, and thought leaders as inspirational role models
- Leverage media and communication channels to raise the visibility and mainstream the adoption of open-source approaches By pursuing these strategies and creating an enabling environment for open-source innovation, Africa can unlock the transformative potential of democratized access to knowledge and technology, empowering marginalized communities as active participants in the digital age and driving inclusive, sustainable development across the continent.

Open Source Community Africa (OSCA): Open Source Community Africa (OSCA) is a community of open-source enthusiasts, advocates and experts in the region interested in increasing the rate of credible open-source contributions from Africa.

OSCA builds communities through Chapters, Open Source Festivals and open-source projects.

V. Empowering marginalized communities through digital inclusion

Bridging the digital divide in Africa requires a targeted focus on empowering marginalized communities, including women, youth, and rural populations, as active participants in the digital ecosystem. By adopting inclusive, community-centric approaches, digital inclusion initiatives can unlock new pathways for social and economic advancement, amplify the voices of underrepresented groups, and promote more equitable development outcomes.

Key strategies for empowering marginalized communities through digital inclusion include (Perez-Escolar & Canet, 2023; Richardson & Wilson, 2024; Munyoka, 2022):

1. Engaging community leaders and local stakeholders
   - Collaborating with community-based organizations, traditional authorities, and grassroots innovators to understand the unique digital needs and barriers faced by marginalized groups.
   - Designing and implementing digital inclusion initiatives that are grounded in the lived experiences and contextual realities of target communities.
2. Fostering gender-responsive digital access and skills
   - Addressing the specific challenges and barriers that women and girls encounter in accessing and utilizing digital technologies, such as sociocultural norms, financial constraints, and limited digital literacy.
   - Implementing targeted digital skills training, mentorship programs, and entrepreneurship support to empower women as active participants and leaders in the digital economy.
3. Integrating digital inclusion into youth development programs
   - Embedding digital literacy, coding, and entrepreneurship skills within education curricula and youth-focused initiatives to equip the next generation with the necessary competencies to thrive in the digital age.
   - Establishing youth-led digital innovation hubs and maker spaces that provide hands-on learning opportunities and pathways for young innovators to develop and scale their ideas.

4. Leveraging mobile technologies for rural digital inclusion
    - Leveraging the ubiquity of mobile phones and mobile money platforms to enhance access to digital services, information, and economic opportunities for rural and remote communities.
    - Designing user-friendly, multilingual mobile applications and digital platforms that address the unique needs and contexts of rural populations.
5. Addressing accessibility for persons with disabilities
    - Ensuring that digital infrastructure, devices, and applications are designed with accessibility features that cater to the diverse needs of persons with disabilities, such as assistive technologies and inclusive user interfaces.
    - Empowering persons with disabilities to actively participate in the development and deployment of inclusive digital solutions.
6. Advocating for inclusive digital rights and data governance
    - Championing the integration of marginalized voices and community interests within digital rights frameworks and data governance policies.
    - Enabling community-driven data collection, management, and utilization to ensure that digital technologies and data-driven decision-making processes benefit local populations.

By adopting these community-centric, equity-focused strategies, digital inclusion initiatives can catalyze the empowerment of marginalized groups, foster their active participation in the digital economy, and unlock new avenues for inclusive and sustainable development across Africa.

VI. Digital Inclusion and the Sustainable Development Goals

The imperative of democratizing access to knowledge and technology, as embodied in the principles of digital inclusion, is intrinsically linked to the realization of the United Nations' Sustainable Development Goals (SDGs). By bridging the digital divide and empowering marginalized communities as active participants in the digital ecosystem, African nations can make significant strides towards achieving the SDGs and fostering a more equitable, prosperous, and sustainable future.

Key areas of alignment between digital inclusion and the SDGs include:

1. Quality Education (SDG 4)
   - Expanding access to digital learning resources, online educational platforms, and technology-enabled training opportunities to enhance the quality and reach of education.
   - Integrating digital literacy and STEM (Science, Technology, Engineering, and Mathematics) education into formal and informal learning environments.
2. Gender Equality (SDG 5)
   - Addressing the gender digital divide and empowering women and girls to actively participate in the digital economy through targeted digital skills development and entrepreneurship support.
   - Ensuring that digital technologies and online platforms are designed and deployed in a manner that promotes gender equality and women's empowerment.
3. Decent Work and Economic Growth (SDG 8)
   - Leveraging digital technologies and platforms to create new economic opportunities, enhance the productivity and competitiveness of businesses, and foster inclusive growth.
   - Equipping marginalized communities, including youth and informal sector workers, with the digital skills and tools required to access dignified employment and income-generating activities.
4. Industry, Innovation, and Infrastructure (SDG 9)
   - Investing in the development of robust, resilient, and inclusive digital infrastructure to enable the widespread adoption and utilization of transformative technologies.
   - Promoting the use of open-source approaches and collaborative innovation models to democratize access to knowledge and technology.
5. Reduced Inequalities (SDG 10)
   - Addressing the multidimensional digital divides that perpetuate socioeconomic inequalities, with a focus on empowering marginalized groups, such as persons with disabilities and rural populations.
   - Ensuring that the benefits of digital transformation are equitably distributed and contribute to the reduction of disparities within and among African countries.

By aligning digital inclusion strategies with the broader SDG framework, African nations can harness the transformative potential of knowledge and technology to drive inclusive and sustainable development, empowering marginalized communities as active participants and beneficiaries of progress.

VII. Measuring the Impact of Digital Inclusion Initiatives

Assessing the impact and effectiveness of digital inclusion initiatives is crucial for informing evidence-based policymaking, refining program design, and scaling successful models across the African continent (Oloyede, Faruk, Noma, Tebepah & Nwaulune, 2023). However, the multifaceted and context-specific nature of digital inclusion efforts presents unique challenges in developing appropriate evaluation frameworks.

Key considerations in measuring the impact of digital inclusion initiatives include:

1. Capturing multidimensional outcomes
   - Evaluating the impact of digital inclusion initiatives beyond just quantitative metrics, such as internet penetration rates or device ownership, to assess the social, economic, and empowerment-related outcomes for marginalized communities.
   - Incorporating indicators that measure the enhancement of digital literacy, the participation of underrepresented groups in the digital economy, and the contribution of digital technologies to improving access to essential services and livelihood opportunities (Kanobe, Ademolu Ajigini, Ssebuggwawo, Alexandra Nantogo, Mukosi & Moyane, 2022; Allen, 2018).
2. Adopting participatory, community-driven approaches
   - Engaging directly with target communities, particularly marginalized groups, in the design and implementation of impact assessments to ensure that the evaluation process reflects their priorities, needs, and perspectives.
   - Empowering community members as active partners in data collection, analysis, and the interpretation of findings to foster a sense of ownership and agency (Rong, Ristevski & Carroll, 2023; Salsberg, Macridis, Garcia Bengoechea, Macaulay, Moore & KSDPP School Travel Planning Committee. 2017).

3. Assessing systemic and sustainable change
   - Examining the extent to which digital inclusion initiatives have contributed to the strengthening of local innovation ecosystems, the development of strategic partnerships, and the integration of inclusive digital policies and regulations.
   - Evaluating the long-term sustainability of digital inclusion programs, including their ability to foster community-driven ownership and ongoing adaptation to evolving needs and contexts (Guandalini, 2022).
4. Fostering cross-learning and knowledge-sharing
   - Establishing collaborative platforms and networks that facilitate the exchange of impact data, best practices, and lessons learned among digital inclusion practitioners, policymakers, and researchers.
   - Promoting the use of open data and open research approaches to enhance the transparency and accessibility of evaluation findings, enabling the replication and scaling of successful models (Ugochukwu & Phillips, 2024).
5. Integrating digital inclusion metrics within broader development frameworks
   - Aligning digital inclusion impact measures with the overarching Sustainable Development Goals and national development strategies to ensure that digital transformation efforts are cohesively contributing to equitable and sustainable progress.
   - Developing comprehensive digital inclusion indices and dashboards that can be integrated into existing monitoring and evaluation systems at the regional, national, and local levels (Sharp, 2024).

By adopting these holistic, participatory, and collaborative approaches to impact measurement, African nations can not only demonstrate the tangible outcomes of their digital inclusion initiatives but also generate valuable insights to guide the continuous improvement and scaling of these transformative efforts across the continent.

References

Allen, M. (2018). The Contribution of Information and Communication Technology to the wellbeing of the urban poor in South Africa.

Amentae, T. K., Song, W., & Wang, J. (2024). Intellectual property rights in the agri-food chains: A systematic review and bibliometric analysis. *World Patent Information*, *77*, 102279.

Ciasullo, M. V., Carli, M., Lim, W. M., & Palumbo, R. (2022). An open innovation approach to co-produce scientific knowledge: an examination of citizen science in the healthcare ecosystem. *European Journal of Innovation Management*, *25*(6), 365-392.

Dewandaru, G., Masih, R., Bacha, O. I., & Masih, A. M. M. (2018). The impact of religious beliefs and practices on cryptocurrency intention to use. *Applied Economics Letters*, 25(17), 1245-1249.

Diga, K. (2019). Digital inequality and the roles of technology in Africa. In *Routledge Handbook of Digital Media and Communication* (pp. 361-372). Routledge.

Erforth, B. (2024). Data extraction, data governance and Africa-Europe cooperation: a research agenda. *Working Paper* 14.

Ghadially, R., & Kumar, P. (2016). Open source software adoption and its implications for ICT diffusion and development. *Education and Information Technologies*, 21(6), 1643-1662.

Grimus, M. (2017). *Enhancing Mobile Learning in a Developing Country (Sub-Saharan Africa) Experiences in a High School in Ghana* (Doctoral dissertation, Graz University of Technology).

Guandalini, I. (2022). Sustainability through digital transformation: A systematic literature review for research guidance. *Journal of Business Research*, *148*, 456-471.

Hassan, M., Mies, R., & Jochem, R. (2023). Key Enablers towards Mature Company-community Collaboration in Open Source Hardware. *Journal of Innovation Economics & Management*, *40*(1), 159-191.

Holloway, C., Morgado Ramirez, D. Z., Bhatnagar, T., Oldfrey, B., Morjaria, P., Moulic, S. G., ... & Sujatha, S. (2021). A review of innovation strategies and processes to improve access to AT: Looking ahead to open innovation ecosystems.

Horrigan, J. B., & Schement, J. R. (2022). *Broadband as civic infrastructure: community empowerment, equity, and a Digital New Deal.* German Marshall Fund of the United States.

Kanobe, F., Ademolu Ajigini, O., Ssebuggwawo, D., Alexandra Nantogo, B., Mukosi, E., & Moyane, L. (2022). An Assessment of Digital Inclusion among Vulnerable Persons in Developing Economies.

Kibala Bauer, G. (2020). Digital solutions to improve basic service provision to the urban poor. *Field Actions Science Reports. The journal of field actions*, (Special Issue 22), 116-124.

Maldonado, U. P. T., Khan, G. F., Moon, J., & Rho, J. J. (2011). E-learning motivation and educational portal acceptance in developing countries. *Online Information Review*.

Masutha, M., & Tengeh, R. K. (2015). Small business development in a township in South Africa: A focus on the critical role of business incubators. *Mediterranean Journal of Social Sciences*, 6(6), 264-264.

Moleka, P. (2024a). Frugal Innovation for Inclusive and Sustainable Development in Africa. *Advanced Research in Economics and Business Strategy Journal*, *5*(1), 107-117.

Moleka, P. (2024b). Empowering Transformation: The Intersection of Information Literacy and Social Change in Academic Libraries. In *Examining Information Literacy in Academic Libraries* (pp. 32-47). IGI Global.

Mukoro, V., Sharmina, M., & Gallego-Schmid, A. (2022). A review of business models for access to affordable and clean energy in Africa: Do they deliver social, economic, and environmental value?. *Energy Research & Social Science*, *88*, 102530.

Munyoka, W. (2022). Inclusive digital innovation in South Africa: Perspectives from disadvantaged and marginalized communities. *Sustainability*, *14*(9), 5372.

Nkomo, S. M. (2009). The seductive power of academic journal rankings: Challenges of searching for the otherwise. *Academy of Management Learning & Education*, 8(1), 106-121.

Nyirenda-Jere, T., Mangwende, T., Nimako, G., Gashami, J. P., Samatar, O. E., ATU, M. S., & Seck, M. (2022). African Union (AU) Data Policy Framework. *Policy*.

Perez-Escolar, M., & Canet, F. (2023). Research on vulnerable people and digital inclusion: toward a consolidated taxonomical framework. *Universal access in the information society*, *22*(3), 1059-1072.

Oloyede, A. A., Faruk, N., Noma, N., Tebepah, E., & Nwaulune, A. K. (2023). Measuring the impact of the digital economy in developing countries: A systematic review and meta-analysis. *Heliyon*, *9*(7).

Phiri, M. (2021). Skills for Employability and Productivity in Africa (SEPA) Action Plan, 2022-2025.

Richardson, P. E., & Wilson, S. (2024). Evaluating a Women's digital inclusion and storytelling initiative through the lens of empowerment. *Digital Geography and Society*, 100092.

Robinson, L., Cotten, S. R., Ono, H., Quan-Haase, A., Mesch, G., Chen, W., ... & Stern, M. J. (2015). Digital inequalities and why they matter. *Information, communication & society*, 18(5), 569-582.

Rong, T., Ristevski, E., & Carroll, M. (2023). Exploring community engagement in place-based approaches in areas of poor health and disadvantage: A scoping review. *Health & Place*, *81*, 103026.

Salsberg, J., Macridis, S., Garcia Bengoechea, E., Macaulay, A. C., Moore, S., & KSDPP School Travel Planning Committee. (2017). Engagement strategies that foster community self-determination in participatory research: Insider ownership through outsider championship. *Family Practice*, *34*(3), 336-340.

Sharp, M. (2024). Revisiting the measurement of digital inclusion. *The World Bank Research Observer*, *39*(2), 289-318.

Sowe, S. K., Zettsu, K., Simintiras, A. C., & Sunami, A. (2012). Towards open and collaborative innovation in Africa. In *Emerging Markets from a Multidisciplinary Perspective* (pp. 159-177). Springer, Boston, MA.

Troxler, P., & Voigt, C. (2014). Fab Labs: A global movement or a local wave of digital fabrication for development?

Ugochukwu, A. I., & Phillips, P. W. (2024). Open data ownership and sharing: Challenges and opportunities for application of FAIR principles and a checklist for data managers. *Journal of Agriculture and Food Research*, 101157.

Union, A. (2020). The Digital Transformation Strategy for Africa (2020-30).

van Dijk, J. A. (2006). Digital divide research, achievements and shortcomings. *Poetics*, 34(4-5), 221-235.

Watkins, A., Papaioannou, T., Mugwagwa, J., & Kale, D. (2015). National innovation systems and the intermediary role of industry associations in building institutional capacities for innovation in developing countries: A critical review of the literature. *Research policy*, *44*(8), 1407-1418.

CHAPTER 7

Inclusive Entrepreneurship: Empowering Marginalized Groups

Entrepreneurship has long been recognized as a driving force for economic and social transformation, with the potential to create jobs, spur innovation, and catalyze sustainable development. However, in many African countries, the landscape of entrepreneurship has been historically skewed, favoring certain demographic groups and excluding others, particularly women, youth, and marginalized communities (Brush et al., 2019). This chapter explores the critical imperative of fostering inclusive entrepreneurship in Africa, where diverse voices and innovative ideas can thrive, and the transformative potential of entrepreneurship can be harnessed to address systemic inequalities and drive equitable progress. By examining the barriers faced by underrepresented entrepreneurs, the innovative support structures and programs that are empowering them, and the policy frameworks required to enable inclusive entrepreneurial ecosystems, this chapter aims to provide a comprehensive blueprint for unlocking the power of entrepreneurship as a tool for inclusive development.

I. The Imperative of Inclusive Entrepreneurship

Inclusive entrepreneurship refers to the process of actively engaging and supporting entrepreneurs from underrepresented and marginalized groups, including women, youth, ethnic minorities, persons with disabilities, and

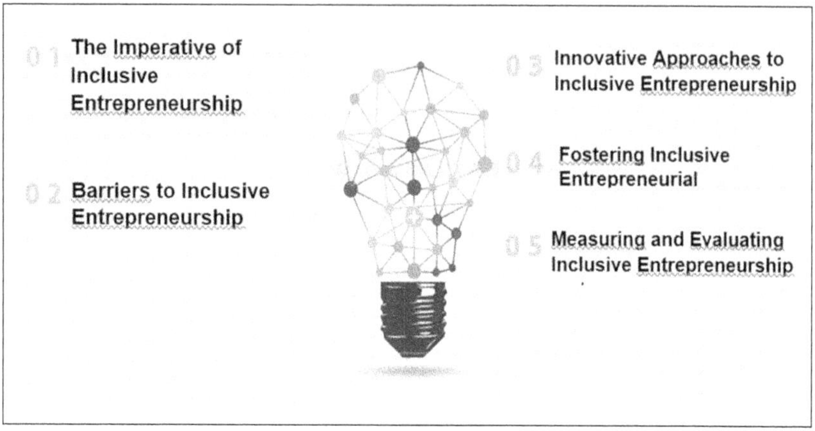

Figure 7.1 Inclusive Entrepreneurship

individuals from low-income backgrounds (Danho, 2023; Dana & Vorobeva, 2021; Acs, Szerb & Autio, 2016). This holistic approach to entrepreneurship development recognizes the inherent value and untapped potential of diverse entrepreneurial talent and seeks to create equitable pathways for participation, funding, and growth. The importance of inclusive entrepreneurship in Africa cannot be overstated.

Across the continent, women, youth, and other marginalized groups face significant barriers to entering and succeeding in the entrepreneurial sphere, including limited access to financing, skills gaps, sociocultural biases, and systemic discrimination (Campos et al., 2015). This exclusion not only deprives these groups of economic opportunities but also robs African societies of the innovative solutions, employment generation, and community empowerment that inclusive entrepreneurship can catalyze. By empowering marginalized entrepreneurs and fostering inclusive entrepreneurial ecosystems, African nations can unlock a wealth of untapped potential, drive sustainable and equitable development, and create more resilient, self-reliant communities (Minniti, 2010). Inclusive entrepreneurship represents a critical lever for addressing poverty, inequality, and social marginalization, aligning with the Sustainable Development Goals (SDGs) and the broader vision of a more just and prosperous Africa.

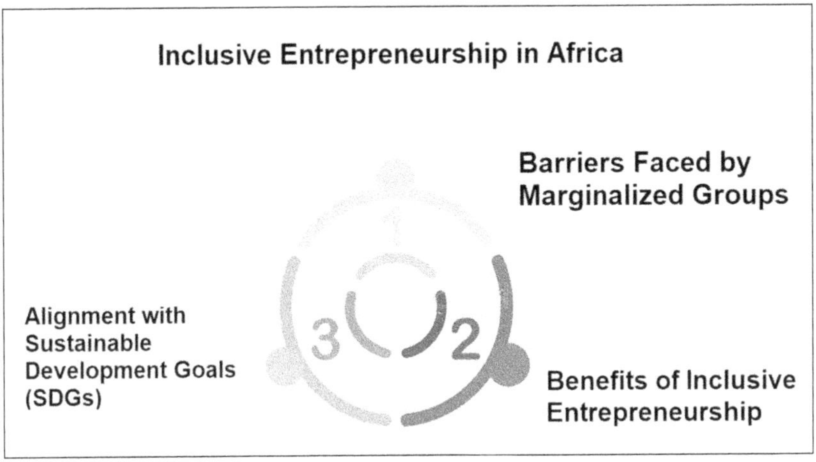

Figure 7.2 Inclusive Entrepreneurship in Africa (Author's own work)

II. Barriers to Inclusive Entrepreneurship

The challenges faced by marginalized entrepreneurs in Africa are multifaceted and deeply rooted in sociocultural, economic, and institutional structures. Key barriers include:

1. Access to finance (Brixiová, Kangoye & Yogo, 2020)
    - Limited access to formal financial services, such as bank loans and venture capital.
    - Lack of collateral and credit history, which disadvantages entrepreneurs from low-income backgrounds.
    - Biases and discrimination in the investment community, which disproportionately impact women and minority entrepreneurs.
2. Skills and capacity gaps (Wang, Li, Yang, Little, Basnight & Fryberger, 2024).
    - Inadequate entrepreneurship education and training opportunities, particularly in marginalized communities.
    - Lack of role models, mentorship, and peer-to-peer learning networks for underrepresented entrepreneurs.
    - Unequal access to business development services, technical assistance, and incubation programs.

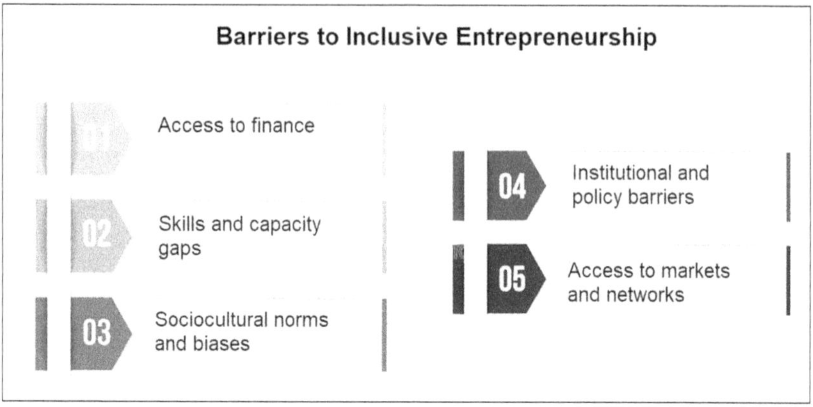

Figure 7.3 Barriers to Inclusive Entrepreneurship (Author's own work)

3. Sociocultural norms and biases (Muñoz Boudet, Petesch & Turk, 2013).
   - Persistent gender norms and stereotypes that discourage women from pursuing entrepreneurial careers.
   - Cultural stigmas and discriminatory attitudes towards entrepreneurs from certain ethnic, religious, or socioeconomic backgrounds.
   - Intra-community power dynamics and hierarchies that limit the participation of marginalized groups.
4. Institutional and policy barriers (Bakker & McMullen, 2023).
   - Absence of targeted policies, programs, and funding mechanisms to support inclusive entrepreneurship.
   - Regulatory environments that do not adequately address the unique challenges faced by marginalized entrepreneurs.
   - Weak enforcement of anti-discrimination laws and limited legal recourse against exclusionary practices.
5. Access to markets and networks (Bonfanti, De Crescenzo, Simeoni & Adaui, 2024).
   - Limited visibility and exposure of marginalized entrepreneurs within mainstream business networks and supply chains.
   - Challenges in accessing procurement opportunities, particularly with larger corporations and government agencies.

- Barriers to entering and navigating international markets due to language, cultural, and logistical hurdles. Overcoming these multifaceted barriers requires a comprehensive, multi-stakeholder approach that addresses the systemic drivers of exclusion and empowers marginalized entrepreneurs as agents of change.

III. Innovative Approaches to Inclusive Entrepreneurship

Across Africa, a growing number of initiatives and programs are pioneering innovative strategies to foster inclusive entrepreneurship and empower marginalized groups. These approaches include (Henry, Wu, Moberg, Singer, Gabriel, Valente... & Fannin, 2024):

1. Targeted entrepreneurship education and training
   - Integrating entrepreneurship curricula into formal education systems, with a focus on underserved communities.
   - Implementing specialized entrepreneurship training programs and accelerators for women, youth, and other marginalized groups.
   - Leveraging digital platforms and online learning to enhance the accessibility and scalability of entrepreneurship education.
2. Accessible financing and investment vehicles
   - Designing alternative financing models, such as microfinance, crowdfunding, and impact investment funds, to address the unique needs of marginalized entrepreneurs.
   - Implementing affirmative action policies and public procurement programs that prioritize the inclusion of women-owned, youth-led, and minority-owned businesses (Coronel-Pangol, Heras-Tigre, Jiménez Yumbla, Aguirre Quezada & Mora, 2023).
   - Fostering angel investor networks and venture capital funds with a specific focus on underrepresented entrepreneurs.
3. Holistic business support and incubation (Awonuga, Mhlongo, Olatoye, Ibeh, Elufioye & Asuzu, 2024)
   - Establishing inclusive entrepreneurship hubs, makerspaces, and incubators that provide tailored mentorship, technical assistance, and access to resources.

- Facilitating peer-to-peer learning and networking opportunities for marginalized entrepreneurs to build social capital and collaborative partnerships.
- Connecting underrepresented entrepreneurs with corporate supply chains and market access opportunities.

Entrepreneurship has long been recognized as a key driver of economic growth, job creation, and social innovation (Minniti, 2008; Ács et al., 2018). However, the benefits of entrepreneurship in Africa have historically been unequally distributed, with marginalized groups such as women, youth, and ethnic minorities often facing significant barriers to starting and scaling successful businesses (Brush et al., 2019; Khoury & Prasad, 2016). Addressing this challenge is crucial for achieving more inclusive and sustainable development across the continent. Cultivating thriving, inclusive entrepreneurial ecosystems in Africa requires the active engagement and coordination of diverse stakeholders, including policymakers, financial institutions, educational institutions, corporate partners, and community-based organizations (Isenberg, 2010; Amoako & Matlay, 2015). This holistic, collaborative

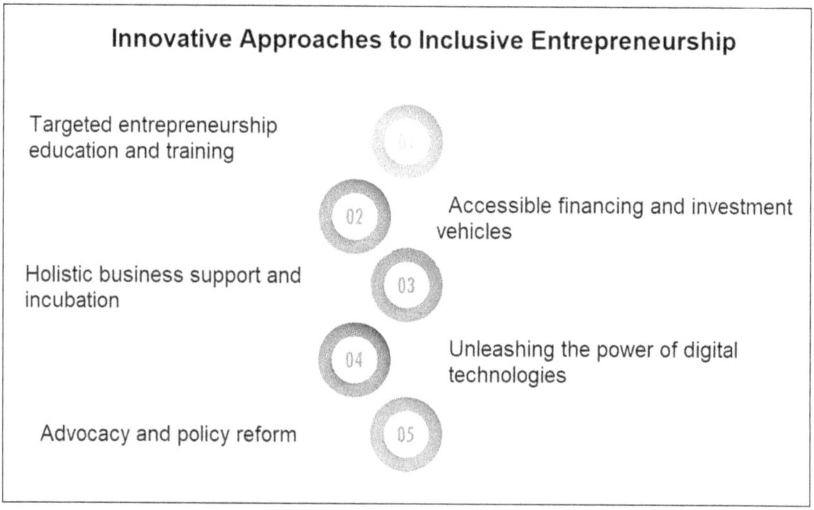

Figure 7.4 Innovative Aproaches to Inclusive Entrepreneurship (Author's own work)

approach is essential for dismantling the systemic barriers that impede the participation and success of marginalized entrepreneurs.

IV. The Role of Key Stakeholders in Fostering Inclusive Entrepreneurial Ecosystems

1. Policymakers and Regulators: Policymakers and regulators play a pivotal role in creating an enabling environment for inclusive entrepreneurship. This can be achieved through the implementation of targeted policies, regulations, and public programs, such as tax incentives, targeted funding schemes, and anti-discrimination measures (Dilli et al., 2018; Hechavarría & Ingram, 2019). Integrating inclusive entrepreneurship strategies into national development plans, industrial policies, and innovation agendas is also crucial (Ács et al., 2014; Schøtt et al., 2015).
2. Financial Institutions and Investors: Financial institutions and investors are instrumental in providing the necessary resources and support for marginalized entrepreneurs. This includes designing and offering tailored financial products and services, such as microfinance, venture capital, and impact investment funds, to meet the unique needs of underrepresented groups (Cassar, 2004; Brush et al., 2002). Inclusive lending practices and capacity-building initiatives can also help to address the barriers faced by women, youth, and other underrepresented groups in accessing finance (Brush et al., 2019; Khoury & Prasad, 2016).
3. Educational Institutions and Training Providers: Educational institutions and training providers play a crucial role in equipping marginalized individuals with the knowledge, skills, and networks necessary for successful entrepreneurship. This can be achieved by integrating entrepreneurship education, with a focus on inclusive and sustainable approaches, into academic curricula at all levels (Nabi et al., 2017; Sieger et al., 2016). Establishing specialized entrepreneurship programs and incubators targeted at marginalized communities can also help to address the unique needs and challenges faced by these groups (ACS & GEM, 2019; Ács et al., 2018).
4. Corporate and Private Sector Partners: Corporate and private sector partners can contribute to the development of inclusive entrepreneurial ecosystems through the implementation of inclusive procurement policies, supplier diversity programs, and corporate social responsibility initiatives (Hechavarría & Ingram, 2019; Brush et al., 2019). These efforts

can increase the participation of women-owned, youth-led, and minority-owned businesses in corporate supply chains, while also providing marginalized entrepreneurs with access to resources, mentorship, and market opportunities.

5. Community-based Organizations and Civil Society: Community-based organizations and civil society play a critical role in facilitating grassroots entrepreneurship development programs, advocating for policy reforms, and amplifying the voices of marginalized entrepreneurs within the broader ecosystem (McKeever et al., 2015; Welter et al., 2017). By mobilizing resources, providing capacity-building support, and fostering collaborative networks, these stakeholders can help to address the systemic barriers faced by underrepresented groups and empower them as active agents of change.

V. Measuring and Evaluating the Impact of Inclusive Entrepreneurship Initiatives

Effective monitoring and evaluation frameworks are crucial for understanding the impact and progress of inclusive entrepreneurship initiatives, as well as informing evidence-based policymaking and program design (Brush et al., 2019;

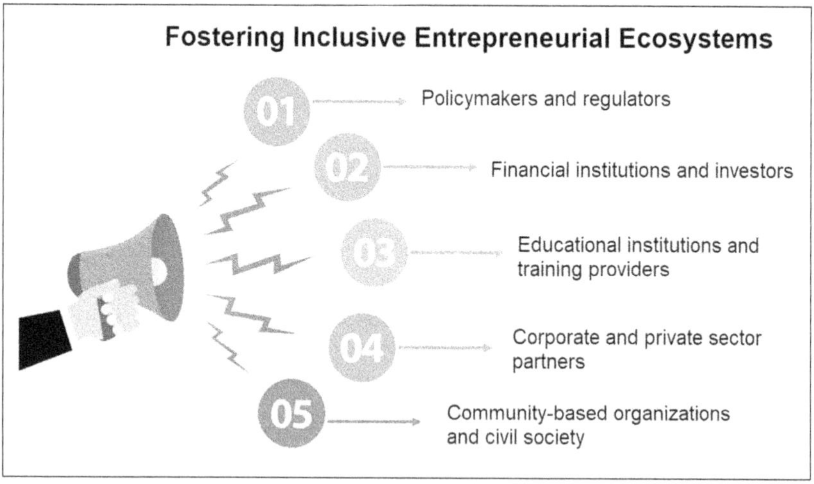

Figure 7.5 Fostering Inclusive Entrepreneurial Ecosystems

Khoury & Prasad, 2016). Key considerations in measuring the success of inclusive entrepreneurship efforts include:

1. Representation and Participation Tracking the demographic diversity of entrepreneurs, including gender, age, ethnicity, and socioeconomic status, as well as measuring the levels of participation and access to entrepreneurship support programs among marginalized groups (Brush et al., 2019; Hechavarría & Ingram, 2019).
2. Access to Resources and Opportunities: Assessing the availability and utilization of inclusive financing, business development services, and market access channels, as well as evaluating the equitable distribution of entrepreneurship awards, grants, and procurement contracts (Cassar, 2004; Brush et al., 2002).
3. Enterprise Performance and Growth: Analyzing the financial and operational performance of enterprises led by marginalized entrepreneurs, and monitoring the employment generation, revenue growth, and scaling trajectories of inclusive enterprises (Minniti, 2008; Ács et al., 2018).
4. Community Impact and Social Value Creation: Measuring the social, economic, and environmental impact of inclusive entrepreneurship initiatives on local communities, and evaluating the extent to which inclusive enterprises contribute to the achievement of the Sustainable Development Goals (Hechavarría & Ingram, 2019; Welter et al., 2017).

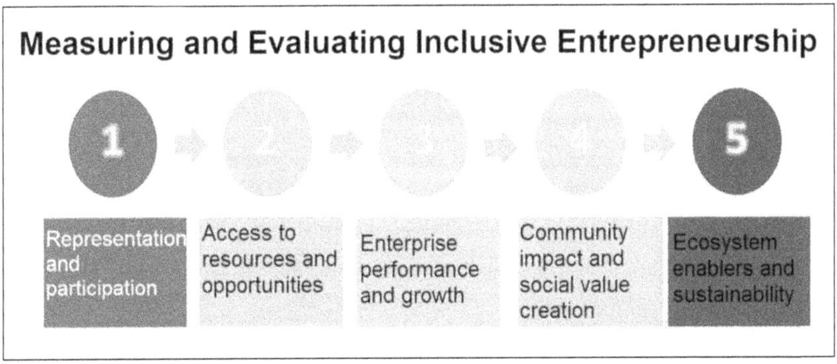

Figure 7.6 Measuring and Evaluating Inclusive Entrereneurship. Source: Author

5. Ecosystem Enablers and Sustainability: Assessing the effectiveness of policy frameworks, institutional support structures, and collaborative partnerships in fostering inclusive entrepreneurship, as well as analyzing the long-term viability and scalability of inclusive entrepreneurship models and their ability to catalyze systemic change (Isenberg, 2010; Amoako & Matlay, 2015). By developing and implementing robust, inclusive, and participatory monitoring and evaluation frameworks, African nations can meaningfully track progress, identify best practices, and continuously refine their strategies for empowering marginalized entrepreneurs and driving equitable, sustainable development.

Fostering inclusive entrepreneurial ecosystems in Africa is essential for unlocking the transformative potential of entrepreneurship and driving sustainable, equitable development across the continent. By adopting a holistic, multi-stakeholder approach that addresses systemic barriers, empowers marginalized groups, and fosters collaborative partnerships, African nations can create an enabling environment for inclusive entrepreneurship to thrive, ultimately contributing to the achievement of the Sustainable Development Goals and the creation of a more just, prosperous, and resilient future.

References

Ács, Z. J., Autio, E., & Szerb, L. (2014). National systems of entrepreneurship: Measurement issues and policy implications. *Research Policy*, 43(3), 476-494.

ACS, Z. J., & GEM. (2019). Global Entrepreneurship Monitor 2018/2019 Global Report. Global Entrepreneurship Research Association.

Acs, Z. J., Szerb, L., & Autio, E. (2016). *Global Entrepreneurship Index 2016*. Washington, DC: The Global Entrepreneurship and Development Institute.

Ács, Z. J., Szerb, L., Ortega-Argilés, R., Ainsworth, E. A., & Meters, D. (2018). The entrepreneurial ecosystem: The regional entrepreneurship and development index. *Small Business Economics*, 51(2), 501-514.

Amoako, I. O., & Matlay, H. (2015). Norms and trust-shaping relationships among food-producing SMEs in Ghana. *The International Journal of Entrepreneurship and Innovation*, 16(2), 123-134.

Aterido, R., Beck, T., & Iacovone, L. (2013). Access to finance in Sub-Saharan Africa: is there a gender gap? *World Development*, 47, 102-120.

Awonuga, K. F., Mhlongo, N. Z., Olatoye, F. O., Ibeh, C. V., Elufioye, O. A., & Asuzu, O. F. (2024). Business incubators and their impact on startup success: A review in the USA. *International Journal of Science and Research Archive*, *11*(1), 1418-1432.

Bakker, R. M., & McMullen, J. S. (2023). Inclusive entrepreneurship: A call for a shared theoretical conversation about unconventional entrepreneurs. *Journal of Business Venturing*, *38*(1), 106268.

Bonfanti, A., De Crescenzo, V., Simeoni, F., & Adaui, C. R. L. (2024). Convergences and divergences in sustainable entrepreneurship and social entrepreneurship research: A systematic review and research agenda. *Journal of Business Research*, *170*, 114336.

Brixiová, Z., Kangoye, T., & Yogo, T. U. (2020). Access to finance among youth and female entrepreneurs: Evidence from Eswatini. *Economic Modelling*, 84, 178-189.

Brush, C., Carter, N., Gatewood, E., Greene, P., & Hart, M. (2002). *The Diana Project: Women business owners and equity capital: The myths dispelled*. Kauffman Center for Entrepreneurial Leadership.

Brush, C. G., Edelman, L. F., Manolova, T., & Welter, F. (2019). A gendered look at entrepreneurship ecosystems. *Small Business Economics*, 53(2), 393-408.

Brush, C. G., Greene, P. G., Balachandra, L., & Davis, A. E. (2019). The gender gap in venture capital-progress, problems, and perspectives. *Venture Capital*, 20(2), 115-136.

Campos, F., Frese, M., Goldstein, M., Iacovone, L., Johnson, H. C., McKenzie, D., & Mensmann, M. (2015). Teaching personal initiative beats traditional training in boosting small business in West Africa. *Science*, 357(6357), 1287-1290.

Cassar, G. (2004). The financing of business start-ups. *Journal of Business Venturing*, 19(2), 261-283.

Coronel-Pangol, K., Heras-Tigre, D., Jiménez Yumbla, J., Aguirre Quezada, J., & Mora, P. (2023). Microfinance, an Alternative for Financing Entrepreneurship: Implications and Trends-Bibliometric Analysis. *International Journal of Financial Studies*, *11*(3), 83.

Dana, L. P., & Vorobeva, E. (2021). Understanding the term 'minority entrepreneurship'. *The Palgrave handbook of minority entrepreneurship*, 15-32.

Danho, E. J. M. (2023). *Toward A More Inclusive Entrepreneurial Ecosystem: An Exploration of the Lived Experience of Disadvantaged Women Entrepreneurs and the Supportive or Barrier-Breaking Role of the French Entrepreneurial Ecosystem* (Doctoral dissertation, University of Essex).

Dilli, S., Elert, N., & Herrmann, A. M. (2018). Varieties of entrepreneurship: Exploring the institutional foundations of different entrepreneurship types through 'Varieties-of-Capitalism' arguments. *Small Business Economics*, 51(2), 293-320.

Goyal, S., Sergi, B. S., & Jaiswal, M. P. (2016). Understanding the challenges and strategic actions of social entrepreneurship at base of the pyramid. *Management Decision*.

Hechavarría, D. M., & Ingram, A. E. (2019). Entrepreneurial ecosystem conditions and gendered national-level entrepreneurial activity: A 14-year panel study of GEM. *Small Business Economics*, 53(2), 431-458.

Henry, C., Wu, W., Moberg, K., Singer, S., Gabriel, B., Valente, R., ... & Fannin, N. (2024). Exploring inclusivity in entrepreneurship education provision: A European study. *Journal of Business Venturing Insights*, *22*, e00494.

Herrington, M., & Kew, P. (2017). Global entrepreneurship monitor 2016/17 report for South Africa. *Development*, 151, 36.

Isenberg, D. J. (2010). How to start an entrepreneurial revolution. *Harvard Business Review*, 88(6), 40-50.

Khoury, T. A., & Prasad, A. (2016). Entrepreneurship amid concurrent institutional constraints in less developed countries. *Business & Society*, 55(7), 934-969.

Kempster, S., Maak, T., & Parry, K. (2019). Editorial introduction for the special issue on responsible leadership in emerging markets. *Asia Pacific Journal of Management*, 36(2), 307-312.

McKeever, E., Jack, S., & Anderson, A. (2015). Embedded entrepreneurship in the creative re-construction of place. *Journal of Business Venturing*, 30(1), 50-65.

Minniti, M. (2008). The role of government policy on entrepreneurial activity: Productive, unproductive, or destructive? *Entrepreneurship Theory and Practice*, 32(5), 779-790.

Minniti, M. (2010). Female entrepreneurship and economic activity. *The European Journal of Development Research*, 22(3), 294-312.

Muñoz Boudet, A. M., Petesch, P., & Turk, C. (2013). *On norms and agency: Conversations about gender equality with women and men in 20 countries*. The World Bank.

Nabi, G., Liñán, F., Fayolle, A., Krueger, N., & Walmsley, A. (2017). The impact of entrepreneurship education in higher education: A systematic review and research agenda. *Academy of Management Learning & Education*, 16(2), 277-299.

Schøtt, T., Kew, P., & Cheraghi, M. (2015). Future Potential: A GEM perspective on youth entrepreneurship 2015. *Global Entrepreneurship Monitor.*

Sieger, P., Fueglistaller, U., Zellweger, T., & Braun, I. (2016). *Student entrepreneurship 2016: Insights from 50 countries*. KMU-HSG/IMU.

Simba, A., & Ojong, N. (2017). Entrepreneurial ecosystems in Africa–a systematic literature review. *African Journal of Economic and Management Studies*.

Wang, Q., Li, Y., Yang, Y., Little, M. G., Basnight, E. B., & Fryberger, C. B. (2024). University-Led Entrepreneurship Ecosystem Building in Underserved Communities: from a Network Perspective. *Geographical Review*, *114*(3), 353-377.

Welter, F., Baker, T., Audretsch, D. B., & Gartner, W. B. (2017). Everyday entrepreneurship—a call for entrepreneurship research to embrace entrepreneurial diversity. *Entrepreneurship Theory and Practice*, 41(3), 311-321.

CHAPTER 8

Grassroots Innovation and Traditional Knowledge Systems

Africa's development landscape is undergoing a remarkable transformation, driven by the dynamic interplay between grassroots innovation and traditional knowledge systems. At the heart of this vibrant innovation ecosystem lies a deep well of Indigenous wisdom that has been cultivated and passed down through generations. These repositories of traditional knowledge encompass a profound understanding of the natural environment, innovative agricultural and crafting techniques, and holistic approaches to community well-being (Agrawal, 1995; Berkes, 2012). Far from being relics of the past, these traditional knowledge systems are increasingly recognized as vital sources of inspiration and innovation for addressing contemporary development challenges across the African continent. By seamlessly blending traditional and modern knowledge, grassroots innovators are creating synergistic solutions that are both culturally relevant and technologically sophisticated, empowering local communities as active agents of change. This chapter delves into the dynamic interplay between grassroots innovation and traditional knowledge systems in Africa, exploring how these complementary paradigms can be leveraged to drive inclusive, sustainable, and equitable development. It examines the power of grassroots innovation, the significance of traditional knowledge systems, the vibrant ecosystem of actors and enablers, the barriers to integration, and the strategies for fostering more inclusive innovation ecosystems. Furthermore, the chapter highlights the transformative potential of grassroots innovation in advancing the Sustainable Development Goals (SDGs), the crucial role of innovation intermediaries, and the importance of comprehensive impact assessment frameworks. Through a holistic, collaborative, and community-driven approach, this chapter aims to illuminate new pathways for unleashing the transformative power of grassroots innovation and traditional knowledge systems, ultimately catalyzing a more equitable, resilient, and sustainable future for Africa.

I. The Power of Grassroots Innovation in Africa

Grassroots innovation, also known as bottom-up or community-based innovation, refers to the creative problem-solving initiatives that emerge organically from local communities in response to their specific needs and contexts. These innovations are often characterized by their frugal, user-centric, and environmentally sustainable nature, leveraging limited resources and indigenous knowledge to address local challenges (Gupta, 2016; Moleka, 2024a; Moleka, 2024b). Across the African continent, grassroots innovators are tackling a wide range of pressing issues, from improving agricultural productivity and food security to developing affordable healthcare solutions, renewable energy technologies, and sustainable urban infrastructure. These homegrown innovations not only serve the immediate needs of their communities but also hold the promise of scalable and replicable models that can be adapted to different contexts (Berdegué, 2005; Moleka, 2024b). The power of grassroots innovation lies in its ability to unlock novel, context-specific solutions that are often overlooked by conventional, top-down approaches to development. By drawing on the intimate understanding of local needs and challenges, grassroots innovators are able to devise innovative, low-cost, and accessible solutions that resonate with the lived experiences and aspirations of marginalized communities (Ely & Oxley, 2014; Fressoli et al., 2014). Moreover, grassroots innovations frequently exhibit a strong emphasis on environmental sustainability, resource efficiency, and the preservation of traditional livelihoods. These characteristics align closely with the principles of sustainable development, making grassroots initiatives particularly relevant and impactful in addressing complex challenges such as climate change, resource scarcity, and socioeconomic inequality (Seyfang & Smith, 2007; Manzini, 2014). The Significance of Traditional Knowledge Systems Integral to the grassroots innovation landscape in Africa are the rich and diverse traditional knowledge systems that have been passed down through generations. These repositories of Indigenous wisdom encompass a deep understanding of the natural environment, innovative agricultural and crafting techniques, and holistic approaches to community well-being (Ely & Oxley, 2014; Lwoga et al., 2010). Traditional knowledge systems in Africa are deeply rooted in the cultural heritages, ancestral practices, and lived experiences of local communities. They reflect a holistic worldview that recognizes the interdependence of human societies and the natural environment, emphasizing the importance of community-based decision-making, ecological stewardship, and collective well-being (Berkes, 2012; Brokensha et al., 1980). Across the African continent, traditional knowledge systems have been instrumental in addressing a wide range of development challenges, from sustainable agriculture and natural resource management to community healthcare and renewable energy solutions. By drawing on the intimate understanding of local contexts, traditional knowledge systems have the potential to inform the design of more culturally-relevant, ecologically-sound, and socially-inclusive innovations (Agrawal, 1995; Sillitoe, 1998). Moreover, these knowledge systems are often imbued with a profound respect for biodiversity, traditional livelihoods, and the preservation of intangible cultural heritage. As such, they represent a crucial counterpoint to the predominantly Western-centric and techno-centric models of innovation, which have frequently failed to account for the diverse lived realities and aspirations of African communities (Briggs & Sharp, 2004; Escobar, 1995).

II. The Synergistic Relationship between Grassroots Innovation and Traditional Knowledge

The synergistic relationship between grassroots innovation and traditional knowledge systems is a key driver of inclusive, sustainable development in Africa. Grassroots innovators, often deeply embedded within their local communities, are uniquely positioned to identify pressing challenges and leverage traditional knowledge to devise innovative, context-appropriate solutions (Gupta, 2016; Kaplinsky, 2011). This fusion of traditional and contemporary knowledge represents a powerful approach to addressing complex development challenges in a manner that is culturally relevant, ecologically sustainable, and empowering for local communities. By blending traditional techniques with modern scientific and technological advancements, grassroots innovators are creating innovative solutions that address a wide range of issues, from improving agricultural productivity and renewable energy access to developing affordable healthcare solutions and water management systems (Ely & Oxley, 2014; Seyfang & Smith, 2007). The success of these grassroots innovations is often rooted in their ability to tap into the rich reservoirs of traditional knowledge, which provide a deep understanding of local environments, socio-cultural dynamics, and community needs. This contextual knowledge, combined with the creativity and problem-solving capacities of grassroots innovators, enables the development of customized solutions that are more likely to be adopted and sustained by local communities (Lwoga et al., 2010; Manzini, 2014). Furthermore, the incorporation of traditional knowledge systems into grassroots innovation processes can help to foster a greater sense of community ownership, cultural resilience, and environmental stewardship – all of which are crucial for the long-term sustainability and scalability of these initiatives (Brokensha et al., 1980; Sillitoe, 1998).

III. Grassroots Innovation Ecosystems: Actors and Enablers

The flourishing of grassroots innovation in Africa is underpinned by a diverse and vibrant ecosystem of actors and enablers, each playing a crucial role in identifying, supporting, and scaling innovative solutions (Clausen & Saeed, 2020; Paunov, 2013).

1. Grassroots Innovators and Community-based Organizations
   At the heart of this ecosystem are the grassroots innovators and community-based organizations that serve as the driving force behind the grassroots innovation movement. These individuals and groups leverage their intimate understanding of local needs and contexts to develop innovative solutions that address pressing challenges (Moleka, 2024b; Fressoli et al., 2014).
2. Civil Society Organizations and Non-governmental Organizations (NGOs)
   Civil society organizations and NGOs often play a crucial role in identifying, supporting, and scaling grassroots innovations through capacity-building, funding, advocacy, and network facilitation efforts. These entities help to bridge the gaps between local communities,

policymakers, and other key stakeholders, amplifying the voices and initiatives of grassroots innovators (Paunov, 2013; Clausen & Saeed, 2020).

3. Academic and Research Institutions
   Universities, research centers, and knowledge hubs are increasingly engaging with grassroots innovators, providing technical expertise, access to facilities, and opportunities for collaborative research and development. These academic and research institutions can help to enhance the rigor, scalability, and impact of grassroots innovations (Krishnan, 2010; Moleka, 2024a).
4. Government Agencies and Policymakers
   Progressive policymakers and government agencies are recognizing the value of grassroots innovations and implementing supportive frameworks, such as inclusive innovation policies, intellectual property protection mechanisms, and public procurement programs. These initiatives help to create an enabling environment for the growth and scaling of grassroots solutions (Kaplinsky, 2011; Ács et al., 2014).
5. Private Sector Partners
   Corporations, social enterprises, and impact investors are forging strategic partnerships with grassroots innovators, leveraging their innovative solutions and providing access to resources, distribution channels, and markets. These private sector collaborations can help to bolster the commercial viability and scalability of grassroots innovations (Fressoli et al., 2014; Brush et al., 2019).

IV. Innovation Intermediaries and Ecosystem Builders

Organizations and initiatives that facilitate knowledge sharing, networking, and the provision of tailored support services to grassroots innovators play a crucial role in strengthening the overall innovation ecosystem. These innovation intermediaries help to address challenges related to funding, capacity building, and policy advocacy, catalyzing the growth and scaling of grassroots innovations (Clausen & Saeed, 2020; Kaplinsky, 2011). By fostering collaborative, multi-stakeholder efforts that align the interests and resources of these diverse ecosystem actors, African nations can create an enabling environment for grassroots innovation and traditional knowledge-based solutions to thrive, ultimately driving inclusive, sustainable, and community-led development.

V. Barriers to Integrating Traditional Knowledge into Innovation Ecosystems

Despite the immense value of traditional knowledge systems, their integration into mainstream innovation ecosystems continues to face significant barriers, hindering the realization of their full potential.

1. Lack of Recognition and Legitimacy
   Traditional knowledge is often marginalized or overlooked in favor of formal, scientific knowledge systems, limiting its influence in decision-making processes and innovation pathways. The persistent bias towards Western-centric models of innovation undermines the legitimacy and recognition of traditional knowledge as a valuable source of inspiration and problem-solving (Briggs, 2005; Briggs & Sharp, 2004).
2. Intellectual Property Rights and Benefit-Sharing Challenges
   The informal and decentralized nature of traditional knowledge makes it difficult to formally recognize and protect the intellectual property rights of local communities. This, in turn, leads to challenges in ensuring equitable benefit-sharing and discourages the active participation of traditional knowledge holders in innovation ecosystems (Srinivas, 2012; Agarwal et al., 2018).
3. Intergenerational Knowledge Gaps
   The erosion of traditional knowledge due to urbanization, modernization, and the loss of cultural traditions threatens the transfer of this vital knowledge to younger generations. Bridging these intergenerational knowledge gaps is critical for sustaining the relevance and dynamism of traditional knowledge systems within innovation ecosystems (Mazzocchi, 2006; Lwoga et al., 2010).
4. Power Imbalances and Cultural Biases
   Deeply entrenched social hierarchies, gender inequalities, and biases against traditional knowledge holders can impede their meaningful participation and empowerment within innovation ecosystems. Addressing these structural inequities is essential for fostering inclusive and collaborative innovation processes (Briggs & Sharp, 2004; Escobar, 1995).

5. Misalignment with Dominant Innovation Models
   The holistic, community-centric nature of traditional knowledge systems may not align with the linear, technology-driven models that often characterize mainstream innovation approaches. Bridging this disconnect and developing frameworks that valorize the unique contributions of traditional knowledge is crucial for its effective integration (Agrawal, 1995; Sillitoe, 1998).

VI. Strategies for Integrating Traditional Knowledge into Inclusive Innovation Ecosystems

To harness the transformative power of traditional knowledge systems and foster more inclusive, sustainable, and culturally-grounded innovation ecosystems in Africa, a range of strategies can be employed.

1. Recognizing and Legitimizing Traditional Knowledge
   Implementing policies and regulatory frameworks that formally recognize the value and legitimacy of traditional knowledge systems is a crucial first step. This can be achieved through the establishment of dedicated institutional mechanisms, such as traditional knowledge councils or knowledge banks, to document, protect, and promote the use of traditional knowledge. Incorporating traditional knowledge-based solutions into national and regional development strategies and public procurement programs can further amplify their recognition and integration (Brokensha et al., 1980; Srinivas, 2012).
2. Protecting Intellectual Property Rights and Ensuring Equitable Benefit-Sharing
   Developing sui generis intellectual property rights frameworks that safeguard the collective ownership and control of traditional knowledge by local communities is essential. This should be coupled with the implementation of mechanisms for the fair and equitable distribution of benefits derived from the use of traditional knowledge in innovative solutions, empowering traditional knowledge holders as active participants in the design and governance of these frameworks (Agarwal et al., 2018; Srinivas, 2012).

i. Bridging Intergenerational Knowledge Gaps
Integrating traditional knowledge curricula and experiential learning into formal and informal education systems can help to bridge the intergenerational knowledge gaps. Establishing mentorship programs and community-based initiatives that facilitate the transfer of traditional knowledge across generations, as well as leveraging digital technologies and platforms to document, archive, and disseminate traditional knowledge in culturally-appropriate formats, can further strengthen these efforts (Lwoga et al., 2010; Mazzocchi, 2006).
ii. Addressing Power Imbalances and Cultural Biases
Implementing inclusive, participatory approaches that empower traditional knowledge holders, particularly women and marginalized groups, as equal partners in innovation ecosystems is crucial. Fostering cross-cultural dialogues and exchanges that promote mutual understanding and respect between traditional and formal knowledge systems, while also developing leadership development programs that cultivate inclusive innovation mindsets, can help to address power imbalances and cultural biases (Briggs & Sharp, 2004; Escobar, 1995).
iii. Aligning Traditional Knowledge with Contemporary Innovation Models
Facilitating the co-creation of innovative solutions that blend traditional and modern approaches, drawing on the complementary strengths of both knowledge systems, can help to bridge the disconnect between traditional knowledge and mainstream innovation models. Developing frameworks and impact assessment methodologies that capture the multidimensional value of traditional knowledge-based innovations, and promoting their integration into the design and implementation of inclusive innovation programs and initiatives, can further strengthen this alignment (Agrawal, 1995; Sillitoe, 1998).
iv. Strengthening Collaborative Ecosystems for Traditional Knowledge-Based Innovation

Establishing innovation hubs, makerspaces, and living labs that serve as collaborative platforms for traditional knowledge holders, grassroots innovators, and other ecosystem actors can foster the exchange of knowledge, resources, and best practices. Fostering cross-sector partnerships and multi-stakeholder networks that leverage the diverse expertise and resources required to scale traditional knowledge-based innovations, as well as mobilizing sustainable funding and financing mechanisms to support their development and scaling, can further strengthen these collaborative ecosystems (Clausen & Saeed, 2020; Fressoli et al., 2014). By adopting a holistic, collaborative, and community-driven approach to integrating traditional knowledge systems into innovation ecosystems, African nations can unlock new pathways for inclusive, sustainable, and culturally-grounded development that empowers local communities as active agents of change.

VII. The Transformative Potential of Grassroots Innovation for Sustainable Development

Grassroots innovation in Africa holds immense potential to drive progress towards the achievement of the Sustainable Development Goals (SDGs). By harnessing the creativity, community-centricity, and environmental stewardship inherent in grassroots innovations, African nations can unlock new pathways for inclusive, sustainable, and culturally-grounded development.

1. Poverty Alleviation and Food Security (SDG 1 and SDG 2)
   Grassroots innovations in sustainable agriculture, agroforestry, and food processing can enhance the productivity, resilience, and incomes of smallholder farmers, contributing to poverty reduction and food security. Community-based initiatives that leverage traditional knowledge and frugal technologies can also improve access to affordable, nutritious foods in underserved areas (Berdegué, 2005; Moleka, 2024b).
2. Good Health and Well-Being (SDG 3)
   Grassroots innovations in traditional and community-based healthcare, such as herbal medicines, preventive care, and assistive technologies, can enhance the accessibility and affordability of essential health services. Community-driven solutions that address social determinants of health, such as access to clean water, sanitation, and waste management, can improve overall community well-being (Paunov, 2013; Ács et al., 2018).

3. Affordable and Clean Energy (SDG 7)
   Grassroots innovations in decentralized renewable energy technologies, such as solar lamps, micro-hydropower, and biomass-based cooking solutions, can drive the expansion of clean energy access in off-grid and underserved communities. Community-managed energy initiatives that integrate traditional knowledge and local resources can promote sustainable and equitable energy transitions (Moleka, 2024a; Ács et al., 2014).
4. Sustainable Cities and Communities (SDG 11)
   Grassroots innovations in sustainable urban design, waste management, and public transportation can contribute to the development of more livable, inclusive, and environmentally-friendly cities and towns. Community-led initiatives that leverage traditional knowledge and local resources can enhance the resilience of urban and peri-urban settlements to climate change and other shocks (Fressoli et al., 2014; Paunov, 2013).
5. Climate Action and Responsible Consumption (SDG 13 and SDG 12)
   Grassroots innovations in natural resource management, agroecology, and climate change adaptation can promote environmentally-sustainable practices and help communities mitigate and adapt to the impacts of climate change. Community-based initiatives that foster circular economy models and responsible consumption patterns can contribute to the reduction of waste and the conservation of natural resources (Seyfang & Smith, 2007; Manzini, 2014).

   By integrating grassroots innovation and traditional knowledge systems into mainstream development efforts, African nations can foster more equitable, sustainable, and culturally-relevant solutions that directly address the diverse needs and priorities of local communities, thereby accelerating progress towards the achievement of the Sustainable Development Goals.

VIII. The Role of Intermediaries in Strengthening Grassroots Innovation Ecosystems

Innovation intermediaries play a crucial role in fostering vibrant, inclusive, and collaborative grassroots innovation ecosystems in Africa. These intermediary organizations and initiatives serve as catalysts, connectors, and capacity builders, helping to bridge the gaps between local communities, policymakers, academic institutions, and other key stakeholders.

1. Identification and Scouting
   Intermediaries proactively identify and scout for grassroots innovations and traditional knowledge-based solutions that have the potential for impact and scaling. They establish community-based networks and outreach programs to ensure that the voices and ideas of marginalized groups are represented (Clausen & Saeed, 2020; Moleka, 2024b).
2. Capacity Building and Technical Assistance
   Intermediaries provide tailored training, mentorship, and access to resources (e.g., funding, infrastructure, and expertise) to strengthen the capacities of grassroots innovators. They also facilitate knowledge exchange, peer-to-peer learning, and collaborative research and development opportunities (Krishnan, 2010; Paunov, 2013).
3. Ecosystem Coordination and Advocacy
   Intermediaries convene multi-stakeholder dialogues and platforms to foster collaborations, align priorities, and address systemic barriers within the grassroots innovation ecosystem. They also advocate for policy reforms, regulatory changes, and institutional support mechanisms that create an enabling environment for grassroots innovation (Kaplinsky, 2011; Ács et al., 2014).
4. Scaling and Replication
   Intermediaries develop strategies and pathways for the scaling and replication of successful grassroots innovations, including through public-private partnerships, social franchising, and digital platforms. They also document and disseminate best practices, case studies, and lessons learned to inspire and inform the broader innovation community (Fressoli et al., 2014; Moleka, 2024a).

   a. Bridging Traditional and Formal Knowledge Systems
      Intermediaries play a crucial role in facilitating the integration of traditional knowledge systems into mainstream innovation processes, ensuring that the contributions of local communities are recognized and valued. They develop frameworks and tools

for the respectful and equitable co-creation of innovative solutions that combine traditional and contemporary knowledge (Agrawal, 1995; Sillitoe, 1998). By playing these multifaceted roles, innovation intermediaries can help to strengthen the overall grassroots innovation ecosystem, foster inclusive development, and unlock the transformative potential of traditional knowledge systems in addressing complex societal challenges.

b. Measuring the Impact and Sustainability of Grassroots Innovation Initiatives
Developing comprehensive impact assessment frameworks is crucial for understanding the multidimensional value and long-term sustainability of grassroots innovation initiatives in Africa. These frameworks should go beyond traditional economic metrics to capture the social, environmental, and community-level outcomes of these innovative solutions.

c. Participatory Evaluation Approaches
Actively engaging grassroots innovators, traditional knowledge holders, and community members in the design and implementation of impact assessment processes ensures that the evaluation reflects their priorities and perspectives. Employing qualitative and ethnographic research methods can capture the lived experiences, narratives, and transformative changes enabled by grassroots innovations (Berdegué, 2005; Seyfang & Smith, 2007).

d. Multidimensional Impact Indicators
Developing a balanced set of indicators that measure the economic, social, environmental, and cultural impacts of grassroots innovations, such as improvements in livelihoods, community well-being, biodiversity conservation, and the preservation of traditional knowledge, can provide a comprehensive understanding of their value. Aligning these impact indicators with the Sustainable Development Goals can demonstrate the contributions of grassroots innovation to the broader development agenda (Paunov, 2013; Ács et al., 2018).

e. Sustainability and Scalability Assessment
Evaluating the long-term viability and adaptability of grassroots innovations, including their ability to withstand shocks, respond

to evolving community needs, and be replicated or scaled across different contexts, is crucial. Assessing the strength of supporting institutional frameworks, collaborative partnerships, and community-level ownership can contribute to understanding the sustainability of these initiatives (Moleka, 2024a; Fressoli et al., 2014).

f. Collaborative Learning and Knowledge Sharing
Establishing platforms and networks that enable the exchange of impact data, case studies, and lessons learned among grassroots innovators, policymakers, researchers, and other stakeholders can foster collaborative learning and knowledge sharing. Promoting the use of open data and open science approaches can enhance the transparency and accessibility of impact assessment findings, catalyzing the replication and scaling of successful models (Clausen & Saeed, 2020; Kaplinsky, 2011).

g. Strengthening Institutional Capacities
Building the evaluation and monitoring capabilities of grassroots organizations, community-based initiatives, and local government agencies can enable them to continuously assess the impact and sustainability of their innovation efforts. Integrating grassroots innovation impact assessment frameworks within national and regional development monitoring systems can ensure that these initiatives are reflected in broader policy and planning processes (Berdegué, 2005; Ács et al., 2014). By adopting these holistic, participatory, and collaborative approaches to impact measurement, African nations can not only demonstrate the transformative potential of grassroots innovation and traditional knowledge systems but also generate valuable insights to guide the scaling and institutionalization of these inclusive, sustainable, and culturally-grounded development models.

By integrating grassroots innovation and traditional knowledge systems into mainstream development efforts, African nations can foster more equitable, sustainable, and culturally-relevant solutions that directly address the diverse needs and priorities of local communities, thereby accelerating progress towards the achievement of the Sustainable Development Goals. Through a holistic, collaborative, and community-driven approach, Africa can unlock new pathways for inclusive, sustainable, and culturally-grounded development that empowers local communities as active agents of change. This requires a strategic and multifaceted approach that recognizes and legitimizes traditional knowledge, protects intellectual property rights and ensures equitable benefit-sharing, bridges intergenerational knowledge gaps, addresses power imbalances and cultural biases, aligns traditional knowledge with contemporary innovation models, and strengthens collaborative ecosystems for traditional knowledge-based innovation. By harnessing the transformative power of grassroots innovation and traditional knowledge systems, African nations can foster a more equitable, resilient, and sustainable future – one that is rooted in the vibrant, creative, and community-driven solutions of the continent's diverse populations.

References

Ács, Z. J., Autio, E., & Szerb, L. (2014). National systems of entrepreneurship: Measurement issues and policy implications. *Research Policy*, 43(3), 476-494.

Ács, Z. J., Szerb, L., Ortega-Argilés, R., Ainsworth, E. A., & Meters, D. (2018). The entrepreneurial ecosystem: The regional entrepreneurship and development index. *Small Business Economics*, 51(2), 501-514.

Agrawal, A. (1995). Dismantling the divide between indigenous and scientific knowledge. *Development and change*, 26(3), 413-439.

Agarwal, N., Brem, A., & Grottke, M. (2018). Towards a higher socio-economic impact through shared understanding of product requirements in emerging markets: The case of jugaad-an innovative problem-solving approach. *Technological Forecasting and Social Change*, 135, 91-98.

Berdegué, J. A. (2005). *Pro-Poor Innovation Systems*. International Fund for Agricultural Development.

Berkes, F. (2012). *Sacred ecology*. Routledge.

Briggs, J. (2005). The use of indigenous knowledge in development: problems and challenges. *Progress in development studies*, 5(2), 99-114.

Briggs, J., & Sharp, J. (2004). Indigenous knowledges and development: a postcolonial caution. *Third World Quarterly*, 25(4), 661-676.

Brokensha, D., Warren, D. M., & Werner, O. (Eds.). (1980). *Indigenous knowledge systems and development* (Vol. 11). University Press of America.

Brush, C. G., Greene, P. G., & Zacharakis, A. (2019). The global entrepreneurship monitor (GEM) national entrepreneurship assessment: United States of America, 2018/2019 report. Global Entrepreneurship Research Association.

Clausen, T. H., & Saeed, A. (2020). Entrepreneurial ecosystems and indigenous entrepreneurship. *Journal of Enterprising Communities: People and Places in the Global Economy*, 14(4), 537-555.

Ely, A., & Oxley, N. (2014). *STEPS Centre Research on Grassroots Innovation Movements*. STEPS Centre.

Escobar, A. (1995). *Encountering development: The making and unmaking of the Third World*. Princeton University Press.

Fressoli, M., Arond, E., Abrol, D., Smith, A., Ely, A., & Dias, R. (2014). When grassroots innovation movements encounter mainstream institutions: implications for models of inclusive innovation. *Innovation and Development*, 4(2), 277-292.

Gupta, A. K. (2016). *Grassroots Innovation: Minds on the Margin are not Marginal Minds*. Penguin Random House India.

Kaplinsky, R. (2011). Schumacher meets Schumpeter: Appropriate technology below the radar. *Research Policy*, 40(2), 193-203.

Krishnan, R. T. (2010). *From Jugaad to Systematic Innovation: The Challenge for India*. Utpreraka Foundation.

Lwoga, E. T., Ngulube, P., & Stilwell, C. (2010). Managing indigenous knowledge for sustainable agricultural development in developing countries: Knowledge management approaches in the social context. *The International Information & Library Review*, 42(3), 174-185.

Manzini, E. (2014). Making things happen: Social innovation and design. *Design Issues*, 30(1), 57-66.

Mazzocchi, F. (2006). Western science and traditional knowledge: Despite their variations, different forms of knowledge can learn from each other. *EMBO reports*, 7(5), 463-466.

Moleka, P. (2024a). Innovative Leadership in Addressing Climate Change: A Pathway Towards Sustainable Futures.

Moleka, P. (2024b). *Grassroots Innovation Ecosystems: Catalyzing Inclusive and Sustainable Development in Africa*. Volume 1, Issue 5. Page: 01-08. www.wjims.com

Paunov, C. (2013). Innovation and Inclusive Development: A Discussion of the Main Policy Issues. *OECD Science, Technology and Industry Working Papers*, 2013/01, OECD Publishing.

Seyfang, G., & Smith, A. (2007). Grassroots innovations for sustainable development: Towards a new research and policy agenda. *Environmental politics*, 16(4), 584-603.

Sillitoe, P. (1998). The development of indigenous knowledge: a new applied anthropology. *Current anthropology*, 39(2), 223-252.

Srinivas, K. R. (2012). Protecting traditional knowledge holders' interests and preventing misappropriation—Traditional knowledge commons and sui generis models. *The WIPO Journal*, 3(2), 167-184.

CHAPTER 9

Policy Frameworks for Inclusive Innovation Ecosystems

Enabling policy and regulatory frameworks play a critical role in shaping the trajectory of inclusive innovation ecosystems in Africa. As the continent grapples with complex development challenges, the need for coherent, forward-looking policy approaches that nurture and empower diverse innovation actors has become increasingly evident. These policy frameworks not only set the stage for the effective deployment of inclusive innovation strategies but also signal the broader societal commitment to fostering equitable, sustainable, and community-driven development. This chapter delves into the pivotal role of policy in cultivating inclusive innovation ecosystems in Africa. It examines the current landscape of innovation-related policies, the key barriers and enablers, and the emerging best practices that are redefining the frontiers of inclusive development. By drawing on illustrative case studies and cutting-edge research, this chapter aims to provide a comprehensive understanding of how policymakers, in collaboration with diverse stakeholders, can design and implement transformative policy frameworks to unleash the full potential of inclusive innovation.

I. The Evolving Policy Landscape for Inclusive Innovation

Over the past decade, Africa has witnessed a growing recognition of the imperative for inclusive innovation among policymakers, governments, and development agencies. This recognition has manifested in the emergence of a diverse array of policy initiatives, strategies, and frameworks aimed at nurturing and empowering inclusive innovation ecosystems across the continent.

1. National Innovation Policies and Strategies
   Many African countries have introduced dedicated national innovation policies or strategies that explicitly recognize and prioritize the principles of inclusive innovation. These policy frameworks often outline clear objectives, targets, and implementation plans for fostering more equitable and participatory innovation ecosystems (Hokoma et al., 2018). For example, the Government of Kenya's National Innovation Agency has developed the Kenya National Innovation System Strategy, which emphasizes the importance of "inclusive innovation" and outlines specific interventions to support grassroots innovators, community-based organizations, and marginalized groups (Government of Kenya, 2020). Similarly, the South African Department of Science and Innovation has implemented the Inclusive Innovation Programme, which aims to "facilitate the inclusion of marginalized groups in the innovation value chain" (Department of Science and Innovation, 2021).
2. Inclusive Entrepreneurship and MSME Support Programs
   Governments and development agencies have rolled out a range of policies and initiatives to promote inclusive entrepreneurship, with a particular focus on supporting the growth and scaling of micro, small, and medium enterprises (MSMEs), which are often pivotal drivers of grassroots innovation (Masutha & Tengeh, 2015). The African Development Bank's Entrepreneurship and Small Business Development Strategy, for instance, emphasizes the need to "create an enabling environment for inclusive and sustainable entrepreneurship" through policy reforms, capacity building, and access to finance (African Development Bank, 2016). Similarly, the International Labour Organization's Start and Improve Your Business (SIYB) program has been implemented across multiple African countries, providing tailored support for the establishment and growth of MSMEs, with a focus on women and youth entrepreneurs (ILO, 2020).
3. Public Procurement and Innovation Incentives
   Some governments have implemented policies and regulations that leverage public procurement as a tool to drive the adoption and scaling of innovative solutions, with a focus on prioritizing inclusive,

community-driven initiatives (Edquist & Zabala-Iturriagagoitia, 2012). The Ugandan government's Public Procurement and Disposal of Public Assets Act, for example, includes provisions that require government agencies to reserve a portion of their procurement budgets for goods and services supplied by local MSMEs and disadvantaged groups (Public Procurement and Disposal of Public Assets Authority, 2003). Similarly, the Kenyan government's Buy Kenya, Build Kenya strategy encourages public institutions to procure locally produced goods and services, with the aim of supporting inclusive economic development (Government of Kenya, 2017).

4. Intellectual Property and Benefit-Sharing Frameworks
   Policymakers have begun to grapple with the need for more equitable and inclusive intellectual property (IP) regimes that recognize and protect the collective rights of local communities, traditional knowledge holders, and grassroots innovators (Srinivas, 2012). The African Regional Intellectual Property Organization (ARIPO) has developed the Swakopmund Protocol on the Protection of Traditional Knowledge and Expressions of Folklore, which provides a framework for the legal protection of traditional knowledge and the equitable sharing of benefits derived from its use (ARIPO, 2010). Similarly, the South African Indigenous Knowledge Systems Policy aims to "promote the protection, development and management of indigenous knowledge systems" and ensure the "equitable sharing of benefits" (Department of Science and Innovation, 2019).
5. Digital Inclusion and Open Data Policies
   Recognizing the centrality of digital technologies and open knowledge in driving inclusive innovation, some African countries have introduced policies and initiatives aimed at bridging the digital divide and promoting open access to data and digital resources (Gurstein, 2003; Diga, 2019). The Ghanaian government's Digital Inclusion Policy, for instance, outlines strategies to expand affordable internet access, enhance digital literacy, and promote the development of inclusive digital services and applications (Ministry of Communications, 2019). Similarly, the Open Data Policy of the African Development Bank commits the institution to "increasing access to and use of open data to foster inclusive development" (African Development Bank, 2020).

Science, Technology, and Innovation (STI) Policy Integration Several African nations have sought to integrate inclusive innovation principles into their broader STI policy frameworks, aligning these with national development priorities and the Sustainable Development Goals (SDGs) (Essegbey et al., 2015). The Senegalese National Strategy for the Development of Science, Technology and Innovation, for example, emphasizes the need to "promote inclusive innovation that addresses the needs of marginalized communities" and outlines specific initiatives to support grassroots innovators and community-based organizations (Government of Senegal, 2017). Similarly, the Ethiopian Science, Technology and Innovation Policy highlights the importance of "inclusive and participatory innovation" in driving sustainable development (Ministry of Science and Higher Education, 2019). While these policy developments represent important strides towards cultivating more inclusive innovation ecosystems, significant challenges and gaps remain, underscoring the need for a more holistic, multi-stakeholder approach to policy design and implementation.

II. Barriers to Effective Policy Implementation

Despite the growing momentum around inclusive innovation policies in Africa, several key barriers continue to hinder their effective implementation and impact.

1. Lack of Policy Coherence and Coordination
   Fragmented and siloed policymaking approaches, often driven by competing priorities and agendas, can undermine the overall effectiveness and synergies of inclusive innovation policies (Borrás & Edquist, 2013). The lack of coordination among different government agencies, as well as between national and subnational levels of government, can lead to duplication, inefficiencies, and the failure to leverage complementary initiatives (Marques et al., 2020).
2. Institutional Capacity Constraints
   Many government agencies and policymaking bodies lack the specialized expertise, resources, and institutional structures required to

effectively design, implement, and monitor inclusive innovation policies (Marques et al., 2020). This can result in the adoption of generic, one-size-fits-all approaches that fail to address the unique needs and contexts of diverse innovation actors.

3. Misalignment with Dominant Innovation Models
   Existing policy frameworks may be biased towards traditional, technology-driven innovation models, failing to adequately recognize and support the diverse manifestations of grassroots, frugal, and social innovation (Agrawal, 1995). This misalignment can lead to the marginalization of alternative innovation practices and the under-prioritization of inclusive innovation in policy agendas.
4. Insufficient Stakeholder Engagement and Participation
   The formulation and implementation of inclusive innovation policies often fall short in meaningfully engaging and empowering diverse ecosystem actors, particularly marginalized communities and grassroots innovators (Briggs & Sharp, 2004). This can result in the development of policies that are misaligned with the needs and priorities of local stakeholders, undermining their effectiveness and legitimacy.
5. Entrenched Power Dynamics and Vested Interests
   Deeply rooted power structures and the resistance of dominant actors to disruptive, community-driven innovation can undermine the effective translation of inclusive innovation policies into tangible outcomes (Marques et al., 2020). Addressing these entrenched power imbalances and vested interests requires a concerted effort to transform existing power dynamics and foster more inclusive governance mechanisms.
6. Challenges in Monitoring, Evaluation, and Learning

The lack of robust, context-appropriate frameworks for measuring the impact and effectiveness of inclusive innovation policies hinders evidence-based policymaking and adaptive learning (Hadfield-Hill & Roulston, 2020). Without a clear understanding of the multidimensional outcomes and systemic effects of these policies, policymakers struggle to identify and scale successful approaches. Overcoming these barriers and creating an enabling policy environment for inclusive innovation requires a multifaceted approach that addresses the systemic, institutional, and sociopolitical dimensions of policymaking.

III. Strategies for Designing Inclusive Innovation Policy Frameworks

To cultivate effective and impactful policy frameworks for inclusive innovation ecosystems in Africa, the following strategies can be employed:

1. Fostering Policy Coherence and Coordination
   - Establish dedicated inter-ministerial or cross-agency coordination mechanisms to align inclusive innovation policies and initiatives across different government departments and levels (Borrás & Edquist, 2013).
   - Promote the integration of inclusive innovation principles into broader national development strategies, industrial policies, and sectoral plans, ensuring policy coherence and alignment (Essegbey et al., 2015).
   - Facilitate regular multi-stakeholder dialogues and policy review processes to ensure continuous alignment and adaptation, responding to evolving ecosystem needs and emerging trends (Marques et al., 2020).
2. Strengthening Institutional Capacities and Structures
   - Invest in the capacity-building of government agencies and policymaking bodies to enhance their understanding of inclusive innovation principles and their ability to design, implement, and monitor relevant policies (Marques et al., 2020).
   - Develop specialized units or innovation policy councils to champion the mainstreaming of inclusive innovation within government institutions, providing technical expertise and coordinating cross-departmental initiatives (Hokoma et al., 2018).
   - Encourage the adoption of flexible, adaptive, and cross-functional organizational structures that enable responsive policymaking, fostering collaboration and knowledge-sharing across different agencies and levels of government (Marques et al., 2020).
3. Aligning Policies with Diverse Innovation Models
   - Conduct in-depth assessments of the diverse innovation landscape, including grassroots, frugal, and social innovation practices, to inform the design of inclusive policy frameworks (Agrawal, 1995).
   - Develop policies that recognize, incentivize, and support a wide range of innovation approaches, from community-driven solutions

to high-tech, knowledge-intensive initiatives, ensuring a level playing field for diverse innovation actors (Gupta, 2016; Moleka, 2024a, 2024b).
- Ensure that policy instruments and implementation mechanisms are tailored to the unique needs and contexts of different innovation actors and communities, promoting inclusivity and responsiveness (Agarwal et al., 2018).

4. Fostering Multi-Stakeholder Engagement and Participation
   - Implement inclusive, participatory policymaking processes that actively engage and empower diverse ecosystem actors, including grassroots innovators, community organizations, civil society groups, and marginalized communities (Briggs & Sharp, 2004).
   - Establish permanent consultation and feedback mechanisms to ensure the continuous incorporation of stakeholder perspectives and lived experiences into policy design and refinement (Ely & Oxley, 2014).
   - Promote the representation and leadership of traditionally underrepresented groups, such as women, youth, and Indigenous communities, in policymaking bodies and decision-making processes, ensuring the equitable distribution of power and decision-making authority (Clausen & Saeed, 2020).
5. Addressing Power Dynamics and Vested Interests
   - Identify and address the underlying power imbalances, social hierarchies, and entrenched interests that may impede the effective implementation of inclusive innovation policies (Escobar, 1995).
   - Implement measures to safeguard the rights and equitable participation of marginalized groups, such as traditional knowledge holders and grassroots innovators, within policy frameworks, ensuring the protection of their intellectual property and fair distribution of benefits (Srinivas, 2012).
   - Foster a culture of transparency, accountability, and strong anti-corruption measures to build trust and ensure the equitable distribution of resources and opportunities within the innovation ecosystem (Marques et al., 2020).
6. Enhancing Monitoring, Evaluation, and Learning
   - Develop comprehensive, context-appropriate monitoring and evaluation frameworks that capture the multidimensional impacts of

inclusive innovation policies, including social, economic, and environmental outcomes (Hadfield-Hill & Roulston, 2020).

- Implement robust data collection, analysis, and knowledge management systems to facilitate evidence-based policymaking and adaptive learning, enabling the continuous refinement and improvement of inclusive innovation policies (Paunov, 2013).
- Establish platforms and mechanisms for the continuous sharing of best practices, lessons learned, and innovative policy approaches across different jurisdictions and levels of government, promoting cross-pollination and collaborative learning (Clausen & Saeed, 2020).

By adopting a holistic, collaborative, and community-centric approach to policymaking, African nations can cultivate an enabling environment that nurtures and empowers inclusive innovation ecosystems, ultimately driving more equitable, sustainable, and impactful development outcomes across the continent.

IV. Aligning Inclusive Innovation Policies with the Sustainable Development Goals

The Sustainable Development Goals (SDGs) provide a compelling and comprehensive framework for aligning inclusive innovation policies in Africa. By harnessing the transformative potential of inclusive innovation to address complex development challenges, policymakers can drive progress towards the achievement of the SDGs.

1. Mapping Inclusive Innovation Initiatives to SDG Targets
   - Conducting in-depth assessments to identify the specific SDG targets and indicators that can be advanced through inclusive innovation policies and programs, such as those related to poverty alleviation, food security, affordable and clean energy, sustainable cities, and climate action (Ács et al., 2014, 2018; Moleka, 2024b).
   - Developing robust monitoring and evaluation frameworks to track the contributions of inclusive innovation interventions to the realization of the SDGs, capturing both quantitative and qualitative outcomes (Paunov, 2013; Hadfield-Hill & Roulston, 2020).

2. Integrating Inclusive Innovation into National Development Plans
   - Embedding inclusive innovation principles and strategies within national development plans, industrial policies, and economic transformation agendas that are aligned with the SDGs (Essegbey et al., 2015).
   - Ensuring that inclusive innovation initiatives are adequately resourced and prioritized within national budgeting and public investment processes, signaling a strong commitment to sustainable and equitable development (Berdegué, 2005).
3. Fostering Multi-Stakeholder Partnerships for SDG-Aligned Innovation
   - Promoting collaborative platforms and mechanisms that bring together diverse ecosystem actors, such as government agencies, private sector, academia, and civil society, to co-create inclusive innovation solutions that address SDG priorities (Fressoli et al., 2014).
   - Leveraging global and regional development cooperation frameworks, such as the African Union's Agenda 2063 and the United Nations' SDG partnerships, to mobilize technical and financial support for the implementation of inclusive innovation policies and programs (Essegbey et al., 2015).
4. Strengthening Policy Coherence and Policy Learning
   - Enhancing coordination and cross-learning among policymakers responsible for inclusive innovation, sustainable development, and other related policy domains to ensure holistic, SDG-aligned approaches (Borrás & Edquist, 2013).
   - Facilitating the exchange of good practices, case studies, and lessons learned across African countries and with the global development community to drive continuous improvement and adaptation of inclusive innovation policies (Clausen & Saeed, 2020).
5. Empowering Marginalized Communities as Innovation Partners
   - Ensuring that the design and implementation of inclusive innovation policies actively engage and empower marginalized communities, including women, youth, and Indigenous groups, as co-creators and beneficiaries, aligned with the SDG principle of leaving no one behind (Briggs & Sharp, 2004; Clausen & Saeed, 2020).
   - Implementing measures to protect the rights, intellectual property, and equitable participation of local communities in the innovation

process, ensuring that the benefits of inclusive innovation are distributed fairly and equitably (Srinivas, 2012).
- By strategically aligning inclusive innovation policies with the Sustainable Development Goals, African nations can unlock synergies, amplify impact, and drive more holistic, equitable, and sustainable development outcomes across the continent.

V. Inclusive Innovation Policies and the Digital Transformation Agenda

The rapid digital transformation sweeping across Africa presents both opportunities and challenges for the design and implementation of inclusive innovation policies. Harnessing the power of digital technologies can enable more inclusive, accessible, and scalable innovation ecosystems, but it also requires proactive measures to address the digital divide and ensure equitable access.

1. Bridging the Digital Divide
   - Implementing policies and public investment programs that expand affordable, reliable, and inclusive digital infrastructure and connectivity, particularly in underserved rural and peri-urban areas (Diga, 2019).
   - Developing digital skills and literacy programs that empower marginalized communities, including women, youth, and persons with disabilities, to actively participate in the digital economy, ensuring that no one is left behind (Gurstein, 2003).
2. Promoting Open Data and Open Innovation
   - Enacting policies and regulations that enable open access to government data, research, and innovation resources, fostering collaborative, community-driven innovation (Gurstein, 2003).
   - Incentivizing the development and deployment of open-source technologies, digital platforms, and collaborative innovation models that are accessible to a wide range of innovation actors, promoting inclusivity and knowledge-sharing (Berdegué, 2005).
   - Implementing policies that support the development and scaling of digital solutions, tools, and services that address the unique needs

and challenges faced by marginalized communities, such as digital platforms for grassroots innovators or mobile-based healthcare applications (Moleka, 2024a, 2024b).
- Fostering public-private partnerships and innovation challenges that leverage emerging digital technologies, such as artificial intelligence, blockchain, and the Internet of Things, to drive inclusive and sustainable development outcomes (Fressoli et al., 2014).

3. Protecting Digital Rights and Data Governance
   - Developing comprehensive data protection, privacy, and digital rights frameworks to safeguard the interests and participation of marginalized groups within the digital economy, ensuring that their data and personal information are secured and their digital rights are protected (Diga, 2019).
   - Empowering local communities, including traditional knowledge holders, to assert their rights and participate in the governance of digital platforms and innovation ecosystems, promoting equitable and community-centric approaches to data ownership and management (Srinivas, 2012).
4. Strengthening Digital Innovation Ecosystems
   - Investing in the establishment of inclusive digital innovation hubs, makerspaces, and incubators that provide tailored support, resources, and networking opportunities for diverse innovation actors, including grassroots innovators and marginalized communities (Clausen & Saeed, 2020).
   - Encouraging the integration of digital skills, tools, and mindsets within inclusive entrepreneurship programs and grassroots innovation initiatives, empowering local communities to leverage digital technologies for their own development needs and priorities (Krishnan, 2010).
   - By strategically aligning inclusive innovation policies with the digital transformation agenda, African nations can harness the power of emerging technologies to drive more equitable, sustainable, and community-centric development outcomes across the continent.

VI. Measuring the Impact of Inclusive Innovation Policies

Effective monitoring and evaluation (M&E) frameworks are crucial for understanding the impact and effectiveness of inclusive innovation policies, as well as informing evidence-based policymaking and continuous improvement.

1. Multidimensional Impact Assessment
   - Evaluating the economic, social, environmental, and community-level impacts of inclusive innovation policies and initiatives, capturing both quantitative and qualitative outcomes aligned with the Sustainable Development Goals (Ács et al., 2014, 2018; Paunov, 2013).
   - Developing a balanced set of impact indicators that measure the contributions of inclusive innovation to poverty alleviation, food security, affordable and clean energy, sustainable cities, climate action, and other relevant SDG targets (Moleka, 2024b).
2. Participatory Evaluation Approaches
   - Engaging diverse ecosystem stakeholders, including marginalized communities, grassroots innovators, and policymakers, in the design and implementation of M&E processes to ensure their perspectives and priorities are reflected (Berdegué, 2005; Seyfang & Smith, 2007).
   - Employing a mix of quantitative and qualitative methods, such as surveys, focus groups, and ethnographic research, to capture the lived experiences and transformative changes enabled by inclusive innovation policies (Ely & Oxley, 2014; Fressoli et al., 2014).
3. Policy Implementation and Ecosystem Analysis
   - Assessing the effectiveness of policy design, coordination, and implementation mechanisms in fostering a conducive environment for inclusive innovation, identifying structural and institutional barriers (Marques et al., 2020).
   - Evaluating the strength and resilience of the broader innovation ecosystem, including the capacity of supporting institutions, the depth of collaborative partnerships, and the sustainability of inclusive innovation models (Clausen & Saeed, 2020; Paunov, 2013).

4. Inclusive Data Collection and Disaggregation
   Ensuring that data collection and analysis processes are inclusive, capturing the participation and outcomes of underrepresented groups, such as women, youth, and ethnic minorities (Paunov, 2013).
   Developing specialized data collection and monitoring tools that empower marginalized communities to actively participate in the assessment of inclusive innovation policies and initiatives, strengthening their agency and ownership (Berdegué, 2005).
5. Collaborative Learning and Knowledge-Sharing
   · Establishing platforms and networks that enable the exchange of M&E findings, best practices, and lessons learned among policymakers, researchers, and practitioners working on inclusive innovation, promoting cross-pollination and continuous improvement (Clausen & Saeed, 2020). - Promoting the use of open data and open science approaches to enhance the transparency and accessibility of policy impact assessments, catalyzing the replication and scaling of successful inclusive innovation models across different contexts (Paunov, 2013).

By adopting a comprehensive, participatory, and collaborative approach to measuring the impact of inclusive innovation policies, African nations can not only demonstrate the tangible outcomes of these transformative efforts but also generate valuable insights to guide the continuous refinement and scaling of inclusive innovation ecosystems across the continent.

VII. Comparative Analysis of Inclusive Innovation Policies: Lessons from Latin America and Southeast Asia

In the quest to develop effective policy frameworks for inclusive innovation, it is valuable to draw insights from other emerging regions, such as Latin America and Southeast Asia. These regions, though geographically and culturally distinct, have shared experiences in fostering inclusive innovation to address issues of inequality, access to technology, and social inclusion. By comparing their experiences with those of African nations, we can identify best practices, lessons learned, and potential pitfalls in shaping inclusive innovation policies that are both locally relevant and globally competitive.

1. Latin America: A Focus on Social Inclusion and Frugal Innovation
   Latin America, particularly countries like Brazil, Mexico, and Argentina, has made significant strides in integrating inclusive innovation into national policy frameworks. A key aspect of their approach has been the emphasis on social inclusion—using innovation to address disparities in education, health, and income among marginalized groups.
   - Social Innovation Initiatives: Latin American countries have implemented various social innovation policies that encourage the development of products and services tailored to the needs of disadvantaged communities. For example, Brazil's Inclusive Innovation Programme supports innovations that create economic opportunities for the poor by promoting affordable healthcare solutions and clean energy technologies (García et al., 2018).
   - Frugal Innovation: The region has also adopted frugal innovation strategies, particularly in sectors like healthcare, where cost-effective technologies have been designed to meet the needs of underserved populations. This approach mirrors similar efforts in Africa, where appropriate technologies are used to address local challenges. For instance, low-cost mobile health solutions have been widely deployed in both Latin America and Africa to improve healthcare access in remote areas (Smith et al., 2020).
   - Public Policy and Engagement: Latin America's experience highlights the role of strong public-private partnerships in supporting inclusive innovation. Mexico's National Institute of Entrepreneurs (INADEM) fosters innovation-driven entrepreneurship, particularly among SMEs, through tailored funding programs and capacity-building initiatives (González-Pérez, 2019). This approach could offer valuable lessons for African nations looking to empower local innovators through similar government-backed support systems.
2. Southeast Asia: Leveraging Technology for Inclusive Growth
   Southeast Asia has also been at the forefront of integrating inclusive innovation into development policies, particularly in countries like Indonesia, the Philippines, and Thailand. The region's focus on technological inclusion has enabled significant strides in providing access to technology and innovation, even in rural and remote areas.

- Digital Inclusion and Technology for Social Impact: Southeast Asian nations have focused on digital inclusion as a pathway to achieving inclusive growth. For example, Indonesia's 100 Smart Cities initiative aims to integrate technology into urban and rural areas to promote inclusive economic opportunities and improve service delivery (Abo et al., 2020). Similarly, Africa could consider expanding its own digital infrastructure to empower marginalized communities with access to innovative solutions.
- Cross-Sectoral Collaboration: Southeast Asia has successfully implemented cross-sectoral innovation programs that align government efforts with the private sector's resources. Thailand's Innovation Development Fund fosters collaboration between universities, government agencies, and private businesses to develop innovative solutions for social and environmental challenges. This multi-stakeholder approach could offer valuable lessons for African policymakers looking to strengthen collaboration across various sectors.
- Inclusive Entrepreneurship Ecosystems: Southeast Asia has created thriving inclusive entrepreneurship ecosystems, particularly through microfinance and small-scale business incubation programs. In the Philippines, organizations like the Philippine Business for Social Progress have supported thousands of micro-entrepreneurs, helping them access finance and market opportunities (Tayag, 2017). African nations can similarly develop policies that encourage the growth of micro-entrepreneurship in marginalized communities, offering financial services and capacity-building programs tailored to local needs.

3. Drawing Parallels: Key Lessons for Africa

1° Emphasis on Community-Centric Innovation: Both Latin America and Southeast Asia have prioritized community-driven innovation, which ensures that policies reflect the needs and aspirations of marginalized groups. For Africa, this underscores the importance of engaging local communities directly in the innovation process to create contextually relevant solutions.

2° Collaboration Between Public and Private Sectors: A standout feature in both Latin America and Southeast Asia is the role of public-private partnerships in driving inclusive innovation. For African nations, fostering collaboration between government agencies, private companies, and civil society is crucial to create a sustainable ecosystem for innovation.

3° Frugal and Appropriate Technologies: Frugal innovation is a common thread in both Latin America and Southeast Asia, where cost-effective solutions are developed to serve low-income populations. African countries can benefit from adopting similar strategies by promoting appropriate technologies tailored to local challenges, particularly in sectors like healthcare, energy, and agriculture.

4° Building Inclusive Entrepreneurship Ecosystems: The support of inclusive entrepreneurship through funding, mentorship, and capacity-building has proven successful in Southeast Asia and Latin America. African nations could scale similar initiatives, fostering a culture of innovation among youth, women, and other marginalized groups.

5° Integrating Digital Technologies for Development: Southeast Asia's focus on digital inclusion and leveraging technology for social good offers a clear roadmap for Africa. Policies that promote internet access and digital literacy in marginalized areas can enhance Africa's innovation capacity.

The comparison with Latin America and Southeast Asia offers several actionable insights for African nations as they design and implement inclusive innovation policies.

Conclusion

By integrating grassroots innovation and traditional knowledge systems into mainstream development efforts, African nations can foster more equitable, sustainable, and culturally-relevant solutions that directly address the diverse needs and priorities of local communities, thereby accelerating progress towards the achievement of the Sustainable Development Goals. Through a holistic, collaborative, and community-driven approach to policymaking, African nations can cultivate an enabling environment that nurtures and empowers inclusive innovation ecosystems. This requires fostering policy coherence and coordination, strengthening institutional capacities, aligning policies with diverse innovation models, facilitating multi-stakeholder engagement, addressing power dynamics and vested interests, and enhancing monitoring, evaluation, and learning. By strategically aligning inclusive innovation policies with the Sustainable Development Goals and the digital transformation agenda, African nations can unlock synergies, amplify impact, and drive more equitable, sustainable, and community-centric development outcomes across the continent. Comprehensive impact assessment frameworks that capture the multidimensional value of inclusive innovation initiatives are crucial for informing evidence-based policymaking and continuous improvement. Through this holistic, inclusive, and collaborative approach to policymaking, Africa can unlock new pathways for unleashing the transformative power of grassroots innovation and traditional knowledge systems, ultimately catalyzing a more equitable, resilient, and sustainable future for all.

References

Abo, A., et al. (2020). Digital Inclusion and Innovation for Sustainable Development in Southeast Asia. *Technology and Development Journal*, 18(3), 123-135.

Ács, Z. J., Autio, E., & Szerb, L. (2014). National systems of entrepreneurship: Measurement issues and policy implications. *Research Policy*, 43(3), 476-494.

Ács, Z. J., Szerb, L., Ortega-Argilés, R., Ainsworth, E. A., & Meters, D. (2018). The entrepreneurial ecosystem: The regional entrepreneurship and development index. *Small Business Economics*, 51(2), 501-514.

Agarwal, N., Brem, A., & Grottke, M. (2018). Towards a higher socio-economic impact through shared understanding of product requirements in emerging markets: The case of jugaad-an innovative problem-solving approach. *Technological Forecasting and Social Change*, 135, 91-98.

Agrawal, A. (1995). Dismantling the divide between indigenous and scientific knowledge. *Development and change*, 26(3), 413-439.

African Development Bank. (2016). Entrepreneurship and Small Business Development Strategy 2016-2020. https://www.afdb.org/en/documents/document/entrepreneurship-and-small-business-development-strategy-2016-2020-87354

African Development Bank. (2020). Open Data Policy. https://www.afdb.org/en/documents/african-development-bank-group-open-data-policy

ARIPO. (2010). Swakopmund Protocol on the Protection of Traditional Knowledge and Expressions of Folklore. https://www.wipo.int/edocs/lexdocs/treaties/en/ap010/trt_ap010.pdf

Berdegué, J. A. (2005). *Pro-Poor Innovation Systems*. International Fund for Agricultural Development.

Berkes, F. (2012). *Sacred ecology*. Routledge.

Borrás, S., & Edquist, C. (2013). The choice of innovation policy instruments. *Technological Forecasting and Social Change*, 80(8), 1513-1522.

Briggs, J., & Sharp, J. (2004). Indigenous knowledges and development: a postcolonial caution. *Third World Quarterly*, 25(4), 661-676.

Briggs, J. (2005). The use of indigenous knowledge in development: problems and challenges. *Progress in development studies*, 5(2), 99-114.

Brokensha, D., Warren, D. M., & Werner, O. (Eds.). (1980). *Indigenous knowledge systems and development* (Vol. 11). University Press of America.

Clausen, T. H., & Saeed, A. (2020). Entrepreneurial ecosystems and indigenous entrepreneurship. *Journal of Enterprising Communities: People and Places in the Global Economy*, 14(4), 537-555.

Department of Science and Innovation. (2019). Indigenous Knowledge Systems Policy. https://www.dst.gov.za/index.php/resource-center/strategies-and-reports/2626-indigenous-knowledge-systems-policy

Department of Science and Innovation. (2021). Inclusive Innovation Programme. https://www.dst.gov.za/index.php/strategic-programmatic-focus/inclusive-innovation-programme

Diga, K. (2019). Digital inequality and the roles of technology in Africa. In *Routledge Handbook of Digital Media and Communication* (pp. 361-372). Routledge.

Edquist, C., & Zabala-Iturriagagoitia, J. M. (2012). Public Procurement for Innovation as mission-oriented innovation policy. *Research Policy*, 41(10), 1757-1769.

Ely, A., & Oxley, N. (2014). *STEPS Centre Research on Grassroots Innovation Movements*. STEPS Centre.

Escobar, A. (1995). *Encountering development: The making and unmaking of the Third World*. Princeton University Press.

Essegbey, G. O., Omolo, A., & Oyelaran-Oyeyinka, B. (2015). Africa-Japan partnership in science, technology and innovation: Challenges, opportunities and the role of TICAD VI. *African Journal of Science, Technology, Innovation and Development*, 7(6), 480-487.

Fressoli, M., Arond, E., Abrol, D., Smith, A., Ely, A., & Dias, R. (2014). When grassroots innovation movements encounter mainstream institutions: implications for models of inclusive innovation. *Innovation and Development*, 4(2), 277-292.

García, J., et al. (2018). "Inclusive Innovation and Social Impact in Latin America: Lessons from Brazil's National Innovation Program." *Latin American Innovation Review*, 12(2), 98-110.

González-Pérez, M. A. (2019). "Government Support for Inclusive Innovation: Mexico's National Institute of Entrepreneurs." *Innovation Policy and Economic Development*, 5(3), 142-160.

Government of Kenya. (2017). Buy Kenya, Build Kenya Strategy. https://www.industrialization.go.ke/images/downloads/buy-kenya-build-kenya-strategy.pdf

Government of Kenya. (2020). National Innovation Agency. https://nia.go.ke/

Government of Senegal. (2017). National Strategy for the Development of Science, Technology and Innovation. https://www.gouv.sn/Strategie-Nationale-de-Developpement-de-la-Science-de-la-Technologie-et-de-l-Innovation.html

Gupta, A. K. (2016). *Grassroots Innovation: Minds on the Margin are not Marginal Minds*. Penguin Random House India.

Gurstein, M. (2003). Effective use: A community informatics strategy beyond the digital divide. *First Monday*, 8(12).

Hadfield-Hill, S., & Roulston, S. (2020). Monitoring and evaluating transdisciplinary research: a systematic approach. *International Journal of Sustainable Development & World Ecology*, 27(6), 517-532.

Hill, S., & Roulston, S. (2020). Monitoring and evaluating transdisciplinary research: a systematic approach. *International Journal of Sustainable Development & World Ecology*, 27(6), 517-532.

Hokoma, M. A., Kader, R. A. A., & Crompton, H. (2018). The current status of technology transfer offices (TTOs) in African universities: Perspectives from the literature. *Journal of Innovation and Entrepreneurship*, 7(1), 1-13.

ILO. (2020). Start and Improve Your Business (SIYB) Programme. https://www.ilo.org/empent/Projects/WCMS_141268/lang--en/index.htm Kaplinsky, R.

(2011). Schumacher meets Schumpeter: Appropriate technology below the radar. *Research Policy*, 40(2), 193-203.

Krishnan, R. T. (2010). *From Jugaad to Systematic Innovation: The Challenge for India*. Utpreraka Foundation.

Lwoga, E. T., Ngulube, P., & Stilwell, C. (2010). Managing indigenous knowledge for sustainable agricultural development in developing countries: Knowledge management approaches in the social context. *The International Information & Library Review*, 42(3), 174-185.

Marques, J. C., Zeng, K., Roberts, J. A., & Roth, C. (2020). Institutional complexity and organizational change: Fostering collaborative innovation in the public sector. *Public Administration Review*, 80(3), 457-472.

Masutha, M., & Tengeh, R. K. (2015). Small business development in a township in South Africa: A focus on the critical role of business incubators. *Mediterranean Journal of Social Sciences*, 6(6), 264-264.

Mazzocchi, F. (2006). Western science and traditional knowledge: Despite their variations, different forms of knowledge can learn from each other. *EMBO reports*, 7(5), 463-466.

Ministry of Communications. (2019). Digital Inclusion Policy. https://moc.gov.gh/sites/default/files/downloads/digital-inclusion-policy.pdf

Ministry of Science and Higher Education. (2019). Science, Technology and Innovation Policy. https://www.most.gov.et/policies-and-strategies
Moleka, P. (2024a). Innovative Leadership in Addressing Climate Change: A Pathway Towards Sustainable Futures.

Moleka, P. (2024b). Grassroots Innovation Ecosystems: Catalyzing Inclusive and Sustainable Development in Africa. Volume 1, Issue 5. Page: 01-08. www.wjims.com

Paunov, C. (2013). Innovation and Inclusive Development: A Discussion of the Main Policy Issues. *OECD Science, Technology and Industry Working Papers*, 2013/01, OECD Publishing.

Public Procurement and Disposal of Public Assets Authority. (2003). Public Procurement and Disposal of Public Assets Act. https://www.ppda.go.ug/wp-content/uploads/2020/05/PPDA-Act-2003.pdf

Seyfang, G., & Smith, A. (2007). Grassroots innovations for sustainable development: Towards a new research and policy agenda. *Environmental politics*, 16(4), 584-603.

Sillitoe, P. (1998). The development of indigenous knowledge: a new applied anthropology. *Current anthropology*, 39(2), 223-252.

Smith, R., et al. (2020). Frugal Innovation and the Global South: Lessons from Latin America and Africa. *Frugal Innovation Journal*, 7(2), 101-120.

Srinivas, S. (2012). Empowering Marginalized Communities: Indigenous Innovations in Latin America. *International Journal of Inclusive Development*, 22(4), 153-169.

Tayag, P. (2017). Microfinance and Inclusive Innovation in Southeast Asia: The Philippine Experience. *Asian Development Review*, 25(2), 89-104.

CHAPTER 10

Inclusive Innovation and the Sustainable Development Goals

The adoption of the United Nations Sustainable Development Goals (SDGs) in 2015 marked a pivotal moment in the global development landscape, ushering in a transformative agenda that calls for integrated, collaborative, and people-centered approaches to addressing the world's most pressing challenges. At the heart of this ambitious framework lies the recognition that meaningful and lasting progress can only be achieved through the active participation and empowerment of marginalized communities, whose needs and perspectives have too often been overlooked in traditional development models. This chapter explores the critical intersection between inclusive innovation and the SDGs, examining how the principles and practices of inclusive innovation can be strategically aligned to drive the realization of this transformative global agenda in the African context. By delving into the diverse ways in which inclusive innovation can contribute to the achievement of the SDGs, this chapter will provide a comprehensive understanding of the key enablers, challenges, and innovative strategies that can help harness the power of inclusive innovation to create a more equitable, sustainable, and prosperous future for all.

I. The Sustainable Development Goals: A Holistic Approach to Global Challenges

Adopted by all United Nations member states in 2015, the Sustainable Development Goals represent a comprehensive framework of 17 interlinked goals and 169 targets that aim to address the most pressing social, economic, and environmental challenges facing the world (United Nations, 2015). In contrast to the Millennium Development Goals (MDGs), which were primarily focused on poverty reduction and basic service delivery, the SDGs take a more holistic and integrated approach, addressing a wide range of interconnected issues, from climate change and sustainable energy to gender equality and inclusive economic growth. The SDGs are underpinned by the principle of leaving no one behind, emphasizing the critical importance of ensuring that the development process benefits all members of society, particularly the most marginalized and vulnerable groups. This inclusive ethos is reflected in the SDGs' emphasis on empowering women and girls, promoting decent work and economic opportunities, reducing inequalities, and fostering participatory decision-making processes (United Nations, 2015). Moreover, the SDGs recognize the pivotal role of innovation, technology, and knowledge-sharing in driving sustainable development.

Goal 9, for instance, explicitly calls for building resilient infrastructure, promoting inclusive and sustainable industrialization, and fostering innovation, while Goal 17 highlights the need for strengthening global partnerships and mobilizing resources to support the achievement of the SDGs (United Nations, 2015).

II. Aligning Inclusive Innovation with the Sustainable Development Goals

The principles and practices of inclusive innovation are inherently aligned with the holistic, people-centered approach embodied by the Sustainable Development Goals. By empowering marginalized communities as active participants in the innovation process, inclusive innovation holds the potential to contribute to the realization of multiple SDGs simultaneously, addressing a wide range of interconnected development challenges (Schillo & Robinson, 2017).

1. Poverty Reduction and Inclusive Growth (SDG 1 and SDG 8)
   - Inclusive innovation can drive the development of affordable and accessible products and services that address the needs of low-income and underserved communities, contributing to poverty reduction and promoting inclusive economic growth.
   - Grassroots innovations and social enterprises can create new livelihood opportunities and pathways for marginalized groups, particularly in

the informal sector, fostering decent work and sustainable economic development.

2. Zero Hunger and Sustainable Agriculture (SDG 2)
   - Inclusive innovation in the agricultural sector can improve food security, enhance agricultural productivity, and promote sustainable farming practices that are responsive to the needs and knowledge of small-scale and subsistence farmers.
   - The integration of traditional knowledge systems and community-based innovations can help develop context-appropriate solutions for sustainable land use, water management, and crop diversification.
3. Good Health and Well-being (SDG 3)
   - Inclusive innovation in the healthcare sector can improve access to affordable, quality medical products and services, particularly in underserved rural and urban communities.
   - Community-driven innovations and traditional medicine practices can complement formal healthcare systems, addressing the unique health needs and preferences of local populations.
4. Quality Education and Lifelong Learning (SDG 4)
   - Inclusive innovation in education can promote access to affordable, culturally-relevant learning materials and tools, empowering marginalized communities and ensuring equal opportunities for quality education. - The integration of traditional knowledge and indigenous pedagogical approaches into educational curricula can foster more inclusive and holistic learning experiences.
5. Gender Equality and Women's Empowerment (SDG 5)
   - Inclusive innovation can create new economic and leadership opportunities for women, addressing systemic barriers and promoting their meaningful participation in the innovation process.
   - The inclusion of women's traditional knowledge and community-based innovations can enhance the development of gender-responsive solutions that address the unique needs and challenges faced by women and girls.
6. Clean Water and Sanitation (SDG 6)
   - Inclusive innovation in water and sanitation can improve access to safe, affordable, and sustainable water resources, particularly in underserved and marginalized communities.

- The integration of traditional water management practices and community-driven innovations can help develop culturally-appropriate and environmentally-friendly water solutions.

7. Affordable and Clean Energy (SDG 7)
   - Inclusive innovation can drive the development and deployment of decentralized, off-grid renewable energy solutions that are tailored to the needs and resources of local communities.
   - Grassroots innovators and traditional knowledge holders can play a vital role in designing and implementing community-based energy systems that promote energy access and self-sufficiency.
8. Decent Work and Economic Growth (SDG 8)
   - Inclusive innovation can foster the growth of sustainable, values-driven enterprises that create quality jobs and livelihood opportunities for marginalized groups, particularly in the informal sector.
   - The integration of traditional knowledge and community-based innovations can help develop new business models and economic activities that are rooted in local contexts and responsive to local needs.
9. Industry, Innovation, and Infrastructure (SDG 9)
   - Inclusive innovation can promote the development of affordable, adaptable, and accessible infrastructure and technological solutions that address the unique needs and constraints of marginalized communities.
   - The incorporation of traditional knowledge and grassroots innovations can inform the design and deployment of more context-appropriate and environmentally-sustainable industrial and infrastructure systems.
10. Reduced Inequalities (SDG 10)
    - Inclusive innovation can help bridge the digital divide and democratize access to knowledge, technology, and economic opportunities, addressing systemic barriers and empowering marginalized groups as active participants in the development process.
    - The amplification of traditional knowledge and community-driven innovations can promote the recognition and valuation of diverse epistemic perspectives, contributing to more inclusive and equitable development outcomes.
11. Sustainable Cities and Communities (SDG 11)

- Inclusive innovation in urban planning and community development can foster the creation of more inclusive, resilient, and livable cities and settlements, addressing the unique needs and aspirations of marginalized urban dwellers.
- The integration of traditional knowledge and community-based practices can inform the design of sustainable, culturally-relevant, and socially-inclusive urban environments.

12. Responsible Consumption and Production (SDG 12)
    - Inclusive innovation can drive the development of circular, resource-efficient, and environmentally-conscious production and consumption models that are tailored to local contexts and community needs.
    - The incorporation of traditional ecological knowledge and indigenous sustainable practices can contribute to the design of more holistic and culturally-grounded approaches to sustainable consumption and production.
13. Climate Action (SDG 13) - Inclusive innovation can foster the development and deployment of climate-resilient technologies and nature-based solutions that are responsive to the specific vulnerabilities and adaptation needs of marginalized communities.
    - The integration of traditional knowledge and community-based practices can inform more effective and equitable climate change mitigation and adaptation strategies that are grounded in local contexts and priorities.
14. Life Below Water (SDG 14)
    - Inclusive innovation can promote the development of sustainable, community-based approaches to marine and coastal resource management, drawing on the traditional ecological knowledge and practices of local fishing communities.
    - The incorporation of grassroots innovations and traditional knowledge can contribute to the design of more holistic and culturally-appropriate solutions for the conservation and sustainable use of marine ecosystems.
15. Life on Land (SDG 15) - Inclusive innovation can drive the development of innovative, community-led approaches to sustainable land use, forest management, and biodiversity conservation, building on the deep understanding and stewardship practices of local communities.

- The integration of traditional ecological knowledge and indigenous resource management practices can inform more effective and equitable strategies for the protection and restoration of terrestrial ecosystems.

16. Peace, Justice, and Strong Institutions (SDG 16)
    - Inclusive innovation can foster the development of participatory governance mechanisms and digital tools that empower marginalized communities to actively engage in decision-making processes and hold institutions accountable.
    - The incorporation of traditional conflict resolution mechanisms and community-based justice systems can contribute to the creation of more inclusive, culturally-relevant, and equitable institutional frameworks.
17. Partnerships for the Goals (SDG 17)
    - Inclusive innovation can catalyze the formation of diverse, cross-sectoral partnerships and collaborative ecosystems that leverage the complementary resources, expertise, and perspectives of multiple stakeholders, including grassroots innovators, community organizations, policymakers, and private sector actors.
    - The amplification of traditional knowledge and community-driven innovations can inform the design of more holistic, contextually-grounded, and mutually beneficial development partnerships and cooperation mechanisms.
    - By strategically aligning the principles and practices of inclusive innovation with the comprehensive framework of the Sustainable Development Goals, African nations can unlock new pathways for driving transformative, equitable, and sustainable development that empowers marginalized communities as active agents of change.

III. Measuring and Evaluating the Impact of Inclusive Innovation on the SDGs

Effectively measuring and evaluating the impact of inclusive innovation initiatives on the achievement of the Sustainable Development Goals is crucial for informing policymaking, guiding investment and resource allocation, and ensuring the long-term sustainability and scalability of these efforts. However, the multidimensional and context-specific nature of both inclusive innovation and the SDGs presents significant challenges in developing robust, standardized impact assessment frameworks. Traditional metrics and evaluation approaches often fail to capture the nuanced, qualitative, and systemic changes that are essential to the realization of the SDGs (Moran et al., 2018). To address these challenges, a multi-stakeholder, participatory approach to impact assessment is required, one that engages diverse ecosystem actors, including grassroots innovators, community representatives, policymakers, and development practitioners, in the co-creation of relevant, context-appropriate measurement frameworks.

Key elements of an effective impact assessment framework for aligning inclusive innovation and the SDGs include:

1. Holistic, multi-dimensional indicators
   - Capturing the social, economic, environmental, and cultural impacts of inclusive innovation initiatives
   - Incorporating both quantitative and qualitative metrics to reflect the multifaceted nature of development outcomes
2. Participatory, community-driven approaches
   - Empowering marginalized communities to define their own indicators of success and well-being
   - Ensuring the meaningful involvement of traditional knowledge holders and grassroots innovators in the design and implementation of impact assessments
3. Systemic, integrated measurement
   - Evaluating the interconnected, synergistic effects of inclusive innovation across multiple SDGs
   - Assessing the broader, long-term transformative impacts on socio-ecological systems and power dynamics
4. Adaptive, iterative evaluation processes
   - Incorporating feedback loops and continuous learning mechanisms to refine and improve inclusive innovation strategies and impact measurement approaches
   - Fostering an environment of transparency and accountability in the reporting and dissemination of evaluation findings
5. Collaborative, multi-stakeholder partnerships
   - Leveraging the diverse expertise and resources of ecosystem actors, including policymakers, academic institutions, civil society organizations, and private sector partners

- Promoting knowledge-sharing and the co-creation of contextualized impact assessment frameworks. By developing and implementing robust, participatory, and integrated impact assessment frameworks, African nations can not only measure the progress towards the SDGs but also gain valuable insights into the most effective and equitable strategies for harnessing the power of inclusive innovation to drive sustainable development.

IV. Overcoming Challenges and Barriers to Aligning Inclusive Innovation and the SDGs

While the synergies between inclusive innovation and the Sustainable Development Goals are well-established, several key challenges and barriers continue to hinder the effective integration and scaling of these complementary approaches:

1. Institutional and policy barriers
    - Lack of coherent policy frameworks and incentive structures that recognize and support the contributions of inclusive innovation to the SDGs
    - Rigid, siloed institutional structures and decision-making processes that impede cross-sectoral collaboration and the mainstreaming of inclusive innovation strategies
2. Capacity and resource constraints
    - Limited technical expertise, financial resources, and organizational capacities among grassroots innovators and community organizations to effectively engage with and contribute to SDG-aligned initiatives
    - Uneven distribution of funding, infrastructure, and other development resources across urban and rural areas, as well as among different socioeconomic groups
3. Misalignment of metrics and evaluation frameworks
    - Disconnect between the quantitative, output-oriented performance indicators often used to measure progress on the SDGs and the more qualitative, process-oriented, and context-specific nature of inclusive innovation impacts
    - Lack of standardized, participatory impact assessment methodologies that can effectively capture the multidimensional value of inclusive innovation initiatives

4. Power imbalances and cultural biases
   - Persistent marginalization and underrepresentation of grassroots innovators, traditional knowledge holders, and other community-based actors in decision-making processes related to the SDGs
   - Dominant development paradigms and narratives that privilege formal, techno centric approaches over more holistic, community-driven innovations
5. Sustaining momentum and scaling impact
   - Challenges in transitioning successful inclusive innovation initiatives from pilot to scale, due to the lack of appropriate financing mechanisms, supportive ecosystems, and integrated policy frameworks
   - Difficulties in replicating and adapting inclusive innovation models across different contexts, given the importance of local knowledge, cultural factors, and community ownership

Overcoming these barriers and fostering more effective alignment between inclusive innovation and the Sustainable Development Goals will require a multi-pronged approach that combines policy reform, capacity-building, collaborative ecosystem development, and the amplification of community voices and perspectives.

Key strategies include:

1. Developing integrated policy frameworks and institutional mechanisms
   - Aligning national development plans, sectoral policies, and public funding mechanisms to incentivize and support the integration of inclusive innovation approaches into SDG implementation

     Establishing dedicated government agencies or innovation councils to coordinate, monitor, and champion the alignment of inclusive innovation and the SDGs
2. Strengthening the capacities and resources of grassroots innovators and community organizations
   - Providing comprehensive training, mentorship, and access to financing for grassroots innovators to enhance their ability to engage with and contribute to SDG-aligned initiatives

   - Investing in the development of inclusive innovation hubs, makerspaces, and community-based infrastructure to foster the growth and scaling of community-driven solutions
3. Co-creating participatory impact assessment frameworks
   - Facilitating multi-stakeholder dialogues and co-design processes to develop contextually-relevant, community-driven impact measurement approaches that capture the multidimensional value of inclusive innovation initiatives
   - Implementing continuous learning and feedback loops to refine these impact assessment frameworks and ensure they remain aligned with evolving community needs and SDG priorities
4. Addressing power imbalances and promoting inclusive governance
   - Empowering grassroots innovators, traditional knowledge holders, and marginalized community representatives as equal partners in SDG policymaking, implementation, and monitoring processes
   - Fostering cross-cultural dialogues and collaboration to bridge the divide between formal and informal knowledge systems and amplify community voices in the development discourse
5. Catalyzing collaborative ecosystems and partnerships
   - Cultivating vibrant, multi-stakeholder innovation ecosystems that bring together diverse actors, including government agencies, academic institutions, private sector partners, and community-based organizations, to collectively drive the alignment of inclusive innovation and the SDGs
   - Mobilizing sustainable, blended financing mechanisms that leverage public, private, and philanthropic resources to support the development, scaling, and replication of inclusive innovation initiatives that contribute to the achievement of the SDGs By pursuing these strategic interventions and fostering a more enabling environment for the integration of inclusive innovation and the Sustainable Development Goals, African nations can unlock new pathways for driving holistic, equitable, and culturally-grounded development that empowers marginalized communities as active agents of change.

V. The Role of Traditional Knowledge in Aligning Inclusive Innovation and the SDGs

A crucial, yet often overlooked, aspect of the intersection between inclusive innovation and the Sustainable Development Goals is the critical role of traditional knowledge systems. Indigenous and local communities across Africa possess a deep, holistic understanding of their natural environments, cultural practices, and societal needs, which can provide invaluable insights for the design and implementation of inclusive, context-appropriate solutions.

Scholars have highlighted how the integration of traditional knowledge can significantly contribute to the achievement of the SDGs. For instance, the incorporation of indigenous land management practices and traditional ecological knowledge can inform more sustainable and equitable approaches to natural resource use, biodiversity conservation, and climate change adaptation (Berkes, 2012; Agrawal, 1995). Similarly, traditional healing practices and community-based healthcare solutions can complement formal healthcare systems, improving access and cultural relevance, especially in underserved areas (Briggs, 2005; Briggs & Sharp, 2004).

By actively engaging with and valuing traditional knowledge holders as key partners in the innovation process, inclusive innovation initiatives can better align with the SDGs' principles of local empowerment, cultural sensitivity, and holistic development. This engagement can take various forms, such as co-design workshops, collaborative research projects, and the establishment of governance structures that ensure the equitable representation and decision-making power of indigenous and local communities.

Moreover, the protection and promotion of traditional knowledge systems can also contribute to the realization of SDG 10 (Reduced Inequalities) and SDG 16 (Peace, Justice, and Strong Institutions) by addressing historical power imbalances, promoting the rights of marginalized groups, and fostering more inclusive and participatory development processes (Ely & Oxley, 2014; Gupta, 2016).

Ultimately, the strategic integration of traditional knowledge within inclusive innovation initiatives can lead to more culturally-grounded, environmentally-sustainable, and socially-equitable solutions that truly align with the transformative vision of the Sustainable Development Goals.

VI. Innovation Hubs and Ecosystems as Catalysts for SDG Alignment

The growing network of inclusive innovation hubs and ecosystems across Africa has emerged as a critical enabler in aligning grassroots-driven innovation with the Sustainable Development Goals. These dynamic, collaborative spaces bring together diverse stakeholders, including grassroots innovators, community organizations, academic institutions, policymakers, and private sector actors, to co-create innovative solutions that address local development challenges.

Inclusive innovation hubs can serve as vital intermediaries, facilitating the integration of community perspectives, traditional knowledge, and inclusive design principles into the development and scaling of SDG-aligned initiatives. By providing access to resources, mentorship, and capacity-building support, these hubs empower marginalized groups, such as women, youth, and rural communities, to actively participate in the innovation process and ensure that the resulting solutions are responsive to their unique needs and aspirations.

Moreover, the collaborative and cross-sectoral nature of these innovation ecosystems can catalyze the formation of multi-stakeholder partnerships that leverage complementary expertise, networks, and resources to drive the implementation of the SDGs. This synergistic approach can lead to the development of more holistic, systemic interventions that address the interconnected nature of the global goals, rather than siloed, fragmented efforts.

Prominent examples of inclusive innovation hubs in Africa that have successfully aligned their work with the SDGs include the Knowledge Hub in South Africa, which focuses on sustainable agriculture and food security (SDG 2), and the iHub in Kenya, which has fostered digital innovations that enhance access to education (SDG 4) and financial inclusion (SDG 8) (Ely & Oxley, 2014).

By strengthening the capacity and connectivity of these inclusive innovation ecosystems, African nations can cultivate vibrant, multi-stakeholder platforms that can serve as catalysts for the effective integration of grassroots-driven solutions and traditional knowledge systems into the achievement of the Sustainable Development Goals.

VII. Financing Inclusive Innovation for SDG Alignment

Securing adequate and sustainable financing is a critical challenge in aligning inclusive innovation initiatives with the Sustainable Development Goals. Traditional funding mechanisms and investment models often prioritize high-growth, technology-driven ventures, neglecting the unique financing needs and challenges faced by grassroots innovators, social enterprises, and community-based organizations.

To address this gap, innovative financing approaches that cater to the diverse funding requirements of inclusive innovation projects are essential. These can include:

1. Impact investment funds: Dedicated impact investment funds that channel patient capital and tailored financial instruments (e.g., equity, debt, grants) to support inclusive innovation initiatives that deliver measurable social and environmental returns aligned with the SDGs.
2. Blended finance mechanisms: Blended finance models that leverage public, private, and philanthropic resources to de-risk and catalyze investment in inclusive innovation projects, particularly in underserved or high-risk areas.
3. Crowdfunding platforms: Community-based crowdfunding platforms that empower grassroots innovators to mobilize funding from diverse sources, including individual donors, local businesses, and community organizations.
4. Inclusive procurement strategies: Public and private sector procurement policies that prioritize the sourcing of goods and services from inclusive innovators, social enterprises, and community-based vendors, creating new market opportunities and revenue streams.
5. Capacity-building and technical assistance: Integrated technical assistance and capacity-building programs that equip inclusive innovators with the skills, tools, and networks to access diverse financing mechanisms and effectively scale their SDG-aligned initiatives.

By developing and implementing these innovative financing approaches, African nations can unlock the necessary resources to support the growth and scaling of inclusive innovation projects that contribute to the realization of the Sustainable Development Goals. Crucially, this financing ecosystem must be accompanied by supportive policy frameworks, collaborative partnerships, and inclusive governance structures to ensure that the benefits of these investments are equitably distributed and aligned with the needs and priorities of marginalized communities.

VIII. Knowledge Sharing and Cross-Pollination of Inclusive Innovation Practices

The effective alignment of inclusive innovation and the Sustainable Development Goals requires robust knowledge-sharing, cross-pollination of practices, and the establishment of collaborative platforms that facilitate the exchange of insights, lessons, and best practices across African nations and beyond.

Scholars have highlighted the importance of creating dedicated knowledge hubs, innovation libraries, and digital repositories that document, analyze, and disseminate the experiences and learnings from successful inclusive innovation initiatives that have contributed to the achievement of the SDGs. These knowledge-sharing platforms can serve as invaluable resources for policymakers, development practitioners, and community-based organizations, enabling them to adapt and scale effective models in their respective contexts.

Furthermore, the establishment of regional and continental networks, such as the Afrilabs network and the Southern African Innovation Support (SAIS) program, can facilitate cross-border collaborations, joint research projects, and the co-creation of inclusive innovation strategies aligned with the SDGs. By leveraging the collective expertise, resources, and diverse perspectives of these collaborative ecosystems, African nations can amplify the impact of inclusive innovation and accelerate progress towards the global goals.

Alongside these formal knowledge-sharing mechanisms, the cultivation of communities of practice, peer-to-peer learning exchanges, and mentorship programs can empower grassroots innovators, traditional knowledge holders, and community-based organizations to share their experiences, challenges, and solutions, fostering a culture of continuous learning and adaptation.

By prioritizing knowledge sharing, cross-pollination, and collaborative networks, African nations can harness the transformative potential of inclusive innovation to drive sustainable development in a more coordinated, scalable, and impactful manner, ultimately contributing to the realization of the Sustainable Development Goals across the continent.

References

Agrawal, A. (1995). Dismantling the divide between indigenous and scientific knowledge. *Development and change*, 26(3), 413-439.

Berkes, F. (2012). *Sacred ecology*. Routledge.

Briggs, J. (2005). The use of indigenous knowledge in development: problems and challenges. *Progress in development studies*, 5(2), 99-114.

Briggs, J., & Sharp, J. (2004). Indigenous knowledges and development: a postcolonial caution. *Third World Quarterly*, 25(4), 661-676.

Ely, A., & Oxley, N. (2014). *STEPS Centre Research on Grassroots Innovation Movements*. STEPS Centre.

Gupta, A. K. (2016). *Grassroots Innovation: Minds on the Margin*.

Moran, M., Rein, M., & Goodin, R. E. (Eds.). (2018). *The Oxford handbook of public policy*. Oxford University Press.

Schillo, R. S., & Robinson, R. M. (2017). Inclusive innovation in developed countries: The who, what, why, and how. *Technology Innovation Management Review*, 7(7), 34-46.

United Nations. (2015). *Transforming our world: The 2030 agenda for sustainable development*. United Nations General Assembly.

CHAPTER 11

Financing Inclusive Innovation: Alternative Models and Mechanisms

Accessing adequate and appropriate financing remains a critical challenge for driving the development and scaling of inclusive innovation initiatives across Africa. The traditional financing landscape, dominated by conventional investment models and profit-driven frameworks, has often failed to

Inclusive Innovation of Africa

cater to the unique needs and constraints faced by grassroots innovators, social enterprises, and marginalized communities (Bates & Robb, 2013). In response to this funding gap, a growing ecosystem of alternative financing models and mechanisms has emerged, offering innovative solutions to unlock the capital required to catalyze inclusive and sustainable development. From impact investing and crowdfunding to blended finance and community-based funding schemes, these alternative approaches are redefining the ways in which resources are mobilized, allocated, and deployed to support the flourishing of inclusive innovation in Africa.

This chapter delves into the evolving landscape of inclusive innovation financing, exploring the diverse array of alternative models, their underlying principles and mechanisms, and the strategies being employed to ensure that marginalized groups and community-driven initiatives can access the resources they need to thrive. By examining illustrative case studies and drawing on cutting-edge research, this chapter aims to equip policymakers, practitioners, and ecosystem builders with a comprehensive understanding of the innovative financing solutions that can unlock the transformative potential of inclusive innovation across the African continent.

I. The Limitations of Traditional Financing Models

Conventional financing approaches, such as venture capital, angel investing, and commercial bank lending, have historically favored high-growth, technology-driven ventures with the potential for outsized financial returns (Moleka, 2024a; Harrison & Mason, 2000).

This profit-centric focus has often resulted in the exclusion of grassroots innovators, social entrepreneurs, and community-based initiatives that prioritize social and environmental impact over pure financial gains (Bates & Robb, 2013). Several key limitations of traditional financing models in the context of inclusive innovation include:

1. Narrow investment criteria and risk aversion: Traditional investors typically focus on scalable, high-growth ventures with proven business models, leaving little room for the riskier, more experimental nature of many inclusive innovation initiatives (Lans et al., 2017).

Table 11.1 Trends in Banking and Financial Inclusion (2004–2018)

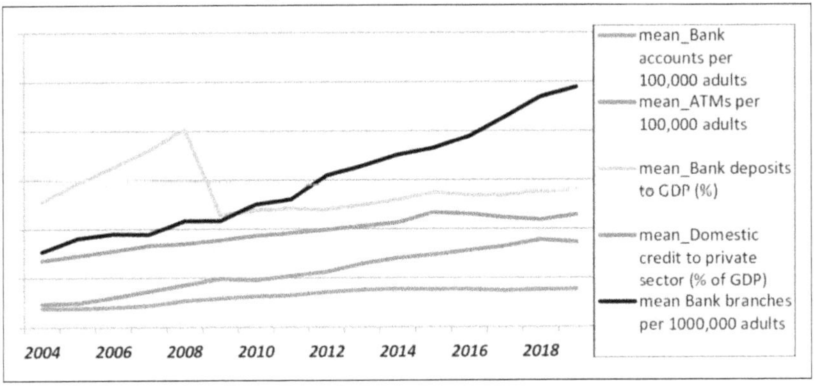

Source: World Bank - *Global Financial Development Database*, **2019. Available at: https://databank.worldbank.org/, IMF** - *Financial Access Survey (FAS)*, **2020. Available at: https://data.imf.org/, BIS** - *Banking Sector Penetration Report*, **2019.**

2. Lack of understanding of local contexts and community needs: Investors often lack the deep contextual knowledge and engagement with marginalized communities required to identify and support locally-relevant, impactful innovations (Bates & Robb, 2013).
3. Misalignment of investment timelines and impact horizons: Inclusive innovation initiatives frequently require longer-term, patient capital to address complex, systemic challenges, which may not align with the shorter investment horizons of traditional financiers (Nicholls & Schwartz, 2020).
4. Absence of tailored support and capacity-building: Grassroots innovators and social enterprises often require more than just financial capital, needing access to business development services, mentorship, and other forms of non-financial support that are not typically provided by traditional investors (Bates & Robb, 2013).
5. Challenges in demonstrating financial viability and scalability: Inclusive innovation initiatives may struggle to meet the financial benchmarks and growth projections demanded by traditional investors, despite their potential for substantial social and environmental impact (Lans et al., 2017).

II. The Rise of Alternative Financing Models for Inclusive Innovation

In response to the limitations of traditional financing approaches, a diverse ecosystem of alternative models and mechanisms has emerged to support the development and scaling of inclusive innovation initiatives in Africa. These innovative financing solutions draw on principles of impact, collaboration, and community-driven resource mobilization to better align with the needs and aspirations of marginalized groups and grassroots innovators (Moleka, 2024b).

Key alternative financing models and mechanisms include:

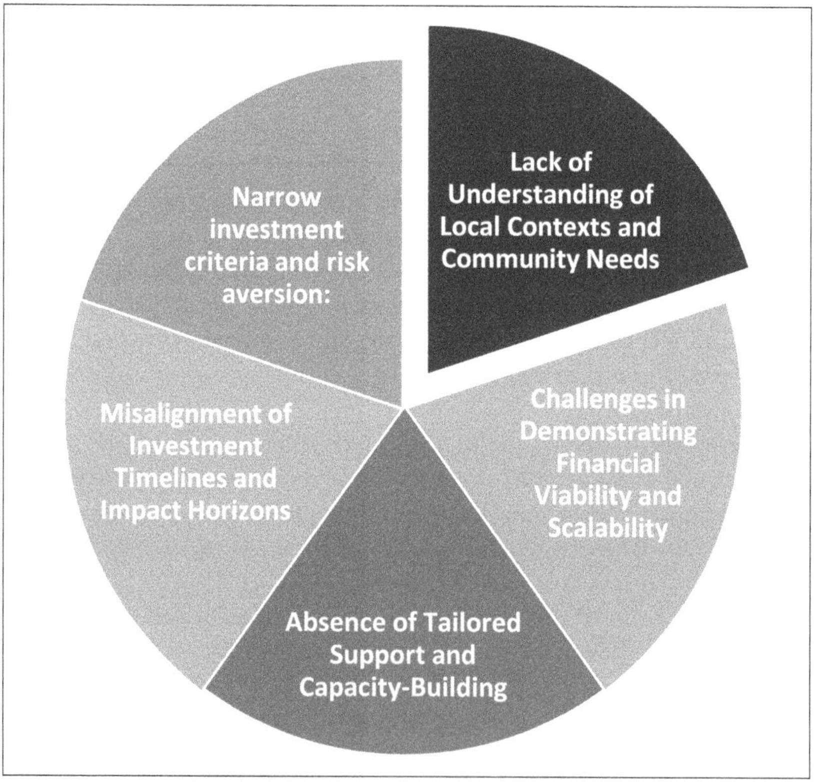

Figure 11.1 The Limitations of Traditional Financing Models (Author's own work)

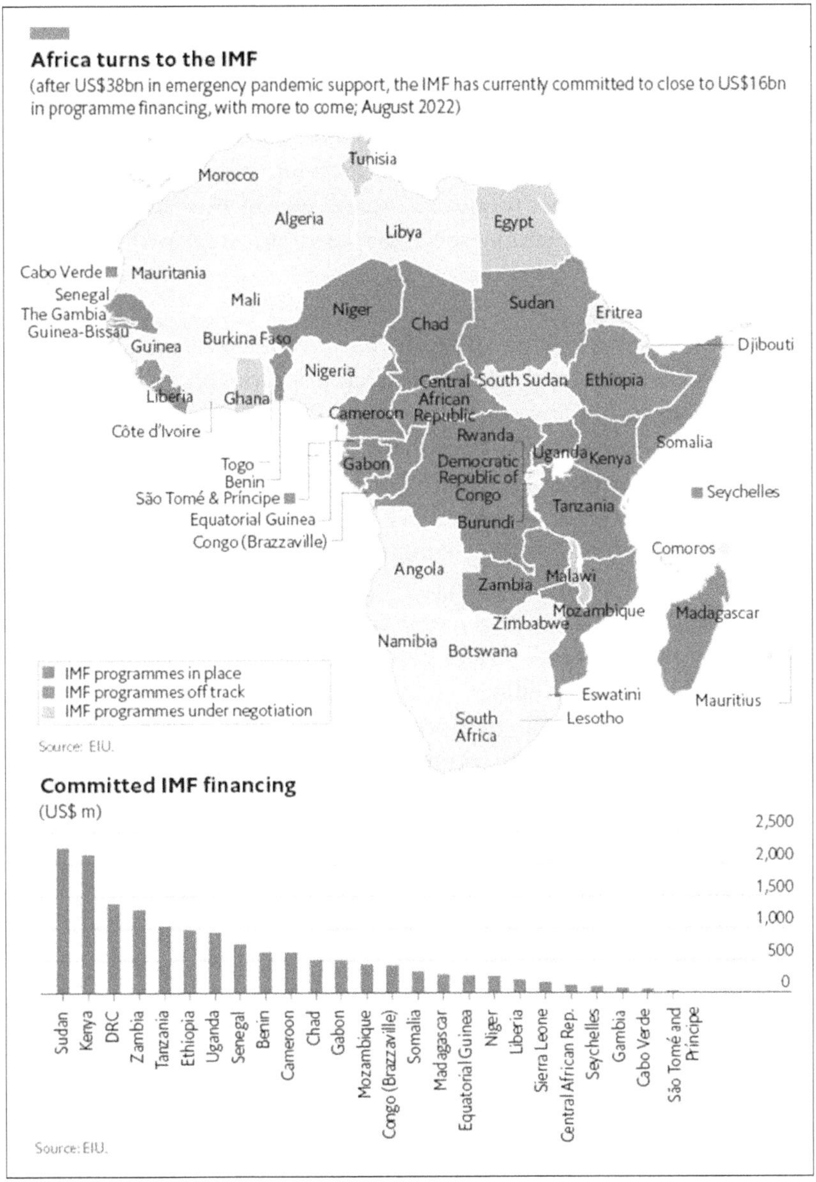

Figure 11.2 Africa's Financial Dependence on the IMF: Programme Status and Committed Financing

1. Impact Investing
    - Investments made with the intention of generating measurable social and environmental impact alongside financial returns
    - Leveraging blended capital from public, private, and philanthropic sources to support inclusive innovation initiatives
    - Employing impact measurement and management frameworks to track and optimize the social and environmental performance of investments
2. Crowdfunding
    - Online platforms that enable the collective mobilization of small-scale contributions from a large number of individuals to fund specific projects or initiatives
    - Providing marginalized communities and grassroots innovators with alternate pathways to access financing beyond traditional sources
    - Fostering a sense of community ownership and engagement in the development and scaling of locally-relevant innovations
3. Community-Based Financing
    - Locally-driven resource mobilization and allocation mechanisms, such as community savings groups, rotating credit associations, and solidarity-based lending
    - Empowering marginalized communities to collectively pool, manage, and deploy financial resources to support their own development priorities
    - Promoting financial inclusion and the development of community-owned and -operated financial institutions
4. Blended Finance
    - Combining public, private, and philanthropic capital to drive the development and scaling of inclusive innovation initiatives
    - Leveraging public funding, risk-sharing mechanisms, and technical assistance to catalyze private sector investment in marginalized communities
    - Fostering innovative partnerships and collaborative platforms that align the motivations and resources of diverse financing actors
5. Social Impact Bonds and Pay-for-Success Models

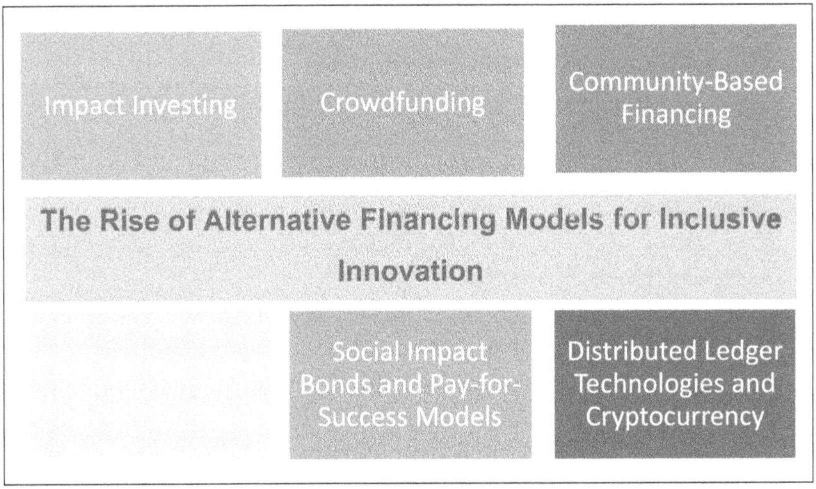

Figure 11.3 The Rise of Alternative Financing Models for Inclusive Innovation. Source: Moleka, 2024

- Outcome-based financing mechanisms that link payments to the achievement of pre-defined social and environmental impact targets
- Shifting the focus from outputs to outcomes, incentivizing the delivery of effective, high-impact inclusive innovation solutions
- Engaging a range of stakeholders, including governments, investors, and service providers, in collaborative risk-sharing and performance-driven models

6. Distributed Ledger Technologies and Cryptocurrency
   - Leveraging blockchain-based platforms and cryptocurrencies to facilitate transparent, secure, and accessible financial transactions
   - Enabling direct, peer-to-peer funding flows that bypass traditional financial intermediaries and reduce barriers to entry for marginalized groups
   - Exploring the use of smart contracts and decentralized autonomous organizations (DAOs) to enhance the transparency and accountability of inclusive innovation financing

III. The Principles and Mechanisms of Alternative Financing Models

Underpinning the diverse array of alternative financing models are several key principles and mechanisms that distinguish them from traditional approaches and better align with the needs of inclusive innovation initiatives (Moleka, 2024a):

1. Impact-Driven Orientation
   - Prioritizing the achievement of measurable social, environmental, and economic impacts alongside financial returns
   - Employing rigorous impact assessment and management frameworks to track, optimize, and communicate the multidimensional value creation of inclusive innovation initiatives
2. Collaborative and Participatory Governance
   - Fostering multi-stakeholder partnerships that bring together public, private, and community actors in the design and deployment of financing solutions
   - Promoting inclusive decision-making processes that empower marginalized communities and grassroots innovators as active participants
3. Flexible and Adaptive Financing Structures
   - Offering patient, long-term capital that aligns with the extended timelines required to address complex, systemic challenges
   - Incorporating flexible financing instruments, such as grants, convertible debt, and revenue-sharing models, to accommodate the unique needs and constraints of inclusive innovation initiatives
4. Capacity-Building and Technical Assistance
   - Providing tailored business development support, mentorship, and access to networks to strengthen the capabilities of grassroots innovators and social enterprises
   - nvesting in the cultivation of an enabling ecosystem that supports the sustainable growth and scaling of inclusive innovation initiatives
5. Community-Driven Resource Mobilization
   - Empowering marginalized communities to collectively pool, manage, and deploy financial resources to address their own development priorities

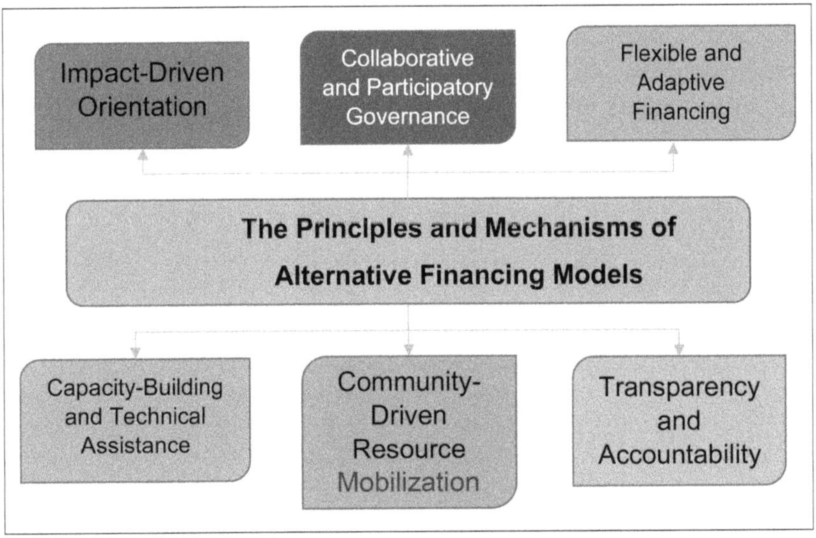

Figure 11.4 The Principles and Mechanisms of Alternative Financing Models (Author's own work)

- Leveraging local knowledge, relationships, and social capital to identify and support context-appropriate inclusive innovation initiatives

6. Transparency and Accountability
   - Implementing robust impact measurement and reporting frameworks to enhance the transparency and accountability of inclusive innovation financing.
   - Exploring the use of distributed ledger technologies and other digital tools to facilitate secure, transparent, and auditable financial transactions By adopting these principles and mechanisms, alternative financing models are better positioned to unlock the transformative potential of inclusive innovation, empowering marginalized communities, grassroots innovators, and social enterprises as active participants in the development and deployment of innovative solutions.

Table 11.2 Account Penetration and Usage in Africa.

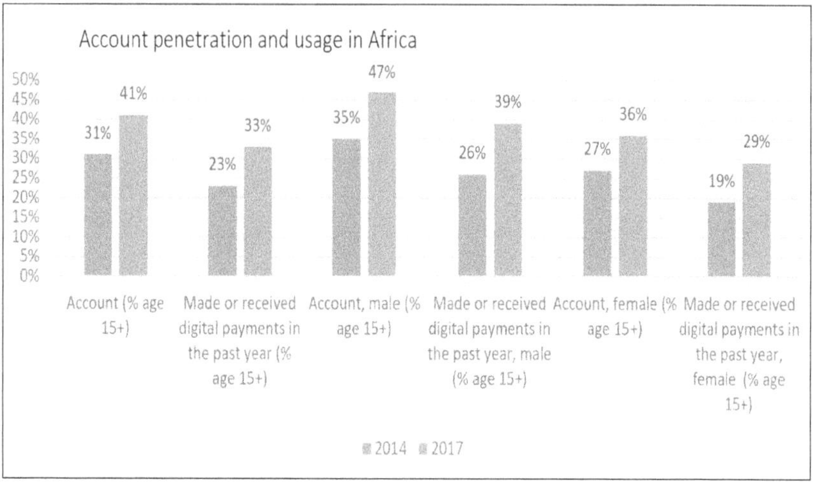

Source: Global Financial Inclusion Database, World Bank.

Impact Investing: Aligning Capital with Social and Environmental Priorities

Impact investing has emerged as a leading alternative financing model for driving inclusive innovation in Africa. This approach to investing aims to generate measurable social and environmental impact alongside financial returns, addressing the limitations of traditional profit-maximizing investment frameworks (Nicholls & Schwartz, 2020). At the core of impact investing is the principle of aligning capital deployment with the achievement of specific impact objectives, such as improving access to healthcare, education, or renewable energy in underserved communities. Impact investors employ a range of financial instruments, including equity, debt, and hybrid structures, to support the development and scaling of inclusive innovation initiatives that deliver on these impact goals (Bates & Robb, 2013).

The impact investing ecosystem in Africa has witnessed significant growth in recent years, with the emergence of dedicated impact investment funds,

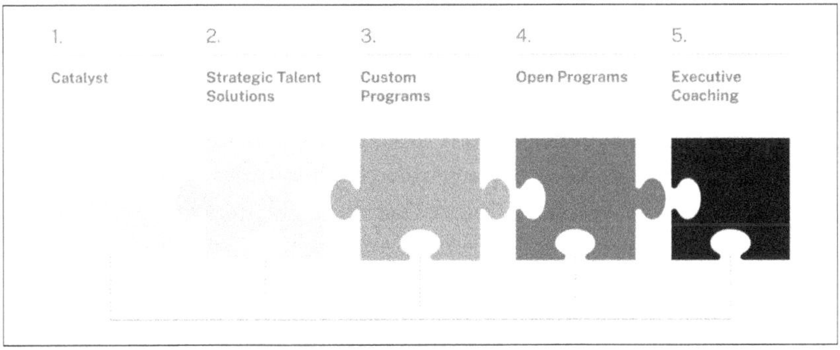

Figure 11.5 Impact Investing (Author's own work)

intermediaries, and collaborative platforms that are channeling capital towards innovative, community-driven solutions. These initiatives not only provide much-needed financing but also often offer tailored capacity-building support, access to networks, and impact measurement assistance to help inclusive innovation ventures thrive (Lans et al., 2017).

Overview of the Impact Investment in Africa Action Plan

IV. United Nations Development Programme

The ultimate aim of the Impact Investment in Africa Action Plan is to support the development a vibrant impact investment sector on the continent. The Roadmap and Logical Framework ("Logframe") presented in this Action Plan illustrate the proposed actions required to achieve this goal. Figure 6 below provides an overview of the

V. Crowdfunding: Democratizing Access to Financing

Crowdfunding has become a transformative force in the world of inclusive innovation financing, empowering marginalized communities and grassroots innovators to access the resources they need to bring their ideas to life. Through online crowdfunding platforms, individuals and communities can collectively mobilize small-scale contributions from a large number of supporters, circumventing the traditional barriers to accessing capital (Datta et al., 2019). Crowdfunding models in the African context have taken diverse forms, from reward-based campaigns that channel resources towards the development of community-driven innovations to equity-based platforms that enable marginalized entrepreneurs to tap into wider investor networks. These collaborative financing approaches not only unlock capital but also foster a sense of community ownership and engagement in the innovation process (Datta et al., 2019).

Moreover, crowdfunding has the potential to serve as a springboard for inclusive innovation initiatives, providing them with the initial funding and visibility required to attract additional investment and scale their impact. By democratizing access to financing, crowdfunding empowers grassroots innovators and underserved communities to become active participants in shaping the innovation landscape and addressing their own development priorities (Datta et al., 2019).

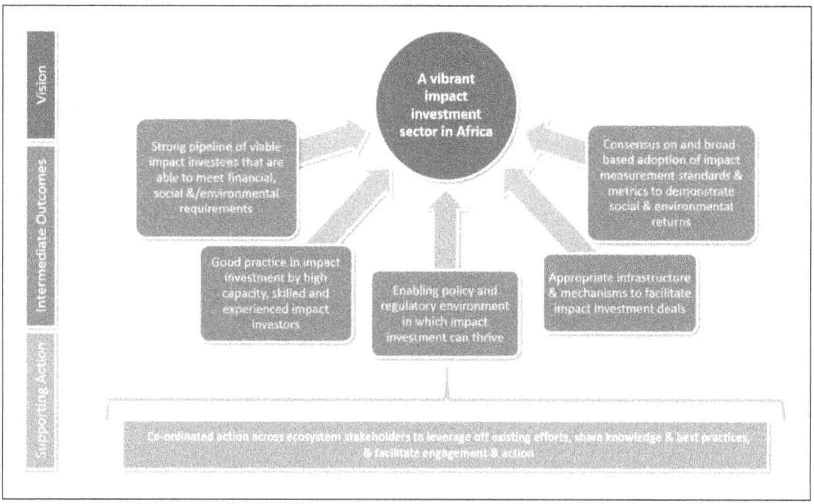

Figure 11.6 Overview of the 'Impact Investment in Africa Action Plan (Author's own work)

Table 11.3 GDP in Africa, 2019-2027

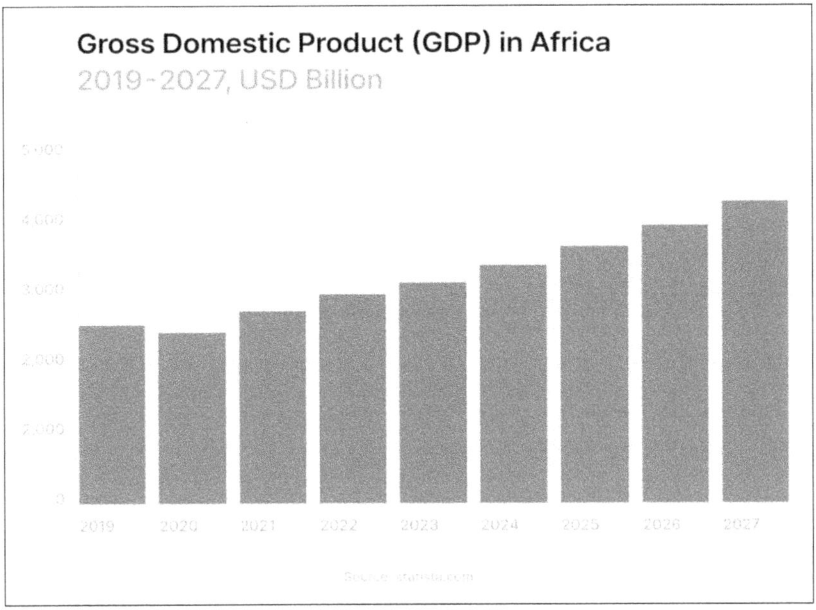

VI. Community-Based Financing: Leveraging Local Resources and Social Capital

Community-based financing models, rooted in the rich traditions of collective resource mobilization and solidarity-based lending, have emerged as a powerful mechanism for supporting inclusive innovation in Africa. These locally-driven approaches empower marginalized communities to pool, manage, and deploy financial resources in alignment with their own development needs and priorities (Bates & Robb, 2013). Initiatives such as community savings groups, rotating credit associations, and community-owned financial institutions tap into the social capital and mutual trust within local communities to facilitate access to affordable financing, particularly for individuals and initiatives that are typically excluded from mainstream financial

systems. By harnessing the collective resources and decision-making capacities of community members, these models foster a sense of ownership and agency, enabling grassroots innovators and social entrepreneurs to secure the funding they require to thrive (Bates & Robb, 2013). Furthermore,

Figure 11.7 Benefits of Community-Based Finance (Author's own work)

community-based financing approaches often incorporate capacity-building and technical assistance components, equipping local communities with the skills and knowledge required to manage their financial resources effectively and deploy them in support of inclusive innovation initiatives. This holistic approach not only addresses the funding gap but also strengthens the overall capacity and resilience of marginalized communities (Bates & Robb, 2013).

VII. Blended Finance: Catalyzing Diverse Capital Sources

Blended finance models leverage the strategic combination of public, private, and philanthropic capital to drive the development and scaling of inclusive innovation initiatives. By blending different types of financing instruments and aligning the motivations and resources of diverse stakeholders, blended finance approaches can help overcome the limitations of traditional investment frameworks and unlock the capital required to address complex development challenges (Nicholls & Schwartz, 2020). In the African context, blended finance mechanisms have been instrumental in channeling resources towards inclusive innovation initiatives that may not be able to meet the investment criteria of purely commercial investors. Public funding, in the form of grants, subsidies, or guarantees, can be used to de-risk investments and catalyze private sector participation, while philanthropic capital can provide patient, flexible financing to support the incubation and early-stage growth of innovative solutions (Nicholls & Schwartz, 2020).

These collaborative financing models often incorporate technical assistance and capacity-building support, empowering inclusive innovation

ventures to strengthen their operational and financial capabilities, improve their impact measurement and reporting, and ultimately, enhance their ability to attract and manage diverse capital sources (Lans et al., 2017). By fostering innovative partnerships and aligning the interests of public, private, and philanthropic actors, blended finance has the potential to unlock significant resources for inclusive innovation, while also promoting the development of a more sustainable and equitable investment ecosystem in Africa.

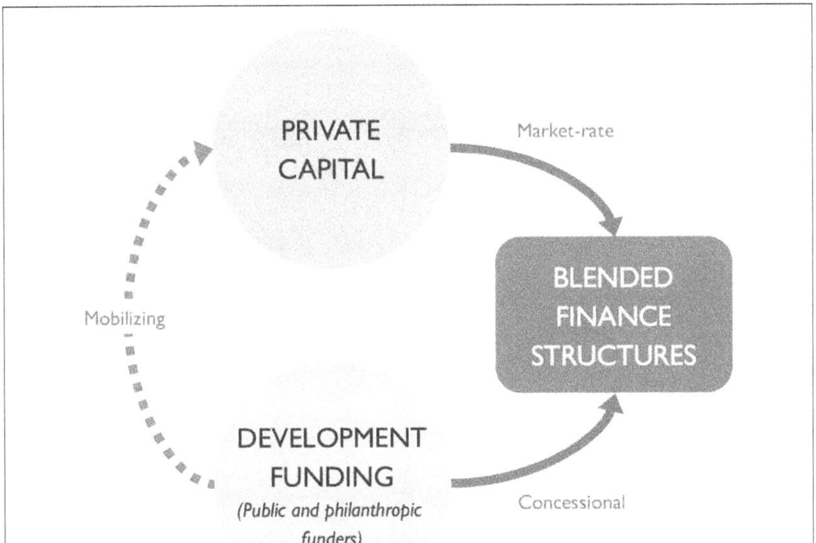

Figure 11.8 Blended Finance (Author's own work)

VIII. Social Impact Bonds and Pay-for-Success Models

Aligning Incentives for Impact Social impact bonds (SIBs) and pay-for-success (PFS) models represent a novel approach to financing inclusive innovation, shifting the focus from inputs and outputs to the achievement of measurable social and environmental outcomes. These outcome-based financing mechanisms engage a range of stakeholders, including governments, investors, and service providers, in a collaborative risk-sharing and performance-driven framework (Nicholls & Schwartz, 2020). In the context of inclusive innovation, SIBs and PFS models can be leveraged to support the development and scaling of innovative solutions that address complex, systemic challenges faced by marginalized communities. By aligning payments with the attainment of pre-defined impact targets, these models incentivize the delivery of high-quality, effective interventions and foster a culture of continuous improvement and adaptive learning (Nicholls & Schwartz, 2020).

Moreover, SIBs and PFS models often incorporate mechanisms for community engagement and co-creation, ensuring that the design and implementation

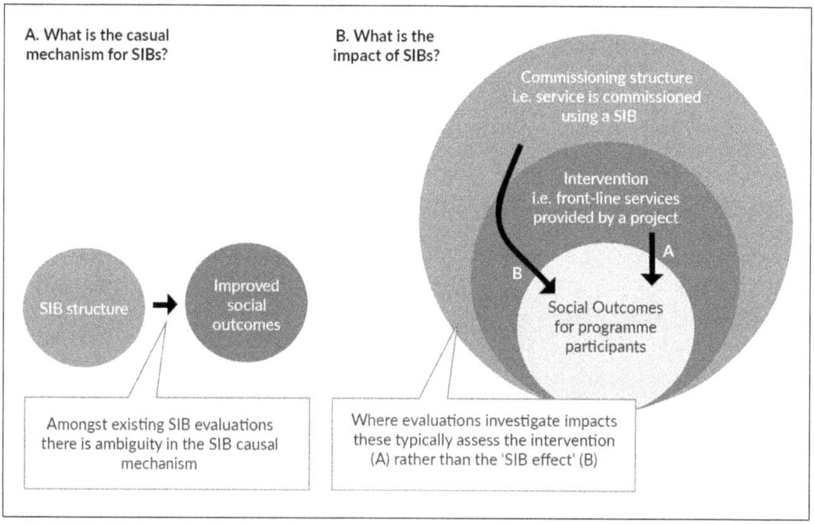

Figure 11.9 Social Impact Bonds (SIBs) and Pay-For-Success (PFS) Models (Author's own work)

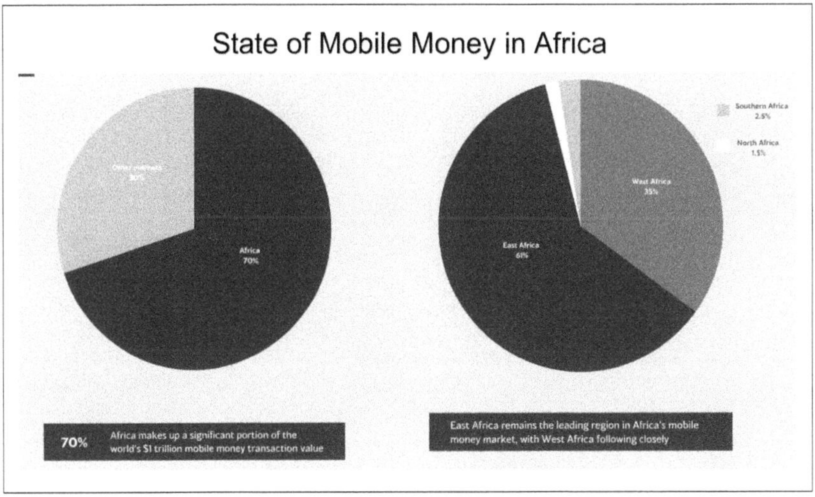

Figure 11.10 State of Mobile Money in Africa. Source: gsma.com/sotir

of inclusive innovation initiatives are responsive to the needs and priorities of local stakeholders. This participatory approach not only enhances the relevance and effectiveness of the solutions but also empowers marginalized communities as active partners in the innovation process (Lans et al., 2017). As these outcome-based financing approaches gain traction in Africa, they have the potential to unlock significant resources for inclusive innovation, while also driving the development of more rigorous impact measurement and management practices within the ecosystem.

IX. Distributed Ledger Technologies and Cryptocurrency: Towards Accessible and Transparent Financing

Emerging technologies, such as blockchain-based platforms and cryptocurrencies, are transforming the landscape of inclusive innovation financing, offering new avenues for direct, peer-to-peer funding flows and enhanced transparency (Datta et al., 2019). Distributed ledger technologies (DLTs), including blockchain, can facilitate secure, transparent, and auditable financial transactions, bypassing traditional financial intermediaries and reducing

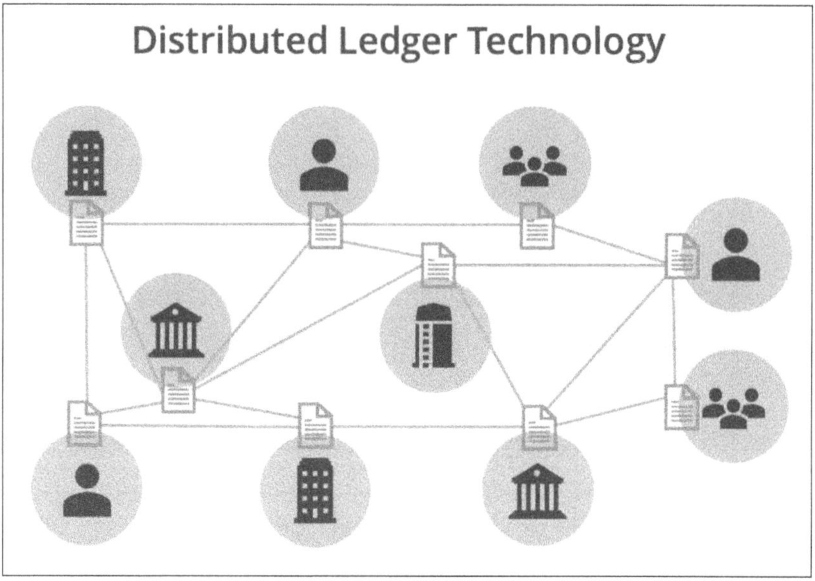

Figure 11.11 Distributed Ledger Technology (Author's own work)

barriers to entry for marginalized groups. This can enable direct funding flows from investors and supporters to grassroots innovators and community-based initiatives, empowering them to access the resources they need to bring their ideas to life (Datta et al., 2019).

Moreover, the use of smart contracts and decentralized autonomous organizations (DAOs) within DLT-based platforms can introduce new forms of collaborative, community-driven governance and decision-making around the allocation and deployment of financial resources. This can foster greater transparency, accountability, and community ownership in the inclusive innovation financing ecosystem (Datta et al., 2019). Cryptocurrencies and digital wallets, in turn, can improve financial inclusion by providing marginalized communities with secure, accessible, and affordable access to digital financial services, enabling them to participate in crowdfunding campaigns, access impact investments, and even create their own community-based financing mechanisms (Datta et al., 2019).

As these innovative technologies continue to evolve and become more widely adopted, they hold immense potential for democratizing access to financing, enhancing the transparency and accountability of inclusive innovation initiatives, and empowering marginalized communities as active participants in the development and deployment of innovative solutions.

The use of blockchain in Africa

The potential blockchain applications can be broadly grouped into three categories: (1) digital payments, (2) contracts, and (3) database and record management.[9] *Based on the PositiveBlockchain.io database, Smart Africa (2020) identifies 69 active blockchain projects across different sectors on the African continent. Financial services and agriculture have the most use cases (Fig. 2). Regional giants Kenya, South Africa, and Nigeria are the top users of blockchain technology.*

According to Smart Africa 2020 the most pertinent blockchain use-cases in Africa would be (1) digital payments, (2) public procurement, (3) decentralised electricity distribution, (4) digital identification and education credentials, (5) digital land administration, (6) agricultural and mining supply chain tracing, and (7) trade facilitation (Smart Africa, 2020).

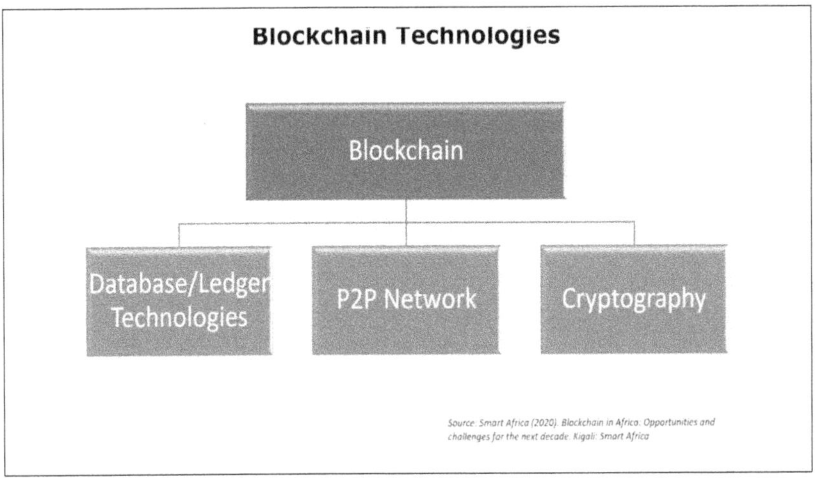

Figure 11.12 Blockchain Technologies

Table 11.4 Blockchain Projects in Africa by Sector

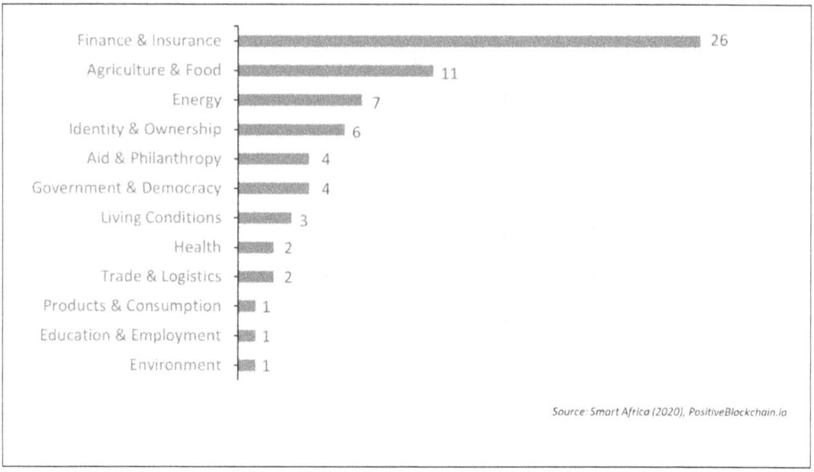

X. Strategies for Scaling and Sustaining Alternative Financing Models

To ensure the long-term viability and scalability of alternative financing models for inclusive innovation in Africa, several key strategies can be employed:

1. Fostering an Enabling Policy and Regulatory Environment
   - Implementing policies and regulations that recognize, protect, and incentivize the use of alternative financing models for inclusive innovation.
   - Developing intellectual property frameworks that safeguard the rights of grassroots innovators and community-based initiatives.
   - Integrating alternative financing approaches into national and regional development strategies and public procurement programs.
2. Strengthening Ecosystem Collaboration and Knowledge-Sharing
   - Facilitating the creation of collaborative platforms, networks, and consortia that bring together diverse financing actors, inclusive innovation ventures, and ecosystem intermediaries.
   - Promoting the exchange of best practices, case studies, and lessons learned to drive the continuous improvement and replication of alternative financing models.

  - Establishing mechanisms for cross-border collaboration and the sharing of resources and expertise within the African inclusive innovation ecosystem.
3. Building Institutional and Organizational Capacities
  - Investing in the training and development of specialized human capital, such as impact investment professionals, crowdfunding platform managers, and community-based financing experts.
  - Strengthening the operational, financial, and impact management capabilities of inclusive innovation ventures and community-based organizations to enhance their investment readiness.
  - Developing standardized impact measurement and reporting frameworks to improve the transparency and credibility of alternative financing models.
4. Diversifying Funding Sources and Blended Finance Approaches
  - Exploring innovative funding mechanisms, such as social impact bonds, development impact bonds, and diaspora investment vehicles, to mobilize diverse capital sources.
  - Leveraging public sector funding, philanthropic grants, and development finance to de-risk and catalyze private sector investment in inclusive innovation.
  - Fostering the creation of specialized impact investment funds, angel investor networks, and other financing vehicles tailored to the needs of inclusive innovation initiatives.
5. Promoting Awareness, Advocacy, and Visibility Raising awareness, amplifying the voices and perspectives of traditional knowledge holders, and advocating for the recognition and integration of traditional knowledge systems within innovation ecosystems are critical strategies for advancing this agenda.

Key initiatives in this area include:

- Implementing educational campaigns and outreach programs: Developing targeted awareness-raising campaigns, leveraging both traditional and digital media platforms, to disseminate information about the value and relevance of traditional knowledge systems. These campaigns should aim to reach diverse stakeholders, including policymakers, researchers, private sector actors, and the general public.

- Facilitating cross-cultural dialogues and exchanges: Organizing forums, workshops, and community events that bring together traditional knowledge holders, grassroots innovators, academics, and other ecosystem actors to foster mutual understanding, shared learning, and the co-creation of inclusive innovation solutions.
- Amplifying the voices and narratives of traditional knowledge holders: Empowering traditional knowledge holders, particularly women and marginalized groups, to share their stories, showcase their innovations, and actively participate in decision-making processes within innovation ecosystems.
- Advocating for policy and regulatory reforms: Engaging in evidence-based advocacy efforts to influence the development of supportive policies, legal frameworks, and institutional mechanisms that recognize, protect, and incentivize the integration of traditional knowledge systems into innovation and development initiatives.
- Documenting and disseminating success stories: Systematically documenting and widely disseminating case studies and best practices of successful

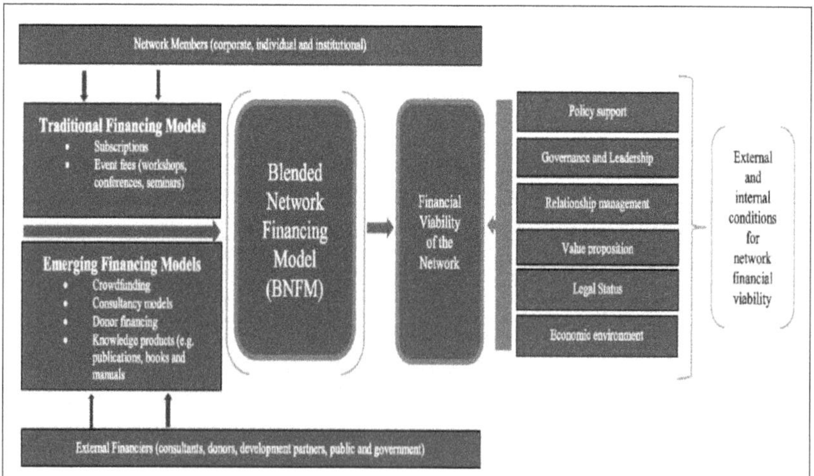

Figure 11.13 BNFM (Author's own work)

traditional knowledge-based innovations, highlighting their social, environmental, and economic impacts, to inspire and guide the replication and scaling of these initiatives.

By implementing these strategies, African nations can foster a more inclusive, equitable, and culturally-grounded innovation landscape that harnesses the transformative power of traditional knowledge systems and empowers local communities as active agents of change.

XI. The Role of Traditional Knowledge in Aligning Inclusive Innovation and the SDGs

A crucial, yet often overlooked, aspect of the intersection between inclusive innovation and the Sustainable Development Goals is the critical role of traditional knowledge systems. Indigenous and local communities across Africa possess a deep, holistic understanding of their natural environments, cultural practices, and societal needs, which can provide invaluable insights for the design and implementation of inclusive, context-appropriate solutions.

Scholars have highlighted how the integration of traditional knowledge can significantly contribute to the achievement of the SDGs. For instance, the incorporation of indigenous land management practices and traditional ecological knowledge can inform more sustainable and equitable approaches to natural resource use, biodiversity conservation, and climate change adaptation (Berkes, 2012; Agrawal, 1995). Similarly, traditional healing practices and community-based healthcare solutions can complement formal healthcare systems, improving access and cultural relevance, especially in underserved areas (Briggs, 2005; Briggs & Sharp, 2004).

By actively engaging with and valuing traditional knowledge holders as key partners in the innovation process, inclusive innovation initiatives can better align with the SDGs' principles of local empowerment, cultural sensitivity, and holistic development. This engagement can take various forms, such as co-design workshops, collaborative research projects, and the establishment of governance structures that ensure the equitable representation and decision-making power of indigenous and local communities.

Moreover, the protection and promotion of traditional knowledge systems can also contribute to the realization of SDG 10 (Reduced Inequalities) and SDG 16 (Peace, Justice, and Strong Institutions) by addressing historical power imbalances, promoting the rights of marginalized groups, and fostering more inclusive and participatory development processes (Ely & Oxley, 2014; Gupta, 2016).

Ultimately, the strategic integration of traditional knowledge within inclusive innovation initiatives can lead to more culturally-grounded, environmentally-sustainable, and socially-equitable solutions that truly align with the transformative vision of the Sustainable Development Goals.

XII. Inclusive Innovation Hubs and Ecosystems as Catalysts for SDG Alignment

The growing network of inclusive innovation hubs and ecosystems across Africa has emerged as a critical enabler in aligning grassroots-driven innovation with the Sustainable Development Goals. These dynamic, collaborative spaces bring together diverse stakeholders, including grassroots innovators, community organizations, academic institutions, policymakers, and private sector actors, to co-create innovative solutions that address local development challenges.

Inclusive innovation hubs can serve as vital intermediaries, facilitating the integration of community perspectives, traditional knowledge, and inclusive design principles into the development and scaling of SDG-aligned initiatives. By providing access to resources, mentorship, and capacity-building support, these hubs empower marginalized groups, such as women, youth, and rural communities, to actively participate in the innovation process and ensure that the resulting solutions are responsive to their unique needs and aspirations.

Moreover, the collaborative and cross-sectoral nature of these innovation ecosystems can catalyze the formation of multi-stakeholder partnerships that leverage complementary expertise, networks, and resources to drive the implementation of the SDGs. This synergistic approach can lead to the development of more holistic, systemic interventions that address the interconnected nature of the global goals, rather than siloed, fragmented efforts.

Prominent examples of inclusive innovation hubs in Africa that have successfully aligned their work with the SDGs include the Knowledge Hub in South Africa, which focuses on sustainable agriculture and food security (SDG 2), and the iHub in Kenya, which has fostered digital innovations that enhance access to education (SDG 4) and financial inclusion (SDG 8) (Ely & Oxley, 2014).

By strengthening the capacity and connectivity of these inclusive innovation ecosystems, African nations can cultivate vibrant, multi-stakeholder platforms that can serve as catalysts for the effective integration of grassroots-driven solutions and traditional knowledge systems into the achievement of the Sustainable Development Goals.

XIII. Financing Inclusive Innovation for SDG Alignment

Securing adequate and sustainable financing is a critical challenge in aligning inclusive innovation initiatives with the Sustainable Development Goals. Traditional funding mechanisms and investment models often prioritize high-growth, technology-driven ventures, neglecting the unique financing needs and challenges faced by grassroots innovators, social enterprises, and community-based organizations.

To address this gap, innovative financing approaches that cater to the diverse funding requirements of inclusive innovation projects are essential. These can include:

1. Impact investment funds: Dedicated impact investment funds that channel patient capital and tailored financial instruments (e.g., equity, debt, grants) to support inclusive innovation initiatives that deliver measurable social and environmental returns aligned with the SDGs.
2. Blended finance mechanisms: Blended finance models that leverage public, private, and philanthropic resources to de-risk and catalyze investment in inclusive innovation projects, particularly in underserved or high-risk areas.
3. Crowdfunding platforms: Community-based crowdfunding platforms that empower grassroots innovators to mobilize funding from diverse sources, including individual donors, local businesses, and community organizations.
4. Inclusive procurement strategies: Public and private sector procurement policies that prioritize the sourcing of goods and services from inclusive

innovators, social enterprises, and community-based vendors, creating new market opportunities and revenue streams.

5. Capacity-building and technical assistance: Integrated technical assistance and capacity-building programs that equip inclusive innovators with the skills, tools, and networks to access diverse financing mechanisms and effectively scale their SDG-aligned initiatives.

By developing and implementing these innovative financing approaches, African nations can unlock the necessary resources to support the growth and scaling of inclusive innovation projects that contribute to the realization of the Sustainable Development Goals. Crucially, this financing ecosystem must be accompanied by supportive policy frameworks, collaborative partnerships, and inclusive governance structures to ensure that the benefits of these investments are equitably distributed and aligned with the needs and priorities of marginalized communities.

XIV. Knowledge Sharing and Cross-Pollination of Inclusive Innovation Practices

The effective alignment of inclusive innovation and the Sustainable Development Goals requires robust knowledge-sharing, cross-pollination of practices, and the establishment of collaborative platforms that facilitate the exchange of insights, lessons, and best practices across African nations and beyond.

Scholars have highlighted the importance of creating dedicated knowledge hubs, innovation libraries, and digital repositories that document, analyze, and disseminate the experiences and learnings from successful inclusive innovation initiatives that have contributed to the achievement of the SDGs. These knowledge-sharing platforms can serve as invaluable resources for policymakers, development practitioners, and community-based organizations, enabling them to adapt and scale effective models in their respective contexts.

Furthermore, the establishment of regional and continental networks, such as the Afrilabs network and the Southern African Innovation Support (SAIS) program, can facilitate cross-border collaborations, joint research projects, and the co-creation of inclusive innovation strategies aligned with the SDGs. By leveraging the collective expertise, resources, and diverse perspectives of these collaborative ecosystems, African nations can amplify the impact of inclusive innovation and accelerate progress towards the global goals.

Alongside these formal knowledge-sharing mechanisms, the cultivation of communities of practice, peer-to-peer learning exchanges, and mentorship programs can empower grassroots innovators, traditional knowledge holders, and community-based organizations to share their experiences, challenges, and solutions, fostering a culture of continuous learning and adaptation.

By prioritizing knowledge sharing, cross-pollination, and collaborative networks, African nations can harness the transformative potential of inclusive innovation to drive sustainable development in a more coordinated, scalable, and impactful manner, ultimately contributing to the realization of the Sustainable Development Goals across the continent.

References

Agarwal, N., Brem, A., & Grottke, M. (2018). Towards a higher socio-economic impact through shared understanding of product requirements in emerging markets: The case of jugaad-an innovative problem-solving approach. *Technological Forecasting and Social Change*, 135, 91-98.

Agrawal, A. (1995). Dismantling the divide between indigenous and scientific knowledge. *Development and change*, 26(3), 413-439.

Berkes, F. (2012). Sacred ecology. Routledge. Briggs, J. (2005). The use of indigenous knowledge in development: problems and challenges. *Progress in development studies*, 5(2), 99-114.

Briggs, J., & Sharp, J. (2004). Indigenous knowledges and development: a postcolonial caution. *Third World Quarterly*, 25(4), 661-676.

Briggs, J. (2005). The use of indigenous knowledge in development: problems and challenges. *Progress in development studies*, 5(2), 99-114.

Brokensha, D., Warren, D. M., & Werner, O. (Eds.). (1980). *Indigenous knowledge systems and development* (Vol. 11). University Press of America.

Ely, A., & Oxley, N. (2014). *STEPS Centre Research on Grassroots Innovation Movements*. STEPS Centre.

Escobar, A. (1995). *Encountering development: The making and unmaking of the Third World*. Princeton University Press.

Gupta, A. K. (2016). *Grassroots Innovation: Minds on the Margin are not Marginal Minds*. Penguin Random House India.

Lwoga, E. T., Ngulube, P., & Stilwell, C. (2010). Managing indigenous knowledge for sustainable agricultural development in developing countries: Knowledge management approaches in the social context. *The International Information & Library Review*, 42(3), 174-185.

Mazzocchi, F. (2006). Western science and traditional knowledge: Despite their variations, different forms of knowledge can learn from each other. *EMBO reports*, 7(5), 463-466.

Mensah, J. (2019). Sustainable development: Meaning, history, principles, pillars, and implications for human action: Literature review. *Cogent social sciences*, 5(1), 1653531.

Moleka, P. (2024a). Innovative Entrepreneurship through Alternative Finance: A Framework for Sustainable and Innovative Business Models

Moleka, P. (2024b). Climate Resilience through Grassroots Innovation: Empowering Congolese Communities to Adapt to Environmental Change.

Moran, M., Rein, M., & Goodin, R. E. (Eds.). (2018). *The Oxford handbook of public policy*. Oxford University Press.

SAIS. (2021). About Southern Africa Innovation Support Programme. Retrieved from https://www.saisprogramme.com/about-sais/

Sá, C., & Lee, H. (2012). Open global networks, positioning BRICS for the post-2015 development agenda. *Journal of International Development*, 24(5), 654-669.

Schillo, R. S., & Robinson, R. M. (2017). Inclusive innovation in developed countries: The who, what, why, and how. *Technology Innovation Management Review*, 7(7), 34-46.

Seyfang, G., & Smith, A. (2007). Grassroots innovations for sustainable development: Towards a new research and policy agenda. *Environmental politics*, 16(4), 584-603.

Sillitoe, P. (1998). The development of indigenous knowledge: a new applied anthropology. *Current anthropology*, 39(2), 223-252.

Srinivas, K. R. (2012). Protecting traditional knowledge holders' interests and preventing misappropriation—Traditional knowledge commons and sui generis models. *The WIPO Journal*, 3(2), 167-184.

United Nations. (2015). *Transforming our world: The 2030 agenda for sustainable development*. United Nations General Assembly.

CHAPTER 12

Collaborative Innovation: Building Transnational Partnerships

In today's increasingly interconnected and globalized world, the imperatives of inclusive and sustainable development in Africa can no longer be addressed in isolation (Mensah, 2019). Innovative solutions to complex challenges require the coming together of diverse stakeholders, knowledge systems, and resources across national and regional boundaries. The power of collaborative innovation, fueled by transnational partnerships, holds immense potential for driving transformative change on the African continent. This chapter explores the critical role of collaborative innovation and transnational partnerships in advancing inclusive innovation ecosystems in Africa. It examines the growing landscape of cross-border collaborations, the unique benefits and challenges they present, and the innovative models and mechanisms that are enabling these partnerships to thrive. By highlighting successful case studies and drawing on cutting-edge research, this chapter provides a comprehensive roadmap for policymakers, practitioners, and community leaders to harness the synergistic power of collaborative innovation for the realization of equitable and sustainable development.

I. The Imperative of Collaborative Innovation in Africa

The complexity of the development challenges facing Africa – from poverty alleviation and food security to climate change adaptation and healthcare access – demands a holistic, multidimensional approach that transcends geographical and institutional boundaries. Collaborative innovation, which leverages the diverse perspectives, expertise, and resources of a wide range of stakeholders (Kruk, Gage, Arsenault, Jordan et al., 2018), has emerged as a crucial strategy for addressing these interconnected challenges in a more effective and impactful manner. Transnational partnerships, in particular, offer a unique opportunity to tap into global knowledge, technology, and financial resources, while simultaneously amplifying the voices and solutions of local communities. By fostering cross-border collaboration and knowledge exchange, these partnerships can contribute to the development of scalable, context-appropriate innovations that are grounded in the lived realities and aspirations of African communities (Sá & Lee, 2012). Moreover, collaborative innovation aligns with the principles of inclusive development, which emphasize the need to empower marginalized groups, promote equity and social justice, and ensure that the benefits of progress are equitably distributed. By engaging a diverse array of stakeholders, including civil society organizations, community-based groups, and informal sector actors, collaborative innovation models can help to redress systematic inequalities and amplify the agency of traditionally excluded populations (Berdegué, 2005).

II. The Landscape of Collaborative Innovation Partnerships in Africa

The African continent has witnessed a flourishing of collaborative innovation initiatives and transnational partnerships in recent years, driven by a range of actors, including:

1. Intergovernmental and regional organizations: Institutions such as the African Union, the United Nations Economic Commission for Africa (UNECA), and the New Partnership for Africa's Development (NEPAD) have spearheaded collaborative frameworks and programs that facilitate cross-border knowledge exchange and solution-sharing.
2. Bilateral and multilateral development agencies: International development organizations, including the World Bank, the United Nations Development Programme (UNDP), and the United States Agency for International Development (USAID), have increasingly invested in collaborative innovation initiatives that leverage global expertise and resources to address local challenges.

3. Private sector entities: Multinational corporations, social enterprises, and impact investment firms have forged strategic partnerships with local actors to co-create innovative business models, products, and services tailored to the unique needs of African markets.
4. Academic and research institutions: Universities, think tanks, and research centers, both within Africa and globally, have established collaborative networks and joint research programs to advance knowledge-sharing and the co-production of innovative solutions.
5. Civil society organizations and community-based groups: Grassroots movements, non-governmental organizations, and community-led initiatives have banded together across national borders to amplify the voices of marginalized groups, share best practices, and advocate for more inclusive innovation policies and programs. These diverse collaborative innovation partnerships have given rise to a rich tapestry of initiatives, ranging from regional innovation hubs and cross-border accelerator programs to joint research projects and transnational advocacy campaigns.
   By leveraging complementary strengths and fostering synergies, these collaborative efforts have the potential to unlock new pathways for inclusive and sustainable development in Africa.

III. Benefits of Collaborative Innovation Partnerships

The adoption of collaborative innovation models in Africa has yielded a wide range of benefits, including:

1. Access to diverse knowledge, expertise, and resources
   - Transnational partnerships enable the exchange of cutting-edge knowledge, technological advancements, and innovative best practices across borders.
   - By pooling financial, technical, and human resources, collaborative initiatives can mobilize the critical mass required to tackle complex development challenges.
2. Contextualization and localization of innovative solutions
   - Collaborative models that bring together global expertise and local community knowledge can foster the development of innovative

solutions that are better tailored to the unique needs and realities of African contexts.
- The active engagement of local stakeholders in the co-creation process helps to ensure the cultural relevance, social acceptability, and long-term sustainability of innovative interventions.

3. Amplification of marginalized voices and perspectives
   - Transnational partnerships that prioritize the inclusion of traditionally underrepresented groups, such as women, youth, and rural communities, can empower these stakeholders to shape the innovation agenda and advocate for more equitable development outcomes.
   - By bridging the divide between global and local knowledge systems, collaborative innovation models can help to elevate the status and agency of Indigenous and community-based innovation practices.
4. Scaling and replication of successful initiatives
   - Collaborative frameworks enable the sharing and adaptation of innovative solutions across national boundaries, facilitating the scaling and replication of successful models in different contexts.
   - Cross-border partnerships can also help to mobilize the resources and networks required to support the long-term sustainability and expansion of inclusive innovation initiatives.
5. Fostering regional integration and economic cooperation
   - Collaborative innovation initiatives can contribute to the strengthening of regional economic integration and the development of shared infrastructure, markets, and value chains across the African continent.
   - By facilitating the cross-pollination of ideas and the co-creation of innovative products and services, these partnerships can enhance the competitiveness and resilience of African economies.

IV. Challenges and Barriers to Collaborative Innovation Partnerships

Despite the significant benefits of collaborative innovation, the establishment and sustenance of transnational partnerships in Africa face several challenges and barriers, including:

1. Navigating cultural, linguistic, and institutional differences
   - Disparities in organizational cultures, decision-making processes, and communication styles can hinder the development of trust and effective collaboration among partners.
   - Linguistic and cultural divides can also pose barriers to the seamless exchange of knowledge and the alignment of goals and priorities.
2. Aligning divergent interests and priorities
   - Partners from diverse backgrounds, such as private sector entities, government agencies, and civil society organizations, may have differing motivations, incentives, and timelines, which can complicate the coordination of collaborative efforts.
   - Reconciling these diverse interests and finding mutually beneficial ways of engaging can be a significant hurdle in establishing and maintaining effective partnerships.
3. Ensuring equitable power dynamics and inclusive participation
   - Existing power imbalances and asymmetries, both at the global and regional levels, can undermine the ability of marginalized stakeholders to meaningfully participate and influence the collaborative innovation process.
   - Addressing these power dynamics and fostering truly inclusive and participatory models of collaboration remains an ongoing challenge.
4. Mobilizing sustainable funding and resources
   - Securing long-term, reliable funding to support the development, implementation, and scaling of collaborative innovation initiatives can be a persistent challenge, particularly for grassroots organizations and community-based groups.
   - Overreliance on external donor funding and the lack of dedicated funding mechanisms designed to catalyze and sustain these partnerships can hamper their long-term viability.
5. Navigating legal and regulatory frameworks
   - Differences in national policies, intellectual property regimes, and cross-border regulations can create administrative and legal obstacles that impede the smooth functioning of collaborative innovation partnerships.

- Developing harmonized frameworks and streamlined processes to facilitate the seamless flow of knowledge, resources, and innovative solutions across borders remains a crucial but complex undertaking.

V. Strategies for Enabling Effective Collaborative Innovation Partnerships

To overcome these challenges and unlock the transformative potential of collaborative innovation in Africa, the following strategies can be employed:

1. Fostering trust, communication, and cultural competence
   - Invest in capacity-building programs and cross-cultural exchange initiatives to enhance mutual understanding, communication, and trust-building among partners.
   - Establish dedicated coordination mechanisms, such as joint steering committees and liaison roles, to facilitate seamless collaboration and the alignment of goals and priorities.
2. Promoting inclusive and equitable participation
   - Adopt participatory, co-creation approaches that empower traditionally marginalized stakeholders, including women, youth, and rural communities, to actively shape the collaborative innovation agenda.
   - Implement mechanisms for equitable decision-making, resource allocation, and benefit-sharing to address power imbalances and ensure the fair distribution of collaborative outcomes.
3. Developing innovative financing and resource mobilization models
   - Explore collaborative funding mechanisms, such as multi-stakeholder innovation funds, cross-border crowdfunding platforms, and blended finance schemes, to diversify and sustain the resource base for collaborative innovation initiatives.
   - Leverage public-private partnerships and engage impact investors to mobilize the necessary financial, technical, and human resources to support the development and scaling of collaborative innovation projects. 4. Harmonizing legal and regulatory frameworks
   - Advocate for the harmonization of national and regional policies, intellectual property regimes, and cross-border regulations to facilitate

the seamless exchange of knowledge, technology, and resources within collaborative innovation ecosystems.
- Establish dedicated institutional mechanisms, such as regional innovation policy taskforces or bilateral/multilateral regulatory sandboxes, to navigate legal and administrative complexities and enable the smooth functioning of collaborative initiatives.

5. Strengthening knowledge management and impact measurement
   - Implement robust knowledge management systems and collaborative platforms to enable the efficient sharing, adaptation, and scaling of innovative solutions across borders.
   - Develop comprehensive impact assessment frameworks and key performance indicators to capture the multidimensional value and long-term sustainability of collaborative innovation initiatives.
6. Championing collaborative innovation at the policy level
   - Integrate collaborative innovation approaches into national and regional development strategies, digital transformation plans, and innovation policy frameworks to create an enabling environment for cross-border partnerships.
   - Leverage the influence of regional economic communities, intergovernmental bodies, and multilateral organizations to advocate for the prioritization of collaborative innovation as a key driver of inclusive and sustainable development in Africa.
   - By adopting these strategies and cultivating an ecosystem that nurtures and supports effective collaborative innovation partnerships, African nations can harness the collective power of global expertise, local knowledge, and multi-stakeholder collaboration to address complex development challenges, unlock new avenues for inclusive growth, and accelerate the realization of the continent's sustainable development aspirations.

VI. Leveraging Regional Economic Communities for Collaborative Innovation

The African continent is home to a vibrant network of regional economic communities (RECs), such as the Economic Community of West African States (ECOWAS), the Southern African Development Community (SADC), and the East African Community (EAC), which have emerged as crucial platforms for fostering collaborative innovation across national borders.

These regional bodies have the potential to play a catalytic role in enabling effective transnational partnerships by leveraging their convening power, policy influence, and access to resources. Some key ways in which RECs can drive collaborative innovation include:

1. Developing regional innovation policies and strategies: RECs can spearhead the creation of harmonized, region-wide innovation policies and strategies that encourage cross-border collaboration, knowledge exchange, and the co-development of innovative solutions.
2. Establishing regional innovation funds and financing mechanisms: By pooling resources and mobilizing diverse funding sources, RECs can establish dedicated regional innovation funds or blended finance schemes to support the incubation, scaling, and replication of collaborative innovation initiatives across member states.
3. Facilitating the creation of regional innovation hubs and networks: RECs can catalyze the development of interconnected regional innovation hubs, accelerators, and knowledge-sharing platforms that bring together diverse stakeholders and foster the cross-pollination of ideas and best practices.
4. Harmonizing legal and regulatory frameworks: RECs can work towards the harmonization of intellectual property regimes, data governance policies, and other cross-border regulations to create an enabling environment for the seamless exchange of knowledge, technology, and resources within collaborative innovation ecosystems.
5. Championing inclusive and participatory approaches: RECs can ensure that the design and implementation of their collaborative innovation initiatives prioritize the meaningful engagement of marginalized communities, grassroots innovators, and civil society organizations, thereby amplifying their voices and perspectives.

Prominent examples of REC-driven collaborative innovation initiatives include the ECOWAS Innovation Initiative, which aims to foster a regional innovation ecosystem, and the Southern Africa Innovation Support (SAIS) program, which has facilitated cross-border collaboration and knowledge exchange among innovation hubs in the SADC region (ECOWAS, 2021; SAIS, 2021).

By leveraging the convening power, policy influence, and resource mobilization capacity of regional economic communities, African nations can unlock new pathways for scaling up collaborative innovation and ensuring that the benefits of these partnerships are equitably distributed across the continent.

VII. The Role of Diaspora Networks in Enabling Collaborative Innovation

The African diaspora, comprising millions of individuals living outside the African continent, represents a significant yet often underutilized resource for promoting innovation and sustainable development in Africa. This diverse and dynamic group, with its wealth of skills, experiences, financial resources, and global networks, plays a critical role in fostering cross-border collaboration and driving the continent's development agenda. By leveraging their unique position, diaspora members can catalyze innovation, bridge knowledge gaps, and bring new financial flows and partnerships to address Africa's most pressing challenges. This section explores how the African diaspora contributes to innovation ecosystems, enhances capacity building, and drives economic growth through strategic collaborations across borders.

1. Diaspora-Led Innovation Ecosystems

Diasporas are increasingly pivotal in the establishment of innovation ecosystems that are contextually relevant to African nations. Often possessing advanced skills and global exposure, diaspora members can offer new perspectives and innovative solutions to local challenges, particularly in sectors such as technology, health, energy, and agriculture. Their involvement can facilitate the creation of ecosystems that blend local knowledge with cutting-edge solutions, fostering the development of high-impact innovations suited to the African context.

Diaspora-led innovation hubs, incubators, and accelerators are increasingly sprouting across Africa, often spearheaded by returnees or diaspora organizations. These initiatives help to bridge the gap between the global innovation landscape and local needs. The African Innovation Foundation, for example, works with the African diaspora to support local innovations through funding, mentorship, and strategic partnerships (Akinbo, 2020). Similarly, the African Diaspora Network, which connects professionals and entrepreneurs, has been instrumental in promoting cross-border innovation through knowledge exchange and partnerships between local innovators and global networks (Cunningham, 2019). Successful examples of diaspora-driven collaborative innovation include the African Diaspora Marketplace, a joint initiative of USAID and Western Union that provides funding and mentorship to diaspora-led enterprises, and the Diaspora Innovation Institute, which connects African diaspora professionals with grassroots innovators in their countries of origin (African Diaspora Marketplace, 2021; Diaspora Innovation Institute, 2021).

By strengthening innovation ecosystems, diasporas can help unlock the creative potential of local communities while simultaneously making African nations more competitive in the global market.

2. Financial Contributions and Investment Flows

The African diaspora is a significant source of financial resources, with remittances constituting a substantial portion of Africa's GDP. In 2020 alone, African countries received over $40 billion in remittances, a figure that is greater than foreign direct investment (FDI) and official development assistance combined (World Bank, 2021). Beyond remittances, the diaspora plays a crucial role in financing development projects, entrepreneurship, and social enterprises in Africa through impact investing, venture capital, and philanthropic activities.

Diaspora investment can directly support the scaling of innovative project, particularly in sectors that face difficulties securing financing from traditional sources. In the clean energy sector, for example, diaspora investors are critical in financing projects such as solar power initiatives or off-grid energy solutions (UNDP, 2020). The "Africa Diaspora Market" initiative, launched by the United Nations Economic Commission for Africa (UNECA), is another example of how diaspora investments are being harnessed to support entrepreneurial ventures and sustainable development projects across the continent (UNECA, 2019). Moreover, diaspora networks can facilitate access to international markets, providing African startups with the necessary business connections and visibility to scale their operations beyond national borders (Graham, 2018).

3. Knowledge Transfer and Capacity Building

One of the most valuable contributions of the African diaspora is the transfer of knowledge and expertise. Many members of the diaspora are highly skilled professionals with substantial experience in sectors such as technology, health, finance, and education. Through capacity-building programs, mentorship, and collaborations, the diaspora helps bridge critical knowledge gaps and enhance local capacities in innovation.

Capacity-building initiatives led by the diaspora have a profound impact, especially in fields such as higher education, healthcare, and science and technology. The African Academy of Sciences, for example, engages diaspora scientists in transnational research initiatives that address critical issues such as climate change, infectious diseases, and sustainable agriculture (Chimuka et al., 2021). Diaspora scientists and professionals have also contributed to building Africa's technological and scientific infrastructure through collaborative research projects and joint training programs (Ogunniyi & Adeoye, 2018). These initiatives help to localize global knowledge, ensuring that innovations are tailored to Africa's socio-economic and cultural contexts.

In the healthcare sector, diaspora professionals have contributed significantly to combating diseases such as malaria, HIV/AIDS, and Ebola by sharing expertise, developing local research capacity, and leading international collaborations. Through programs like the African Health Diaspora Initiative (AHDI), healthcare professionals in the diaspora work with local governments and international organizations to strengthen health systems and improve access to healthcare (Gyakye, 2017).

4. Diaspora Networks and Collaborative Platforms

Diaspora networks provide crucial platforms for knowledge exchange, cross-border collaboration, and advocacy. These networks create opportunities for diaspora members to engage with local communities, innovators, and policymakers, facilitating the sharing of best practices, lessons learned, and successful models for innovation and development.

Diaspora-led platforms, such as the African Diaspora Network (ADN) and the African Network of Entrepreneurs (ANE), provide valuable spaces for cross-border collaboration, connecting African innovators with global markets, investors, and experts. These networks facilitate the formation of partnerships that lead to shared solutions and mutually beneficial outcomes. For example, the ADN's annual Global Diaspora Week provides a forum for discussing opportunities for diaspora engagement in African development (Cunningham, 2019). Furthermore, platforms like the Pan-African Diaspora Alliance (PADA) and the African Union's Diaspora Policy Framework enable diaspora members to collaborate on the continent's long-term development goals, particularly in fostering sustainable innovations in technology and entrepreneurship.

By creating these collaborative spaces, diaspora networks strengthen the transnational bonds necessary for achieving inclusive growth and innovation across African countries. These platforms also enhance the visibility of African innovators and foster global collaboration, positioning Africa as a key player in the global innovation economy.

5. Policy Advocacy and Institutional Support

The African diaspora plays a key role in advocating for policies that promote innovation and development. By engaging with policymakers, diaspora members can drive the creation of an enabling environment for innovation through advocacy for favorable policies, funding mechanisms, and infrastructure improvements. The diaspora's international perspective also provides them with the ability to influence global policies that can benefit Africa, such as trade agreements, intellectual property rights, and climate change initiatives.

For instance, the African Union's Diaspora Division has worked closely with diaspora organizations to enhance the engagement of the African diaspora in Africa's development initiatives (African Union, 2019). By advocating for policies that prioritize innovation and entrepreneurship, the diaspora ensures that African nations adopt frameworks that attract investment, foster creativity, and promote sustainable growth.

Governments can further institutionalize diaspora engagement by establishing dedicated ministries or units to coordinate diaspora relations and leverage their expertise. Initiatives like the "African Diaspora Volunteer Program" offer practical avenues for diaspora members to contribute to local development by volunteering their skills and knowledge on specific projects (Muleya, 2020).

6. Challenges and Strategic Approaches to Harnessing Diaspora Potential

Despite its significant potential, the full engagement of the African diaspora in cross-border innovation and sustainable development is hindered by several challenges. These include issues related to regulatory frameworks, difficulties in managing diaspora investments, and the lack of cohesive diaspora engagement policies. Moreover, the political and economic instability in some African countries can limit the diaspora's willingness to engage or invest in home-country projects (Chikweche & Fletcher, 2014).

To effectively harness the potential of the African diaspora, African governments must implement policies that facilitate engagement, incentivize investments, and streamline collaboration between diaspora members and local actors. Governments should also work to improve infrastructure, such as digital platforms for knowledge exchange, and ensure that regulatory environments are conducive to cross-border partnerships.

The African diaspora represents a powerful and underutilized resource for driving sustainable development and fostering innovation in Africa. By strategically leveraging their intellectual, financial, and networked capital, the diaspora can play a critical role in transforming Africa's innovation landscape. To realize the full potential of the diaspora, African nations must create an enabling environment that encourages collaboration, facilitates knowledge transfer, and builds long-term partnerships. In doing so, Africa can harness the collective power of its diaspora to tackle its most pressing development challenges and accelerate the achievement of its sustainable development goals.

VIII. Measuring the Impact and Evaluating the Effectiveness of Collaborative Innovation Partnerships

Robust impact measurement and evaluation frameworks are essential for understanding the effectiveness and long-term viability of collaborative innovation partnerships in Africa. However, the complex, multi-stakeholder, and cross-border nature of these initiatives presents unique challenges in developing appropriate evaluation approaches.

Key considerations in measuring the impact and effectiveness of collaborative innovation partnerships include:

1. Capturing multidimensional value creation: Evaluation frameworks should go beyond purely economic or output-oriented metrics to assess the social, environmental, and systemic impacts of collaborative initiatives, including their contributions to capacity building, empowerment, and the strengthening of innovation ecosystems.
2. Embracing participatory and community-driven approaches: The design and implementation of evaluation processes should actively involve diverse stakeholders, including local communities, grassroots innovators, and marginalized groups, to ensure that the measurement of impact aligns with their needs and perspectives.
3. Assessing the quality of collaboration and partnership dynamics: Evaluation should examine the quality of the collaborative process, including factors such as trust-building, power dynamics, and the equitable distribution of benefits, to inform the continuous improvement of partnership models.
4. Evaluating the scalability and replicability of collaborative solutions: Assessments should examine the potential for collaborative innovations to be scaled up and adapted across different contexts, as well as the mechanisms and enablers that support successful replication.
5. Integrating learning and feedback loops: Evaluation should be embedded within a broader learning and adaptive management framework, enabling partners to continuously refine their collaborative approaches and strategies based on evidence-based insights.

6. Fostering cross-border knowledge sharing and comparative analysis: Establishing collaborative platforms for the exchange of evaluation findings, case studies, and lessons learned can enhance the collective understanding of what works in enabling effective transnational partnerships for inclusive innovation.

By developing and implementing comprehensive, participatory, and collaborative evaluation frameworks, African nations can not only measure the impact of their cross-border innovation initiatives but also generate valuable insights to guide the design and scaling of future collaborative endeavors, ultimately strengthening the continent's capacity to address complex development challenges through the power of collective action.

References

Adeoti, J. O. (2012). Building technological capability in the less developed countries: the role of a national system of innovation. *Science and Public Policy*, 39(2), 187-206.

African Diaspora Marketplace. (2021). About the African Diaspora Marketplace. Retrieved from https://africandiarasporamarketplace.org/about/

Akinbo, O. (2020). Harnessing Diaspora Expertise for Africa's Sustainable Development: A Critical Review. *African Journal of Development*, 15(2), 103-119.

Arocena, R., & Sutz, J. (2000). Looking at national systems of innovation from the South. *Industry and innovation*, 7(1), 55-75.

Berdegué, J. A. (2005). Pro-poor innovation systems.

Bergek, A., Jacobsson, S., Carlsson, B., Lindmark, S., & Rickne, A. (2008). Analyzing the functional dynamics of technological innovation systems: A scheme of analysis. *Research policy*, 37(3), 407-429

Chataway, J., Hanlin, R., & Kaplinsky, R. (2014). Inclusive innovation: an architecture for policy development. *Innovation and Development*, 4(1), 33-54.

Chikweche, T., & Fletcher, R. (2014). A Study of the Impact of Diaspora Communities in Africa's Development. *Journal of African Business*, 15(4), 213-228.

Chimuka, L., Dube, S., & Mhlanga, N. (2021). Diaspora and Science: Empowering Africa's Future through Knowledge Transfer. *African Science Review*, 9(1), 45-60.

Cunningham, W. (2019). Global Diaspora Engagement and Africa's Development. *The African Development Review*, 31(3), 318-332.

Diaspora Innovation Institute. (2021). About the Diaspora Innovation Institute. Retrieved from https://diaspirainnovation.org/about/

ECOWAS. (2021). ECOWAS Innovation Initiative. Retrieved from https://www.ecowas.int/ecowas-innovation-initiative/

Gyakye, A. (2017). The Role of the African Diaspora in Public Health Initiatives: Lessons from the Ebola Crisis. *African Health Journal*, 20(2), 81-92.

Graham, J. (2018). Cross-Border Investment by the African Diaspora: Emerging Trends and Opportunities. *Journal of African Economics*, 27(3), 341-356.

Kaplan, D. (2008). South African innovation policy: Potential and limitations. *Science & Public Policy (SPP)*, 35(1).

Kruk, M. E. et l. (2018). High-quality health systems in the Sustainable Development Goals era: time for a revolution. *The Lancet. Global health*, 6(11), e1196–e1252. https://doi.org/10.1016/S2214-109X(18)30386-3

Lundvall, B. Å. (2007). National innovation systems—analytical concept and development tool. *Industry and innovation*, 14(1), 95-119.

Mensah, J. (2019). Sustainable development: Meaning, history, principles, pillars, and implications for human action: Literature review. *Cogent social sciences*, *5*(1), 1653531.

OECD. (2015). *Innovation Policies for Inclusive Development: Scaling Up Inclusive Innovations*. OECD Publishing, Paris.

Ogunniyi, M., & Adeoye, O. (2018). Diaspora and the Growth of Innovation Systems in Africa. *Journal of Innovation and Technology*, 11(2), 113-126.

Oyelaran-Oyeyinka, B., & Kaushalesh, L. (2006). Inter-firm collaboration and competitive strategy in the mobile telecommunications industry of China. *Technovation*, 26(2), 277-290.

SAIS. (2021). About Southern Africa Innovation Support Programme. Retrieved from https://www.saisprogramme.com/about-sais/

Sá, C., & Lee, H. (2012). Open global networks, positioning BRICS for the post-2015 development agenda. *Journal of International Development*, 24(5), 654-669.

Schillo, R. S., & Robinson, R. M. (2017). Inclusive innovation in developed countries: The who, what, why, and how. *Technology Innovation Management Review*, 7(7).

Sutz, J. (2012). Measuring innovation in developing countries: some suggestions to achieve more accurate and useful indicators. International *Journal of Technological Learning, Innovation and Development*, 5(1-2), 40-57.

UNECA (United Nations Economic Commission for Africa). (2019). *Leveraging Diaspora Resources for African Development*. UNECA Policy Brief, 58, 2-6.

World Bank. (2021). *Remittances to Sub-Saharan Africa: Trends and Impact*. World Bank Report, 15(1), 1-12.

CHAPTER 13

Inclusive Innovation and the Future of Work

The rapid emergence of transformative technologies, from artificial intelligence and automation to digital platforms and the gig economy, is profoundly reshaping the world of work (Moleka, 2024), presenting both opportunities and challenges for Africa's workforce and economic development. As the continent grapples with high youth unemployment, informality, and widening inequalities, the imperative to harness the potential of inclusive innovation to foster a more equitable and sustainable future of work has become increasingly urgent. This chapter explores the nexus between inclusive innovation and the evolving African job market, examining the impact of emerging technologies on employment patterns, skills requirements, and the livelihoods of diverse communities. It delves into the strategies and models that can enable the development of inclusive workforce programs, skills training initiatives, and social protection mechanisms to ensure that the benefits of technological progress are equitably distributed and empower marginalized groups. By drawing on cutting-edge research, case studies, and insights from policymakers, industry leaders, and community innovators, this chapter charts a comprehensive roadmap for cultivating an inclusive innovation ecosystem that empowers African workers, nurtures resilient livelihoods, and unlocks new avenues for sustainable development. The chapter will address critical themes such as the future of work in an age of automation, the role of digital platforms and the gig economy, and the importance of reskilling and upskilling initiatives that cater to the diverse needs of Africa's workforce.

I. The Transformative Impact of Emerging Technologies on African Job Markets

The rapid advancement of emerging technologies, such as artificial intelligence (AI), automation, and digital platforms, is profoundly reshaping the future of work in Africa, presenting both opportunities and challenges for inclusive development. On one hand, these transformative technologies hold the potential to boost productivity, enhance efficiency, and drive economic growth, creating new categories of jobs and expanding access to digital work opportunities. AI-powered assistants, for example, can augment human capabilities and increase the efficiency of various industries, while digital platforms can facilitate the participation of underserved communities in the gig economy (Acemoglu & Restrepo, 2018). However, the disruptive nature of these technological advancements also poses significant risks, particularly for marginalized groups and informal sector workers who lack the resources, skills, and social protections to adapt to the changing labor market. Widespread automation and the proliferation of platform-based work can lead to job displacement, the erosion of traditional employment models, and the widening of existing socioeconomic divides (Frey & Osborne, 2017). The impact of these technological shifts is particularly acute in the African context, where informal and precarious forms of employment already dominate the labor landscape. The susceptibility of many African jobs to automation, combined with the limited availability of comprehensive social safety nets and reskilling programs, threatens to exacerbate the continent's persistent challenges of youth unemployment, income inequality, and poverty (ILO, 2019).

II. Navigating the Paradoxes of the Gig Economy and Digital Platforms

The rise of the gig economy and digital labor platforms in Africa presents both opportunities and challenges for inclusive development. On one hand, these platforms can provide previously marginalized individuals, particularly women and youth, with unprecedented access to flexible, on-demand work opportunities, enabling them to supplement their incomes and diversify their livelihood strategies (Graham et al., 2017). However, the inherent precarity and lack of social protections associated with gig work can also amplify the vulnerabilities of these workers, exposing them to unstable earnings, limited job security, and the absence of benefits such as healthcare and retirement plans. The gendered dynamics of platform-based work further exacerbate these challenges, with women often facing additional barriers to accessing and thriving within these digital ecosystems (Rani & Furrer, 2019). Moreover, the algorithms and data-driven decision-making processes that govern the operations of many digital platforms can perpetuate existing biases and discriminatory practices, leading to the exclusion of certain groups from job opportunities or the unfair treatment of workers. The opacity and lack of worker agency within these platform-based systems can further undermine principles of fairness, accountability, and worker empowerment (Fairwork, 2020). Navigating the paradoxes of the gig economy and digital platforms requires the development of innovative policy frameworks, institutional mechanisms, and community-driven initiatives that can harness the potential benefits of these emerging work models while mitigating their inherent risks and ensuring the protection of workers' rights and well-being.

III. Upskilling, Reskilling, and Lifelong Learning for Inclusive Innovation

As the African job market undergoes profound transformations driven by technological change, the imperative to develop inclusive workforce development programs and skills training initiatives has become paramount.

Equipping workers, particularly those from marginalized communities, with the knowledge, skills, and mindsets required to thrive in the evolving innovation landscape is crucial for fostering inclusive and sustainable development. However, the traditional educational and vocational training systems in many African countries often fail to keep pace with the rapidly shifting skills demands, leaving workers ill-equipped to adapt to the changing nature of work. Addressing this mismatch requires a multifaceted approach that prioritizes the following strategies:

1. Demand-driven skills development
   - Engaging closely with industry, academia, and community stakeholders to identify emerging skills gaps and design responsive, context-specific training programs that equip workers with the competencies required by the job market.

   - Fostering collaborative models that integrate work-based learning, apprenticeships, and on-the-job training to bridge the divide between classroom-based education and real-world application.
2. Lifelong learning and reskilling initiatives
   - Implementing comprehensive upskilling and reskilling programs that enable workers to continuously adapt their skills in response to technological and economic shifts, ensuring their long-term employability and adaptability.
   - Leveraging digital learning platforms, micro-credentials, and flexible training modalities to provide workers, particularly those in the informal sector or remote areas, with accessible and affordable opportunities for ongoing skills development.
3. Inclusive and equitable access to skills training
   - Designing targeted workforce development programs that actively reach out to and empower marginalized groups, such as women, youth, and people with disabilities, to access the skills, resources, and support required to thrive in the innovation economy.
   - Addressing systemic barriers to skills acquisition, including gender-based biases, financial constraints, and cultural norms that limit the participation of certain groups in education and training.
4. Strengthening the innovation capabilities of workers
   - Integrating design thinking, problem-solving, and entrepreneurial mindsets into skills training curricula to cultivate the creativity, adaptability, and innovative capacities of the workforce.
   - Fostering cross-disciplinary collaboration and the integration of diverse knowledge systems to enable workers to tackle complex challenges through innovative, holistic approaches.
5. Aligning skills development with the future of work
   - Anticipating and adapting skills training programs to address the evolving needs of the labor market, including the growing demand for digital, green, and social innovation-oriented competencies.
   - Developing strong partnerships between educational institutions, industry, and policymakers to ensure the continuous alignment of skills development initiatives with the changing nature of work and the emerging innovation landscape. By embracing these strategies and investing in inclusive, future-oriented workforce development

programs, African nations can empower their workers to actively participate in and drive the transformation of innovation ecosystems, ultimately unlocking new pathways for equitable and sustainable economic growth.

IV. Inclusive Social Protection for Workers in the Innovation Economy

As the African job market becomes increasingly volatile and uncertain, the need for comprehensive, inclusive social protection systems has become paramount. Traditional social security frameworks, often linked to formal employment, frequently fail to extend coverage to the growing number of workers in the informal sector, gig economy, and other non-standard forms of employment. Addressing this gap requires the development of innovative, context-appropriate social protection mechanisms that can safeguard the livelihoods and well-being of all workers, regardless of their employment status or income level.

Key elements of this inclusive social protection agenda include:

1. Universal basic income and social assistance programs
   - Exploring the feasibility and viability of universal basic income (UBI) schemes and other forms of unconditional cash transfers to provide a reliable safety net and cushion workers against economic shocks and uncertainties.
   - Expanding the reach and adequacy of social assistance programs, such as targeted income support, food security initiatives, and housing subsidies, to ensure that the most vulnerable individuals and households can meet their basic needs.
2. Portable and adaptable social security systems
   - Designing social security frameworks that are decoupled from traditional employment models, enabling workers in the informal sector, gig economy, and other non-standard forms of work to access benefits such as healthcare, pensions, and unemployment insurance.
   - Leveraging digital technologies and innovative financing mechanisms to facilitate the portability and adaptability of these social protection schemes, ensuring their reach and responsiveness to the evolving nature of work.

3. Strengthening workers' collective bargaining and representation
   - Supporting the organization and collective mobilization of workers, including the formation of trade unions, cooperatives, and worker associations, to amplify their voices, advocate for their rights, and negotiate improved working conditions and social protections.
   - Promoting social dialogue and collaborative governance models that bring together workers, employers, and policymakers to co-create inclusive and equitable social protection frameworks.
4. Integrating social protection with skills development and innovation support
   - Aligning social protection initiatives with workforce development programs and innovation ecosystems to provide a comprehensive suite of support that enables workers to navigate the changing labor market, access reskilling opportunities, and participate in the innovation economy.
   - Leveraging the synergies between social protection, skills training, and innovation support to foster more resilient and inclusive pathways for sustainable livelihoods and economic empowerment.
5. Harnessing technology for inclusive social protection
   - Leveraging digital technologies, such as mobile money, biometric identification, and data analytics, to enhance the reach, efficiency, and responsiveness of social protection systems, particularly in reaching marginalized communities.
   - Exploring the potential of blockchain-based social protection frameworks and other innovative financing mechanisms to improve transparency, accountability, and the portability of benefits across diverse employment models. By embracing these inclusive social protection strategies, African nations can safeguard the well-being and livelihoods of all workers, empower them to participate in and contribute to the innovation economy, and foster a more equitable and resilient future of work.

V. Empowering Women and Marginalized Groups in the Innovation Economy

The evolving landscape of work driven by emerging technologies and the innovation economy presents both opportunities and challenges for women and other marginalized groups in Africa. On one hand, the flexibility and accessibility offered by digital platforms and gig work can create new avenues for economic participation and income generation, particularly for those facing structural barriers to traditional employment. However, these transformative shifts also risk exacerbating existing gender inequalities and the exclusion of marginalized communities if not accompanied by intentional, inclusive strategies.

Addressing the unique needs and barriers faced by women, youth, and other underrepresented groups in the innovation economy requires a multipronged approach that includes:

1. Targeted skills development and entrepreneurship support: Designing and implementing skills training programs, business incubation initiatives, and mentorship opportunities that are tailored to the specific needs and circumstances of women and marginalized entrepreneurs.
2. Enhancing access to digital infrastructure and technologies: Investing in the expansion of affordable, reliable, and inclusive digital connectivity and technological resources to empower marginalized communities to actively participate in the innovation economy.
3. Fostering inclusive platforms and algorithmic accountability: Ensuring that digital labor platforms and the algorithms that govern them are designed and operated in a manner that promotes fairness, transparency, and the equal treatment of all workers, regardless of their gender, race, or social status.
4. Advocating for gender-responsive policies and regulations: Engaging in policy advocacy to ensure that the regulatory frameworks governing the innovation economy, gig work, and social protection systems address the unique challenges and needs of women and marginalized groups.
5. Mobilizing community-driven financing and support networks: Empowering women and marginalized innovators to collectively pool resources, share knowledge, and access tailored financial and non-financial support through community-based initiatives and peer-to-peer networks.
6. Documenting and amplifying the experiences and contributions of underrepresented groups: Elevating the narratives, innovations, and success stories of women, youth, and other marginalized individuals

within the African innovation ecosystem to inspire and encourage their broader participation.

By adopting these strategies and fostering an inclusive innovation ecosystem that proactively addresses the unique needs and barriers faced by diverse communities, African nations can unlock the transformative potential of emerging technologies and the future of work to drive more equitable and sustainable development outcomes.

VI. Harnessing the Potential of the Informal Sector for Inclusive Innovation

The informal sector, which accounts for a significant portion of employment and economic activity in many African countries, presents both challenges and opportunities in the context of inclusive innovation and the future of work. While the precarious nature of informal work and the lack of social protections pose significant risks, the diverse, grassroots-driven innovations and adaptability of informal sector actors can also serve as a valuable resource for inclusive development.

Strategies for harnessing the potential of the informal sector for inclusive innovation include:

1. Integrating informal innovators into formal innovation ecosystems: Establishing dedicated programs, intermediary organizations, and collaborative platforms that bridge the divide between the formal and informal sectors, enabling the exchange of knowledge, resources, and opportunities.
2. Providing tailored capacity-building and business support: Designing and delivering customized training, mentorship, and advisory services that address the unique needs and constraints of informal sector entrepreneurs and workers, empowering them to scale their innovations and improve their livelihoods.
3. Facilitating access to inclusive financing mechanisms: Developing alternative financing models, such as community-based savings groups, cooperative-linked credit schemes, and flexible microcredit programs, that cater to the specific requirements of informal sector actors.

4. Strengthening social protection and formalization pathways: Implementing social protection frameworks that are adaptable and portable, ensuring that informal sector workers can access essential benefits and services. Simultaneously, promoting policy and regulatory reforms that facilitate the gradual formalization of informal enterprises while preserving their innovative potential.
5. Leveraging digital technologies for informal sector inclusion: Exploring the use of digital platforms, mobile applications, and other technological solutions to enhance the productivity, market access, and social protection of informal sector workers, while addressing the risks of digital exclusion.
6. Amplifying the voices of informal sector innovators: Creating dedicated platforms and advocacy channels that elevate the perspectives, experiences, and innovative solutions of informal sector actors, ensuring that their needs and priorities are reflected in policymaking and development agendas.

By adopting a more inclusive and holistic approach that recognizes the value of informal sector innovation and empowers these grassroots actors, African nations can foster a thriving, equitable, and resilient future of work that harnesses the full breadth of the continent's diverse workforce.

VII. Aligning Inclusive Innovation with the Sustainable Development Goals

The linkages between inclusive innovation and the Sustainable Development Goals (SDGs) become particularly salient in the context of the future of work. As African nations grapple with the disruptive impacts of emerging technologies, the imperative to align workforce development, social protection, and inclusive entrepreneurship initiatives with the global development agenda becomes increasingly crucial.

Key areas of alignment include:

1. Decent Work and Economic Growth (SDG 8): Fostering inclusive innovation ecosystems that create new categories of dignified, sustainable jobs and secure livelihoods, particularly for marginalized communities.

2. Industry, Innovation, and Infrastructure (SDG 9): Developing innovation-driven industries and technological infrastructure that are accessible, adaptable, and responsive to the needs of diverse workforce groups.
3. Reduced Inequalities (SDG 10): Ensuring that the benefits of technological progress and the innovation economy are equitably distributed, empowering historically disadvantaged individuals and communities.
4. Sustainable Cities and Communities (SDG 11): Leveraging inclusive innovation to create urban environments and community-based enterprises that are resilient, socially inclusive, and environmentally sustainable.
5. Responsible Consumption and Production (SDG 12): Fostering inclusive innovation in the design and deployment of circular, resource-efficient production models that generate decent work opportunities.
6. Climate Action (SDG 13): Harnessing inclusive innovation to develop climate-resilient livelihoods, green jobs, and sustainable solutions that safeguard the well-being of workers and communities.

By aligning inclusive innovation strategies with the broader SDG framework, African nations can cultivate a future of work that not only harnesses the transformative power of technology but also advances social, economic, and environmental justice, ultimately contributing to the realization of the continent's sustainable development aspirations.

References

Acemoglu, D., & Restrepo, P. (2018). The race between man and machine: Implications of technology for growth, factor shares, and employment. *American Economic Review*, 108(6), 1488-1542.

Asongu, S. A., & Odhiambo, N. M. (2019). Enhancing ICT for quality education in sub-Saharan Africa. *Education and Information Technologies*, 24(5), 2823-2839.

Beeharry, G. (2016). *Leapfrogging: The key to Africa's development?* Center for Global Development.

Brynjolfsson, E., & McAfee, A. (2014). *The second machine age: Work, progress, and prosperity in a time of brilliant technologies*. WW Norton & Company.

Castells, M. (2010). *The rise of the network society* (Vol. 1). John Wiley & Sons.
D. P. (2017). *The risks and rewards of online gig work at the global margin*. Oxford Internet Institute.
Fairwork. (2020). Fairwork Ethiopia Scores 2020: Labour Standards in the Gig Economy.
Graham, M., Lehdonvirta, V., Wood, A., Barnard, H., Hjorth, I., & Simon, Frey, C. B., & Osborne, M. A. (2017). The future of employment: How susceptible are jobs to computerisation? *Technological forecasting and social change*, 114, 254-280.
Graham, M., Hjorth, I., & Lehdonvirta, V. (2017). Digital labour and development: impacts of global digital labour platforms and the gig economy on worker livelihoods. *Transfer: European Review of Labour and Research*, 23(2), 135-162.
ILO. (2019). *Work for a brighter future – Global Commission on the Future of Work*. International Labour Organization.
Malik, K., Nicholson, B., & Heeks, R. (2018). Examining institutional influences on the retention and attrition of digital labour in global impact sourcing. *The Electronic Journal of Information Systems in Developing Countries*, 84(6), e12058.
Moleka, P. (2024). *The future of workplace spirituality as science*. GRIN: Verlag.
Rani, U., & Furrer, M. (2019). Digital labour platforms and new forms of flexible work in developing countries: The case of Rwanda. *Competition & Change*, 23(4), 401-419.
Rodrik, D., & Sabel, C. F. (2019). Building a good jobs economy. Unpublished manuscript, Harvard University.
World Bank. (2019). *World Development Report 2019: The Changing Nature of Work*. The World Bank.

CHAPTER 14

Inclusive Innovation Leadership: Cultivating a New Generation of Visionaries

In the rapidly evolving landscape of innovation and development in Africa, the critical role of inclusive leadership has emerged as a driving force for transformative change. The ability to effectively navigate complex challenges, foster collaborative ecosystems, and champion the empowerment of marginalized communities has become increasingly essential for unlocking the continent's immense potential. This chapter delves into the distinctive qualities, competencies, and behaviors that define inclusive innovation leaders – individuals who are committed to advancing social justice, amplifying diverse perspectives, and harnessing the collective power of communities to drive sustainable progress. By examining the lived experiences and insights of pioneering inclusive innovation champions, as well as drawing on cutting-edge research and leadership development frameworks, this chapter provides a comprehensive roadmap for nurturing and empowering the next generation of visionary leaders. The chapter will explore key aspects of inclusive innovation leadership, such as the importance of systems thinking, community-centric approaches, and the ability to navigate power dynamics and institutional barriers. It will also highlight successful models and strategies for cultivating inclusive leadership capacities within both the public and private sectors, as well as at the grassroots level, to ensure that the innovation agenda is firmly anchored in the principles of equity, sustainability, and social impact. Ultimately, this chapter aims to inspire and equip a diverse array of stakeholders – from policymakers and ecosystem builders to social entrepreneurs and community organizers – with the knowledge, tools, and mindsets required to foster a new era of inclusive innovation leadership, one that can propel the African continent towards a more prosperous, equitable, and sustainable future.

I. The Imperative of Inclusive Innovation Leadership

Across the African continent, the pressing need to address complex, interconnected development challenges – from poverty alleviation and food security to climate change adaptation and healthcare access – has underscored the critical importance of inclusive innovation leadership. These multifaceted, systemic issues demand a holistic, collaborative, and community-centric approach that transcends traditional boundaries and hierarchies. Inclusive innovation leaders, who prioritize the empowerment of marginalized groups, the integration of diverse knowledge systems, and the co-creation of transformative solutions, are uniquely positioned to navigate these challenges and catalyze lasting change. By amplifying the voices and perspectives of traditionally underrepresented communities, fostering cross-sectoral partnerships, and championing innovative, context-appropriate interventions, these visionary leaders can unlock new pathways for sustainable development that leave no one behind (Mazzucato, 2018). Moreover, the cultivation of inclusive innovation leadership aligns with the broader principles of equitable, participatory, and mission-oriented innovation – a fundamental shift in the way we conceptualize and approach the innovation process. This shift recognizes that innovation is not merely a linear, technology-driven endeavor, but a dynamic, socially-embedded, and value-laden undertaking that must be harnessed to address pressing societal challenges and promote the well-being of all people (Schot & Steinmueller, 2018). By empowering a new generation of inclusive innovation leaders, African nations can harness the transformative potential of their diverse populations, mobilize the collective intelligence and creativity of their communities, and drive the realization of the Sustainable Development Goals and the African Union's Agenda 2063. This imperative not only serves to promote social justice and inclusive development, but also holds the key to unlocking the continent's full economic and social potential.

II. Defining the Competencies of Inclusive Innovation Leaders

Inclusive innovation leaders possess a unique set of competencies that enable them to navigate complex challenges, foster collaborative ecosystems, and champion the empowerment of marginalized communities.

These competencies can be broadly categorized as follows:

1. Systems Thinking and Holistic Problem-Solving (Moleka, 2024)
   - Ability to understand and navigate the interconnected, multidimensional nature of development challenges, recognizing the interdependencies and feedback loops within complex socio-ecological systems.
   - Capacity to adopt a holistic, integrated approach to problem-solving, drawing on diverse disciplines, knowledge systems, and perspectives to devise innovative, context-appropriate solutions.
2. Participatory Leadership and Community Engagement
   - Commitment to inclusive, collaborative, and community-centric approaches that empower the active participation of marginalized groups in the innovation process.
   - Skill in facilitating inclusive dialogues, building trust, and fostering co-creation and collective decision-making with diverse stakeholders.
3. Adaptive Mindset and Continuous Learning
   - Openness to experimentation, risk-taking, and learning from failure, enabling the agile and iterative development of innovative solutions.
   - Capacity to continuously adapt to changing contexts, anticipate emerging challenges, and champion the acquisition of new knowledge and skills within their teams and communities.
4. Advocacy and Institutional Transformation
   - Ability to navigate complex power dynamics, institutional inertia, and policy frameworks to advocate for the integration of inclusive innovation principles within mainstream development agendas.
   - Skill in leveraging diverse communication strategies, data-driven evidence, and collaborative partnerships to drive institutional and ecosystem-level change.

5. Ethical Decision-Making and Social Impact Orientation
   - Grounding in ethical principles, such as social justice, environmental sustainability, and equitable distribution of benefits, to guide the innovation process and ensure positive societal impact.
   - Capacity to assess and mitigate potential unintended consequences of innovative interventions, while prioritizing the needs and wellbeing of marginalized communities.
6. Emotional Intelligence and Collaborative Leadership
   - Self-awareness, empathy, and interpersonal skills that enable inclusive innovation leaders to build trust, foster cross-cultural understanding, and inspire diverse teams and communities to work towards shared goals.
   - Ability to facilitate collective leadership, nurture the agency and leadership capacities of others, and create an enabling environment for collaborative innovation.
   - By cultivating these multifaceted competencies, inclusive innovation leaders can drive transformative change, catalyze the development of equitable and sustainable innovation ecosystems, and empower marginalized communities to become active agents of progress.

III. Inclusive Innovation Leadership in Action: Successful Case Studies

Across the African continent, a growing number of visionary leaders have emerged, showcasing the transformative impact of inclusive innovation approaches. These changemakers have spearheaded innovative initiatives that have positively impacted the lives of marginalized communities, while also inspiring and empowering others to follow in their footsteps.

1. Fatima Oyiza Abubakar, Nigeria: Founder of Farmcrowdy, a digital agricultural platform that connects smallholder farmers with investors and resources, empowering rural communities and promoting food security.
   - Key competencies: Systems thinking, community engagement, adaptive mindset, advocacy, and social impact orientation.
   - Impact: Farmcrowdy has enabled over 25,000 Nigerian farmers to access financing, training, and market linkages, while providing investors with opportunities to support sustainable agriculture.

2. Tito Ovia, Kenya: Co-founder of Havelock, a social enterprise that develops inclusive, last-mile distribution solutions for essential products and services, with a focus on women and youth.
   - Key competencies: Participatory leadership, collaborative innovation, adaptive mindset, and ethical decision-making.
   - Impact: Havelock's innovative distribution models have improved access to affordable healthcare, clean energy, and other critical resources for underserved communities across Kenya.
3. Leila Ndiaye, Senegal: Director-General of the Initiative for the Adaptation of African Agriculture, an organization that promotes climate-smart agriculture and the integration of traditional knowledge systems.
   - Key competencies: Systems thinking, advocacy, community engagement, and ethical decision-making.
   - Impact: Through innovative programs and policy advocacy, the Initiative has empowered smallholder farmers, particularly women, to adapt to the impacts of climate change and enhance food security.
4. Nkosana Mafico, Zimbabwe: Founder of Unlock Rural, a social enterprise that leverages digital technologies to connect rural entrepreneurs with resources, markets, and skills development opportunities.
   - Key competencies: Adaptive mindset, collaborative leadership, community engagement, and social impact orientation.
   - Impact: Unlock Rural has enabled over 15,000 rural entrepreneurs, the majority of them women, to grow their businesses and access new market opportunities, contributing to inclusive economic development.
5. Elsa Majimbo, Kenya: Comedian and social media influencer who has used her platform to amplify the voices of young Africans, challenge societal norms, and promote mental health awareness.
   - Key competencies: Advocacy, emotional intelligence, and community engagement.
   - Impact: Majimbo's bold, relatable content has inspired youth across the continent, fostering a sense of empowerment, self-acceptance, and collective action among marginalized communities. These are just a few examples of the inclusive innovation leaders who are driving transformative change and inspiring a new generation of visionaries across Africa. By studying their approaches, mindsets, and the

impact of their work, we can gain valuable insights into the critical competencies and strategies required to cultivate inclusive innovation leadership at scale.

IV. Nurturing Inclusive Innovation Leadership: Strategies and Models

Fostering the development of inclusive innovation leadership requires a multifaceted, collaborative approach that spans the public, private, and community sectors.

Key strategies and models for nurturing this transformative cadre of leaders include:

1. Inclusive Innovation Leadership Development Programs
   - Designing comprehensive leadership development programs that integrate systems thinking, community engagement, adaptive management, and ethical decision-making, with a focus on empowering marginalized groups, such as women, youth, and people from rural communities.
   - Leveraging mentorship, peer-to-peer learning, and immersive field experiences to enable aspiring inclusive innovation leaders to develop the necessary competencies and mindsets.
2. Collaborative Ecosystem-Building Initiatives
   - Fostering multi-stakeholder coalitions and innovation hubs that bring together diverse actors, including policymakers, industry leaders, civil society organizations, and community representatives, to collectively identify and address systemic barriers to inclusive innovation leadership. - Implementing co-creation workshops, knowledge-sharing platforms, and joint initiatives that enable inclusive innovation champions to learn from one another, share best practices, and amplify their collective impact.
3. Inclusive Innovation Leadership Fellowships and Awards
   - Establishing prestigious fellowship programs and recognition awards that celebrate the achievements of inclusive innovation leaders, amplify their stories, and provide them with the resources, networks, and visibility required to scale their impact.

- Ensuring that the selection process for these programs is inclusive, transparent, and responsive to the unique challenges faced by marginalized groups.

4. Integrating Inclusive Innovation Leadership into Education and Training
   - Embedding inclusive innovation leadership competencies and mindsets within the curricula of higher education institutions, vocational training programs, and lifelong learning initiatives to nurture the next generation of changemakers.
   - Collaborating with educational institutions to develop immersive, project-based learning experiences that enable students to apply inclusive innovation principles in real-world contexts.
5. Inclusive Innovation Leadership Coaching and Mentorship
   - Establishing dedicated coaching and mentorship programs that pair aspiring inclusive innovation leaders with experienced practitioners, community elders, and subject matter experts, enabling the transfer of knowledge, skills, and wisdom.
   - Fostering intergenerational and cross-cultural mentorship relationships that bridge the gap between traditional and emerging innovation models, and empower marginalized groups to lead with confidence.
6. Policy and Institutional Reforms
   - Advocating for the integration of inclusive innovation leadership competencies and criteria within public sector recruitment, promotion, and training frameworks to ensure that government institutions and policymaking bodies are equipped with the necessary mindsets and capabilities.
   - Promoting the development of inclusive innovation leadership development initiatives within the private sector, social enterprises, and civil society organizations through targeted incentives, partnerships, and capacity-building programs. By implementing these multifaceted strategies and models, African nations can nurture a vibrant ecosystem of inclusive innovation leaders who are poised to drive transformative, community-centered change and propel the continent towards a more equitable, sustainable, and prosperous future.

V. The Role of Inclusive Innovation Leaders in Addressing Systemic Challenges

Inclusive innovation leaders play a pivotal role in addressing the complex, interconnected challenges that African nations face, leveraging their unique competencies and community-centric approaches to drive systemic change. Some of the key areas where inclusive innovation leaders can have a transformative impact include:

1. Fostering Inclusive and Sustainable Development
   - Championing the integration of marginalized voices and traditional knowledge systems into the design and implementation of development programs, ensuring that the benefits of progress are equitably distributed.
   - Advocating for the alignment of innovation ecosystems with the Sustainable Development Goals and the principles of environmental sustainability, social justice, and community empowerment.
2. Addressing Climate Change and Environmental Degradation
   - Bridging the gap between scientific and traditional ecological knowledge to devise innovative, context-appropriate solutions for climate change adaptation and natural resource management.
   - Mobilizing community-based initiatives and multi-stakeholder partnerships to address environmental challenges in a holistic, participatory manner.
3. Promoting Gender Equality and Women's Empowerment
   - Championing the meaningful inclusion and leadership of women within innovation ecosystems, challenging gender stereotypes, and addressing the systemic barriers that impede women's participation.
   - Designing and scaling innovative solutions that address the unique needs and priorities of women, particularly in areas such as healthcare, education, and financial inclusion.
4. Enhancing Access to Essential Services and Infrastructure
   - Leveraging community engagement, collaborative partnerships, and innovative business models to improve the reach and affordability of critical services, such as healthcare, clean energy, and digital connectivity, in underserved and marginalized communities.

- Advocating for inclusive, pro-poor policies and targeted investments that prioritize the equitable provision of infrastructure and basic services. 5. Promoting Youth Empowerment and Decent Job Creation
- Fostering youth-led innovation and entrepreneurship initiatives that provide young people with the skills, resources, and platforms to become active agents of change within their communities.
- Collaborating with public and private sector stakeholders to design inclusive workforce development programs and skills training interventions that prepare the youth for the evolving demands of the innovation economy.

6. Building Resilient and Inclusive Communities
   - Strengthening the adaptive capacities of marginalized communities to withstand and recover from shocks and crises, such as economic downturns, health emergencies, and natural disasters.
   - Championing the integration of traditional community-based support systems, social safety nets, and disaster risk reduction strategies within inclusive innovation ecosystems. By embracing these multifaceted roles and leveraging their unique competencies, inclusive innovation leaders can catalyze systemic transformations that address the root causes of societal challenges, empower marginalized communities, and chart a more equitable and sustainable course for Africa's development.

VI. Bridging Traditional and Emerging Leadership Paradigms

The imperative of inclusive innovation leadership in Africa requires a critical examination of the relationship between traditional leadership models and the evolving paradigms of innovative, community-centric approaches. By bridging these often-disparate frameworks, African nations can cultivate a new generation of visionary leaders who can effectively harness the strengths of both approaches.

Traditional African leadership models, rooted in principles of collectivism, consensus-building, and the stewardship of communal resources, hold valuable lessons for inclusive innovation leadership. These time-honored approaches emphasize the importance of community engagement, the integration of diverse knowledge systems, and the empowerment of marginalized groups – all of which are central to the inclusive innovation agenda (Peredo & Chrisman, 2006). By drawing inspiration from these traditional leadership models and incorporating their core tenets into contemporary frameworks, aspiring inclusive innovation leaders can develop a deeper understanding of their local contexts, build trust within their communities, and leverage indigenous problem-solving strategies.

Conversely, emerging leadership paradigms, such as systems thinking, adaptive management, and collaborative governance, can complement and strengthen traditional approaches, equipping inclusive innovation champions with the tools and mindsets required to navigate the complexities of the modern innovation landscape (Holling, 2001; Westley et al., 2013). These contemporary frameworks emphasize the ability to navigate interconnected sociopolitical, economic, and environmental systems, foster cross-sectoral partnerships, and champion flexible, iterative, and community-driven solutions.

By fostering intergenerational dialogue and mentorship opportunities, African nations can enable the cross-pollination of traditional wisdom and innovative leadership competencies. This synergistic approach can empower a new generation of inclusive innovation leaders to draw upon the rich heritage of their communities while also embracing the transformative power of emerging frameworks and technologies.

VII. Inclusive Innovation Leadership and the Sustainable Development Goals

The cultivation of inclusive innovation leadership aligns closely with the overarching vision and principles of the United Nations' Sustainable Development Goals (SDGs). By nurturing a cadre of visionary leaders who prioritize equity, sustainability, and community empowerment, African nations can directly contribute to the realization of the SDGs and the broader African Union's Agenda 2063.

Key areas of alignment between inclusive innovation leadership and the SDGs include:

1. No Poverty (SDG 1) and Zero Hunger (SDG 2): Inclusive innovation leaders can champion the development of innovative, community-driven

solutions that address the root causes of poverty and food insecurity, empowering marginalized communities as active agents of change.

2. Good Health and Well-Being (SDG 3) and Quality Education (SDG 4): Inclusive innovation leaders can leverage their systems thinking and collaborative skills to devise holistic, context-appropriate interventions that improve access to healthcare, education, and other essential services.
3. Gender Equality (SDG 5) and Reduced Inequalities (SDG 10): Inclusive innovation leaders can champion the meaningful inclusion and leadership of women, youth, and other marginalized groups, addressing systemic barriers and promoting equitable development outcomes.
4. Sustainable Cities and Communities (SDG 11) and Climate Action (SDG 13): Inclusive innovation leaders can bridge the gap between scientific and traditional ecological knowledge to co-create innovative, community-based solutions for climate change adaptation and sustainable urban development.
5. Partnerships for the Goals (SDG 17): Inclusive innovation leaders can foster collaborative, multi-stakeholder ecosystems that mobilize diverse resources, expertise, and knowledge to drive the implementation of the SDGs and the African Union's Agenda 2063.

By aligning the development of inclusive innovation leadership with the broader sustainable development agenda, African nations can ensure that the continent's next generation of visionary leaders are equipped to tackle complex, interconnected challenges in a manner that is holistic, equitable, and community-centric. This strategic alignment can further strengthen the impact and scalability of inclusive innovation initiatives, ultimately contributing to the realization of a more prosperous, sustainable, and inclusive future for all Africans.

VIII. Measuring the Impact of Inclusive Innovation Leadership

Assessing the impact and effectiveness of inclusive innovation leadership initiatives is crucial for understanding their long-term outcomes, refining their approaches, and scaling their influence. However, the multidimensional and context-specific nature of these efforts presents unique challenges in developing appropriate measurement frameworks.

Key considerations in measuring the impact of inclusive innovation leadership include:

1. Capturing Multidimensional Value Creation: Impact assessments should go beyond traditional metrics, such as economic growth or project outputs, to also evaluate the social, environmental, and systemic changes catalyzed by inclusive innovation leaders. This can include indicators related to community empowerment, equity, and the strengthening of local innovation ecosystems.
2. Embracing Participatory Evaluation Approaches: The design and implementation of impact measurement frameworks should actively involve the diverse stakeholders impacted by inclusive innovation initiatives, including marginalized communities, to ensure that the evaluation process is truly reflective of their needs and perspectives.
3. Assessing Capacity-Building and Sustainability: Evaluations should examine the extent to which inclusive innovation leadership initiatives have contributed to the long-term capacity, resilience, and self-reliance of the communities and organizations they serve, cultivating a sustainable foundation for continued progress.
4. Documenting and Disseminating Lessons Learned: The systematic documentation and dissemination of case studies, best practices, and lessons learned from inclusive innovation leadership initiatives can inform the continuous improvement of these approaches and inspire the replication of successful models across different contexts.
5. Fostering Collaborative Learning and Knowledge-Sharing: Establishing platforms for the exchange of impact data, evaluation findings, and collaborative research among inclusive innovation leaders and their supporting ecosystems can enhance collective understanding and drive the development of more robust, evidence-based practices.

   The cultivation of inclusive innovation leadership is not merely a laudable aspiration, but a critical imperative for unlocking Africa's immense potential and driving transformative change across the continent. By nurturing a new generation of visionary leaders who are committed to the principles of equity, sustainability, and community empowerment, African nations can harness the collective intelligence, creativity, and resilience of their diverse populations to address complex, interconnected challenges. The strategies and models outlined in this chapter provide a roadmap for policymakers, ecosystem builders, and community organizations to strategically invest in the development of inclusive innovation leaders. From comprehensive leadership programs and collaborative ecosystem-building initiatives to integrating inclusive innovation competencies within education and training, these multifaceted approaches can equip aspiring changemakers with the knowledge, skills, and mindsets required to navigate the complexities of the innovation landscape and drive lasting, community-centered impact. Ultimately, the emergence of a thriving ecosystem of inclusive innovation leaders holds the key to realizing the African Union's Agenda 2063 and the United Nations' Sustainable Development Goals. These visionary individuals, grounded in ethical principles and committed to social justice, will be the architects of a more equitable, sustainable, and prosperous future – one that celebrates the diverse contributions of all Africans and empowers marginalized communities as active agents of change. As we embark on this transformative journey, the time is ripe to champion the rise of inclusive innovation champions, who will inspire, mobilize, and empower the next generation of leaders to harness the power of innovation for the betterment of all. By doing so, we can unlock a future where the African continent's immense potential is fully realized, and where the principles of equity, sustainability, and community-driven progress become the foundational pillars of inclusive development.

References

Gupta, J., & Vegelin, C. (2016). Sustainable development goals and inclusive development. *International environmental agreements: Politics, law and economics*, 16(3), 433-448.

Holling, C. S. (2001). Understanding the complexity of economic, ecological, and social systems. *Ecosystems*, 4(5), 390-405.

Mazzucato, M. (2018). Mission-oriented innovation policies: challenges and opportunities. *Industrial and Corporate Change*, 27(5), 803-815.

Moleka, P. (2024). Innovative Leadership in Addressing Climate Change: A Pathway Towards Sustainable Futures.

Peredo, A. M., & Chrisman, J. J. (2006). Toward a theory of community-based enterprise. *Academy of Management Review*, 31(2), 309-328

Ramalingam, B., Sharma, B., Hernandez, K., & Butti, L. (2018). *Distributed Innovation Systems: A new way to leverage global development cooperation.* Institute of Development Studies.

Schot, J., & Steinmueller, W. E. (2018). Three frames for innovation policy: R&D, systems of innovation and transformative change. *Research Policy*, 47(9), 1554-1567.

Westley, F. R., Tjornbo, O., Schultz, L., Olsson, P., Folke, C., Crona, B., & Bodin, Ö. (2013). A theory of transformative agency in linked social-ecological systems. *Ecology and Society*, 18(3).

CHAPTER 15

Innovationology: Towards a Holistic and Systemic Understanding of Innovation in Africa

Innovation, long celebrated as the engine of economic growth, social progress, and technological advancement, has traditionally been studied through fragmented, discipline-specific lenses (Hadhri, Arvanitis & M'Henni, 2016). Economists have focused on the role of innovation in driving productivity and competitiveness; management scholars have examined the organizational and managerial factors that enable innovative outcomes; and science and technology studies researchers have explored the sociocultural dimensions of technological change (Fagerberg et al., 2005; Tidd & Bessant, 2018; Jasanoff, 2004). However, the complexity and multifaceted nature of innovation have increasingly led to the recognition that a more holistic, systemic approach is needed to fully understand this phenomenon (Lundvall, 2010; Ritala & Hurmelinna-Laukkanen, 2013; Bogers, Zobel, Afuah, Almirall, Brunswicker, Dahlander ... & Ter Wal, 2017). The transdisciplinary field of innovationology, which is devoted to the methodical investigation of innovation in all of its forms, is founded within this framework.

This vision for Innovationology transcends the traditional, fragmented approaches to innovation research, offering a groundbreaking, systemic perspective that can capture the inherent complexity, uncertainty, and non-linearity that characterize the innovation process. By adopting a systemic lens, Innovationology can uncover the multilayered, co-evolutionary dynamics that shape the emergence, diffusion, and impact of innovations across diverse contexts, ultimately contributing to the advancement of innovation theory, practice, and policymaking. At the heart of Innovationology, lies a deep commitment to interdisciplinarity. The field draws on a wide range of academic disciplines, including economics, management, sociology, political science, and science and technology studies, to develop a rich and nuanced understanding of the innovation phenomenon (Moleka, 2023; Moleka, 2024). This multidisciplinary foundation allows Innovationology to address the inherent complexity of innovation, fostering cross-pollination of ideas and the integration of diverse analytical perspectives. Through a comprehensive, rigorous, and authoritative treatment, this article positions the field as a groundbreaking, highly impactful, and globally relevant domain of study. It offers a transformative vision for the future of innovation research and practice, one that embraces systemic thinking, fosters cross-disciplinary collaboration, and empowers researchers, practitioners, and policymakers to navigate the dynamic and ever-evolving innovation landscape.

I. The Systemic Foundations of Innovationology

At the core of Innovationology, is a deep commitment to a systemic perspective – the recognition that innovation is the product of a dynamic, interconnected ecosystem of actors, institutions, and processes (Coletto, Caliari, Bernardes-de-Souza & Callegaro-de-Menezes, 2024; Granstrand & Holgersson, 2020). This systemic approach rejects the reductionist and linear models that have historically dominated the field, instead embracing the inherent complexity, uncertainty, and nonlinearity that characterize the innovation phenomenon.

1° Transcending Linear Models of Innovation: Traditional innovation research has often been characterized by linear, stage-gate models that depict the innovation process as a sequential progression from idea generation to commercialization (Tidd & Bessant, 2018). While these models have provided valuable insights, they have also been criticized for their oversimplification of the innovation phenomenon, failing to capture the iterative, feedback-driven, and contextually embedded nature of the innovation process. Innovationology offers a fundamentally different perspective, embracing a systemic view of innovation that recognizes the complex, multidimensional, and co-evolutionary dynamics that shape innovative outcomes. This systemic approach rejects the notion of innovation as a linear, deterministic process, instead acknowledging the inherent uncertainty, emergence, and nonlinearity that characterize the innovation landscape. By adopting a systemic lens, Innovationology can uncover the multilayered interactions and feedback loops that occur between various innovation actors, institutions, and processes, shedding light on the complex, contextually situated nature of innovation. This systemic understanding can inform the development of more effective innovation policies, the design of supportive innovation ecosystems, and the implementation of transformative innovation strategies.

2° Innovationology's Interdisciplinary Foundations: Integral to vision for Innovationology is the field's deep commitment to interdisciplinarity. Rather than being confined to a single academic discipline, Innovationology draws on and integrates insights from a wide range of scholarly traditions, including economics, management, sociology, political science, neurosciences, quantic physics, sustainability science, transition study, post-normal science, science of integration, and science and technology studies. This multidisciplinary foundation allows Innovationology to capture the inherent complexity of innovation, fostering a rich and nuanced understanding of the phenomenon. By drawing on diverse analytical perspectives and methodological approaches, the field can address the multilayered, co-evolutionary dynamics that shape the emergence, diffusion, and impact of innovations across various contexts. For example, Innovationology integrates economic perspectives on the role of innovation in driving productivity and competitiveness with management insights on the organizational and managerial factors that enable innovative outcomes. It also incorporates sociological analyses of the sociocultural dimensions of technological change, as well as political science perspectives on the role of institutions and policymaking in shaping innovation trajectories. By embracing this interdisciplinary approach, Innovationology can foster cross-pollination of ideas, the integration of diverse theoretical frameworks, and the development of holistic, systemic solutions to complex innovation-related challenges.

3° Innovationology's Systemic Perspective on Innovation Ecosystems: A key tenet of Innovationology is the field's focus on innovation ecosystems – the dynamic and interconnected networks of actors, institutions, and processes that collectively shape the innovation landscape (Ritala & Hurmelinna-Laukkanen, 2013; Fransman, 2018). Innovationology recognizes that innovation does not occur in isolation, but rather emerges from the complex interactions and interdependencies within these innovation ecosystems (Moleka, 2023). This systemic perspective demands a deep understanding of the diverse stakeholders involved, including entrepreneurs, firms, research institutions, government agencies, and civil society organizations, as well as the institutional frameworks, resource flows, and knowledge-sharing mechanisms that enable their collaborative innovation efforts. By adopting a systemic lens, Innovationology can uncover the multilayered, co-evolutionary dynamics that shape the emergence, diffusion, and impact of innovations within these ecosystems. This understanding can inform the design of more effective innovation policies, the development of supportive infrastructure and incentive structures, and the facilitation of collaborative innovation initiatives that foster the sustained growth and transformation of innovation ecosystems. Moreover, Innovationology recognizes the importance of contextual factors in shaping the dynamics and performance of innovation ecosystems. The field acknowledges that innovation ecosystems are inherently situated within specific geographical, cultural, and institutional contexts, and that these contextual factors can profoundly influence the nature, pace, and direction of innovation.

4° Innovationology's Commitment to Multidimensional Innovation Impact: A hallmark of Innovationology, is its commitment to understanding the multidimensional impacts of innovation. Rather than focusing solely on economic or technological outcomes, the field embraces a holistic perspective that considers the social, environmental, and sociopolitical implications of innovation. Innovationology recognizes that innovation can have far-reaching consequences that extend beyond narrow measures of commercial success or technological advancement (Moleka, 2024a). The field explores how innovations can contribute to the achievement of broader societal goals, such as enhancing social welfare, promoting environmental sustainability, and fostering more inclusive and equitable development pathways. By adopting a systemic and multidimensional approach to innovation impact, Innovationology can inform the design of innovation strategies, policies, and programs that are aligned with the diverse needs and aspirations of various stakeholders, including marginalized communities, vulnerable populations, and the natural environment. This commitment to multidimensional innovation impact reflects Innovationology's fundamental purpose: to advance the understanding and practice of innovation in ways that contribute to the creation of a more sustainable, equitable, and prosperous world. Through these interconnected tenets – the systemic perspective on innovation, the interdisciplinary foundations, the focus on innovation ecosystems, and the commitment to multidimensional innovation impact – Innovationology offers a groundbreaking, highly impactful, and globally relevant approach to the study of innovation. By embracing complexity, fostering cross-disciplinary collaboration, and prioritizing the diverse societal impacts of innovation, the field can make vital contributions to the advancement of innovation theory, practice, and policymaking worldwide.

II. The Theoretical Foundations of Innovationology

Innovationology draws on a robust body of theoretical perspectives and analytical frameworks to develop a comprehensive, systemic understanding of the innovation phenomenon. These theoretical foundations, which span multiple academic disciplines, allow the field to capture the inherent complexity, dynamism, and multifaceted nature of innovation.

1° Systems Theory and the Complexity of Innovation: At the core of Innovationology's theoretical foundations lies systems theory, which provides a robust conceptual framework for understanding the systemic nature of innovation (Bertalanffy, 1968; Meadows, 2008). Systems theory emphasizes the interconnectedness and interdependence of various elements within a larger system, recognizing that the behavior and outcomes of the system cannot be fully explained by examining its individual components in isolation. Innovationology applies systems theory to the study of innovation, recognizing that the innovation process is shaped by the dynamic interactions and feedback loops among a diverse array of actors, institutions, and processes. This systemic perspective rejects the linear, stage-gate models that have historically dominated innovation research, instead embracing the inherent complexity, uncertainty, and nonlinearity that characterize the innovation landscape. By drawing on systems theory, Innovationology can uncover the multilayered, co-evolutionary dynamics that influence the emergence, diffusion, and impact of innovations. This includes, for example, understanding how the actions and decisions of individual innovators or firms are shaped by the broader innovation ecosystem, and how these ecosystems, in turn, evolve and transform in response to the innovative outputs they generate.

2° Evolutionary Economics and the Dynamics of Innovation: Innovationology also draws extensively on the theoretical insights of evolutionary economics, which emphasizes the dynamic, path-dependent, and uncertainty-driven nature of technological change and innovation (Nelson & Winter, 1982; Dosi, 1982). Evolutionary economists view innovation as an inherently evolutionary process, characterized by variation, selection, and retention mechanisms that shape the trajectories of technological development over time. This perspective acknowledges the crucial role of entrepreneurial experimentation, institutional frameworks, and selection pressures in driving the emergence and diffusion of innovations. Innovationology integrates evolutionary economic theory to explore how the innovation process unfolds within complex, co-evolving systems. This includes examining the diverse sources of variation (e.g., new ideas, technologies, business models), the mechanisms of selection (e.g., market forces, regulatory regimes, user preferences), and the processes of retention (e.g., organizational routines, institutional norms, technological standards) that collectively shape the innovation landscape. By embracing an evolutionary perspective, Innovationology can offer insights into the dynamic, path-dependent, and often unpredictable nature of innovation, informing the design of more effective innovation policies and the development of supportive innovation ecosystems.

3° Sociotechnical Systems Theory and the Co-Evolution of Technology and Society: Innovationology also draws on sociotechnical systems theory, which emphasizes the mutually constitutive relationship between technological change and social, cultural, and institutional transformations (Geels, 2004; Bijker et al., 1987). Sociotechnical systems theory posits that innovations do not emerge in a vacuum, but rather are shaped by the complex interplay between technological elements and the broader societal context. This includes the role of user practices, cultural meanings, policy frameworks, and power dynamics in shaping the development, diffusion, and impacts of new technologies. By integrating sociotechnical systems theory, Innovationology can explore how innovations both influence and are influenced by the societal structures, norms, and institutions within which they are embedded. This perspective allows the field to shed light on the co-evolutionary dynamics that drive the emergence of new sociotechnical configurations, as well as the social, environmental, and political implications of technological change.

4° Multi-Level Perspectives on Innovation: Innovationology also draws on multi-level perspectives to understand the multilayered nature of innovation (Geels, 2002; Rip & Kemp, 1998). This approach recognizes that innovation occurs across multiple levels of analysis, from the micro-level of individual innovators and firms to the meso-level of innovation ecosystems and the macro-level of broader societal transformations. By adopting a multi-level lens, Innovationology can explore how innovation processes at different levels interact, influence, and co-evolve with one another. This includes, for example, examining how individual-level creativity and entrepreneurial activity shape the dynamics of innovation ecosystems, and how these ecosystems, in turn, are shaped by broader institutional, cultural, and technological trends at the societal level. This multi-level perspective allows Innovationology to capture the inherent complexity and dynamism of the innovation phenomenon, informing the development of more comprehensive and nuanced innovation theories, policies, and strategies. Through the integration of these diverse theoretical foundations – systems theory, evolutionary economics, socio-technical systems theory, and multi-level perspectives – Innovationology offers a robust, interdisciplinary framework for understanding the innovation phenomenon in all its complexity. By drawing on this rich theoretical tapestry, the field can contribute to the advancement of innovation research, practice, and policymaking worldwide.

III. Methodological Approaches in Innovationology

Innovationology embraces a diverse array of methodological approaches to capture the inherent complexity and multifaceted nature of the innovation phenomenon. Recognizing the limitations of traditional, reductionist research methods, the field adopts a pluralistic, interdisciplinary approach to data collection, analysis, and interpretation.

1° Qualitative Approaches in Innovationology: Qualitative methodologies allow Innovationology researchers to delve deeply into the lived experiences, motivations, and decision-making processes of diverse innovation actors, such as entrepreneurs, firms, policymakers, and end-users. These methods facilitate a rich, contextualized understanding of the complex, socially embedded nature of innovation, uncovering the multilayered dynamics that shape the emergence, diffusion, and impact of innovations. For example, ethnographic studies can provide valuable insights into the innovation practices and organizational cultures within firms, while in-depth interviews can shed light on the challenges, opportunities, and strategic considerations that guide the innovation-related decisions of entrepreneurs and policymakers. Narrative analyses, on the other hand, can illuminate the role of storytelling and meaning-making in the innovation process, revealing how innovations are perceived, interpreted, and legitimized within specific sociocultural contexts. By embracing these qualitative approaches, Innovationology can develop a rich, nuanced, and contextualized understanding of the innovation phenomenon, complementing the insights gained from more quantitative methods.

2° Quantitative Approaches: While qualitative methods are central to Innovationology, the field also recognizes the value of quantitative research approaches in capturing certain aspects of the innovation process. These include large-scale surveys, econometric analyses, network analyses, and simulation modeling (Wooldridge, 2010; Wasserman & Faust, 1994; Gilbert & Troitzsch, 2005). Quantitative methods can provide Innovationology researchers with the ability to identify patterns, trends, and causal relationships within innovation-related data, offering insights that complement the depth and richness of qualitative investigations. For example, econometric analyses can shed light on the macroeconomic drivers and impacts of innovation, while network analyses can uncover the structural dynamics of innovation ecosystems. Moreover, simulation modeling techniques, such as agent-based modeling, can allow Innovationology researchers to explore the emergent, nonlinear, and dynamic properties of innovation systems, testing hypotheses and experimenting with different policy interventions or innovation strategies. By integrating quantitative approaches with the field's qualitative orientation, Innovationology can develop a more comprehensive, multifaceted understanding of the innovation phenomenon, drawing on the complementary strengths of both methodological traditions.

3° Mixed Methods and Interdisciplinary Collaboration: Reflecting its strong commitment to interdisciplinarity, Innovationology embraces a mixed methods approach that combines qualitative and quantitative research techniques. This methodological pluralism allows the field to leverage the unique strengths and insights of different analytical perspectives, fostering a richer, more nuanced understanding of the innovation process. Moreover, Innovationology's interdisciplinary foundations encourage close collaboration among researchers from diverse academic backgrounds, such as economics, management, sociology, political science, and science and technology studies. This cross-disciplinary collaboration facilitates the integration of multiple analytical frameworks and the development of innovative, holistic research designs that can capture the inherent complexity of innovation. By drawing on the diverse methodological expertise and substantive knowledge of this interdisciplinary community of scholars, Innovationology can produce research outputs that are both rigorously grounded in empirical evidence and conceptually sophisticated in their treatment of the innovation phenomenon.

4° Engaged Scholarship and Collaborative Research: Innovationology also embraces the principles of engaged scholarship, which emphasizes the active collaboration between researchers and various innovation stakeholders, including practitioners, policymakers, and community members (Van de Ven, 2007; Greenwood & Levin, 2007). This approach to research acknowledges the importance of incorporating diverse perspectives and lived experiences into the innovation research process, fostering a more nuanced and practically relevant understanding of the phenomenon. Innovationology researchers actively engage with innovation actors in the field, co-creating research agendas, co-designing research methodologies, and co-interpreting the findings to ensure their relevance and applicability. Moreover, Innovationology's commitment to engaged scholarship aligns with its overarching praxis of transformation, in which the production of knowledge is intrinsically linked to the goal of fostering more sustainable, equitable, and impactful innovation pathways. By collaborating closely with innovation stakeholders, Innovationology researchers can not only advance theoretical and empirical understanding, but also directly contribute to the development of innovative solutions that address pressing societal challenges. Through this pluralistic, interdisciplinary, and engaged approach to research methods, Innovationology can produce rigorous, contextually grounded, and impactful knowledge that can inform the ongoing transformation of innovation research, practice, and policymaking worldwide.

IV. Innovationology's Contributions to Innovation Theory, Practice, and Policy

Innovationology has the potential to make significant and far-reaching contributions to the advancement of innovation theory, the enhancement of innovation practice, and the formulation of more effective innovation policies. By embracing a systemic, interdisciplinary, and engaged approach, the field can offer novel insights and practical solutions to the complex challenges facing innovation ecosystems globally.

1° Advancing Innovation Theory: One of the key contributions of Innovationology is its potential to advance the theoretical understanding of the innovation phenomenon. By drawing on a diverse array of theoretical perspectives, from systems theory to evolutionary economics, the field can develop more comprehensive and nuanced models of innovation that capture the inherent complexity, dynamism, and contextual embeddedness of the innovation process. For example,

Innovationology's systemic perspective can lead to the development of new theoretical frameworks that explain how the interactions and interdependencies among innovation actors, institutiossns, and processes shape the emergence, diffusion, and impact of innovations. Similarly, the field's integration of sociotechnical systems theory can yield insights into the co-evolutionary dynamics between technological change and broader societal transformations. Moreover, Innovationology's commitment to interdisciplinarity can foster the cross-pollination of ideas and the integration of diverse analytical lenses, leading to the creation of innovative theoretical hybrids that can better account for the multifaceted nature of innovation. This theoretical advancement can, in turn, inform the design of more effective innovation policies, the implementation of more impactful innovation strategies, and the development of more supportive innovation ecosystems.

2° Enhancing Innovation Practice: Innovationology also has the potential to enhance the practice of innovation by providing practitioners, such as entrepreneurs, firms, and innovation intermediaries, with a more comprehensive and actionable understanding of the innovation process. By embracing a systemic and multidimensional approach, Innovationology can offer practitioners valuable insights into the complex, interconnected factors that shape innovative outcomes. This may include, for example, a deeper understanding of the dynamics of innovation ecosystems, the role of institutional frameworks in enabling or constraining innovation, and the diverse sources of innovation-related knowledge and resources. Moreover, Innovationology's engagement with innovation practitioners through collaborative research and participatory approaches can lead to the co-creation of innovative solutions that are tailored to the specific needs and contexts of diverse innovation stakeholders. This collaborative process can help bridge the gap between innovation research and practice, ensuring that the knowledge generated by Innovationology is directly applicable and responsive to the real-world challenges faced by innovation practitioners. By enhancing the practical relevance and applicability of innovation research, Innovationology can contribute to the more effective design, implementation, and scaling of innovative initiatives, ultimately fostering the sustained growth and transformation of innovation ecosystems worldwide.

3° Informing Innovation Policymaking: Innovationology can also play a pivotal role in informing the development of more effective innovation policies. By providing policymakers with a comprehensive, systemic understanding of the innovation phenomenon, the field can help guide the formulation of policies, programs, and institutional frameworks that are better aligned with the complex realities of innovation ecosystems. For instance, Innovationology's insights into the multilayered, co-evolutionary dynamics that shape innovation can inform the design of innovation policies that strike a balance between top-down and bottom-up approaches, recognizing the importance of both macro-level structural conditions and micro-level entrepreneurial agency. Similarly, the field's commitment to multidimensional innovation impacts can encourage policymakers to consider the social, environmental, and sociopolitical implications of innovation, rather than narrowly focusing on economic or technological outcomes. Furthermore, Innovationology's engagement with diverse innovation stakeholders, including policymakers, can facilitate the co-creation of innovation policies that are responsive to the needs and aspirations of various societal groups. This collaborative approach can help ensure that innovation policymaking is more inclusive, equitable, and aligned with the broader goals of sustainable development. By informing the development of more comprehensive, contextually grounded, and transformative innovation policies, Innovationology can contribute to the creation of innovation ecosystems that are better equipped to address the complex challenges facing societies worldwide. Through its contributions to innovation theory, practice, and policymaking, Innovationology emerges as a groundbreaking, highly impactful, and globally relevant field of study. By embracing a systemic, interdisciplinary, and engaged approach, the field can foster the co-creation of more sustainable, equitable, and impactful innovation pathways, ultimately contributing to the transformation of the global innovation landscape.

Innovationology and Innovation in Africa

1. The Need for a Systemic Approach to Innovation in Africa: The complex challenges facing the African continent require a holistic understanding of innovation, moving beyond traditional linear models. Innovationology, with its systemic perspective, can unveil the intricate and contextual dynamics that shape innovation in Africa (Hadhri et al., 2016; Tidd & Bessant, 2018).
2. Interdisciplinarity in Service of African Innovation: The interdisciplinary approach of Innovationology is particularly relevant for apprehending the diversity of innovation experiences and trajectories in Africa. By mobilizing the resources of multiple disciplines, it fosters the emergence of innovative solutions that address the economic, social, environmental, and political challenges of the continent in an integrated manner (Moleka, 2024c; 2024d; 2024e;2024f).
3. Strengthening African Innovation Ecosystems: Innovationology emphasizes the identification and understanding of the actors, institutions, and processes that shape African innovation ecosystems, in all their complexity (Ritala & Hurmelinna-Laukkanen, 2013; Fransman, 2018). This in-depth knowledge of ecosystem dynamics enables the design of policies and programs that foster their inclusive and resilient development.
4. Measuring the Multidimensional Impact of Innovation in Africa: Beyond traditional economic indicators, Innovationology advocates for the adoption of holistic evaluation frameworks that reflect the priorities of sustainable development and equity in Africa (Bogers et al., 2017; Jasanoff, 2004). This multidimensional approach to innovation impact will guide strategies and investments towards solutions that bring tangible value to African communities.

Conclusion: Innovationology, a Path Forward for Inclusive and Sustainable Innovation in Africa

Innovationology, with its systemic, interdisciplinary, and multidimensional perspective, offers a powerful conceptual framework for rethinking innovation in Africa. By embracing this transformative approach, African innovation actors - researchers, practitioners, and policymakers - can design strategies and programs that holistically address the continent's complex challenges, thereby stimulating inclusive innovation, grounded in local realities, and oriented towards equitable and sustainable development for all Africans.

References

Bertalanffy, L. von. (1968). *General System Theory: Foundations, Development, Applications*. New York, NY: George Braziller.

Bijker, W. E., Hughes, T. P., & Pinch, T. J. (Eds.). (1987). *The Social Construction of Technological Systems: New Directions in the Sociology and History of Technology*. Cambridge, MA: MIT Press.

Bogers, M. et al. (2017). The open innovation research landscape: Established perspectives and emerging themes across different levels of analysis. *Industry and Innovation*, *24*(1), 8-40.

Coletto, C., Caliari, L., Bernardes-de-Souza, D., & Callegaro-de-Menezes, D. (2024). Dynamics of actors in innovation ecosystems' analytical structures. *Innovation & Management Review*.

Dosi, G. (1982). Technological Paradigms and Technological Trajectories: A Suggested Interpretation of the Determinants and Directions of Technical Change. *Research Policy*, 11(3), 147-162.

Eisenhardt, K. M., & Graebner, M. E. (2007). Theory Building from Cases: Opportunities and Challenges. *Academy of Management Journal*, 50(1), 25-32.

Fagerberg, J., Mowery, D. C., & Nelson, R. R. (Eds.). (2005). *The Oxford Handbook of Innovation*. Oxford, UK: Oxford University Press.

Fransman, M. (2018). *Innovation Ecosystems: Increasing Competitiveness*. Cambridge, UK: Cambridge University Press.

Geels, F. W. (2002). Technological Transitions as Evolutionary Reconfiguration Processes: A Multi-Level Perspective and a Case-Study. *Research Policy*, 31(8-9), 1257-1274.

Geels, F. W. (2004). From Sectoral Systems of Innovation to Socio-Technical Systems: Insights about Dynamics and Change from Sociology and Institutional Theory. *Research Policy*, 33(6-7), 897-920.

Gilbert, N., & Troitzsch, K. G. (2005). *Simulation for the Social Scientist* (2nd ed.). Maidenhead, UK: Open University Press.

Godin, S. (2015). *The Invention of Science: A New History of the Scientific Revolution*. New York, NY: Harper.

Granstrand, O., & Holgersson, M. (2020). Innovation ecosystems: A conceptual review and a new definition. *Technovation*, *90*, 102098.

Greenwood, D. J., & Levin, M. (2007). *Introduction to Action Research: Social Research for Social Change* (2nd ed.). Thousand Oaks, CA: SAGE Publications.

Hadhri, W., Arvanitis, R. & M'Henni, H. (2016). Determinants of innovation activities in small and open economies: the Lebanese business sector. *Journal of Innovation Economics & Management*, (n°21) (3), 77-107. https://doi.org/10.3917/jie.021.0077.

Jasanoff, S. (2004). *States of knowledge: the co-production of science and the social order.* Routledge.

Kaplinsky, R. (2011). Scumpe Research for Scumpe People: The Origins and Use of Rapid Rural Appraisal. *World Development*, 39(10), 1742-1755.

Lundvall, B. Å. (Ed.). (2010). *National Systems of Innovation: Toward a Theory of Innovation and Interactive Learning.* London, UK: Anthem Press.

Meadows, D. H. (2008). *Thinking in Systems: A Primer.* White River Junction, VT: Chelsea Green Publishing.

Moleka, P. (2023). *A Catalyst for Sustainable Digitalization in Asian Economies*. GRIN: Verlag.

Moleka, P. (2024a). Frugal Innovation for Inclusive and Sustainable Development in Africa. *Advanced Research in Economics and Business Strategy Journal*, 5(1), 107-117. https://doi.org/10.52919/arebus.v5i1.58

Moleka, P. (2024b). *Lexique des Mots Techniques dans le Domaine d'Innovation*. EUE.

Moleka, P. (2024c). *Holistic Education. Enhancing the Mind, Body and Soul*. The Innovationology Series / TOME V. GRIN: Verlag.

Moleka, P. (2024d). *Innovationology and the Geoeconomics of the BRICS. Towards a Sustainable and Equitable Global Order.* The Innovationology Series / TOME VII. GRIN: Verlag.

Moleka, P. (2024e). Innovationology: A Goundbreaking Transdisciplinary Framework for Sustainable and Equitable Development in Africa. *International Journal of Social Sciences and Management Review*. 7(5):178-193.

Moleka, P. (2024f). Innovation Metrics for the 21st Century: An Innovationology-based Comprehensive, Multidimensional Framework. *International Journal of Social Sciences and Management Review*. 7(5):199-210.

Nelson, R. R., & Winter, S. G. (1982). *An Evolutionary Theory of Economic Change*. Cambridge, MA: Belknap Press of Harvard University Press.

Ritala, P., & Hurmelinna-Laukkanen, P. (2013). Incremental and Radical Innovation in Coopetition: The Role of Absorptive Capacity and Appropriability. *Journal of Product Innovation Management*, 30(1), 154-169.

Rip, A., & Kemp, R. (1998). Technological Change. In S. Rayner & E. L. Malone (Eds.), *Human Choice and Climate Change* (Vol. 2, pp. 327-399). Columbus, OH: Battelle Press.

Tidd, J., & Bessant, J. R. (2018). *Managing Innovation: Integrating Technological, Market and Organizational Change* (6th ed.). Chichester, UK: John Wiley & Sons.

Van de Ven, A. H. (2007). *Engaged Scholarship: A Guide for Organizational and Social Research*. Oxford, UK: Oxford University Press.

Wasserman, S., & Faust, K. (1994). *Social Network Analysis: Methods and Applications*. Cambridge, UK: Cambridge University Press.

Wooldridge, J. M. (2010). *Econometric Analysis of Cross Section and Panel Data* (2nd ed.). Cambridge, MA: MIT Press.

Yin, R. K. (2018). *Case Study Research and Applications: Design and Methods* (6th ed.). Thousand Oaks, CA: SAGE Publications.

CHAPTER 16

Towards an Integrated Vision for Inclusive and Sustainable African Development

The preceding chapters have explored the multifaceted landscape of inclusive innovation in Africa, examining the critical role of traditional knowledge systems, collaborative partnerships, the empowerment of women and youth, and the evolving future of work. As we synthesize these insights, a clear imperative emerges: the need to chart an integrated, holistic, and collaborative path towards realizing inclusive and sustainable development across the African continent.

This final chapter aims to weave together the key frameworks, strategies, and perspectives presented throughout the book, distilling a comprehensive vision for the role of inclusive innovation in transforming Africa's development trajectories. By highlighting the interconnected nature of the challenges and the synergistic potential of the solutions, this chapter provides a roadmap for policymakers, practitioners, and community leaders to collectively harness the power of inclusive innovation and catalyze a new era of equitable, resilient, and environmentally-conscious progress. The chapter will delve into the fundamental principles and values that should underpin this integrated vision, drawing from the insights and best practices showcased in previous chapters. It will also explore the importance of fostering multi-stakeholder collaboration, strengthening institutional and governance frameworks, and aligning inclusive innovation with the broader sustainable development agenda. By synthesizing the key learnings and charting a collaborative path forward, this chapter aims to inspire and empower a diverse array of actors to embrace inclusive innovation as a transformative engine for Africa's sustainable future.

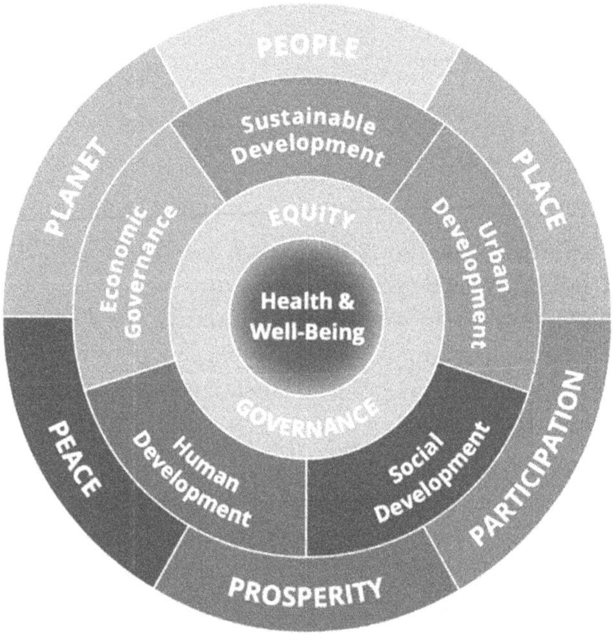

I. Principles and Values for an Integrated Inclusive Innovation Agenda

At the heart of the inclusive innovation agenda lies a set of core principles and values that must guide the development and implementation of strategies, policies, and programs across the African continent. These guiding principles include:

1. Equity and Social Justice
   - Prioritizing the needs, perspectives, and agency of marginalized communities, including women, youth, Indigenous peoples, and those living in poverty, to ensure that the benefits of innovation are equitably distributed.
   - Addressing systemic inequities and power imbalances within innovation ecosystems to create a level playing field and enable the meaningful participation of traditionally underrepresented groups.
2. Environmental Sustainability
   - Aligning inclusive innovation initiatives with the imperatives of environmental protection, climate change mitigation, and the regeneration of natural resources to foster a sustainable, eco-conscious development paradigm.
   - Harnessing the innovative capacities of local communities to devise solutions that tackle pressing environmental challenges, such as renewable energy, sustainable agriculture, and waste management.
3. Community Ownership and Self-Determination
   - Recognizing and empowering local communities as the primary agents and decision-makers in the design, implementation, and governance of inclusive innovation initiatives.
   - Respecting and integrating diverse knowledge systems, cultural practices, and traditional forms of innovation into the inclusive innovation agenda, positioning them as equal and complementary to formal, scientific knowledge.
4. Collaborative Partnerships and Cross-Sectoral Synergies
   - Fostering robust, transparent, and mutually beneficial partnerships among diverse stakeholders, including governments, private sector entities, civil society organizations, academia, and community-based groups.
   - Catalyzing cross-cutting, interdisciplinary collaboration and the co-creation of innovative solutions that address the interconnected challenges facing African societies.
5. Adaptability and Contextual Responsiveness
   - Developing inclusive innovation frameworks and interventions that are flexible, iterative, and tailored to the unique socio-cultural, economic, and environmental contexts of different regions and communities.

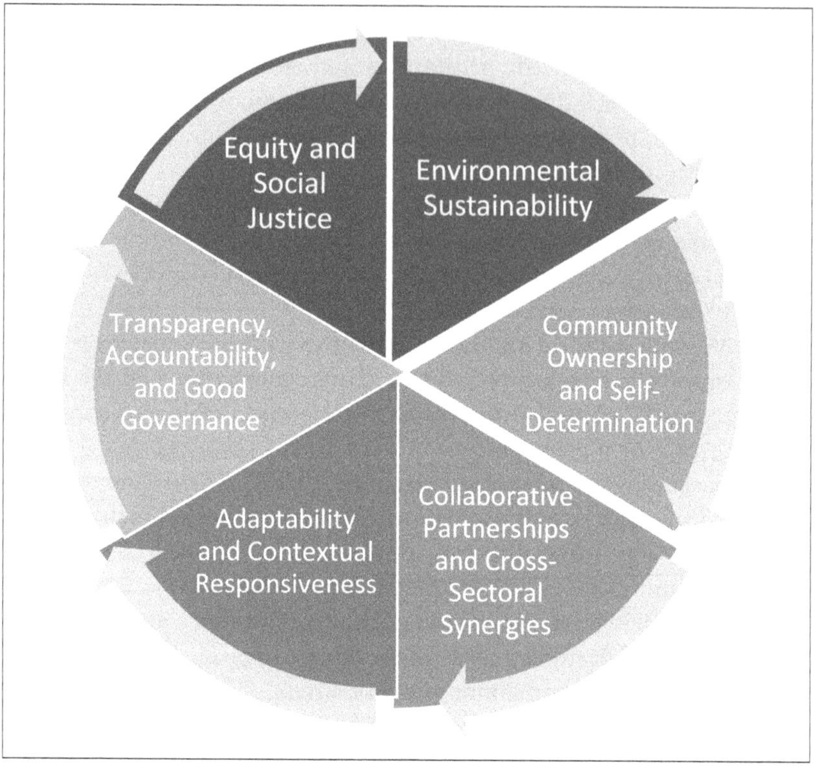

Figure 16.1 Principles and Values for an Integrated Inclusive Innovation Agenda (Author)

- Embracing a culture of continuous learning, experimentation, and adaptation to ensure the long-term relevance and impact of inclusive innovation initiatives.

6. Transparency, Accountability, and Good Governance
   - Fostering transparent and accountable governance structures that uphold the principles of democracy, the rule of law, and inclusive decision-making processes.
   - Implementing robust monitoring, evaluation, and impact assessment mechanisms to ensure the equitable distribution of benefits

and the transparent utilization of resources within inclusive innovation ecosystems.

By anchoring the inclusive innovation agenda in these core principles and values, African nations can cultivate a development paradigm that is truly transformative, empowering, and sustainable – one that addresses the fundamental needs and aspirations of all members of society.

II. Strengthening Institutional and Governance Frameworks for Inclusive Innovation

The realization of an integrated vision for inclusive and sustainable African development requires the establishment of robust, enabling institutional and governance frameworks that can support the seamless implementation and

Table 16.1 Global Youth Population Projections

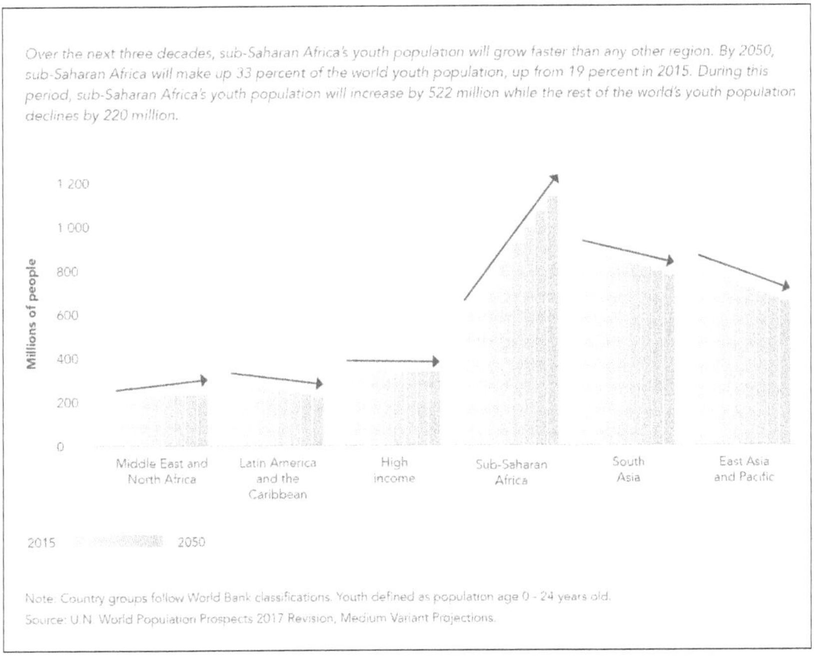

scaling of inclusive innovation initiatives. Key elements of this institutional and governance architecture include:

1. Inclusive Innovation Policies and Strategies
   - Developing comprehensive national and regional policies, strategies, and action plans that explicitly prioritize the principles of inclusive innovation, providing a clear policy framework and resource allocation to drive their adoption and implementation.
   - Ensuring the participatory and collaborative formulation of these policies, with the active involvement of diverse stakeholders, including marginalized communities, to ensure their relevance and responsiveness to local needs.
2. Dedicated Institutional Mechanisms
   - Establishing dedicated government agencies, innovation authorities, or cross-sectoral councils that are mandated to coordinate, facilitate, and monitor the integration of inclusive innovation principles across different ministries, departments, and development programs.
   - Empowering these institutional mechanisms with the necessary resources, decision-making authority, and convening power to effectively harmonize policies, mobilize funding, and drive the collaborative implementation of inclusive innovation initiatives.

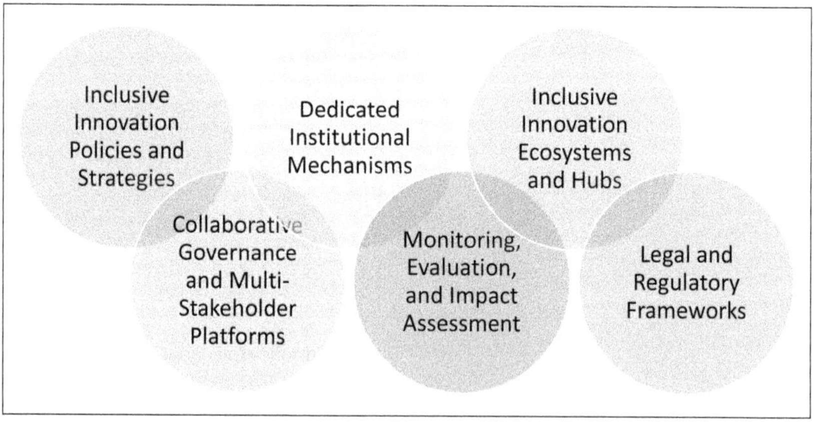

Figure 16.2 Strengthening Institutional and Governance Frameworks for Inclusive Innovation (Moleka, 2024)

3. Inclusive Innovation Ecosystems and Hubs
   - Fostering the development of inclusive innovation hubs, incubators, and accelerators that provide tailored support, resources, and networking opportunities for marginalized innovators, entrepreneurs, and community-based groups.
   - Ensuring the equitable distribution of these inclusive innovation ecosystem entities across different regions and communities to enhance geographic accessibility and local relevance.
4. Collaborative Governance and Multi-Stakeholder Platforms
   - Establishing multi-stakeholder platforms, advisory bodies, and collaborative governance mechanisms that bring together representatives from government, private sector, academia, civil society, and community-based organizations to jointly shape the inclusive innovation agenda and oversee its implementation.
   - Empowering these collaborative governance structures with the decision-making authority, resource mobilization capabilities, and conflict resolution mechanisms required to foster transparent, accountable, and equitable outcomes.
5. Monitoring, Evaluation, and Impact Assessment
   - Developing comprehensive monitoring, evaluation, and impact assessment frameworks that capture the multidimensional outcomes and long-term sustainability of inclusive innovation initiatives, ensuring their alignment with the broader sustainable development agenda.
   - Leveraging data-driven insights and community feedback to continuously refine and improve the design and implementation of inclusive innovation programs, fostering a culture of evidence-based policymaking and adaptive management.
6. Legal and Regulatory Frameworks
   - Harmonizing legal and regulatory frameworks across national and regional boundaries to facilitate the seamless exchange of knowledge, technology, and resources within inclusive innovation ecosystems.
   - Ensuring that these legal and regulatory frameworks uphold the principles of intellectual property rights protection, data privacy, and environmental sustainability, while also safeguarding the rights and interests of marginalized innovators and communities. By establishing

Over the next three decades, sub-Saharan Africa's youth population will grow faster than any other region. By 2050, sub-Saharan Africa will make up 33 percent of the world youth population, up from 19 percent in 2015. During this period, sub-Saharan Africa's youth population will increase by 522 million while the rest of the world's youth population declines by 220 million.

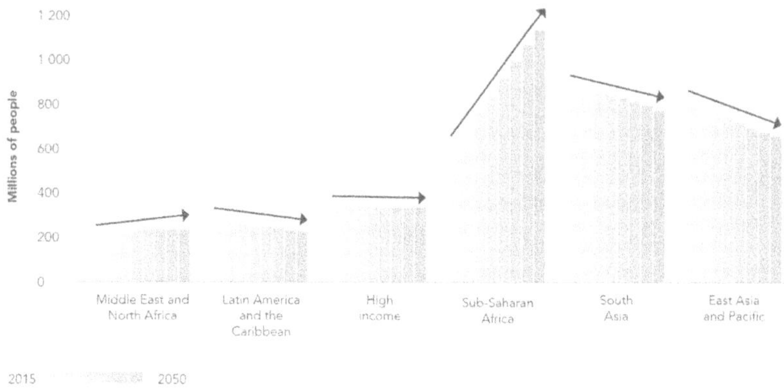

Note: Country groups follow World Bank classifications. Youth defined as population age 0 - 24 years old.
Source: U.N. World Population Prospects 2017 Revision, Medium Variant Projections.

these robust institutional and governance structures, African nations can create an enabling environment that nurtures and sustains the inclusive innovation agenda, empowering diverse stakeholders to collaborate effectively and drive transformative, equitable, and sustainable development outcomes.

III. Aligning Inclusive Innovation with the Sustainable Development Agenda

The vision for inclusive and sustainable African development outlined in this book is inherently aligned with the broader Sustainable Development Goals (SDGs) adopted by the United Nations in 2015. The core principles and strategies of inclusive innovation – from empowering marginalized communities to harnessing traditional knowledge and fostering collaborative partnerships – are intricately woven into the, interconnected framework of the 2030 Agenda for Sustainable Development. By intentionally aligning inclusive innovation initiatives with the SDGs, African nations can leverage the synergies and complementarities between these two transformative agendas, amplifying their collective impact and accelerating progress towards a more equitable, resilient, and environmentally-conscious future. Some of the key areas of alignment between inclusive innovation and the SDGs include:

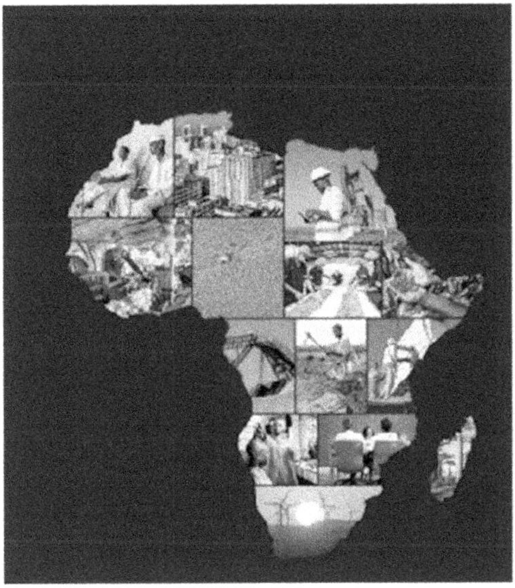

1. Poverty Reduction and Shared Prosperity (SDG 1 and 10)
   - Inclusive innovation's focus on empowering marginalized communities, improving access to resources, and creating livelihood opportunities can contribute directly to the eradication of poverty and the reduction of inequality.
2. Food Security and Sustainable Agriculture (SDG 2)
   - Grassroots innovations in sustainable agriculture, water management, and post-harvest technologies can enhance food production, improve nutrition, and promote environmentally-friendly farming practices.
3. Good Health and Well-being (SDG 3)
   - Inclusive innovations in healthcare delivery, access to medicines, and community-based wellness solutions can improve the health and quality of life for underserved populations.

4. Quality Education and Lifelong Learning (SDG 4)
   - Inclusive innovation in education, from digital learning platforms to community-based skills development programs, can enhance access to quality education and promote lifelong learning.
5. Gender Equality and Women's Empowerment (SDG 5)
   - The intentional integration of gender-responsive approaches within inclusive innovation ecosystems can contribute to the advancement of women's rights, leadership, and economic empowerment.
6. Clean Water and Sanitation (SDG 6)
   - Grassroots innovations in water infrastructure, purification, and waste management can improve access to clean water and sanitation services for marginalized communities.
7. Affordable and Clean Energy (SDG 7)
   - Inclusive innovations in renewable energy technologies and decentralized energy solutions can expand energy access and promote sustainable energy systems.
8. Decent Work and Economic Growth (SDG 8)
   - Inclusive innovation's focus on supporting grassroots enterprises, empowering informal workers, and fostering equitable job opportunities can contribute to sustainable economic development and decent work for all.
9. Sustainable Consumption and Production (SDG 12)
   - Inclusive innovation in the circular economy, waste management, and sustainable product design can promote more environmentally-conscious patterns of production and consumption.
10. Climate Action and Environmental Sustainability (SDG 13, 14, and 15)
    - Grassroots innovations that address climate change adaptation, biodiversity conservation, and natural resource management can contribute to the protection of the planet and the achievement of sustainability. By proactively aligning inclusive innovation initiatives with the Sustainable Development Goals, African nations can ensure the holistic, integrated, and systemic transformation of their development trajectories, while also contributing to the overall global progress towards a more just, equitable, and sustainable future.

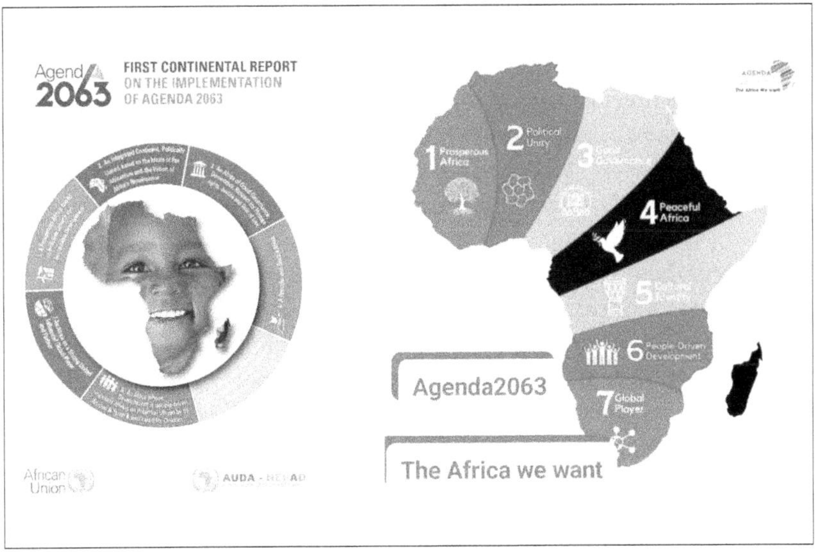

Figure 16.3 Agenda 2063: The Africa We Want

Agenda 2063: The Africa We Want.

AGENDA 2063 is Africa's blueprint and master plan for transforming Africa into the global powerhouse of the future. It is the continent's strategic framework that aims to deliver on its goal for inclusive and sustainable development and is a concrete manifestation of the pan-African drive for unity, self-determination, freedom, progress and collective prosperity pursued under Pan-Africanism and African Renaissance The genesis of Agenda 2063 was the realisation by African leaders that there was a need to refocus and reprioritise Africa's agenda from the struggle against apartheid and the attainment of political independence for the continent which had been the focus of The Organisation of African Unity (OAU), the precursor of the African Union; and instead to prioritise inclusive social and economic development, continental and regional integration, democratic governance and peace and security amongst other issues aimed at repositioning Africa to becoming a dominant player in the global arena

IV. Pathways for Collaborative Implementation and Scaling

Realizing the integrated vision for inclusive and sustainable African development will require a collaborative, multi-stakeholder approach that harnesses the diverse expertise, resources, and networks of a wide range of actors. Key pathways for collaborative implementation and scaling include:

1. Strengthening Regional and Pan-African Cooperation
   - Fostering greater collaboration and knowledge exchange among African nations, regional economic communities, and continental bodies, such as the African Union, to harmonize policies, share best practices, and collectively drive the inclusive innovation agenda.
   - Developing joint funding mechanisms, shared innovation infrastructure, and cross-border innovation corridors that enable the scaling and replication of successful inclusive innovation initiatives across the continent.
2. Catalyzing Public-Private Partnerships
   - Cultivating strategic partnerships between government agencies, private sector entities, and civil society organizations to leverage

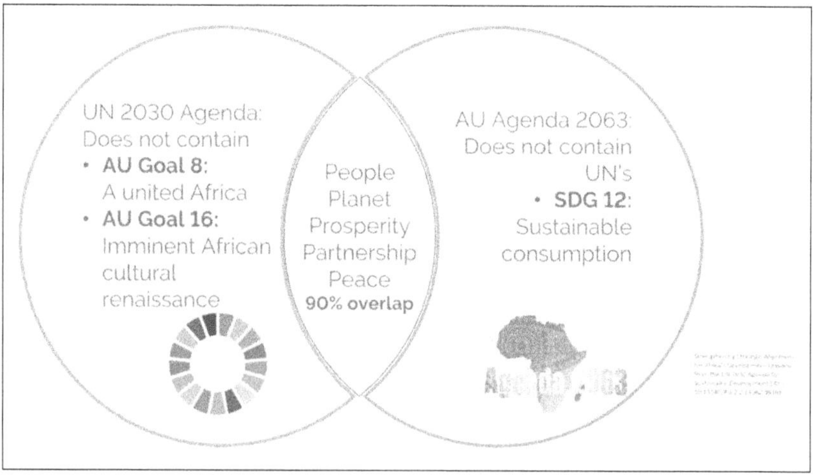

Figure 16.4 Comparison Between UN 2030 Agenda and AU Agenda

complementary strengths, mobilize resources, and co-create inclusive innovation solutions that address pressing development challenges.
- Promoting the active participation of the private sector in inclusive innovation ecosystems, incentivizing their investments, and aligning their business models with the principles of sustainability and social impact.

3. Empowering Community-Based Organizations and Social Enterprises - Strengthening the capacity, resources, and networks of grassroots organizations, community-based groups, and social enterprises that are spearheading inclusive innovation initiatives at the local level.
   - Enabling these community-driven actors to participate in decision-making processes, access financing and technical support, and scale their innovative solutions through collaborative partnerships and ecosystem-level interventions.

Figure 16.5 Pathways for Collaborative Implementation and Scaling

4. Fostering University-Industry-Community Collaborations
   - Facilitating the development of vibrant, cross-cutting innovation ecosystems that bring together academic institutions, private sector entities, and community-based organizations to co-create, prototype, and scale inclusive innovations.
   - Embedding inclusive innovation principles and community engagement within the core functions of universities, research centers, and technical training institutes to nurture the next generation of inclusive innovation champions.
5. Leveraging South-South and North-South Cooperation
   - Strengthening collaboration and knowledge exchange between African nations and their counterparts in the Global South, sharing innovative practices and co-developing context-appropriate solutions to shared development challenges.
   - Cultivating mutually beneficial partnerships with actors in the Global North, leveraging their expertise, resources, and networks to support the scaling and replication of inclusive innovation initiatives across the African continent.
6. Engaging Development Finance Institutions and Impact Investors
   - Mobilizing dedicated funding streams from development finance institutions, impact investment funds, and blended finance mechanisms to provide the necessary financial resources and risk capital to support the development and scaling of inclusive innovation initiatives.
   - Incentivizing and empowering these financial actors to adopt inclusive and sustainable investment strategies that prioritize community-driven solutions and marginalized innovators.

By embracing these collaborative pathways and leveraging the capacities and resources of diverse stakeholders, African nations can unleash the transformative potential of inclusive innovation and accelerate the realization of the continent's sustainable development aspirations.

V. Nurturing Inclusive Innovation Champions and Visionary Leadership

At the heart of the integrated vision for inclusive and sustainable African development lies the crucial role of visionary leadership and the empowerment of inclusive innovation champions. These are the individuals, organizations, and communities that possess the courage, creativity, and commitment to challenge the status quo, amplify marginalized voices, and spearhead the transformative change required to build a more equitable, resilient, and environmentally-conscious future.

Strategies for nurturing and empowering these inclusive innovation champions include:

1. Identifying and Showcasing Inclusive Innovation Role Models
   - Highlighting the inspiring stories, innovative solutions, and transformative impact of grassroots innovators, community leaders, and social entrepreneurs who are driving inclusive innovation at the local level.
   - Leveraging diverse media platforms and recognition programs to amplify the visibility and influence of these inclusive innovation champions, inspiring and motivating others to follow in their footsteps.
2. Investing in Capacity-Building and Leadership Development
   - Implementing comprehensive training, mentorship, and networking initiatives that equip individuals and organizations with the knowledge, skills, and support systems required to effectively lead and sustain inclusive innovation initiatives.
   - Fostering the development of inclusive innovation leadership competencies, such as systems thinking, collaborative decision-making, and community engagement, within educational curricula and professional development programs.
3. Embedding Inclusive Innovation within Institutional Structures
   - Ensuring the meaningful representation and participation of inclusive innovation champions within key decision-making bodies, policy advisory councils, and innovation governance frameworks at the national and regional levels.
   - Empowering these inclusive innovation leaders to shape the strategic vision, resource allocation, and implementation of inclusive innovation policies and programs across different sectors and institutions.

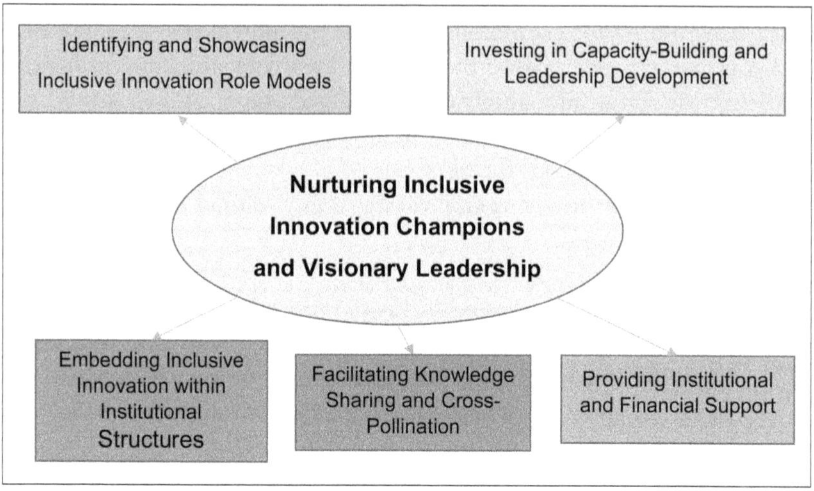

Figure 16.6 Nurturing Inclusive Innovation Champions and Visionary Leadership (Author)

4. Facilitating Knowledge Sharing and Cross-Pollination
   - Creating dedicated platforms, forums, and virtual communities that enable inclusive innovation champions to connect, exchange ideas, and collaborate on joint initiatives across geographic and institutional boundaries.
   - Fostering cross-pollination of innovative practices, collaborative problem-solving, and the co-creation of scalable solutions through these knowledge-sharing networks and communities of practice.
5. Providing Institutional and Financial Support
   - Establishing dedicated funding streams, incubation programs, and technical assistance initiatives that specifically target and empower inclusive innovation champions, particularly those from marginalized backgrounds, to transform their ideas into sustainable, high-impact initiatives.
   - Leveraging the influence and convening power of inclusive innovation champions to mobilize broader institutional and financial support for the inclusive innovation agenda within their respective spheres of influence. By nurturing and empowering a new generation of inclusive innovation champions, African nations can cultivate a cadre

of visionary leaders who possess the mindsets, competencies, and agency to drive transformative change, challenge entrenched power structures, and mobilize diverse stakeholders towards the realization of an inclusive and sustainable development future.

As the African continent stands at the crossroads of a profound developmental transition, the imperative to harness the power of inclusive innovation has never been more urgent or impactful. By embracing the principles, strategies, and collaborative frameworks outlined in this book, African nations can chart a path towards a future where sustainable progress, social justice, and equitable prosperity are not mere aspirations, but tangible realities. The integrated vision for inclusive and sustainable African development presented in this chapter represents a clarion call to action – a rallying cry for policymakers, practitioners, community leaders, and global partners to come together and collectively transform the innovation landscape. It is a vision that recognizes the inherent value and agency of marginalized communities, the indispensable role of traditional knowledge systems, and the immense potential of collaborative, cross-cutting partnerships. As we embark on this transformative journey, we must remain steadfast in our commitment to the core principles of equity, environmental sustainability, community ownership, and good governance. We must be willing to challenge entrenched power structures, disrupt traditional development models, and empower the voices and innovations of those who have been historically excluded and overlooked. By doing so, we can unlock a future where innovation is not the exclusive domain of the elite, but a democratic and inclusive force that empowers all members of society to shape their own destinies. A future where sustainable and resilient livelihoods, thriving local economies, and vibrant, resilient communities are the norm, rather than the exception. This is the African future that lies within our grasp – a future where inclusive innovation becomes the driving force that propels the continent towards a more equitable, prosperous, and environmentally-conscious tomorrow.

It is a future that we must collectively embrace, nurture, and celebrate, for the sake of present and future generations on the African continent. Embracing inclusive innovation as the foundation for a transformative African future requires a collaborative, holistic, and long-term vision that transcends institutional, sectoral, and geographical boundaries. This final chapter synthesizes the key frameworks, insights, and strategies presented throughout the book, charting a unified path forward for policymakers, practitioners, and African communities to collectively realize the promise of inclusive and sustainable development.

VI. Towards an Integrated Vision for Inclusive and Sustainable African Development

The imperative of fostering inclusive innovation ecosystems that empower marginalized groups, harness traditional knowledge systems, and drive equitable progress has been a recurrent theme throughout this book. However, realizing this vision requires the integration of these diverse perspectives and strategies into a cohesive, collaborative, and action-oriented framework for African development. This integrated vision for inclusive and sustainable development rests on the following pillars:

1. Whole-of-society engagement and multi-stakeholder collaboration
   - Cultivating innovation ecosystems that bring together a diverse array of stakeholders, including policymakers, industry leaders, academia, civil society, and community-based organizations, to collectively shape the innovation agenda and drive inclusive development.
   - Fostering cross-sectoral partnerships and knowledge-sharing platforms that facilitate the co-creation of innovative solutions and the equitable distribution of their benefits.
2. Centering the voices and perspectives of marginalized groups
   - Ensuring the meaningful participation and leadership of women, youth, Indigenous communities, and other underrepresented groups in all stages of the innovation and development process, from agenda-setting to implementation and evaluation.
   - Developing targeted policies, programs, and support mechanisms that address the unique needs and challenges faced by these marginalized stakeholders, empowering them as agents of change.
3. Integrating traditional knowledge systems and grassroots innovations
   - Recognizing, validating, and proactively incorporating the wisdom, practices, and solutions embedded within traditional knowledge systems into innovation ecosystems and development initiatives.

- Amplifying the voices and narratives of grassroots innovators, particularly those from marginalized communities, and creating enabling environments for the scaling and replication of their impactful solutions.

4. Aligning innovation with the Sustainable Development Goals
   - Harnessing the transformative power of inclusive innovation to address the multifaceted development challenges articulated in the UN Sustainable Development Goals, fostering synergies and coherence across economic, social, and environmental domains.
   - Implementing comprehensive monitoring and evaluation frameworks that capture the multidimensional impacts of inclusive innovation initiatives, ensuring their alignment with the SDG targets and principles of equity and sustainability.
5. Nurturing inclusive innovation leadership and champions
   - Identifying, empowering, and celebrating a new generation of inclusive innovation leaders who embody the values of collaboration, empathy, and social impact, and who can inspire and catalyze transformative change at all levels of society.
   - Investing in capacity-building programs, mentorship initiatives, and succession planning to cultivate a pipeline of inclusive innovation visionaries and champions across the African continent.
6. Responsive, adaptive, and future-oriented policymaking
   - Developing flexible, context-specific policy frameworks that can anticipate and respond to the evolving nature of innovation, technological change, and development challenges, while remaining anchored in the principles of inclusivity and sustainability.
   - Fostering continuous dialogue, evidence-based policymaking, and iterative learning to ensure the relevance, effectiveness, and adaptability of inclusive innovation policies and programs. By embracing this integrated vision and translating it into coordinated, collaborative, and impactful action, African nations can unlock new pathways for inclusive and sustainable development, empowering marginalized communities, harnessing the power of traditional and grassroots innovations, and positioning the continent as a global leader in the pursuit of equitable progress.

VII. Actionable Operational Recommendations for an Integrated Vision

1. Strengthening Multi-Stakeholder Collaboration
   - Establish National Innovation Platforms: Governments, civil society, and the private sector should jointly create national innovation platforms where stakeholders can regularly meet to align on priorities and coordinate efforts. These platforms should include marginalized groups, such as women, youth, and local entrepreneurs, ensuring that their voices are integrated into policy development.
   - Create Regional Innovation Hubs: Develop physical or virtual regional hubs where communities, researchers, and business leaders can collaborate on localized innovations. These hubs should focus on identifying scalable, community-driven solutions and offer infrastructure, mentorship, and networking opportunities.
   - Public-Private Partnerships (PPP) for Innovation: Strengthen PPPs that fund inclusive innovation projects. These collaborations can leverage private-sector investment alongside government incentives and support, fostering innovative projects that benefit marginalized populations.
2. Promoting Inclusive Innovation Leadership
   - Leadership Training Programs: Create programs at national universities and local leadership institutes to train leaders who focus on inclusive innovation. These programs should emphasize skills like systems thinking, community engagement, and collaborative problem-solving.
   - Incentivizing Inclusive Leadership: Governments and international organizations should create recognition programs for leaders who implement successful inclusive innovation projects. This can include funding or awards to expand successful initiatives.
   - Mentorship and Capacity Building: Develop mentorship programs that pair young leaders and entrepreneurs from marginalized communities with experienced innovators and policymakers. This provides knowledge transfer and ensures the sustainability of inclusive innovation practices.

3. Leveraging Traditional Knowledge
   - Integrate Indigenous Knowledge into Policy Design: Governments and development organizations should work closely with local communities to document and integrate traditional knowledge into national policies, especially in sectors like agriculture, healthcare, and resource management.
   - Support Community-Led Knowledge Networks: Establish community-led platforms where traditional knowledge holders and scientists can collaborate to innovate solutions. These networks should include mechanisms for knowledge protection and fair compensation for traditional knowledge.
   - Promote Co-Design Approaches: Ensure that innovation projects, particularly in agriculture and resource management, adopt co-design models that blend modern science with traditional practices. Pilot projects that integrate both should be funded and scaled.
4. Sustainable Infrastructure and Technology Access
   - Develop Green Infrastructure Policies: Governments should establish policies that prioritize green infrastructure in public projects. This can include tax incentives for companies that adopt sustainable building practices and renewable energy solutions in urban and rural settings.
   - Expand Digital Access: The government should ensure nationwide internet access through public-private partnerships, focusing on rural and underserved areas. In parallel, digital literacy programs should be implemented in schools and communities to ensure equitable access to technology.
   - Incentivize Local Tech Startups: Provide grants, low-interest loans, and tax breaks for startups focusing on sustainable technologies, particularly those addressing local challenges like clean energy, water management, and waste reduction.
5. Ensuring Social and Economic Inclusion
   - Support Social Entrepreneurs: Create funding opportunities and support for social entrepreneurs, particularly in marginalized communities. This could include micro-loans, grant programs, and technical assistance to launch businesses that focus on community welfare, education, and healthcare.

- Expand Access to Quality Education and Skills Training: Invest in educational programs that equip marginalized groups with the skills needed to engage in and benefit from inclusive innovation. This includes vocational training, STEM education for women and youth, and entrepreneurship courses tailored to local needs.
- Establish Inclusive Safety Nets: Governments should create social safety nets for individuals and communities affected by rapid technological change. These could include unemployment benefits, retraining programs, and universal health coverage to mitigate the adverse effects of economic transitions.

6. Monitoring, Evaluation, and Scaling Impact
   - Develop a National Inclusive Innovation Index: Establish an inclusive innovation index to monitor and evaluate the progress of inclusive innovation efforts across the country. This index should measure key indicators such as the number of inclusive businesses, access to education and healthcare, and the participation of marginalized groups in the innovation process.
   - Create Scaling Programs for Successful Initiatives: Once successful grassroots innovations are identified, governments and development partners should provide scaling programs that offer resources, funding, and mentorship to expand these initiatives to other regions or sectors.
   - Support Impact Evaluation: Design and fund independent, participatory impact evaluations of inclusive innovation projects to understand their outcomes and identify best practices for replication.
7. Financial Instruments and Investment Models
   - Create Impact Investment Funds: Governments and private investors should collaborate to create impact investment funds that specifically target inclusive innovation initiatives. These funds can provide both early-stage and growth-stage capital to local entrepreneurs and social enterprises.
   - Facilitate Access to Credit for Marginalized Innovators: Work with banks and microfinance institutions to develop inclusive financial products that allow marginalized innovators, especially women and

youth, to access capital. This could include low-interest loans, micro-loans, and risk-sharing mechanisms.

- Implement Tax Incentives for Inclusive Innovations: Governments should offer tax breaks or incentives for businesses that invest in inclusive innovation, particularly those that serve marginalized communities or contribute to sustainable development.
- To realize the integrated vision for inclusive and sustainable African development, these actionable recommendations provide a clear pathway for transforming ideas into tangible outcomes. Through coordinated multi-stakeholder collaboration, empowered leadership, the integration of traditional knowledge, and targeted investments in infrastructure and economic inclusion, African nations can advance toward a future where innovation benefits all citizens, especially those traditionally left behind. These recommendations offer a roadmap for turning the vision of inclusive innovation into reality and achieving the Sustainable Development Goals for the continent.

References

Acemoglu, D., & Restrepo, P. (2018). The race between man and machine: Implications of technology for growth, factor shares, and employment. *American Economic Review*, 108(6), 1488-1542.

Agrawal, A. (1995). Dismantling the divide between indigenous and scientific knowledge. *Development and change*, 26(3), 413-439.

Arocena, R., & Sutz, J. (2000). Looking at national systems of innovation from the South. *Industry and innovation*, 7(1), 55-75.

Bergek, A., Jacobsson, S., Carlsson, B., Lindmark, S., & Rickne, A. (2008). Analyzing the functional dynamics of technological innovation systems: A scheme of analysis. *Research policy*, 37(3), 407-429.

Briggs, J., & Sharp, J. (2004). Indigenous knowledges and development: a postcolonial caution. *Third World Quarterly*, 25(4), 661-676.

Briggs, J. (2005). The use of indigenous knowledge in development: problems and challenges. *Progress in development studies*, 5(2), 99-114.

Brokensha, D., Warren, D. M., & Werner, O. (Eds.). (1980). *Indigenous knowledge systems and development* (Vol. 11). University Press of America.

Brynjolfsson, E., & McAfee, A. (2014). *The second machine age: Work, progress, and prosperity in a time of brilliant technologies*. WW Norton & Company.

Ely, A., & Oxley, sN. (2014). *STEPS Centre Research on Grassroots Innovation Movements*. STEPS Centre.

Escobar, A. (1995). *Encountering development: The making and unmaking of the Third World.* Princeton University Press.

Fairwork. (2020). Fairwork Ethiopia Scores 2020: Labour Standards in the Gig Economy.

Frey, C. B., & Osborne, M. A. (2017). The future of employment: How susceptible are jobs to computerisation? *Technological forecasting and social change*, 114, 254-280.

Graham, M., Hjorth, I., & Lehdonvirta, V. (2017). Digital labour and development: impacts of global digital labour platforms and the gig economy on worker livelihoods. *Transfer: European Review of Labour and Research*, 23(2), 135-162.

Graham, M., Lehdonvirta, V., Wood, A., Barnard, H., Hjorth, I., & Simon, D. P. (2017). *The risks and rewards of online gig work at the global margin*. Oxford Internet Institute.

Gupta, A. K. (2016). *Grassroots Innovation: Minds on the Margin are not Marginal Minds*. Penguin Random House India.

ILO. (2019). *Work for a brighter future – Global Commission on the Future of Work*. International Labour Organization.

Lundvall, B. Å. (2007). National innovation systems—analytical concept and development tool. *Industry and innovation,* 14(1), 95-119.

Lwoga, E. T., Ngulube, P., & Stilwell, C. (2010). Managing indigenous knowledge for sustainable agricultural development in developing countries: Knowledge management approaches in the social context. *The International Information & Library Review*, 42(3), 174-185.

Malik, K., Nicholson, B., & Heeks, R. (2018). Examining institutional influences on the retention and attrition of digital labour in global impact sourcing. *The Electronic Journal of Information Systems in Developing Countries*, 84(6), e12058.

Mazzocchi, F. (2006). Western science and traditional knowledge: Despite their variations, different forms of knowledge can learn from each other. *EMBO reports*, 7(5), 463-466.

OECD. (2015). *Innovation Policies for Inclusive Development: Scaling Up Inclusive Innovations*. OECD Publishing, Paris.

Rani, U., & Furrer, M. (2019). Digital labour platforms and new forms of flexible work in developing countries: The case of Rwanda. *Competition & Change*, 23(4), 401-419.

Rodrik, D., & Sabel, C. F. (2019). Building a good jobs economy. Unpublished manuscript, Harvard University.

Seyfang, G., & Smith, A. (2007). Grassroots innovations for sustainable development: Towards a new research and policy agenda. *Environmental politics*, 16(4), 584-603.

Sillitoe, P. (1998). The development of indigenous knowledge: a new applied anthropology. *Current anthropology*, 39(2), 223-252.

Srinivas, K. R. (2012). Protecting traditional knowledge holders' interests and preventing misappropriation—Traditional knowledge commons and sui generis models. *The WIPO Journal*, 3(2), 167-184.

United Nations. (2015). *Transforming our world: The 2030 Agenda for Sustainable Development*. United Nations.

World Bank. (2016). *World Development Report 2016: Digital Dividends*. The World Bank.

World Bank. (2019). *World Development Report 2019: The Changing Nature of Work*. The World Bank.

Conclusion

As we reach the end of this groundbreaking exploration of inclusive innovation in Africa, it is clear that we stand at a pivotal moment in the continent's history. The time has come to embrace a new paradigm of development that puts equity, sustainability, and the empowerment of marginalized communities at the forefront. The insights and case studies presented throughout this book have demonstrated the immense potential of inclusive innovation to address the pressing challenges facing African nations. From frugal solutions that improve access to essential goods and services, to social enterprises that tackle complex societal problems, to grassroots initiatives that amplify traditional knowledge systems – the diversity and dynamism of African innovation landscapes offer a glimpse into a future of shared prosperity. Yet, realizing this vision will require a fundamental shift in mindsets, policies, and institutional practices. It will necessitate a collaborative effort among policymakers, entrepreneurs, civil society organizations, and local communities to dismantle the barriers that have long excluded the most vulnerable groups from the innovation ecosystem. By democratizing access to knowledge, technology, and resources, we can unlock the creative potential of Africa's youth, women, and underserved populations. By valuing and integrating indigenous wisdom with cutting-edge solutions, we can create context-appropriate innovations that are truly responsive to local needs. And by forging cross-border partnerships and regional networks, we can amplify the impact of inclusive innovation initiatives and inspire a new generation of visionary leaders. As we look to the future, the path forward is clear: we must embrace inclusive innovation as a transformative force for sustainable development in Africa. This will require bold steps, a willingness to challenge the status quo, and a deep commitment to empowering the most marginalized members of our societies. But if we rise to this challenge, we can shape a future where innovation truly serves the interests of all Africans, leaving no one behind. The journey ahead may be complex, but the rewards of success are immeasurable. By harnessing the power of inclusive innovation, we can build a more equitable, resilient, and prosperous Africa – one that serves as a beacon of hope and inspiration for the entire world. Let us, therefore, embark on this transformative path with unwavering determination and a steadfast belief in the limitless potential of the African continent.

Praxis Toolkit for Chapter 1: The Imperative of Inclusive Innovation

This praxis toolkit provides a set of actionable strategies and practical steps to operationalize the concepts and principles discussed in Chapter 1: The Imperative of Inclusive Innovation. The toolkit is designed for policymakers, practitioners, researchers, community leaders, and development organizations aiming to foster inclusive innovation in Africa.

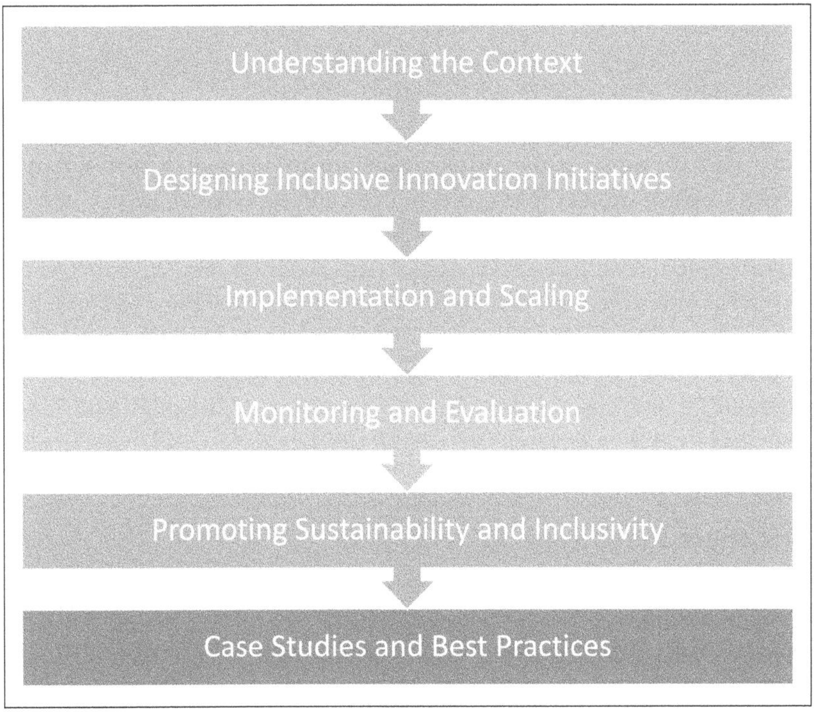

Praxis Toolkit for Chapter 1 The Imperative of Inclusive Innovation (Author)

I. Understanding the Context

Before implementing inclusive innovation initiatives, it is crucial to thoroughly understand the local context and the specific needs of marginalized communities.

Importance of Inclusive Innovation

In recent years, there has been a growing recognition of the importance of inclusive innovation in driving economic growth and development in Africa. Traditional innovation models often exclude marginalized populations, perpetuating inequality and hindering overall progress. Inclusive innovation, on the other hand, emphasizes involving a broader range of stakeholders in the innovation process, including women, youth, and rural communities. By harnessing the creativity and knowledge of diverse groups, inclusive innovation can generate new solutions to pressing challenges and ensure that the benefits of innovation are more equitably distributed.

Governance Practices and Innovation Policies

In examining the background of inclusive innovation in Africa, it is important to consider the complexities and challenges inherent in governance practices related to innovation policies on the continent. Innovation governance focuses on aligning goals, allocating resources, and assigning decision-making authority for innovation across various sectors and levels. Implementing transformative innovation policies, such as the National Accelerated Language Programme (NALAP) in Ghana, highlights the importance of language and cultural context in shaping inclusive innovation strategies. This underscores the need for a nuanced approach to innovation governance in Africa that addresses local nuances and fosters inclusive practices to drive sustainable development and societal change.

Challenges and Opportunities

Inclusive innovation in Africa comes with unique challenges such as limited access to resources, infrastructure constraints, and a lack of supportive policies and institutions. Despite these obstacles, there are inspiring case studies from various African countries demonstrating the transformative power of inclusive innovation in addressing local needs and promoting social progress.

II. Designing Inclusive Innovation Initiatives

The design phase involves creating innovative solutions that are community-centric, participatory, and sustainable.

Action Steps:

1. Community Assessments:
   - Conduct participatory rural appraisals (PRAs) to gather insights directly from community members.
   - Utilize surveys, focus group discussions, and ethnographic studies to understand local challenges, needs, and aspirations.
2. Stakeholder Mapping:
   - Identify key stakeholders, including local communities, civil society organizations, grassroots innovators, and local governments.
   - Develop a comprehensive map of existing resources, capabilities, and potential partners within the community.
3. Contextual Analysis:
   - Analyze socio-cultural, economic, and environmental factors that influence the community.
   - Leverage existing local knowledge and traditional practices to inform the innovation process.
4. Co-Creation Workshops:
   - Organize co-creation workshops with community members and stakeholders to collaboratively identify problems and brainstorm solutions.
   - Ensure diverse representation, including women, youth, and other marginalized groups to capture a wide range of perspectives.
5. Participatory Design:
   - Engage community members in the design and prototyping of solutions.
   - Use human-centered design principles to ensure that innovations are user-friendly and contextually appropriate.
6. Integration of Local Knowledge:
   - Incorporate traditional and indigenous knowledge systems into the innovation process.
   - Recognize and validate the expertise of local artisans, farmers, healers, and other community members.

III. Implementation and Scaling

Effective implementation and scaling of inclusive innovation require strategic planning, capacity building, and continuous engagement with the community.

Action Steps:

1. Pilot Projects:
   - Start with small-scale pilot projects to test and refine innovations.
   - Use feedback loops to continuously improve solutions based on community input and performance data.
2. Capacity Building:
   - Provide training and support to community members to enhance their skills and knowledge.
   - Develop local leadership and entrepreneurship through workshops, mentorship, and access to resources.
3. Collaborative Partnerships:
   - Foster partnerships with local, national, and international organizations to support implementation and scaling.
   - Leverage resources, expertise, and networks of partners to enhance the impact and reach of innovations.

IV. Monitoring and Evaluation

Regular monitoring and evaluation (M&E) are critical to assess the effectiveness, sustainability, and impact of inclusive innovation initiatives.

Action Steps:

1. Develop M&E Frameworks:
   - Create comprehensive M&E frameworks that include both qualitative and quantitative indicators.
   - Ensure that M&E frameworks are participatory and involve community members in data collection and analysis.
2. Impact Assessment:
   - Conduct periodic impact assessments to evaluate the social, economic, and environmental outcomes of innovations.

   - Use impact assessment findings to inform adaptive management and continuous improvement.
3. Feedback Mechanisms:
   - Establish robust feedback mechanisms to capture the experiences and suggestions of community members.
   - Use feedback to make iterative adjustments to the innovation process and ensure that it remains aligned with community needs.

V. Promoting Sustainability and Inclusivity

Ensuring the long-term sustainability and inclusivity of innovations requires ongoing commitment and adaptation.

Action Steps:

- 1. Institutional Support:
   - Advocate for policies and frameworks that support inclusive innovation at local, national, and regional levels.
   - Work with governments and institutions to integrate inclusive innovation into development agendas and funding mechanisms.
- 2. Sustainable Business Models:
   - Develop and promote business models that ensure the financial viability and sustainability of innovations.
   - Explore social enterprises, cooperatives, and community-based organizations as potential models.
- 3. Continued Engagement:
   - Maintain ongoing engagement with communities to monitor changes and emerging needs.
   - Foster a culture of innovation and continuous learning within communities.

VI. Case Studies and Best Practices

Learning from successful inclusive innovation initiatives can provide valuable insights and inspiration.

Action Steps:

1. Document Case Studies:

  - Collect and document case studies of successful inclusive innovation projects in Africa and beyond.
  - Highlight best practices, challenges, and lessons learned.
2. Knowledge Sharing:
   - Facilitate knowledge-sharing platforms such as workshops, conferences, and online forums to disseminate best practices.
   - Encourage peer-to-peer learning and networking among communities and practitioners.
3. Replication and Adaptation:
   - Identify scalable models and adapt successful innovations to different contexts.
   - Support replication efforts through technical assistance, funding, and mentorship.

The praxis toolkit for inclusive innovation provides a comprehensive guide for translating the theoretical concepts and principles discussed in Chapter 1 into practical actions. By adopting community-centric, participatory, and sustainable approaches, stakeholders can foster inclusive innovation that addresses the unique challenges and leverages the strengths of African communities, ultimately contributing to more equitable and sustainable development across the continent.

In Africa, inclusive innovation plays a crucial role in driving sustainable development and addressing the continent's socio-economic challenges. By involving a diverse range of stakeholders, including marginalized communities, women, and youth in the innovation process, a more inclusive and equitable society can be fostered. Inclusive innovation can lead to the creation of products and services that cater to the needs of underserved populations, ultimately improving their quality of life and promoting social inclusion. Moreover, by harnessing local knowledge and resources, inclusive innovation can stimulate entrepreneurship and job creation, contributing to economic growth and poverty alleviation. Embracing inclusive innovation is essential for Africa to harness its full potential and achieve meaningful progress towards the United Nations Sustainable Development Goals. It is imperative for policymakers, businesses, and civil society to collaborate and ensure that innovation benefits all segments of society.

Praxis Toolkit for Fostering African Innovation Ecosystems

Innovation ecosystems are crucial drivers of economic growth, social progress, and sustainable development. In Africa, a diverse and dynamic innovation ecosystem is emerging, characterized by grassroots initiatives, collaborative networks, and local problem-solving. This toolkit aims to provide practical guidance for stakeholders looking to nurture and sustain inclusive innovation ecosystems in Africa. By focusing on the key features, drivers, and enabling conditions that underpin the growth of inclusive innovation, this toolkit will help to unlock new pathways for equitable and sustainable development across the continent.

I. The Diverse Actors Shaping African Innovation Ecosystems

1. Identify Key Stakeholders
   - Grassroots Communities: Engage with community-based organizations, social enterprises, and informal networks that have a deep understanding of local challenges and innovative problem-solving strategies.
   - Intermediary Organizations: Support innovation hubs, accelerators, and incubators that provide crucial resources, including access to funding, mentorship, and capacity-building programs.
   - Academic Institutions: Collaborate with universities and research centers to leverage their expertise, infrastructure, and networks.
   - Public Sector: Partner with government agencies, policymakers, and regulatory bodies to shape the enabling environment for inclusive innovation.
   - Private Sector: Engage with multinational corporations, local businesses, and impact investors to contribute financial resources, technical expertise, and market access.

Praxis Toolkit for Fostering African Innovation Ecosystems

I. Diverse Actors Shaping African Innovation Ecosystems

- Identify Key Stakeholders
- Foster Cross-Sector Collaboration

Example: Bertha Centre for Social Innovation and Entrepreneurship
Example: xHub Addis

II. Grassroots Innovation and Local Knowledge

- Integrate Traditional Knowledge Systems
- Promote Peer-to-Peer Learning

Example: Sahel Region Agroecological Practices
Example: Kibera Hamlets Project

- Establish Innovation Hubs and Incubators
- Develop Collaborative Research Initiatives

Example: Kigali Innovation City
Example: Mzuzu Innovation Hub

IV. [illegible]

- Assess and Improve Policy Landscape
- Foster Multi-Stakeholder Collaboration
- Strengthen Intellectual Property Rights
- Invest in STEM Education
- Adopt Inclusive Public Procurement Strategies

Example: Kenya's Digital Economy Blueprint
Example: Rwanda's National Policy on Science, Technology, and Innovation

2. Foster Cross-Sector Collaboration
   - Intermediary Organizations: Facilitate the exchange of knowledge, resources, and connections between grassroots initiatives and broader innovation ecosystems.
   - Public-Private Partnerships: Mobilize resources, share knowledge, and align incentives across the innovation ecosystem.

Case Studies:

- Bertha Centre for Social Innovation and Entrepreneurship: Supports social enterprises and community-based organizations through tailored acceleration programs and cross-sector collaborations (Bertha Centre, 2020).
- xHub Addis: Provides resources and connections to social entrepreneurs and grassroots innovators in Ethiopia (xHub Addis, 2021).

II. Grassroots Innovation and the Centrality of Local Knowledge

1. Integrate Traditional Knowledge Systems
   - Blend Knowledge Sources: Combine traditional knowledge with modern scientific and technological advancements to create context-appropriate solutions.
   - Community Ownership: Ensure that initiatives emerge from the lived experiences and contextual understanding of the communities themselves.
2. Promote Peer-to-Peer Learning
   - Knowledge-Sharing Networks: Encourage local innovators and problem-solvers to engage in peer-to-peer learning and exchange best practices.
   - Intermediary Support: Utilize innovation hubs and community-based organizations to facilitate the exchange of knowledge and resources.

Case Studies:

- Sahel Region Agroecological Practices: Combines traditional land management techniques with modern sustainable farming methods (Altieri & Nicholls, 2017; Reij et al., 2009).

- Kibera Hamlets Project: Uses recycled plastic bottles to create affordable, durable housing solutions in Nairobi (Kibera Hamlets, 2021).

III. Collaborative Innovation and Cross-Sector Synergies

1. Establish Innovation Hubs and Incubators
   - Provide Resources: Offer access to funding, mentorship, and networking opportunities to enable grassroots initiatives to scale and thrive.
   - Facilitate Cross-Sector Partnerships: Bring together entrepreneurs, researchers, policymakers, and community representatives.
2. Develop Collaborative Research Initiatives
   - Leverage Collective Knowledge: Partner with academic institutions, public sector agencies, and community-based organizations to tackle interdisciplinary development challenges.
   - Promote Inclusive Governance: Ensure marginalized groups are represented in decision-making processes and the benefits of innovation are equitably distributed.

Case Studies:

- Kigali Innovation City: Drives Rwanda's digital transformation through knowledge-sharing, capacity-building, and cross-sector partnerships (Kigali Innovation City, 2021).
- Mzuzu Innovation Hub: Works with smallholder farmers and local enterprises in Malawi to develop and scale innovative agricultural technologies (Mzuzu Innovation Hub, 2021).

IV. Enabling Environments and Policy Frameworks for Inclusive Innovation

1. Assess and Improve Policy Landscape
   - Implement Targeted Policies: Provide tax incentives for innovative startups and prioritize underrepresented vendors in public procurement strategies.
   - Establish Innovation Hubs: Develop hubs and accelerators in underserved communities.

2. Foster Multi-Stakeholder Collaboration
   - Public-Private Partnerships: Organize joint innovation challenges and create innovation hubs that bring together diverse stakeholders.
   - Promote Access to Finance: Develop targeted funding mechanisms such as impact investment funds and crowd-sourcing platforms.
3. Strengthen Intellectual Property Rights
   - Protect Traditional Knowledge: Develop frameworks for fair and transparent sharing of benefits derived from traditional knowledge.
4. Invest in STEM Education
   - Strengthen Education Programs: Reform curricula, provide scholarships, and create partnerships with academic institutions and industry.
5. Adopt Inclusive Public Procurement Strategies
   - Prioritize Underrepresented Vendors: Focus on products and services from women-led, youth-led, and community-based enterprises.

Case Studies:

- Kenya's Digital Economy Blueprint: Outlines a comprehensive strategy for harnessing digital technologies for inclusive growth.
- Rwanda's National Policy on Science, Technology, and Innovation: Emphasizes community-based innovation and traditional knowledge systems.

By fostering cross-sector partnerships, leveraging traditional knowledge, and creating enabling policy environments, African innovation ecosystems can address complex development challenges in a holistic and impactful way. This toolkit provides practical steps for stakeholders to nurture and sustain inclusive innovation ecosystems, unlocking new pathways for equitable and sustainable development across the African continent.

References

Arocena, R., & Sutz, J. (2000). Looking at National Systems of Innovation from the South. *Industry and Innovation*, 7(1), 55-75.

Berdegué, J. A. (2005). *Pro-poor innovation systems*. IFAD.

Bertha Centre for Social Innovation and Entrepreneurship. (2020). Annual Report.

Byanyima, W. (2018). *Empowering Marginalized Communities through Innovation*. Oxfam International.

Chataway, J., Hanlin, R., & Kaplinsky, R. (2014). Inclusive Innovation: An Architecture for Policy Development. *Innovation and Development*, 4(1), 33-54.

Cozzens, S. E., & Sutz, J. (2014). *Innovation in Informal Settings: A Research Agenda*. IDRC.

Grobbelaar, S., & Boshoff, N. (2019). Inclusive Innovation and Transformative Change in South Africa. *African Journal of Science, Technology, Innovation and Development*, 11(3), 279-291.

Kigali Innovation City. (2021). Annual Report.

Léautier, F. (2012). *Innovation in Africa: Harnessing the Power of Inclusive Development*. African Development Bank.

Omidyar Network. (2013). Accelerating Entrepreneurship in Africa.

Reij, C., Tappan, G., & Smale, M. (2009). *Agroenvironmental Transformation in the Sahel: Another Kind of Green Revolution*. IFPRI.

SAIS. (2021). Southern African Innovation Support Program Annual Report. Technology Innovation Agency. (2021). Annual Report.

Wamae, W. (2009). *Building Science, Technology and Innovation Capacity in Rwanda*. UNU-MERIT.

Praxis Toolkit: Policy Frameworks for Inclusive Innovation Ecosystems

This toolkit aims to provide practical guidance and strategies for policymakers, development practitioners, and stakeholders involved in fostering inclusive innovation ecosystems in Africa. By translating the theoretical insights and best practices from Chapter 9 into actionable steps, this toolkit will help in designing, implementing, and monitoring effective policy frameworks that support equitable, sustainable, and community-driven innovation.

I. Understanding the Policy Landscape

Conduct a Policy Audit

- Review existing national innovation policies and strategies to identify gaps and areas for improvement.
- Analyze the alignment of these policies with inclusive innovation principles and broader national development goals.

Engage in Comparative Analysis

- Study successful inclusive innovation policies from other countries or regions to draw lessons and best practices.
- Identify adaptable elements that can be integrated into local policy frameworks.

II. Overcoming Barriers to Policy Implementation

Enhancing Policy Coherence and Coordination

- Establish inter-ministerial or cross-agency task forces to ensure policy alignment and address fragmentation.
- Develop a comprehensive policy framework that integrates inclusive innovation across various sectors.

Building Institutional Capacity

- Invest in training and capacity-building programs for government officials and policymakers on inclusive innovation.

- Create dedicated units or councils within government agencies to champion inclusive innovation.

Promoting Stakeholder Engagement

- Organize regular multi-stakeholder forums to gather input and feedback from diverse ecosystem actors.
- Ensure the inclusion of marginalized groups, such as women, youth, and Indigenous communities, in the policymaking process.

Addressing Power Dynamics and Vested Interests

- Conduct power mapping exercises to identify key stakeholders and potential resistances.
- Implement measures to safeguard the rights and participation of marginalized groups.

Developing Robust Monitoring and Evaluation Frameworks

- Design context-appropriate indicators to measure the impact of inclusive innovation policies.
- Establish data collection and analysis systems to support evidence-based policymaking.

III. Strategies for Effective Policy Design

Fostering Policy Coherence

- Align inclusive innovation policies with national development strategies, industrial policies, and SDGs.
- Facilitate continuous policy review and adaptation processes through regular multi-stakeholder dialogues.

Strengthening Institutional Capacities

- Provide ongoing training and support for policymakers to enhance their understanding of inclusive innovation.
- Promote flexible and adaptive organizational structures that can respond to changing needs and contexts.

Aligning with Diverse Innovation Models

- Conduct assessments of local innovation landscapes to identify and support diverse innovation approaches.
- Tailor policy instruments to meet the unique needs of different innovation actors and communities.

Encouraging Multi-Stakeholder Participation

- Implement participatory policymaking processes that actively engage diverse ecosystem actors.
- Establish permanent consultation mechanisms to incorporate stakeholder perspectives continuously.

Addressing Power Imbalances

- Develop policies that explicitly address and mitigate power imbalances and vested interests.
- Foster a culture of transparency and accountability in policy implementation.

Enhancing Monitoring, Evaluation, and Learning

- Develop comprehensive monitoring and evaluation frameworks that capture the multidimensional impacts of policies.
- Establish knowledge-sharing platforms to disseminate best practices and lessons learned.

Leveraging Regional and Global Frameworks

- Align national policies with regional and global development agendas, such as the African Union's Agenda 2063.
- Facilitate cross-border policy harmonization and leverage international cooperation for technical and financial support.

IV. Practical Steps for Policy Implementation

Policy Formulation

- Conduct stakeholder consultations to identify key priorities and objectives for inclusive innovation.
- Draft policy documents that outline clear goals, targets, and implementation plans.

Policy Implementation

- Mobilize resources and establish implementation teams to drive policy execution.
- Develop partnerships with civil society, private sector, and international organizations to support implementation.

Policy Monitoring and Evaluation

- Implement continuous monitoring to track progress and identify challenges.
- Conduct regular evaluations to assess policy impact and inform necessary adjustments.

V. Case Studies and Examples

South Africa's Support for MSMEs

- Analyze the country's policies and programs aimed at promoting inclusive entrepreneurship and supporting MSMEs.

Kenya's Digital Inclusion Initiatives

- Examine Kenya's efforts to bridge the digital divide and promote open access to data and digital resources.

Ethiopia's Public Procurement for Innovation

- Review Ethiopia's policies that leverage public procurement to drive inclusive, community-driven innovation.

By adopting a holistic, collaborative, and community-centric approach to policymaking, African nations can create enabling environments that nurture inclusive innovation ecosystems. This toolkit serves as a practical guide to translate the theoretical insights of Chapter 9 into actionable steps, driving more equitable, sustainable, and impactful development outcomes across the continent.

Business & Innovation

Vol. 37

The creation of new activities, of news production and consumption modes, of new goods and services, of new markets and new jobs (etc.) depends as much on the heroic action of entrepreneurs as on the strategies of big corporations which develop their activities at a global scale. Innovation and business are interlinked. The main themes of the books published in this series are: Entrepreneurship, enterprise and innovation; Innovation strategies in a global context; Innovation policies and business climate; Innovation, business dynamics and socio-economic change. The synergies between innovative entrepreneurship, firms' strategies and innovation policies is of major importance in the explanation of technological paradigms change and of the transformations in economic and social structures of wealthy and less wealthy countries. In this series are published books in English or in French specialized in economics, management and sociology of innovation and also dealing with change and entrepreneurship in a local, national or international perspective.

This series is supported by the Research Network on Innovation.

Published Volumes

Vol. 38 – Pitshou Moleka, Empowering Africa: Harnessing Inclusive Innovation for Sustainable Development. 2025.

Vol. 37 – Son Thi Kim LE (ed.), Innovation in East Asia. Contexts and relevant cases, 2024.

Vol. 36 – Dominique Desjeux, The Market of the Gods. How religious innovations emerge. From Judaism to Christianity, 2024.

Vol. 35 – Fedoua Kasmi, Mauricio Camargo, Laurent Dupont (dir.), Territoires en transition et innovation. Enjeux et outils d'accompagnement, 2024.

Vol. 34 – Hubert Bonin, Les responsabilités de l'entreprise, 2024.

Vol. 33 – Nathalie Dupont, Laetitia Garcia (dir.), Tourisme, arts et territoires. Impacts réciproques à travers des études de cas, 2024.

Vol. 32 – Elachhab Fathi, Macroéconomie quantitative et théorie des fluctuations. Applications aux pays en développement, 2024.

Vol. 31 – Laurent Adatto, Camille Aouinaït, Son Thi Kim Le and Michelle Mongo (Eds.), Innovation Ecosystems in the New Economic Era. Digital Revolution and Ecological Transition, 2023.

Vol. 30 – Joëlle Forest et Bertrand Bocquet (dir.), Imaginer le futur à partir du passé, 2023.

Vol. 29 – Manon Enjolras, Mauricio Camargo, Christophe Schmitt (eds.), Innovation and Internationalization of Small and Medium Enterprises. A Crossroads Perspective, 2022.

Vol. 28 – Samuel-Jacques Priso-Essawe, Intégration régionale « appropriée » en Afrique. Éléments juridiques d'effectivité, 2021.

Vol. 27 – Vincent Herbert (dir.), Tourisme et Territoires. Espaces d' innovations, 2021.

Vol. 26 – Jean-Alain Héraud et Nathalie Popiolek, L'organisation et la valorisation de la recherche. Problématique européenne et étude comparée de la France et de l'Allemagne, 2021.

Vol. 25 – Stéphanie Lachaud-Martin, Corinne Marache, Julie McIntyre, Mikaël Pierre (eds.), Wine, Networks and Scales. Intermediation in the Production, Distribution and Consumption of Wine, 2021.

Vol. 24 – Verónica González-Araujo, Roberto-Carlos Álvarez-Delgado, Ángel Sancho-Rodríguez (eds.), Ethics in Business Communication. New Challenges in the Digital World, 2020.

Vol. 23 – Didier Caveng, L' éthique dans la finance. Les banques genevoises à l' épreuve des faits, 2019.

Vol. 22 – André Tiran et Dimitri Uzunidis (dir.), Libéralisme et protectionnisme, 2019.

Vol. 21 – Dominique Desjeux, The anthropological perspective of the world. The inductive method illustrated, 2018.

Vol. 20 – Benoît Bernard, Management Public. 65 schémas pour analyser et changer les organisations publiques, 2018.

Vol. 19 – Dimitri Uzunidis (dir.), Recherche académique et innovation. La force productive de la science, 2018.

Vol. 18 – Jean Vercherand, Le marché du travail. L'esprit libéral et la revanche du politique, 2018. Vol. 17 – Dominique Desjeux (dir.), L'empreinte anthropologique du monde. Méthode inductive illustrée, 2018.

Vol. 16 – Sophie Boutillier, Entrepreneuriat et innovation, 2017.

Vol. 15 – Arvind Ashta, Microfinance. Battling a Wicked Problem, 2016.

Vol. 14 – Jean Vercherand, Microéconomie. Une approche critique : Théorie et exercices, 2016.

Vol. 13 – Réseau de Recherche sur l'innovation, Blandine Laperche (dir.), Géront' innovations. Trajectoires d' innovation dans une économie vieillissante, 2016.

Vol. 12 – Société Internationale Jean-Baptiste Say, Dimitri Uzunidis (dir.), Et Jean- Baptiste Say… créa l'Entrepreneur, 2015.

Vol. 11 – Faïz Gallouj, Francois Stankiewicz (dir.), Le DRH innovateur. Management des ressources humaines et dynamiques d' innovation, 2014.

Vol. 10 – Charlotte Fourcroy, Services et environnement. Les enjeux énergétiques de l' innovation dans les services, 2014.

Vol. 9 – Rémy Herrera, Wim Dierckxsens, Paulo Nakatani (eds.), Beyond the Systemic Crisis and Capital-Led Chaos. Theoretical and Applied Studies, 2014.

Vol. 8 – Réseau de Recherche sur l'Innovation, Sophie Boutillier, Joëlle Forest, Delphine Gallaud, Blandine Laperche, Corinne Tanguy, Leïla Temri (dir.), Principes d' économie de l' innovation, 2014.

Vol. 7 – Michel Santi, Capitalism without Conscience, 2013.
Vol. 6 – Arnaud Diemer, Jean-Pierre Potier, Léon Walras, Un siècle après (1910–2010), 2013.
Vol. 5 – Sophie Boutillier, Faridah Djellal, Dimitri Uzunidis (Réseau de Recherche sur l'Innovation) (dir.), L' innovation. Analyser, anticiper, agir, 2013.
Vol. 4 – Aurélie Trouvé, Marielle Berriet-Solliec, Denis Lépicier (dir.), Le développement rural en Europe. Quel avenir pour le deuxième pilier de la Politique agricole commune ?, 2013.
Vol. 3 – Sophie Boutillier, Faridah Djellal, Faïz Gallouj, Blandine Laperche, Dimitri Uzunidis (dir.), L' innovation verte. De la théorie aux bonnes pratiques, 2012.
Vol. 2 – Faridah Djellal, Faïz Gallouj, La productivité à l' épreuve des services, 2012.
Vol. 1 – Abdelillah Hamdouch, Sophie Reboud, Corinne Tanguy (dir.), PME, dynamiques entrepreneuriales et innovation, 2011

www.ingramcontent.com/pod-product-compliance
Ingram Content Group UK Ltd.
Pitfield, Milton Keynes, MK11 3LW, UK
UKHW020154290926
15471UKWH00005B/859

9 783034 361149